Natural Resources in U.S.-Canadian Relations

Volume I
The Evolution of Policies and Issues

Other Volumes

Natural Resources in U.S.-Canadian Relations, Volume II: Patterns and Trends in Resource Supplies and Policies, edited by Carl E. Beigie and Alfred O. Hero, Jr.

Natural Resources in U.S.-Canadian Relations, Volume III: Perspectives, Prospects, and Policy Options, edited by Carl E. Beigie and Alfred O. Hero, Jr.

About the Book and Editors

Natural Resources in U.S.-Canadian Relations
Volume I
The Evolution of Policies and Issues

edited by Carl E. Beigie and Alfred O. Hero, Jr.

The combined efforts of the World Peace Foundation, the C. D. Howe Research Institute, and the Centre Québécois de Relations Internationales have culminated in a comprehensive three-volume study of critical U.S.-Canadian resource issues. Motivated initially by the tensions of the mid-1970s and by U.S. concern about the actions of its major non-energy resource supplier, Canada, the study grew to examine bilateral resource issues from a long-term perspective.

The first volume traces the background of the U.S.-Canadian resource connection, analyzes the evolution of resource policies and processes in the two countries, and introduces the domestic and bilateral policy issues that have emerged regarding natural resource development and trade. Contributors examine the possibility that Canada might seek to exploit its resource position by taking actions detrimental to U.S. interests.

Volume II, *Patterns and Trends in Resource Supplies and Policies*, presents detailed case studies of nine specific resources of interest to both countries. Volume III, *Perspectives, Prospects, and Policy Options*, examines the resource sector from the perspectives of corporate investors, workers, and environmentalists and concludes with a review of policy options and prospects for the bilateral relationship.

Carl E. Beigie, president of the C. D. Howe Research Institute in Montreal, is a specialist in Canadian-U.S. economic relations. Alfred O. Hero, Jr., director of the World Peace Foundation in Boston, is a political scientist who specializes in U.S.-Canadian, and particularly U.S.-Quebec, relations.

Published in cooperation with
The World Peace Foundation
and
The C. D. Howe Research Institute

Natural Resources in U.S.-Canadian Relations

Volume I
The Evolution of Policies and Issues

edited by
Carl E. Beigie and Alfred O. Hero, Jr.

Westview Press / Boulder, Colorado

This book was prepared with the support of NSF Grant AER 76-07304. However, opinions, findings, conclusions, and/or recommendations herein are those of the authors and do not necessarily reflect the views of NSF.

Published in 1980 in the United States of America by
  Westview Press, Inc.
  5500 Central Avenue
  Boulder, Colorado 80301
  Frederick A. Praeger, Publisher

This book is available in Canada from:
  C. D. Howe Research Institute
  2064 Sun Life Building
  Montreal, Quebec H3B 2X7

Library of Congress Cataloging in Publication Data
Main entry under title:
Natural resources in U.S.-Canadian relations.
  Includes index.
  CONTENTS: v. 1. The evolution of policies and issues.
  1. United States—Foreign economic relations—Canada—Addresses, essays, lectures.
2. Canada—Foreign economic relations—United States—Addresses, essays, lectures.
3. Natural resources—United States—Addresses, essays, lectures.   4. Natural resources—Canada—Addresses, essays, lectures.   I.Beigie, Carl E.   II.Hero, Alfred O.
HF1456.5.C2N37   1980   382'.0971'073   79-25103
ISBN: 0-89158-554-0 (v. 1)
ISBN: 0-89158-877-9 (v. 1) pbk.

Printed and bound in the United States of America

Contents

Preface

This volume is the first of three volumes of a comprehensive study of U.S.-Canadian resource linkages. A detailed review of the scope and contents of the entire project is contained in the first chapter of this volume.

The project is a joint effort of the World Peace Foundation in Boston, the C. D. Howe Research Institute in Montreal, and the Centre Québécois de Relations Internationales in Quebec City. The directors of these organizations — Alfred O. Hero, Jr., Carl E. Beigie, and Albert Legault, respectively — are jointly responsible for the design of the project and for editorial supervision. Valuable assistance in all phases of the enterprise has been provided by a research committee consisting of Robert W. Cox, professor of political science, York University; William Diebold, Jr., senior research fellow, Council on Foreign Relations; and Roger Frank Swanson, former acting director of the Center of Canadian Studies, Johns Hopkins School of Advanced International Studies, and now a member of the staff of the U.S. Chamber of Commerce.

Each author involved in the project commented on the drafts of several of the chapters. Particularly valuable were the detailed contributions made by John H. Ashworth, D. J. Daly, and Garth Stevenson. In addition, a steering committee of academic and industrial experts provided essential guidance, particularly during the formative stages of the project. Each chapter was circulated in draft to specialists in government and industry for comment. The project directors are indebted to all those who provided assistance, but responsibility for the contents of each chapter lies solely with the author or authors.

From the outset of this endeavor, the directors recognized that the desire to remain up to date on late-breaking developments in a rapidly changing environment would present problems. Nonetheless, they underestimated the seriousness of these problems. Finalizing some of the chapters took as long as a year, which made it necessary to revise those chapters completed more promptly. This created problems for several authors, but in each case they responded cooperatively, and we greatly appreciated their efforts. At the end of this process the chapters generally reflected information available as of mid- to late 1978, but in a few instances it was impossible to incorporate recent developments, for which the authors cannot be held accountable.

Financial support for this project came from several sources. The World Peace Foundation received partial support from the National Science Foundation (Grant AER 76-07304) and covered the rest of the U.S. input from its own endowment income. The C. D. Howe Research Institute's contribution was made possible from general membership funds. The Quebec Ministry of Natural Resources provided a generous contribution on behalf of the Centre Québécois de Relations Internationales. However, the opinions, findings, conclusions, and/or recommendations that have emerged from the project are those of the authors and do not necessarily reflect the views of the project's sponsors.

A particular expression of appreciation is due three members of the staff of the C. D. Howe Research Institute. Richard Shaffner, a senior member of the economics staff, was exceptionally helpful in filling in data gaps, revising wording of complex passages, and providing effective commentary. Connie Parsons, editor, and Romana Cap, assistant editor, provided painstaking attention under considerable pressure to all the often-overlooked details that go into completing a multi-author volume. Their efforts, and the able assistance of the Institute's secretarial staff, have been crucial to the successful completion of this project.

Carl E. Beigie
Alfred O. Hero, Jr.

The Contributors

John H. Ashworth is an associate of the Solar Energy Research Institute in Golden, Colorado.

Carl E. Beigie, president of the C. D. Howe Research Institute in Montreal, is a specialist in Canadian-U.S. economic relations.

D. J. Daly, a professor in the faculty of administrative studies at York University in Ontario, is a leading analyst of Canadian economic performance and trade policy.

Paul Daniel is a graduate student in economics at McMaster University in Ontario. His work for this volume was carried out while he was a temporary member of the staff of the C. D. Howe Research Institute.

William Diebold, Jr., senior research fellow at the Council on Foreign Relations in New York, is the author of numerous books and articles on international economic policy issues.

Gérard Gaudet is associate professor and chairman of the Department of Economics at Laval University in Quebec.

Jacob Kaplan, who is with the firm International Finance and Economics in Washington, D.C., was formerly director of senior staff at AID.

Kenneth H. Norrie, associate professor of economics at the University of Alberta in Edmonton, is the author of studies covering a broad range of Canadian economic policy issues.

Donald J. Patton is director of the Centre for International Business Studies at Dalhousie University in Nova Scotia.

Richard Shaffner, an associate economist at the C. D. Howe Research Institute, is director of research in Montreal for the Canadian-American Committee.

Garth Stevenson, associate professor of political science at the University of Alberta in Edmonton, is a specialist in the study of federalist political systems and institutions in Canada and Australia.

1

An Introductory Overview

CARL E. BEIGIE

Changing Policy Landscapes, Persisting Realities

The 1970s may well go down in history as the decade when Murphy's Law was dominant in the world economy — whatever could go wrong did. Great expectations for prosperity and stability were nurtured by the experiences of the 1960s; this expectational bubble has been burst by the events and the uncertainties of the 1970s. Growth has slowed, inflation and unemployment have become persistent and highly resistant to conventional correctives, and balance-of-payments problems have been magnified to the point of causing continuing turmoil in international currency markets.

Because of the bleak record of the 1970s, there appears to be a psychological depression as the nations of the world confront their individual and collective futures. The virtues of liberalization in domestic and international relations continue to be extolled, but specific policy decisions have been characterized increasingly by retrenchment and defensiveness. While there is recognition of the appropriateness of — indeed, the necessity for — coordinated policy actions to reflect the increased degree of international economic integration that has developed during the postwar era, domestic political realities have become such that governments must act to ensure that first priority is given to national concerns and preoccupations.

It is not surprising that in this environment there is a tendency for the focus of public policy concern to bounce around among various "fundamental" issues. There is pessimism about the long term because so few of these issues seem to be resolved or capable of resolution. But the public's capacity for concentrating on any one issue for very long is finite; and as the apparent severity of one problem or another ebbs and flows, there are pressures to try to deal with the most immediate concerns in an *ad hoc* fashion.

This process of constantly changing policy priorities has been apparent in the area of ensuring secure access to natural resources in sufficient quan-

1

tities and at low enough prices to sustain economic growth and prosperity. In a very real sense, natural resources are the core ingredients in the economic-growth process, and the imperative of assuring access to essential resources has played a key role throughout history in relations among regions and nations.

The threat of natural resource scarcity has been raised on numerous occasions in the past. A re-emergence of Malthusian pessimism about the earth's capacity to sustain — much less to expand significantly upon — current living standards has recently appeared in the world policy environment. This pessimism has had a marked impact upon public attitudes toward economic growth in general and toward resource policies in particular. The period from about 1972 to 1974 witnessed a peaking of this pessimism. The publication in 1972 of *The Limits to Growth* provided a deceptively sophisticated foundation for pessimism about supplies of resources that was quickly subscribed to by many who felt that the prosperity of the 1960s just had to be too good to endure.[1] It was also during the early 1970s that global excess-demand inflation, which had as its inevitable counterpart generalized shortages, seemed to provide confirmation of predictions of an imminent end to prodigal affluence. The lean years, it appeared, were upon us.

A crushing blow to the perceived invulnerability of the industrialized world was administered in 1973-74 by the actions of the Organization of Petroleum Exporting Countries (OPEC) oil cartel. The economic impact of the dramatic increase in world oil prices during this period has been captured in the following statement:

> Almost overnight, it turned a routine slowdown of the world economy into a major depression, by far the worst since the 1930s. It brought to a bitter end the thirty-year Keynesian boom, resurrected the spectre, indeed the reality, of mass unemployment in the advanced states, cut growth rates to nil, or even to reverse growth, and induced a new and highly destructive crisis of confidence in the free economy and in free societies everywhere.[2]

The economic repercussions of OPEC's pricing actions have been serious indeed, but they can be dealt with if appropriate adjustment policies are adopted.[3] Much less easily accommodated, however, are the psychological impacts resulting from the perceptions of vulnerability that arose in the wake of the Arab oil embargo in late 1973. This perceived vulnerability led to some exaggeration of the prospects for similar actions affecting other commodities as part of a strategic approach among resource exporters in the Third World. Even when this "threat" is put into its proper perspective, however, there can be little doubt that the importance in foreign-policy decisions of secure access to natural resource supplies has been increased in relation to that in the 1960s.

The current environment in world commodity markets is far different from that in 1972-74. As recession set in during 1974 and then deepened in 1975, shortages disappeared, and commodity prices, particularly when deflated by the general rate of inflation, fell—in many instances quite dramatically. On the basis of this experience, one might be tempted to argue that we have now witnessed another example, albeit acute, of commodity markets' coming full circle in a pattern that has been repeated throughout history.

Looking to the future, it may be that concern over natural resource supplies will subside as a foreign-policy imperative. It is increasingly apparent that, while the notion of a fixed "limit" to economic expansion is deceptively simple and appealing—especially as applied to "non-renewable" natural resources—extreme forms of pessimism about resource supplies give inadequate weight to the adaptability of man and of markets. Numerous examples from recent experience can be cited to illustrate how adaptations to emerging "scarcities" come about through conservation (better insulation of homes to contain heat); substitution (plastics for wood); the development of previously uneconomic sources of supply (the reopening of "spent" gold mines); and expanded exploration activity (the reinvigorated search for oil and natural gas). These and other adaptations (for example, the recycling of metals) will continue, as in the past, to counteract the cost-increasing effects of more intensive exploitation of the earth's natural resource supplies.[4]

Having said this much, however, it would be cavalier to treat concern about natural resource supplies as a purely temporary phenomenon. Three fundamental resource issues are likely to exhibit some permanence in terms of the conduct of foreign economic policies:

- The real-cost issue: Is the world in, or rapidly approaching, a situation in which the real costs of obtaining supplies of certain basic resources are rising along a curve with a significant upward slope?
- The "commodity-power" issue: To what extent, and in what ways, might governments in resource-surplus areas be able to use their export potential as a lever in international economic and political relations?
- The investment-frustration issue: Will government policies, or lack of policies, relating to natural resources handicap the orderly development and marketing of resources to meet the needs of balanced economic expansion?

We shall explore each of these issues briefly below in order to provide an

overview of the general policy context for the discussion in this volume of
natural resources in the U.S.-Canadian relationship.

Three Central Resource Issues

The Real-Cost Issue

Has the rate of actual and projected demand for certain natural resources
reached a point where it will become progressively more costly, in terms of
the labor and capital required, to meet this demand? The evidence is
mixed. On the one hand, the historical record does not appear to support a
conclusion that there has been any persistent shift in terms of trade in favor
of the resource sector. Indeed, the traditional issues in this sector have been
seen as just the opposite: declining terms of trade, making it necessary for
exporters of resources to increase volumes to offset the deterioration in
what these exports could buy in terms of manufactured imports. On the
other hand, a need to rely increasingly on more marginal and/or more
remote resources of supply to sustain high rates of total consumption growing by exponentially expanding amounts may make it impossible to
duplicate past experience indefinitely.

If one adopts as a premise that the continued availability of natural
resources at constant — much less at diminishing — real costs can no longer
be taken for granted, certain important conclusions follow for economic
and political policy. For example:

- Real-income growth expectations may have to be revised downward
  as a greater percentage of new capital formation and increases in the
  labor force are devoted to the expansion of the production of
  resources.
- Income shares may have to be redistributed, both globally and na-
  tionally, toward owners of resources; resistance to this redistribution
  would generate continuing inflationary pressures.
- Economic "rents" arising from wider variations in cost conditions — including considerations of location — experienced in different supply areas may increase in magnitude, with governments
  in these areas pressing, and being pressed, to maximize the capture
  of these "rents."
- Rates of resource exploitation and/or exportation in potential supply areas may be restricted by governments to preserve supplies for
  their own residents or to keep domestic prices below world prices.

Generalizations about the validity of the real-cost issue are not very useful. Instead, careful analysis on a case-by-case basis, as carried out in Volume II of this project, is essential.

The "Commodity-Power" Issue

Concern over the issue of "commodity power" surged immediately following the success of the OPEC oil cartel, which some commentators argued would mark the start of a pattern that would spread over a wide range of resources.[5] It is now widely recognized, however, that oil is a special case among resources with respect to both economic fundamentals and the political factors involved, as Paul Daniel and Richard Shaffner explain in Chapter 10. Therefore, group action to enforce successfully a several-fold increase in the prices of numerous commodities is not a very likely near-term prospect.

Such weak world markets as existed in the mid-1970s for most commodities may, however, give a very misleading impression concerning the viability of concerted action among nations with exportable surpluses of important natural resources. Governments have been exercising much more active control over the production of, and returns from, resources within their territories. In exercising this control, they may be more susceptible to pressures to maintain output — and therefore employment and foreign exchange earnings — in slack markets than private firms would be.

Formal cartels are not essential for the effective exercise of commodity power, especially in those instances in which supplies of a particular resource are relatively concentrated geographically, real costs appear to be rising, and/or opportunities for substitution are limited or very expensive. Informal understandings, or simply "conscious parallel action," may be enough to produce restrictions on the rate of output or export growth, thereby raising prices to consuming nations in periods of market firmness.

The effectiveness of commodity power, particularly over time, depends to a large extent on economic fundamentals of the sort that have always limited the durability of private cartels. Sanctions against cartels or cartel-like behavior, however, are more difficult when governments, as opposed to private firms, are involved. Furthermore, resource-exporting nations perceive themselves as having received the "short end of the stick" in their transactions with consuming nations and with their assumed agents, multinational enterprises. This perception might lead to common action on a variety of fronts, particularly in the areas of resource taxation and demands for further processing of resources prior to export.

Some of the policy implications likely to result from increased government activism in the control of resources are the following:

- Governments in producer countries will probably find it fairly easy to coordinate demands for more information on transfer pricing, exploration results, reserves, production costs, and so forth, from multinational enterprises.

- Pressures to promote upgrading of resources prior to export, to link conditions relating to access to supplies with those relating to access to markets, and to stabilize commodity markets will probably be major preoccupations in future negotiations regarding reforms to international trading rules and institutions.
- Differential pricing systems and preferential terms of supply as between domestic and export markets are likely to become more prevalent, especially in high-income, industrialized countries that are also resource producers, leading to international conflict.

Commodity power, then, boils down to the systematic efforts of governments in producing nations to improve the terms under which their resources are developed and exported. Even if these efforts should prove unsuccessful in the longer run because of economic realities, they can have disruptive impacts on resource supplies over the short and medium terms. Vulnerability to such disruptions raises serious policy concerns for resource importers.

The Investment-Frustration Issue

Even though natural resources account directly for a relatively low percentage of total economic activity in industrialized nations (in most cases, less than 10 percent of GNP), they are an essential indirect input to a wide range of production processes. Price increases in this sector tend to cascade through the entire economic system, and supply shortages tend to have a pronounced negative multiplier effect on an economy's output. In short, this is a sector within which the consequences of supply bottlenecks can have severe repercussions.

Another characteristic of the resource sector is the length of time it takes to find and develop new sources of supply. If the basic transportation infrastructure is lacking, the time and the capital costs involved in bringing new supplies to market will be even greater. In addition, capital commitments for new projects are substantial (and have been increasing rapidly); investment risks—physical, economic, and political—are high; and financing is often difficult to obtain.

These characteristics suggest that, even if adequate resources are available for development, a reasonably predictable planning environment is important in this sector, for the sake not only of investors but also of those consumers of resources dependent upon stable supplies as inputs to the production of final goods. In recent years the planning environment for natural resource investment has become increasingly unstable, and investment plans have been frustrated and even shelved.[6] Some of the reasons for the instability in the investment climate concern issues covered earlier: uncertainty about future economic conditions and the impact of government attempts to exercise greater control over domestic resource endowments. Other reasons include such factors as regulatory delays in granting exploration permits and in approving the construction of transportation facilities, inability on the part of governments to develop and enact legislation relating to resource policies, and competing claims for scarce investment capital.

Because of the risky nature of many resource ventures, private investors must be motivated by prospects of returns well above normal on some of their activities to compensate for the likelihood of lower-than-normal, or even zero, returns on others. With increasing tax burdens imposed on successful resource ventures and the experience of government takeovers in recent years, the chances of realizing above-normal gains are perceived to have diminished, as have incentives for private investors to take risks.

It is possible, of course, that government investment will replace private investment as a source of expansion of resource supplies. Indeed, it is even possible that the rate of investment might accelerate as government-controlled resource enterprises are subjected to pressures to stimulate supply expansion in order to generate employment and foreign-exchange earnings. There is, however, at least one respect in which government enterprises are likely to be ineffective substitutes for investor-owned multinationals — the global diversification of investment.

Multinationals' planning horizons are far wider than those of national and, by extension, local governments. Earnings from one region can be invested, at risk, in promising regions in another part of the world. In contrast, national governments may be more reluctant to invest in speculative exploration activities outside their borders. Governments in promising, but risky, areas are, in turn, not as likely to be able to come up with the funds to finance exploration as are multinationals, who use a high proportion of internally generated financing for this purpose. Therefore, replacing private with government-controlled producers could well lead to a reduction in the overall level of risk-taking in resource sectors.

The U.S.-Canadian Resource Connection

It is difficult to isolate resource issues truly unique to the U.S.-Canadian context. A combination of factors, however, makes this particular bilateral context of interest in relation to the three central resource issues outlined in the preceding section.

- *The proximity and complementarity of the two economies.* The magnitude of trade flows and economic linkages between these two countries is

larger than between any other two nations in the world. Of particular interest for the project of which this volume is a part is the
pattern of bilateral trade. Resources flow in both directions, but
movements from north to south dominate. In south-to-north movements, finished goods and product components are dominant.
Because of proximity, Canada has become the dominant supplier of
a wide range of U.S. natural resource imports, especially in northern states. While alternative sources of supply exist, disruptions to
Canadian supplies would impose costly adjustments on particular
U.S. markets.

- *The degree of U.S. ownership in certain Canadian resource sectors.*
  U.S.-based multinationals control a substantial amount of energy
  and non-energy mineral production in Canada. Nationalism, the
  perception of foreign "domination," and a sense that Canada has
  received a "raw deal" in its resource transactions with the United
  States have been familiar themes in Canadian history. Global trends
  toward greater government efforts to control resource-based activities are illustrated in Canada in a variety of actions at both the
  federal and the provincial levels.

- *Asymmetries in the overall bilateral relationship.* The potential for supplying natural resources to export markets is essentially the only area in
  which Canadian economic aggregates are significantly greater than
  one-tenth those in the United States. But Canada is seeking to
  diversify its economy away from excessive reliance upon that sector
  in which it has a natural comparative advantage — resources. This
  search could affect the size and form of resources that Canada supplies to the United States. Canada is likely to seek to employ its
  resource export potential to improve its terms of access to U.S.
  markets for more highly processed resources and for manufactured
  products, particularly those for which considerations of economies of
  scale and specialization are important in determining cost competitiveness. Therefore, resource and general economic-policy issues
  are bound to be linked for policy purposes in future bilateral relations.

The Scope and Purposes of This Project

This volume is the first of three in a comprehensive project examining
the U.S.-Canadian resource connection. The contents of this volume,
which provides historical background and commentary on the bilateral
relationship, are summarized in the next section. Volume II consists of a
series of in-depth case studies of selected commodities — asbestos, bauxite
and aluminum, copper, forest products, iron ore, nickel, uranium, and
phosphate rock, potash, and fertilizers — and a brief compendium of some

additional resources for which detailed case studies were impractical. Volume III examines bilateral resource issues from the perspectives of corporations investing in the development of resources, of those employed in resource industries, and of environmentalists. Volume III also examines government institutions for dealing with bilateral resource matters and evaluates options for the future of the bilateral resource relationship. The unifying purpose of the three volumes is to assess factors likely to influence the evolution of this relationship, which has been going through a transition toward a still-uncertain outcome.

Those responsible for launching this project intended from the outset that it should be comprehensive rather than exhaustive. The topics chosen for investigation cover a broad range of issues, perspectives, and methodologies. Selection of the resources for which in-depth studies were to be provided was based on several criteria, including volume of bilateral trade involved, types of policy issues that had arisen, research already published in the area, and availability of authors. Virtually all the authors engaged in this project are political scientists or economists who have specialized in resource studies. Many topics required familiarity with the disciplines of political science and economics, although the blending of the two was easier for the research coordinators to request than for the authors to achieve. All the authors, however, have worked hard to provide the material requested of them.

The project was initiated in the hope that it would:

- put basic resource issues into a perspective that avoids the extremes of panic or of complacency;
- improve public understanding in the United States and Canada of the bilateral resource relationship and of the domestic developments that have shaped natural-resource-policy initiatives in both countries;
- evaluate objectively the options for the future of the bilateral resource relationship and the implications that might arise from various courses of action.

Outline of This Volume

The remaining chapters in this volume contain background material essential to the preparation of Volumes II and III.

Chapter 2 provides a detailed statistical account of the production and consumption of various natural resources in the United States and Canada, of the importance of these resources to the two economies, and of the extent to which the two nations have become linked through their bilateral trade in natural resources.

The authors of Chapters 3 and 4 describe, respectively, the policy process and the evolution of policy pertaining to natural resources in the United States, focusing particularly on points relevant to the bilateral context. Parallel material concerning Canada is contained in Chapters 6 and 7. Natural resource production and trade play a comparatively much larger role in the Canadian than in the U.S. economy. This fact has created policy concerns and tensions in Canada that differ in both degree and kind from those in the United States. Therefore, the section of this volume dealing with Canada begins, in Chapter 5, with a description and analysis of the basic context within which natural-resource-policy issues have been widely perceived in that country.

Furthermore, in Canada much more so than in the United States, national policies regarding natural resources must seek to accommodate often quite divergent regional interests. The current internal challenges to Canadian confederation highlight long-standing federal-provincial tensions. These tensions have been particularly acute in the area of natural resources. where the provinces have substantially greater powers than do the states. Accordingly, Chapters 8 and 9 consider natural-resource-policy issues from the perspectives of two regions of Canada whose impact on national policy decisions has become increasingly important—Quebec and the western provinces, particularly Alberta.

So much has been written about bilateral trade in oil and natural gas, and changes in the supply and demand positions respecting these energy sources have been occurring so rapidly, that the decision was made early in this project not to do new in-depth studies for these resources. But during the mid-1970s the bilateral relationship was influenced dramatically by policy developments involving oil and natural gas. Did these developments signal trends that might find broader applicability in the future? Or did they represent unique responses to a crisis situation that should not be regarded as a norm in considering future prospects? These questions are addressed in Chapter 10.

Finally, Chapter 11 synthesizes the material in this volume, focusing attention on issues meriting detailed examination in Volumes II and III of the project. It also places topics relevant to the bilateral context within a broader international framework.

Notes

1. D. H. Meadows *et al., The Limits to Growth* (New York: Universe Books, 1972).

2. Paul Johnson, *Enemies of Society* (London: Weidenfeld & Nicholson, 1977), p. 100.

3. Carl E. Beigie, *HRI Observations,* No. 5, *Oil Prices, Inflation, and Economic Growth* (Montreal: C. D. Howe Research Institute, 1974).

4. For a penetrating analysis of these and related resource issues, see John E. Tilton, *The Future of Nonfuel Minerals* (Washington, D.C.: The Brookings Institution, 1977).

5. See C. Fred Bergsten, "The Threat from the Third World," *Foreign Policy,* No. 11, Summer, 1973, pp. 102-24. Note that this article predated the surge in oil prices.

6. This instability is described in British–North American Committee, *Mineral Development in the Eighties: Prospects and Problems* (Montreal, London, and Washington, D.C.: C. D. Howe Research Institute, 1976).

2

The Resource Sectors of the United States and Canada: An Overview

RICHARD SHAFFNER

Introduction

For the industrial countries of the Western world, the twentieth century has been a period of strong economic growth and tremendous increases in individual material welfare. The availability of abundant supplies of raw materials, the ultimate source of all goods produced, has been an important factor behind this economic achievement. At the same time, resource industries have become more capital-intensive, and the share of the labor force they have employed has declined. Therefore, the supply of labor available to produce the other goods and services that have contributed so significantly to current individual and collective well-being has increased.

Resource industries in recent years have thus been characterized both by their continuing importance to the economy and by decreases in their relative size. This chapter considers the dimensions of their role in the economy by providing a general, and largely statistical, description of the resource sectors of the United States and Canada. Discussion will be confined to the three resource sectors that dominate in terms of economic importance: agriculture, mining, and forestry. The mineral industry will be subdivided for purposes of analysis into the metal, non-metal, and mineral-fuel sectors.

Several general trends in the resource sectors of the United States and Canada have been evident in recent years:

1. The resource sectors, both individually and in total, have been the source of a declining share of gross national product. Between 1963 and 1972, for example, raw-materials-producing industries, measured in terms of value added, declined as a share of GNP from 5.7 to 4.8 percent in the United States and from 11.5 to 8.1 percent in Canada (see Table A.5 in the statistical appendix at the end of this chapter). It should be pointed out,

The author would like to acknowledge the research assistance of Brian Jardim.

13

however, that the industries were not getting smaller in absolute terms; they were only growing more slowly than the total economy.

2. Per capita consumption of raw materials has been growing. As Figure 2.1 shows, per capita consumption of raw materials in the United States is estimated to have grown at an annual rate of 1.9 percent over the period 1920-69, compared to an average annual population growth of 1.3 percent. The mineral sector has been the main area of growth in raw materials consumption, while agricultural-product consumption has grown slightly faster than population and forest-product consumption has grown more slowly.

3. Production of raw materials by a particular country depends on its resource endowment — that is, on its mineral deposits, arable land, and forests. In total, both the United States and Canada have rich resource bases. However, production of raw materials in the United States, particularly of certain minerals, has not been increasing as rapidly as consumption. The resulting increased reliance on foreign sources of supply has led to concern about the long-range security of those supplies.

4. The uneven distribution of resource endowments makes trade in resource commodities essential. The United States is a net importer of resource commodities, and Canada is its largest supplier. Conversely, Canada is a net exporter of resource commodities, and the United States is its most important market.

The purpose of this chapter is to provide a systematic background for the more specific and detailed studies in this series. Three main areas are covered: the patterns of production and consumption of resource products in the United States and Canada and of trade in these commodities between the two countries; the significance of the resource sectors in the economies of the two countries; and the size of the resource bases of the various sectors. In putting this chapter together, it has been necessary to be selective; not all natural resource data and issues could be covered. Moreover, in some cases it might have been possible for the examination of an issue that is covered to have proceeded in a different way. Nevertheless, the chapter should provide a useful description of a major element in the U.S.-Canadian relationship.

The United States and Canada As Producers and Consumers of Resources

The United States and Canada are both major world producers of resource products. Unlike Japan and the countries of Western Europe, which must rely on imports for a large proportion of most raw materials, the United States and Canada are self sufficient in, or at least have significant domestic production of, many resource products.

FIGURE 2.1
Consumption of Raw Materials, United States, 1920-69[a]
(billion constant 1967 dollars)

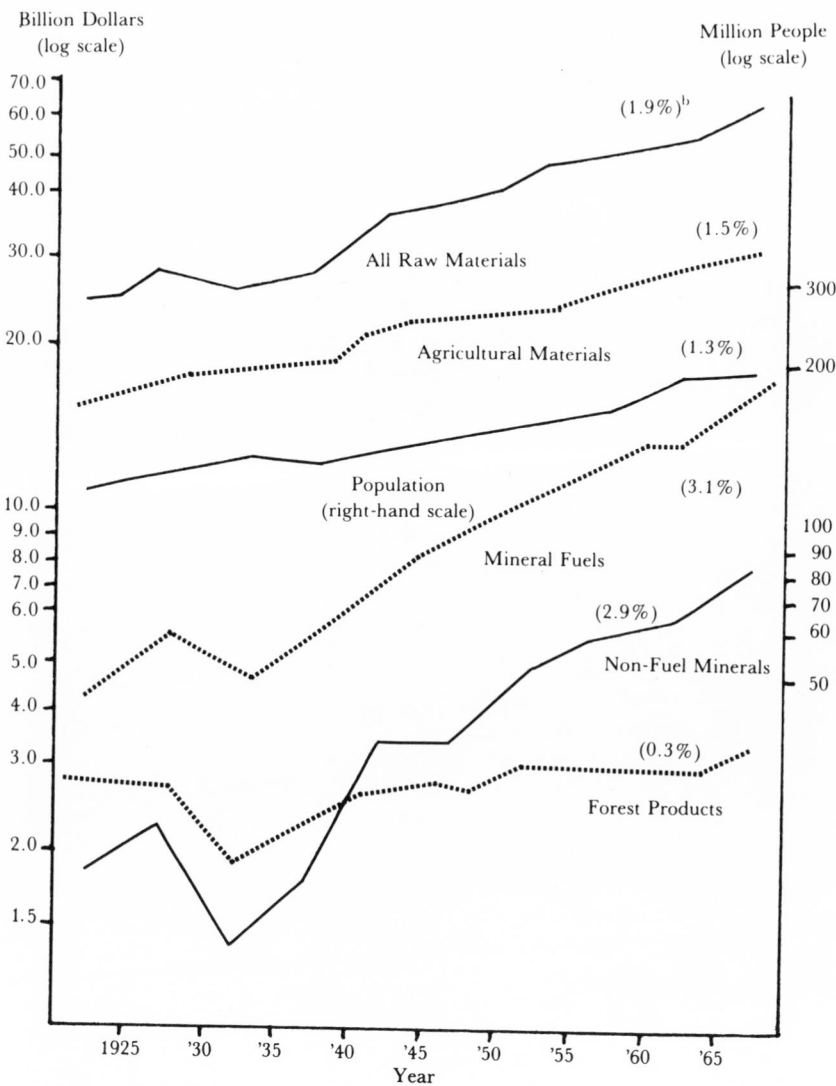

[a]Averages for five-year periods 1920-24 to 1965-69.

[b]Figures in brackets indicate average annual growth rates from 1920 to 1969.

Source: Vivian Eberle Spence, *Raw Materials in the United States Economy: 1900-1969,* U.S. Bureau of Mines and U.S. Bureau of Census Working Paper No. 35 (Washington, D.C.: U.S. Government Printing Office, 1972), pp. 13, 38-39.

In aggregate, the United States is by far the larger producer. The total value of production of primary mineral, forest, and agricultural products in the United States was $168 billion in 1975, compared to $24 billion in Canada.[1] Table 2.1 shows how this raw materials production is allocated among sectors, and Appendix Table A.1 provides details for major commodities.[2] Because raw materials production is not in proportion to the relative sizes of the two economies, however, it plays a considerably larger role in the total economy of Canada than in that of the United States. For example, the value of production on a per capita basis in 1975 was $1,056 in Canada compared to $795 in the United States.[3]

There are deep historical roots behind the relative importance of the resource sectors in the two countries. With the principal exception of the cotton and tobacco trades, the resource industries of the United States developed mainly in response to domestic demand for resource products.

TABLE 2.1
Value of Raw Materials Production,
United States and Canada, 1975
(million U.S. dollars)

	United States	Canada
Minerals:[a]		
Metals	5,196	4,712
Non-metals	9,518	923
Fuels	47,561	6,531
	62,275	12,167
Forest products[b]	13,788	1,882
Agricultural products:[c]		
Crops	46,661	4,689
Livestock	42,902	4,814
	89,563	9,503
Total raw materials	165,626	23,552

[a]Mine production.
[b]Industrial roundwood from logging operations — that is, the value of the cut logs that are used for the production of lumber, plywood and veneer, and pulp and paper products.
[c]Cash receipts from farming operations.

Source: Table A.1

In contrast, it is widely accepted that the establishment of a series of resource industries to supply markets first in Europe and later in the United States was a major driving force behind Canada's economic development.[4] Among the succession of resource products that provided stimulus to the Canadian economy were cod, furs, timber, wheat, and minerals.

The historical pattern is reflected in the relative positions of the various resource sectors in the two countries over the past forty years, as shown in Figure 2.2. The per capita value of forest-product production, for example, has been consistently higher in Canada than in the United States. Canada's lumber industry was developed in the early 1800s to supply markets in Europe. Later, a large part of the North American pulp and paper industry established itself in eastern Canada after U.S. import restrictions were eliminated in the early 1900s. The U.S. forest-product industry, on the other hand, was developed mainly to supply U.S. markets.

Canada's mining industry, in contrast, was slower to develop than that of the United States. Until the early 1950s the per capita value of mineral production in the United States exceeded that in Canada. The origin of the shift in relative positions can be traced to concern in the United States about the adequacy of domestic sources of mineral supplies following World War II.[5] The result was a sharp upswing in mineral development activity in foreign countries by U.S. mining interests. Canada became one of the main areas of interest for U.S. investors because it was close and politically stable. Prior to that time, even though large deposits had been identified, the Canadian mineral industry had remained relatively undeveloped: deposits were often great distances from markets, transportation facilities frequently did not exist, and labor was scarce.

In the agricultural sector, per capita U.S. production has consistently exceeded that in Canada. From the earliest settlement, agriculture developed in close symmetry with population growth in both countries. Today, both countries are major exporters of cereals to other parts of the world. The United States is a slightly more important per capita producer of agricultural products than Canada, mainly because it has a better endowment of arable land and because its climate is more favorable for agriculture.

Even though production of resource commodities in the United States is great, total consumption is even greater. The United States, as a result, can be classified as a "consumer country." Canada, on the other hand, is a "producer country" because overall production exceeds consumption. There is no strict definition for the use of these terms, and although the United States is not a consumer country to the degree that Japan or the countries of the European Community are, Table 2.2 shows that it must depend on imports for a significant share of its raw materials needs. In the period 1972-75, production in the United States exceeded domestic consumption

FIGURE 2.2

Trends in Raw Materials Production on a Per Capita Basis,
United States and Canada, 1936-75[a]
(U.S. dollars)

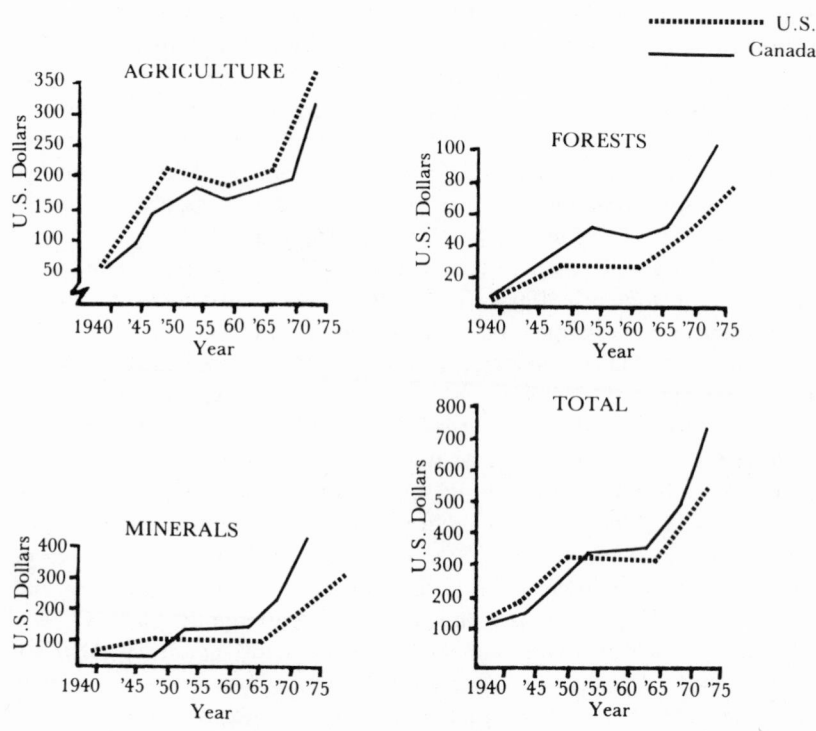

[a]Figures based on five-year averages.

Sources: U.S. Department of the Interior, Bureau of Mines, *Mineral Industry in Early America* (Washington, D.C.: U.S. Government Printing Office, 1977), p. 62; U.S. Department of Commerce, Bureau of the Census, *Historical Statistics of the United States: Colonial Times to 1957* (Washington, D.C.: U.S. Government Printing Office, 1960); U.S. Department of Agriculture, *Agricultural Statistics,* 1972, 1976 (Washington, D.C.: U.S. Government Printing Office, 1972, 1976); U.S. Department of Agriculture, Forest Service, *The Demand and Price Situation for Forest Products,* 1964, 1974-75 (Washington, D.C.: U.S. Government Printing Office, 1965, 1975); Food and Agriculture Organization of the United Nations, *Yearbook of Forest Products,* 1974 (Rome, 1976), and *World Forest Products Statistics: A Ten-Year Summary, 1954-1963* (Rome, 1965); Statistics Canada, *Quarterly Bulletin of Agricultural Statistics,* October-December, 1975 (Ottawa: Information Canada, 1976); A. E. Spoerri, *Mineral Production of Canada by Province, 1931-1975* (Ottawa: Energy, Mines and Resources Canada, 1976); M. C. Urquhart, ed., *Historical Statistics of Canada* (Toronto: Macmillan Company of Canada, 1965); Department of Finance, *Economic Review,* April, 1976 (Ottawa, 1976); U.S. Department of Commerce, Bureau of Economic Analysis, *Business Statistics,* 1975 (Washington, D.C.: U.S. Government Printing Office, 1976); Bank of Canada, *Review,* various issues.

TABLE 2.2
Ratio of Production to Consumption for Selected
Raw Materials, United States and Canada
(averages for the period 1972-75)

	Ratio of Production to Consumption	
	United States	Canada
Minerals:[a]		
Metals:		
Bauxite	0.12	0.0
Chromium	0.0	0.0
Cobalt	0.02	8.82
Copper	0.97	3.55
Gold	0.58	n.a.
Iron ore	0.62	3.61
Lead	0.87	3.51
Manganese	0.0	0.0
Mercury	0.27	11.08
Molybdenum	1.78	8.37
Nickel	0.30	23.11
Silver	0.46	3.73
Tin	0.28	0.04
Tungsten	0.48	3.54
Uranium	1.76	n.a.
Zinc	0.43	9.06
Non-metals:		
Asbestos	0.16	43.02
Phosphate rock	1.37	0.0
Potash	0.48	21.97
Fuels:		
Coal	1.12	0.90
Natural gas	0.98	2.42
Petroleum	0.73	0.97
Forest products:[b]		
Lumber	0.85	2.44
Plywood and veneer	0.93	0.95
Wood pulp	0.97	1.49
Paper and paperboard	0.92	3.00
Agricultural products:		
Wheat	2.79	2.80
Rice	1.66	0.0
Barley	1.14	1.64
Corn	1.28	0.66
Meat	0.98	1.00

[a]Includes production from domestic mines and secondary sources, such as recycling of scrap.
[b]Measured in terms of domestically produced industrial roundwood used in the production of each product.

Sources: U.S. Department of the Interior, Bureau of Mines, *Commodity Data Summaries,* 1977 (Washington, D.C.: U.S. Government Printing Office, 1977); U.S. Department of Agriculture, Forest Service, *The Demand and Price Situation for Forest Products,* 1974-75 (Washington, D.C.: U.S. Government Printing Office, 1975); Food and Agriculture Organization of the United Nations, *Production Yearbook,* 1975, and *Yearbook of Forest Products,* 1975 (Rome, 1977); Energy, Mines and Resources Canada, *Canadian Minerals Yearbook,* 1974, and pre-release data for 1975.

for only 4 of 22 major minerals, and consumption of forest products exceeded production by a small margin as well. In Canada, meanwhile, production was in excess of consumption for 13 of the 21 minerals for which data are available, and in all cases production was more than twice domestic needs. Canada also had production considerably in excess of domestic demand in lumber and pulp products. In terms of agricultural commodities, the United States is, like Canada, a producer country. Both are large exporters of wheat and relatively self-sufficient in, or have slight surpluses of, other major products.

One reason why the United States is a consumer country to the extent that it is has been the slow growth in its production of resource commodities relative to the rest of the world. Between the early 1950s and the early 1970s, the rate of growth in production in the United States exceeded or equaled the rate of growth in the world in total for only 2 of 19 major mineral commodities for which data are available (see Appendix Table A.2 for details). Growth in U.S. production of forest products and most major agricultural commodities also lagged behind world trends. Over the same period, growth in Canadian production of 10 of the 13 mineral commodities for which data are available was faster than for the world in total.

The Bilateral Trade Picture

The extent to which the United States is a consumer country and Canada a producer country is perhaps best illustrated by examining each country's trade in resource products. In 1975, U.S. exports of crude and fabricated resource commodities were 36.7 percent of total U.S. exports, while imports of crude and fabricated resource commodities were 52.7 percent of total imports (see Table 2.3). In Canada, in contrast, exports of resource commodities were 62.3 percent of total exports, and imports of resource commodities were only 30.5 percent of total imports. In dollar terms, U.S. exports of resource commodities, which totaled $38.9 billion, were almost double Canadian resource-commodity exports of $19.6 billion. However, the United States imported $50.7 billion in resource commodities, while Canada imported only $10.4 billion. Thus the United States is a net importer of resource commodities, and Canada is a net exporter.[6]

To a large degree the resource products that Canada produces in abundance are those the United States must import. This is hardly coincidental; the Canadian mining and forest-product industries have been developed perhaps as much in response to demand in the United States as to demand in Canada. In 1975, 57.4 percent of Canada's exports of crude and fabricated raw materials were to the United States. As a share of total U.S. imports of resource commodities, however, shipments from Canada

TABLE 2.3
Summary of Trade in Crude and Fabricated
Resource Commodities, United States and Canada, 1975

UNITED STATES

	Percentage of Total U.S. Exports	Percentage of Total U.S. Imports	Percentage Exported to Canada	Percentage Imported from Canada
Mineral commodities:				
Metals	5.4	9.7	19.1	22.7
Non-metals	2.6	2.4	16.6	31.5
Fuels	4.2	27.5	19.4	18.0
Total	12.2	39.6	18.7	20.0
Forest commodities	3.8	4.4	18.4	84.2
Agricultural commodities	20.6	8.7	5.6	4.4
Total, resource commodities	36.7	52.7	11.3	22.8
Total, all commodities	100.0	100.0	20.2	22.9

CANADA

	Percentage of Total Canadian Exports	Percentage of Total Canadian Imports	Percentage Exported to the U.S.	Percentage Imported from the U.S.
Mineral commodities:				
Metals	15.4	7.1	49.6	60.0
Non-metals	2.9	1.6	57.1	74.3
Fuels	16.3	12.0	89.9	16.4
Total	34.6	20.7	68.4	35.2
Forest commodities	15.8	2.0	66.6	88.7
Agricultural commodities	11.9	7.8	13.0	55.2
Total, resource commodities	62.3	30.5	57.4	43.9
Total, all commodities	100.0	100.0	65.2	67.8

Source: Table A.3.

amounted to only 22.8 percent. This is partly a reflection of the size of the U.S. economy relative to that of Canada, but it is also because, as Appendix Table A.3 shows, Canada provides relatively little of the large mineral fuel and agricultural-commodity requirements of the United States.

The extent to which Canada relies on the United States as a market for specific resource commodities and the extent to which the United States relies on Canada as a source of supply are shown in Table 2.4.

The share of resource commodities in the flow of goods from Canada to the United States has been relatively stable. Table 2.5 shows that Canada's exports of resource commodities to the United States are much the same now as in 1956 and that imports of Canadian resource commodities are of about the same importance in terms of total imports in the United States. (For details of the trends in the trade of mineral, forest, and agricultural commodities, see Appendix Table A.4.) Table 2.5 indicates several other interesting trends. To those who contend that Canada relies too heavily on the exports of its primary industries, the table suggests that resource-commodity exports have been declining over time as a share of total Canadian exports. To those in the United States who worry about that country's dependence on imported raw materials, it suggests that resource-commodity imports have been decreasing as a percentage of total U.S. imports. Finally, Table 2.5 indicates that the reverse flow of resource commodities, from the United States to Canada, has been declining in importance in terms of the total resource-commodity trade of both countries.

Despite the importance of the resource-product trade between the United States and Canada, it is interesting to observe that Canada's exports of crude and fabricated resource commodities were only 57.4 percent of total Canadian exports to the United States in 1975.[7] This figure is less than the 62.3 percent of total Canadian exports to all countries accounted for by exports of crude and fabricated resource commodities. One reason for this is the large trade in automobiles and automobile parts that has grown up between the United States and Canada. As a result of the 1965 U.S.-Canadian automotive agreement, the value of Canadian exports of end products to the United States has greatly increased. When the automobile trade is removed from the calculation, however, resource-commodity exports to the United States are still a smaller proportion than those to all countries. By this calculation, 75.5 percent of all exports to the United States in 1975 were resource commodities, compared to 77.3 percent of exports to all countries.[8] Thus while the United States is the dominant market for Canada's resource-commodity exports, the proportion of non-resource commodities that it imports from Canada is higher than that of the other countries to which Canada exports.

In analyzing trade in resource products among the United States,

TABLE 2.4
Flow of Selected Crude and Fabricated Resource Commodities from Canada to the United States, 1975

	Total Value of Canadian Exports (mil. U.S.$)	Exports to the U.S. As Percentage of Total Canadian Exports	Total Value of U.S. Imports (mil. U.S.$)	Imports from Canada As Percentage of Total U.S. Imports
Mineral commodities:				
Metals:				
Aluminum	456.4	61.8	442.5	63.7
Bauxite	—	0.0	267.0	0.0
Chromium	—	0.0	68.7	0.0
Cobalt	4.0	82.7	25.6	5.6
Copper	792.3	23.1	423.8	48.1
Gold	284.1	54.4	456.6	43.0
Iron	1,437.6	66.4	5,608.9	15.8
Lead	105.0	23.2	50.5	29.5
Manganese	—	0.0	77.1	0.0
Molybdenum	71.8	5.5	6.2	62.9
Nickel	913.2	40.6	460.5	69.3
Platinum	52.5	8.9	123.6	4.0
Silver	154.7	80.9	395.4	38.0
Tin	2.2	78.7	360.3	0.04
Uranium	46.3	59.8	24.5	97.0
Zinc	498.2	34.7	340.9	51.4
Non-metals:				
Asbestos	310.2	34.5	116.6	88.5
Phosphate rock	—	0.0	27.5	0.0
Potash	287.2	81.0	317.2	94.2
Fuels:				
Coal	489.8	3.4	205.4	20.9
Natural gas	1,073.6	100.0	1,071.1	99.6
Petroleum	3,606.6	96.5	25,169.9	14.6
Forest commodities:				
Lumber	1,028.4	77.5	1,115.8	84.2
Plywood and veneer	88.2	44.8	363.1	17.7
Wood pulp	1,782.9	54.6	1,039.4	97.5
Newsprint	1,712.4	78.0	1,427.3	99.5
Other paper and paperboard	278.3	40.5	262.8	45.8
Agricultural commodities:				
Wheat	2,055.9	0.5	5.0	5.6
Barley	425.7	12.1	56.8	0.1
Oilseeds	340.7	4.7	37.5	45.7
Live animals and meat	247.6	47.6	1,283.0	10.3
Fruits and vegetables	106.6	37.4	992.6	4.2
Sugar	70.3	51.2	2,070.3	1.5
Coffee	—	0.0	1,672.8	0.0
Cocoa	—	0.0	433.8	0.0

Sources: U.S. Department of Commerce, Bureau of the Census, *U.S. Imports: Commodity by Country,* December, 1975 (Washington, D.C.: U.S. Government Printing Office, 1976); Statistics Canada, *Summary of External Trade,* December, 1975, and *Exports by Commodity,* December, 1975 (Ottawa: Information Canada, 1976).

TABLE 2.5

Summary of Trends in Resource-Commodity Trade,
United States and Canada,[a] 1956, 1965, and 1975

UNITED STATES

	1956	1965	1975
Resource-commodity exports as percentage of total U.S. exports	39.7	38.9	36.7
Resource-commodity imports as percentage of total U.S. imports	69.0	57.6	52.7
Resource-commodity exports to Canada as percentage of all resource-commodity exports	17.9	14.8	11.3
Resource-commodity imports from Canada as percentage of all resource-commodity imports	24.8	27.2	22.8

CANADA

	1956	1965	1975
Resource-commodity exports as percentage of total Canadian exports	81.8	83.5	62.3
Resource-commodity imports as percentage of total Canadian imports	41.4	27.8	30.5
Resource-commodity exports to the United States as percentage of all resource-commodity exports	58.9	53.5	57.4
Resource-commodity imports from the United States as percentage of all resource-commodity imports	61.9	46.5	43.9

[a]Includes crude and fabricated resource commodities.

Source: Table A.4.

Canada, and other countries, it should be recognized that trade is not entirely a function of resource endowment. Resource industries operate mainly on the basis of their economic competitiveness in world markets. Because a country is a net importer of a certain raw material does not necessarily mean that it could not satisfy its requirements from domestic resources. It possibly means only that foreign sources of supply are cheaper than the domestic sources that might be developed. In such cases, however, bringing domestic sources of supply into production would probably take a number of years. In addition, it is possible for a country to produce roughly what it consumes of a particular resource commodity and still have significant exports and imports of that commodity. This is particularly true of large countries like the United States and Canada, where transportation costs of moving a commodity within a country may exceed those involved in trade with another country. For example, Canada exports coal mined from its large western deposits, while industries in eastern Canada use coal imported from the United States.

Resource Industries and the Two Economies

Resource industries have long played major roles in the economies of the United States and Canada. The availability of land with potential for agricultural development was the primary driving force behind the westward movement of the American population in the nineteenth century, and settlement of the Canadian West somewhat later followed a similar pattern. In both countries, towns — and, eventually, cities — grew up to serve the agrarian population, and railways and highways were built to move the produce. Communities were also established, and transportation links constructed to serve forest-product industries and to exploit mineral deposits sometimes far removed from existing centers of population. Several entirely new communities have been constructed in Canada since 1950 to serve new, remote mining areas.

Measuring the overall impact of resource industries in terms of settlement, the growth of cities, and the development of transportation systems, however, is very difficult. Instead, economists tend to concentrate on the direct effects of resource sectors — such measures as employment, shares of national income, and the value of exports generated. There is also increasing interest in the indirect, or linkage, effects of resource industries with other industries. These include linkages with the industries that supply the resource industries or that provide services for their labor forces (so-called "backward" linkages) and linkages with industries that the resource industries supply with raw materials (or "forward" linkages).

Direct Economic Contributions

The simplest way to evaluate the importance of the resource industries is to look at their share of the principal measures of the size of the economy. These are measures of the direct contribution of the resource industries to the total economy. Four main measures of the size of the resource industries in the United States and Canada are shown in Table 2.6.

The most fundamental is value added as a share of gross national product. Value added is the value of production less the cost of intermediate inputs such as materials, fuel, and contract work. The value added of any industry, consequently, is what that industry contributes to national in-

TABLE 2.6
Indicators of the Importance of Resource Industries
in the Economies of the United States and Canada, 1972
(percentages)

	Value Added As Percentage of GNP		Employment As Percentage of the Labor Force		Wages and Salaries As Percentage of Total[a]		Capital Stock As Percentage of Total[b]	
	U.S.	Canada	U.S.	Canada	U.S.	Canada	U.S.	Canada
Primary industries:								
Agriculture	2.5	3.2	4.0	5.4	2.9	2.8	8.8	8.0
Forestry	0.1	0.8	0.1	0.5	0.1	0.8	0.1	0.7
Mining	2.3	4.1	0.7	1.2	1.0	1.8	9.1	8.8
	4.8	8.1	4.8	7.2	3.9	5.4	18.0	17.5
Secondary industries:								
Food manufacturing	2.5	2.5	1.6	2.1	1.7	2.2	2.0	2.0
Forest-based manufacturing	1.9	3.2	1.4	2.5	1.6	3.2	3.5	4.8
Mineral manufacturing	2.5	3.2	1.5	2.0	2.2	3.0	5.5	5.8
	6.8	8.9	4.5	6.7	5.5	8.4	11.0	12.6
Total, resource industries	11.7	17.0	9.3	13.8	9.4	13.8	29.0	30.1
Total, manufacturing industries	30.1	23.4	21.9	18.8	27.5	22.6	26.6	22.2

[a]Total wages and salaries is assumed to be non-military wages and salaries as derived from the national accounts plus the net income of farm operators from farm production. Wages and salaries in agriculture is assumed to be the net income of farm operators from farm production.
[b]Gross capital stock, excluding government, in historical dollars.

Sources: See Tables A.5 and A.6; Statistics Canada, Fixed Capital Flows and Stocks, 1970-74 (Ottawa, 1975); U.S. Department of Labor, Bureau of Labor Statistics, unpublished data.

come. The sum of the value added in each industry should equal gross national product. In 1972 the value added in the primary resource industries was 4.8 percent of gross national product in the United States and 8.1 percent in Canada. Value added in secondary resource industries was another 6.8 percent of GNP in the United States and 8.9 percent in Canada, making the totals for the primary and secondary resource industries combined 11.7 and 17.0 percent, respectively. Secondary resource industries include the resource processing and resource-based manufacturing that follow from the primary activity — that is, the extraction or harvesting of the raw materials. Secondary industries include manufacturing up to a semifabricated stage, but not to the end-product stage.[9]

Secondary resource industries are included in this analysis because of their close association with the primary industries. Because data are usually collected on the basis of a firm's main activity, for example, it is possible that there will be an overlapping of data between the two, thereby causing imprecision in the figures for the primary and secondary industries separately, although not necessarily for the total. In addition, it may be that the major part of the economic activity will be at the secondary level. This is the case in forest products, where the value of making lumber, plywood, and paper products far exceeds the value of the cut logs that go into these products. It should be noted, however, that the secondary activity indicated for each sector does not follow directly from the primary activity indicated in that country. Some of the raw materials on which the secondary activities are based may be imported, and some primary products may be exported prior to the secondary industry stage.

A note of caution is in order on the subject of the data that are being used. Table 2.6 shows that Canada's resource industries are larger relative to its total economy than are the resource industries of the United States. A general statement like this can be made safely enough, but it should be noted that the definitions of primary and secondary industries are not identical for the United States and Canada and, therefore, that the data are not fully comparable between the two countries. The data in this section, consequently, should be used only to evaluate the structure of the resource industries within each country, and not to make intercountry comparisons.

In terms of value added, the mining industry is the most important primary industry in Canada, and the combination of mining and mineral manufacturing is largest in total. Agriculture is the largest primary industry in the United States, and agriculture and food manufacturing are the largest combined. In both cases, however, the mineral industries are very nearly as large.

Another fundamental measure of the size of the resource industries is the employment they generate. In Canada, 7.2 percent of the 1972 labor force was employed in primary resource industries, and 13.8 percent in primary and secondary resource industries. The sector with the largest share is agriculture, with over half of the total. In the United States, 4.8 percent of the total labor force was employed in the primary sector, and another 4.5 percent in the secondary sector. Here again over half the employment is in agriculture and food manufacturing.

Table 2.6 also shows the shares of wages and salaries received by the various resource sectors and the distribution of private capital stock. The latter accounts for a much larger share of the total than is the case with the other three measures. Part of this difference can be explained by the exclusion of government investment from the total. This has been done because an estimate for government-sector capital stock in the United States is not available. If government investment is included in the total for Canada, however, resource industries in total still account for 24.3 percent.[10]

On the basis of these measures it is possible to develop some basic data about the relative uses of capital and labor inputs in the various resource industries. Table 2.7 shows that mining is clearly the most labor-efficient sector; both value added relative to man-hours of production-worker time and value added relative to total wages paid to production workers are considerably above the levels indicated for the other resource industries and for total manufacturing. In forestry, on the other hand, these measures indicate a much greater dependence on labor as an input. The secondary resource industries generally lie between these two extremes. Unfortunately, comparative data for agriculture are not available. When output per unit of labor is high, it can generally be assumed that the capital each unit of labor has to work with is quite high. As one would expect, therefore, Table 2.7 shows that mining is the most capital-intensive of the resource industries. The value added per dollar of capital spending in mining is the lowest of any of the industries, and capital spending per man-hour of production-worker time is the highest. Conversely, these measures indicate relatively low capital intensity in forestry. It is also worth noting that the secondary resource industries tend to be more capital-intensive than do manufacturing industries in total.

A final measure of the economic importance of resource industries is their impact on a country's balance of trade. Table 2.8 summarizes the trade-balance effect of exports and imports of crude and fabricated resource commodities. A positive trade-balance effect for a particular resource sector means that exports exceed imports, with the number indicating net exports as a percentage of total exports for the sector. Conversely, a negative number means that imports exceed exports for a certain resource sector, with the number indicating net imports as a percentage of total imports for

TABLE 2.7

Indicators of Relative Labor and Capital Intensity in Resource Industries, United States and Canada, 1972

	Value Added per Man-Hour		Value Added/ Production Wages		Production Wages per Man-Hour		Value Added/ Capital Stock		Capital Stock per Man-Hour	
	U.S.	Canada	U.S.	Canada	U.S.	Canada	U.S.	Canada	U.S.	Canada
Primary industries:										
Agriculture	—	—	—	—	—	—	0.30	0.18	—	—
Forestry	8.9	9.1	2.6	2.1	4.0	4.3	0.76	0.50	11.8	18.1
Mining	29.1	28.3	6.2	6.4	6.8	4.4	0.24	0.22	121.0	130.9
Total, primary resource industries	—	—	—	—	—	—	0.27	0.21	—	—
Secondary industries:										
Food manufacturing	14.8	9.5	4.1	3.2	5.5	3.0	1.29	0.56	11.4	16.9
Forest-based manufacturing	10.7	8.8	2.8	2.3	5.0	3.8	0.58	0.31	18.3	28.4
Mineral manufacturing	14.2	11.9	2.8	2.9	6.7	4.2	0.48	0.26	29.7	46.2
Total, secondary resource industries	13.2	9.9	3.3	2.7	5.7	3.7	0.66	0.33	19.9	30.5
Total, manufacturing industries	13.3	9.5	3.4	2.8	6.5	3.4	1.20	0.49	11.0	19.6

Sources: See Table 2.6; Statistics Canada, *Fixed Capital Flows and Stocks, 1970–74;* U.S. Department of Labor, Bureau of Labor Statistics, unpublished data.

the sector. Table 2.8 shows that resource trade has had a substantial
positive effect on Canada's merchandise trade balance. In 1975, exports of
mineral, forest, and agricultural materials all exceeded imports. In the
United States, trade in resource commodities had a large negative impact
on the trade balance. The cause of the negative effect was the mineral sector, and mineral fuels in particular. At the same time, U.S. exports of
agricultural materials had a substantial positive effect on the country's trade
balance, and the negative effect of trade in forest materials was very small.
If trade in mineral fuels is excluded, in fact, the United States would have
had a sizable surplus in resource-commodity trade.

TABLE 2.8

*Net Trade-Balance Effect of Trade in Crude and Fabricated
Resource Commodities, United States and Canada, 1975[a]*

	United States	Canada
Mineral commodities:		
Metals		
Crude	– 0.6	+ 5.5
Fabricated	– 3.1	+ 2.3
Non-metals		
Crude	+ 0.4	+ 1.9
Fabricated	+ 0.5	– 0.6
Fuels		
Crude	– 18.0	+ 2.4
Fabricated	– 4.9	+ 1.1
	– 26.5	+ 12.2
Forest commodities:		
Crude	+ 0.7	–
Fabricated	– 0.9	+ 13.6
	– 0.2	+ 13.6
Agricultural commodities	+ 12.7	+ 3.5
Total, resource commodities	– 12.6	+ 29.3

[a]Net trade balances are calculated by subtracting imports from exports for each commodity
group and, if positive, by dividing by total exports; if negative, by dividing by total imports.

Source: See Table A.3.

Indirect Economic Contributions

In addition to their direct contributions to the economy, the resource industries also make indirect contributions through a series of backward and forward linkages. Backward linkages refer to the benefits that accrue to other sectors of the economy from supplying resource industries with the goods and services they need. These include the machinery used in the resource industries, the transportation systems that serve them, and facilities such as stores and schools for the work force and their families. Forward linkages refer to the benefits from upgrading industries that may result because of the existence of resource industries. Actually, the secondary resource industries included in the analysis of the previous section are largely examples of forward linkages from primary resource industries. There are probably also many instances where firms manufacturing products for final consumption exist in an area because of the presence of a particular resource industry supplying a basic raw material.

The effect of the backward and forward linkages of resource industries in the United States and Canada is probably several times the direct contribution of these industries. Measuring these indirect contributions, however, is much more complex. It is done by input-output analysis, a technique that relates each sector in the economy to every other sector. Studies have been done in both countries to determine the total impact of various resource sectors on the economy, but the results are too involved to be presented here.[11] An indication of the linkages that exist between the resource sector and other sectors is given elsewhere in this volume.[12]

The Shrinking Relative Role of the Resource Sector

Describing the economic significance of a sector at a particular point in time tells only part of the story; it is also useful to know what has been happening to that sector over time. In the case of the resource industries, the trend in both the United States and Canada has been toward a smaller role in the total economy. This trend has been evident for many years in the case of employment as labor-saving machinery has increasingly replaced manual operations, but it is also true for value of output.

In the period 1963-72, value added as a share of gross national product in Canada increased at an average annual rate of 5.3 percent in the primary resource industries and 6.6 percent in the secondary resource industries, compared to 7.6 percent in all manufacturing industries and 9.5 percent in total GNP (see Table 2.9). Only the mining industry, with a growth rate of 9.7 percent annually, exceeded the rate of increase in GNP. Mining consequently replaced agriculture as the most important primary industry (see Appendix Tables A.5 and A.6 for these and many other numbers used in

TABLE 2.9

Changes in the Shares of Value Added and Employment of
Resource Industries, United States and Canada, 1963–72
(average annual growth rates)

	Value Added		Employment	
	U.S.	Canada	U.S.	Canada
Primary industries:				
Agriculture	5.6	2.5	– 3.4	– 3.3
Forestry	9.3	0.9	0.9	– 2.7
Mining	5.8	9.7	– 0.3	1.3
Total, primary resource industries	5.7	5.3	– 2.9	– 2.6
Secondary industries:				
Food manufacturing	5.4	6.7	– 0.7	0.4
Forest-based manufacturing	8.2	7.4	1.5	1.9
Mineral manufacturing	5.0	6.0	0.0	1.8
Total, secondary resource industries	5.9	6.6	0.2	1.2
Total, resource industries	5.8	6.0	– 1.5	– 0.9
Total, manufacturing industries	7.0	7.6	1.2	1.8
Gross national product	7.8	9.5		
Civilian labor force			2.1	3.2

Sources: Tables A.5 and A.6.

this section). As a result of the slow growth pattern, value added as a share of GNP in the primary resource industries declined from 11.5 percent in 1963 to 8.1 percent in 1972, and in the secondary resource industries dropped from 11.2 to 8.9 percent in the same period.

Meanwhile, employment in Canadian primary resource industries in the 1963-72 period declined at an average annual rate of 2.6 percent and in the secondary resource industries increased at an average rate of only 1.2 percent per year. By comparison, employment in total manufacturing grew at an average annual rate of 1.8 percent, and growth in the total labor force was 3.2 percent. Of the three primary resource sectors, only in mining was there a positive change in employment. In the secondary resource industries, however, both forest-based manufacturing and mineral manufacturing recorded growth rates in employment about in the range of the growth rates in total manufacturing. The share of the Canadian labor force in primary resource industries declined from 11.9 percent in 1963 to 7.2 percent in 1972, and the share in secondary resource industries declined from 7.8 percent to 6.7 percent in the same period.

Quite similar trends have prevailed in the resource industries of the United States. Value added as a share of GNP increased at an average annual rate of 5.7 percent in the primary resource industries and at a rate of 5.9 percent in the secondary resource industries in the period 1963-72. These compare with growth rates of 7.0 percent in total manufacturing and 7.8 percent in GNP. The only resource industries that grew faster than GNP were forestry, with an annual rate of increase of 9.3 percent, and forest-based manufacturing, which grew at a rate of 8.2 percent per year. Between 1963 and 1972, value added in primary resource industries as a share of GNP slipped from 5.7 percent to 4.8 percent, and value added in secondary resource industries declined from 8.0 percent of GNP to 6.8 percent.

Employment in U.S. primary resource industries, meanwhile, declined at an average annual rate of 2.9 percent and in secondary resource industries grew at only 0.2 percent per year. Only forestry and forest-based manufacturing recorded positive growth in employment, and in both instances the growth was slower than the 2.1 percent average annual rate of increase in the labor force. In total, the share of the U.S. labor force employed in primary resource industries declined from 7.5 percent in 1963 to 4.8 percent in 1972, and in secondary resource industries, from 5.3 percent to 4.5 percent.

Regional Impact of Resource Industries

Another aspect of the economic significance of resource industries is the difference in their impact on the various regions of a country. No industries situate themselves uniformly across a country; but in the case of primary resource industries, location depends explicitly on the distribution of mineral deposits, forests, and arable land.

Table 2.10 shows how the production of raw materials is distributed, by region, in the United States and Canada. In most cases one region predominates in the production of a particular resource. For example, British Columbia is by far the major producing region for forest products in Canada, and the Pacific region of the United States is almost equally dominant. The Prairie provinces (Alberta, Saskatchewan, and Manitoba) are the source of more than 40 percent of the value of both agricultural and mineral production in Canada. The Prairies dominate mineral production because they account for 91 percent of Canadian mineral-fuel production.[13] The West South Central similarly dominates U.S. mineral

34

TABLE 2.10
Production of Primary Resource Products, by Region, United States and Canada, 1972[a]
(percentage shares)

Region	Mineral Products	Forest Products	Agricultural Products
United States:			
New England	0.5	2.4	1.4
Middle Atlantic	5.2	2.4	4.0
North East Central	8.1	3.9	16.2
North West Central	6.4	2.1	27.5
South Atlantic	9.1	10.8	11.0
South East Central	5.8	6.4	6.5
South West Central	43.7	5.9	12.5
Mountain	14.0	14.9	8.9
Pacific	7.3	51.3	12.2
	100.0	100.0	100.0
Canada:			
Atlantic provinces	7.3	8.4	3.4
Quebec	12.3	18.8	14.3
Ontario	24.0	13.3	29.8
Prairie provinces	42.3	2.6	47.9
British Columbia	10.6	56.9	4.6
Yukon and Northwest Territories	3.5	–	–
	100.0	100.0	100.0

[a]Derived from values of production in 1972, except for forest products in the United States, which is derived from volume of production in 1970.

Sources: U.S. Department of Commerce, Bureau of the Census, Statistical Abstract of the United States, 1976 (Washington, D.C.: U.S. Government Printing Office, 1976), pp. 678, 703; U.S. Department of Commerce, Bureau of the Census, Statistical Abstract of the United States, 1974 (Washington, D.C.: U.S. Government Printing Office, 1974), p. 611; Statistics Canada, General Review of the Mineral Industries, 1974 (Ottawa, 1976), pp. 8-9; Statistics Canada, Canadian Forestry Statistics, 1974 (Ottawa, 1976), pp. 12-13; Statistics Canada, Quarterly Bulletin of Agricultural Statistics, October-December, 1975 (Ottawa, 1976), p. 219.

production because it is the source of 58 percent of mineral-fuel output.[14] Production of selected individual mineral products, by region, in the United States and Canada is provided in Appendix Table A.7. The industry in which production is most evenly balanced among regions is U.S. agriculture, in which five of the nine regions have at least 10 percent of the total.

For the location of secondary resource industry, the nature of the resource base is less of a factor. For example, British Columbia accounts for only 34 percent of Canada's forest-based manufacturing, and the Prairie provinces for only 14 percent of the Canadian food-manufacturing industry.[15] One reason why an area that is a major raw materials producer may not be as significant at the secondary stage is that processing and manufacturing operations usually need not be located adjacent to the source of the raw materials. It is often advantageous to move the raw material to an area where, perhaps, there is a large supply of labor available to operate the processing industries. Another factor is that the degree of processing varies with the industry and product—much of the value of the Prairie provinces' farm output, for example, is wheat, which is exported in an unprocessed form.

Resource Industries As a Source of Government Revenue

Like all industries, resource industries are important to the economy for the revenue they provide governments. In addition to income taxes, which businesses of all types pay, firms in the resource industries must also pay royalties, or severance taxes, and other user fees that represent a direct charge by the government of a country for the use of its natural resources.

In 1974, mining companies in Canada paid $685.3 million in federal and provincial income taxes and another $2,027.4 million in provincial royalties and other user charges.[16] Of the latter, $1,707.6 million was for royalties on oil and gas. The income taxes on mineral-manufacturing firms, meanwhile, were another $649.9 million, making total government revenue from the primary and secondary sectors $3,362.6 million.[17] In the forest industries, provincial and federal income taxes on logging activity were $16.0 million, and on forest-based manufacturing companies, $369.8 million. With the addition of provincial user charges of $254.6 million on the use of forest resources, total government revenue from the primary and secondary forest industries came to $640.4 million. This revenue from the mineral and forest sectors was 6.7 percent of the total revenue of all levels of government in Canada in 1974.[18]

Mining companies in the United States paid state severance taxes of $1,254.2 million in 1974 and had a federal income tax liability of $1,061.3 million. Mineral-manufacturing firms, in addition, had to pay federal income taxes of $4,176.0 million. The federal tax liability of primary and secondary forest-industry firms was $1,672.0 million in 1974.[19]

Determining just how important the resource sectors are as a source of government revenue is more difficult than assessing these sectors in terms of most other measures. One reason is that government revenue from resource industries may fluctuate quite substantially, since changing market conditions cause sharp changes in the profit patterns of resource companies. In general, there has been in recent years considerable questioning of taxation of resource industries. One question that has been debated extensively is whether the government, and consequently the inhabitants, of an area is getting an appropriate return from the use of its natural resources. This applies especially when non-renewable resources are involved.[20] A second question is how the tax levels on resource industries compare with those in other industries.[21]

The Resource Base

It has long been recognized that there are physical limits to the quantities of resource materials that can be obtained from the earth for man's use. As has been postulated over a period of time lasting from Malthus to the recent reports of the Club of Rome, the ultimate effects of the interaction of a rising demand with a finite supply of raw materials must be, at some point, a sharp decrease in mankind's overall welfare.[22] So far the threat posed by these limits has remained a distant prospect. Nevertheless, it is an aspect of the analysis of the resource sectors of a country that cannot be ignored. It may help somewhat at the outset of this volume, however, to suggest that the limits that attract attention in this context are of three types:

- For regenerable resources, like forests, the limits are set not by the amount of the resource (that is, wood) that exists, but by the amount of land available for growing wood. Thus it is the productive capacity, the wood-growing land, that is finite.
- For mineral products, the limits of production are absolute because the earth contains a finite amount of each mineral, and physical depletion is possible.
- Short of physical depletion of a resource, it is possible for economic depletion to occur. Higher costs of mineral production result as higher-grade ores are depleted and society is forced to turn to lower-grade ores. Higher costs result in higher prices for mineral products, which may ultimately choke off demand and could create hardships not too dissimilar from those of physical depletion.[23]

Estimates of potential resources are important because they give an indication of a country's ultimate producibility of resource products. If a country does not have an abundant resource base, obtaining secure sources of supply from other countries becomes vital.

The literature on potential supplies of resources is extensive, and this section is only a brief introduction to a few considerations pertinent to the United States and Canada.

Mineral Reserves and Mineral Resources

The earth contains enormous quantities of minerals. It has been estimated that, if the world's minerals were distributed homogeneously in the earth's crust, each cubic mile would contain 1 billion tons of aluminum, 625 million tons of iron, 12 million tons of manganese, 1 million tons of zinc, 650 thousand tons of copper, 185 thousand tons of lead, and 60 tons of gold.[24]

Because the crust is far from homogeneous, though, man has been able to utilize mineral deposits that are in much greater concentrations than the hypothetical crustal average: iron concentrations can be ten times greater, copper 1,000 times greater, and lead 3,000 times greater.[25] The hydrocarbon fuels — petroleum, natural gas, and coal — occur in many instances in a virtually pure state or not at all.

When a material in a particular location in the earth's crust or in the oceans is in such a form that a usable mineral commodity can be extracted from it, it is defined as a mineral resource. If a mineral resource can be extracted at a profit and if there is a high degree of certainty about its existence, it is classified as a mineral reserve.[26] The concept of reserves has been a source of some confusion in discussions of long-term supplies of minerals. Reserves are not the ultimate stock of recoverable minerals; they comprise only what has been discovered to supply current productive capacity and to provide a buffer to allow for the discovery and development of new resources.

Figure 2.3 illustrates how reserves comprise only a part of total mineral resources. Moving from bottom to top indicates increasing feasibility of economic recovery and moving from right to left indicates increasing certainty of existence. The left side of the diagram indicates resources that have been discovered; the top of the diagram, resources that are economically recoverable. Therefore the top left-hand section represents reserves — those resources that have been identified and are economically recoverable. The lower left-hand section represents discovered deposits that are not economic. These "conditional" resources might become reserves if the price of the mineral increases or if some new technology permits utilization of the resources at a low cost. The right side of the diagram represents

38

FIGURE 2.3
Classification of Mineral Resources

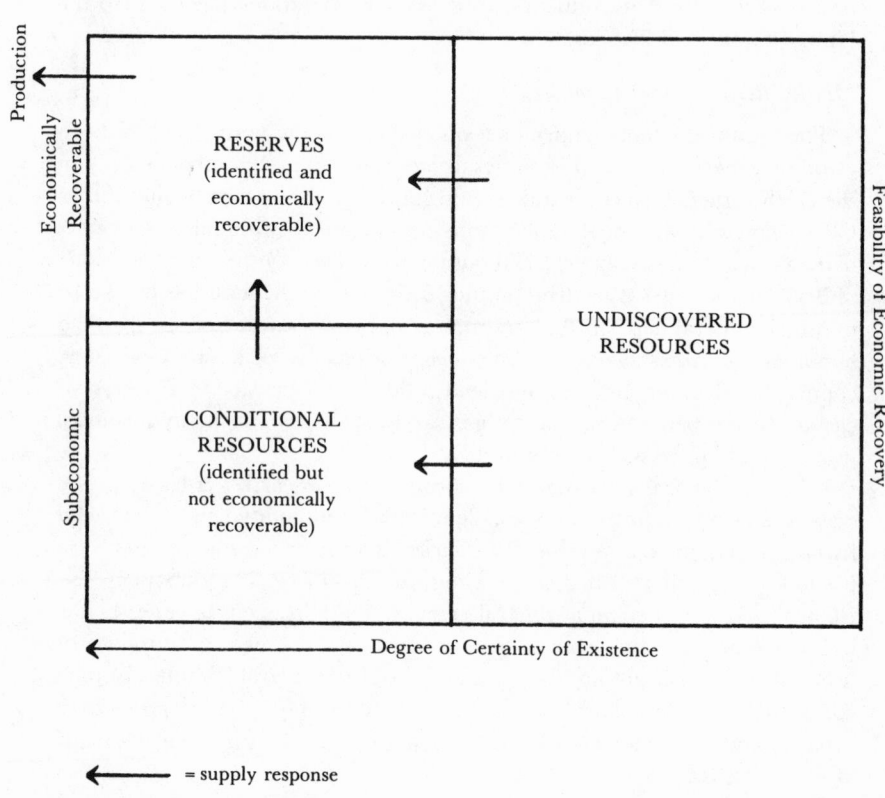

Source: Adapted from work by the U.S. Geological Survey. (See U.S. Department of the Interior, *United States Mineral Resources,* Geological Survey Professional Paper No. 820, ed. Donald A. Brobst and Walden P. Pratt [Washington, D.C.: U.S. Government Printing Office, 1973], pp. 3-5, 11-12.)

undiscovered resources; these, when they are discovered, may or may not be immediately economic.[27] The situation illustrated by these boxes is not a static one. As reserves are mined and fed into the industrial system, they are replenished with supplies from conditional resources as increasing price or technological progress makes utilization feasible, or because of discoveries of new deposits. These supply responses are shown by the arrows in Figure 2.3.

A failure to recognize the dynamic nature of the mineral supply system can result in misleading conclusions. For example, if current rates of production are compared with identified reserves for particular minerals, it is likely to appear that supply shortages will emerge in a few years. What will probably happen instead is that other mineral resources will become classified as reserves. In fact, there have been continuous increases in world reserves of minerals over time, as Table 2.11 shows. One reason for frequent reports that only twenty to thirty years of reserves are known to exist is that most mineral exploration is done by mining companies and there is little value for them in delineating precisely deposits that will not be needed

TABLE 2.11

*Change in World Known Reserves of Selected
Minerals, 1950-70*

(percentages)

Mineral	Percentage Change
Bauxite	279
Chromium	675
Copper	179
Iron	1,221
Lead	115
Tin	10
Tungsten	– 30
Zinc	61
Phosphate rock	4,430
Potash	2,360
Petroleum	507

Sources: National Commission on Supplies and Shortages, *Government and the Nation's Resources* (Washington, D.C.: U.S. Government Printing Office, 1976), p. 16 (data obtained from Bureau of World Metal Statistics, *World Metal Statistics,* 1961-62, and U.S. Department of the Interior, Bureau of Mines, *Minerals Yearbook,* 1954, 1959, 1967, 1970).

for more than twenty years. World reserves that are sometimes reported as being much in excess of twenty to thirty years of production result from "bonanza" discoveries.

Reserves data, therefore, should not be used to indicate more than they are intended to show—the known quantities of minerals that are economically recoverable with present technology and prices. Some efforts have been made to estimate total mineral resources, but these estimates are based on existing geological knowledge, and so much of the world remains relatively unexplored that even these numbers may not give a very satisfactory picture of the ultimately recoverable supplies of a mineral.[28] In the case of copper, for example, the U.S. Geological Survey has estimated that, in addition to reserves of 506 million short tons, 800 million tons of subeconomic deposits have been identified, and undiscovered resources probably amount to another 800 million tons.[29]

The United States and Canada have abundant supplies of many mineral resources. The U.S. and Canadian shares of world reserves of selected major minerals are shown in Table 2.12. In recognition of this wealth of minerals, the Canadian ministers of mines, both federal and provincial, declared in 1974 that they considered expansion of Canadian mineral production and exports to represent a major source of future economic growth.[30] In many cases the United States imports minerals and mineral products it could produce domestically only because foreign sources of supply are cheaper.

There is quite widespread acceptance that there is no fundamental general shortage of minerals in the world today. The U.S. National Commission on Supplies and Shortages, for example, suggests that, in the immediately foreseeable future (that is, "at least the next quarter century and probably many generations thereafter"), "the physical volume of the earth's resources will not prove a serious constraint on economic growth."[31] If a problem exists, it is with the flow capability of the mineral supply system, which requires technological advances to improve. An example of technology's easing an apparent impending mineral shortage occurred in the 1950s with the introduction of beneficiating and agglomeration processes for iron ore. Some feel that too much faith is being placed in future technological innovations.[32] If there are exceptions to the general optimism about supplies of mineral resources, they occur in the areas of oil and gas. Even in the case of oil, where the depletion of deposits in a relatively pure form can be predicted with some confidence in the not-too-distant future, there are still large additional supplies in the tar sands and the oil shales available to be exploited. This is an instance, though, where there will be much pressure on technology to lower the cost of such exploitation.

TABLE 2.12

Reserves of Selected Mineral Resources
As a Share of the World Total, United States and Canada, 1977

Resource	World Reserves	Percentage of World Reserves in United States	Percentage of World Reserves in Canada
Asbestos	96 million short tons	4.2	42.7
Bauxite	24 billion long tons	0.2	–
Chromium	1.9 billion short tons	–	–
Coal	8.6 trillion short tons	5.1	1.4
Cobalt	1.6 million short tons	–	2.1
Copper	506 million short tons	18.4	6.8
Gold	1.12 billion troy ounces	8.9	3.6
Iron ore	102.6 billion short tons recoverable iron	3.9	11.7
Lead	160 million short tons	36.9	8.1
Manganese	6 billion short tons	–	–
Mercury	5.23 million 76-pound flasks	8.2	1.9
Molybdenum	19.1 billion pounds	37.2	8.4
Natural gas	2,330 trillion cubic feet	9.8	2.4
Nickel	61 million short tons ore	0.3	15.7
Petroleum	658.7 billion barrels	5.0	1.2
Phosphate rock	20.4 billion short tons	12.3	–
Platinum group	560 million troy ounces	0.2	1.8
Potash	11.2 billion short tons	1.8	44.6
Silver	6.1 billion troy ounces	24.8	11.6
Tin	10.2 million metric tons metal	0.4	–
Tungsten	4.0 billion pounds	6.0	13.5
Uranium	2.4 million short tons U_3O_8	27.7	9.4
Zinc	175 million short tons metal	17.1	21.1

Sources: U.S. Department of the Interior, Bureau of Mines, *Commodity Data Summaries;* petroleum (Canada) from Canadian Petroleum Association.

Forest Resources

Unlike mineral resources, for which the supply is ultimately finite, forests can be regenerated. The land available for forests is, however, a limiting factor, since there is only a certain amount of the earth's surface where trees can grow. At any time much of that area is being used for other purposes. In fact, on a world scale the supply of productive forest land has been shrinking at an accelerating rate because land is being converted for farming and grazing and forest management is being neglected, particularly in the developing world.[33]

Both the United States and Canada have large supplies of forest land.

Total forest land in the United States was estimated in 1970 at 754 million acres, or 33.2 percent of the total land area. Of this, commercial timberland—that is, "land both available and suitable for growing continuous crops of saw logs or other industrial timber products"—accounted for 500 million acres, or 22.0 percent of the total land area.[34] By comparison, total forest land in Canada was estimated in 1967 at 796 million acres, or 35.2 percent of total land area, and forest land suitable for regular harvest at 588 million acres, or 26.0 percent of the total land area.[35]

The area of forest land suitable for regular harvest in the United States and Canada has not changed much in the postwar period. The net change in the United States between 1952 and 1970, for example, was an increase of 1.0 percent.[36] Forest land in both countries has been lost for urban development, highway construction, reservoirs, parks, and—in a few cases—agriculture. At the same time, new forest land has been created by the abandonment of agricultural acreage. This has occurred mainly in the Appalachian region of the United States and, to a lesser extent, in eastern Canada, where the terrain has limited the benefits of using the modern farm equipment that has so increased farm efficiency in other areas.

Although the area of forest land is similar in the two countries, it is the volume of wood that can be produced on a sustainable basis that is the real measure of the resource. By this criterion, the United States is much better endowed than Canada, partly because the climate of the United States is generally more amenable to rapid growth and partly because much of the Canadian inventory of trees is mature and overmature stock in which there is little growth. As Table 2.13 shows, wood production in terms of tree growth in the United States is more than twice that in Canada. However, the timber cut in the United States is proportionally even greater. Hence Canada has proportionally greater forest-resource potential, as indicated by its high ratios of net growth to removals.

Softwood usage in the United States is indicated as being close to the maximum in Table 2.13. In fact, removals of sawtimber, which is used primarily for making lumber and plywood, exceeded net growth by 18 percent in 1970. Canada, on the other hand, still appears to have considerable potential for increasing its cut of softwoods. In the United States the key to increasing timber production must be found in better management of standing timber and in more complete use of the harvested trees. Forest management includes increased tree planting, better fire protection, better protection against insects and disease, and periodical timber-stand improvements such as thinning. Net growth in both softwoods and hardwoods in U.S. forests increased by about one-third between 1952 and 1970 as a result of improvements in forest management.[37] Some improvement in the efficiency with which harvested trees are used has been occurring as well.

TABLE 2.13

Net Annual Growth of, and Removals from, Forests
Suitable for Regular Harvest, United States and Canada, 1970

	Net Growth (in billion cubic feet)	Removals (in billion cubic feet)	Ratio of Net Growth to Removals
United States:			
Softwoods	10.7	9.6	1.1
Hardwoods	7.9	4.4	1.8
	18.6	14.0	1.3
Canada:[a]			
Softwoods	6.3	3.9	1.6
Hardwoods	1.7	0.4	4.3
	8.0	4.3	1.9

[a]Net growth for Canada is considered to be the annual allowable cut on acres physically accessible.

Source: U.S. Department of Agriculture, Forest Service, *The Outlook for Timber in the United States,* Forest Service Report No. 20 (Washington, D.C.: U.S. Government Printing Office, 1974), pp. 28, 136.

Industrial wood-product consumption in the United States increased 65 percent in the period 1942-72, while consumption of the roundwood required to make these wood products increased by just 56 percent.[38]

Agricultural Land

The ultimate limit for agricultural production is the availability of suitable land. On a global basis, total land under cultivation is about 3,600 million acres, or just over 11 percent of the earth's total land surface.[39] Increases in agricultural-commodity production can be achieved either by bringing more land under cultivation or by improving the output from land already under cultivation. In some parts of the world there are still large quantities of land that could be brought under cultivation, but in most cases the capital costs involved would be very high. Improved production on existing cropland can be achieved by increasing applications of fertilizers, pesticides, and herbicides, by better irrigation or drainage, and by greater use of modern farm machinery.

The United States and Canada already have agricultural sectors that are highly developed in these respects relative to most parts of the world. Although technological advances can be expected to continue to expand the potential production per acre, yield increases will be relatively less important in the United States and Canada as the source of increase in production than in most other countries. The marginal increase in production diminishes with the application of each additional unit of fertilizer, for example. Consequently, the United States and Canada will have to rely to a relatively greater extent on bringing new land under cultivation to increase production.

The United States has a much greater quantity of land in agricultural use and with the capability for agricultural use than has Canada. The United States has generally better soil quality and decidedly better climatic conditions for agriculture than Canada. According to the U.S. Department of Agriculture, cropland in use or temporarily idle in the United States in 1974 was 382 million acres. In addition, there were another 84 million acres in cropland pasture, bringing total cropland to 466 million acres.[40] By comparison, improved farmland in Canada in 1971 was 108 million acres, of which 10 million acres were classified as improved pasture.[41] Cropland in use and idle in the United States represented 16.8 percent of total land area, while improved land less improved pasture in Canada was only 4.3 percent of total land area.

Table 2.14 summarizes some estimates of the land that could be brought into agricultural production in the two countries. The U.S. Department of Agriculture estimates that 266 million acres not used as cropland in 1974 could produce crops if needed. The Canada Land Inventory put land suitable for crops at 180 million acres, or 82 million acres more than was considered cropland (that is, improved farmland less improved pasture) in 1971.

This potential new farmland is, on average, of much lower quality than that already in use, so the output per acre that could be expected would be lower than the average for existing farmland. For example, 58 percent of the 266 million acres of potential agricultural land in the United States would be Class 3 land, whereas only 39 percent of existing cropland is Class 3, the rest being high-quality Class 1 and Class 2 land.[42] Converting potential farmland to agricultural use is also inhibited by the tendency of this land to be located in climatically inferior areas. Common problems are a short growing season, a lack of moisture, or too much moisture. When irrigation or drainage projects are necessary, large capital expenditures are involved in converting land to agricultural use. In general, then, bringing new land into production is a slow process; it is estimated that only 37 percent of potential cropland in the United States could be "considered to be physically well adapted for conversion to cropland in one or two decades."[43]

TABLE 2.14

Recent Estimates of
Agricultural Land, United States and Canada

	Million Acres	Share of Total Land Area
United States:		
Total cropland	466	20.5
Total cropland less cropland pasture	382	16.8
Potential cropland	266	11.7
Total land suitable for crops	648	28.5
Canada:		
Total improved land	108	4.8
Improved land less improved pasture	98	4.3
Land potential suitable for crops	82	3.6
Total land suitable for crops	180	8.0

Sources: U.S. Department of Agriculture, Economic Research Service, *Cropland for Today and Tomorrow,* Agricultural Economic Report No. 291 (Washington, D.C., 1975), p. 6; Statistics Canada, 1971 Census of Canada, *Agriculture* (Ottawa: Information Canada, 1973), Table 1.

In Canada most of the undeveloped agricultural land is north of existing farming regions—in the Peace River country of Alberta, the Interlake region of Manitoba, and the northern clay belt of Ontario and Quebec. These areas, in addition to obvious climatic limitations, are at a disadvantage in terms of transportation costs because they are far removed from market areas.

The amount of land used for agriculture has been essentially unchanged in the United States in the past quarter century, but this does not mean that the land base has remained the same. In Canada, improved land increased by about 11 million acres from 1951 to 1971, an average annual growth rate of 0.6 percent.[44] In both countries there has been a constant shifting of agricultural land into such uses as urban development, new highways, and recreational facilities. This trend has attracted considerable attention in Canada, where the principal cities are on, and adjacent to, prime agricultural land. It has been estimated that 46.8 percent of the total value of Canadian agricultural production in 1971 was derived from land within fifty miles of twenty-two major urban centers.[45] Decreases in farmland have also resulted from the abandoning of small farms, mainly in the eastern states and provinces, as a result of economic obsolescence. Counteracting these trends has been some development of new farmland.

In the United States, reclamation has been made possible by various combinations of clearing, drainage, irrigation, and improved dry-land-farming techniques. The main areas of reclamation have been in the Mississippi delta, Florida, Texas, California, Washington, and Montana. Expansion of agricultural land in Canada has been mainly in the four western provinces, and it has been in a northward direction, since the southern areas have come close to being completely utilized.

In considering agricultural-land potential, it is important to recognize that land quality in terms of soil, moisture, and temperature varies greatly. The best land in both countries is already in use. The United States still has a significant quantity of land that has potential for growing crops, but in most cases the costs of bringing that land into production would be high. A significant increase in real market prices for farm products would probably be necessary to cause an appreciable net increase in cropland. Canada has less good farmland, and less land with potential to be farmland, and faces a greater danger of land currently in agricultural use being lost to other uses, especially urban development. Canada's agricultural-land potential, therefore, is probably even more limited relative to the United States than the data suggest.

Conclusions and Major Policy Issues

The resource sectors form a major component of the economies of the United States and Canada. Both countries have large resource bases that support substantial resource industries and have potential for expanded output of many, although not all, raw materials. The resource industries have played a central role in the historical pattern of development, and they currently generate significant shares of national product and are important for both their direct and their indirect contributions to the economy. In addition, resource-commodity trade comprises a large proportion of the flow of goods between the United States and Canada.

The picture of the resource sectors that emerges from measures of economic performance such as those provided in this chapter, however, is only a partial one. To complete the picture, one must take into account a large number of policy issues that hinge on institutional structures, at both the national and the international levels, and that are at least as important in explaining the functioning of the resource sectors. Many of these policy issues will be considered in depth in the following chapters in this study, so what follows only outlines briefly the main issues.

Institutional policy issues basically involve artificial limitations on supplies of resource commodities. Two key factors seem to underlie these issues: first, each country is concerned about gaining the optimal benefit from its resource sectors; second, each country's position is interrelated with supply and demand conditions in world markets for many resource commodities. Depending on the resource involved, specific policy issues may be of quite dissimilar importance to different countries.

The main current policy issues as they relate to the resource sectors of the United States and Canada are as follows:

Commodity pricing. Resource-commodity prices have been a major cause of concern over a long period because they have experienced severe fluctuations that have alternately hurt both producers and consumers of raw materials and because there has been a tendency for resource-commodity prices to fall over time relative to the prices of manufactured goods. Measures introduced or extensively discussed in the past few years to overcome these problems include the pricing of the same resource commodity at different levels on domestic and foreign markets (two-price systems), the managing of supplies of a resource commodity by producers so that the price can be more stable than it would be if it were market-determined (cartels), the tying of prices of primary commodities to the prices of manufactured goods to prevent divergence of relative prices (indexation), and the building up of stocks of a commodity for release when prices start to rise in response to an increase in demand (buffer stocks). Resource-pricing problems are of great concern to the United States and Canada not only because of their effects on the prices of the resource commodities the two countries must import, but also because of their implications for the conditions under which U.S. and Canadian resource companies must operate.

Security of supply. When a country does not have a resource base from which it can obtain the major resource commodities it requires, having access to supplies of resources from another country is very important. One way to counteract any sudden loss of supplies from sources that might seem especially risky is the establishment of stockpiles of the resource commodities involved. Stockpiling can also be used to protect against sudden large increases in price even if unaccompanied by a disruption in supply. The United States has had strategic stockpiles for about ninety commodities since 1946.

Allocation of the economic rents. When a natural resource is harvested or mined, there arises a question of who should get the direct benefit, the operator of the mine or logging camp or the people of the country to whom the resource originally belonged. The name "economic rent" is given to the return — normally the difference between a low-cost producer's costs and those of the highest-cost producer — that accrues to a scarce, non-reproducible asset, such as land or a mine. In recent years there has been a struggle over the allocation of the economic rents going on between the governments of resource-rich areas and the privately owned enterprises engaged in resource developments in these areas. In Canada, there have been instances where governments have made such determined efforts to increase their shares that much of the incentive for private resource companies to invest in an area has been lost.

Foreign ownership. Foreign ownership of resource industries has a long history because resources are fixed by geography, while capital—and, to some extent, labor—is mobile. One of the main concerns about a business that is foreign-owned is whether appropriate benefits are accruing to the host country from the the company's use of its natural resources. Foreign-owned resource companies tend to be vertically integrated with, for example, their mines in one country and their smelters and other processing facilities in another. This kind of structure may permit a multinational firm, through the transfer-pricing mechanism it uses, to have its profits accrue in the country where the tax burden is least. It may also mean that a company's after-tax profits may be channeled into its operations in another part of the world rather than ploughed back into the economy of the country where the profits originated.

Further processing. The desire to realize greater secondary benefits from resource industries by more upgrading of resource commodities in the countries where they are mined or harvested has been widely advocated in recent years. In some cases, further processing may not be feasible on economic grounds: domestic markets may be too small, or—because of the economies of bulk shipping—transportation costs may be greater for processed than for crude materials. However, there are also some artificial barriers that have inhibited further processing in raw-materials-producing countries, such as tariff structures that allow imports of crude materials duty-free or at lower rates than those for processed materials.

Access to the resource base. Production of any resource commodity depends, initially, on access to areas where the resource is located. Much of the forest and mineral land in the United States and Canada is government-owned. In general, governments permit access to their lands through a leasing system; the company that leases the resource rights pays a royalty based on the amount of timber it harvests or ore it extracts. The tenure power that the government holds gives it authority to prohibit access to resources on certain lands, and with growing demands for competing uses such as national parks and wilderness areas, such prohibitions have been of increasing importance.

Effects on the environment. Production of resource commodities has also been increasingly affected in recent years by concerns about the environment. The environmental-impact study has become a standard feature of any new resource development or expansion. The internalizing of environmental costs has meant that the costs of producing resource commodities have generally increased and that, in some cases, resource developments have been prevented from continuing in operation or from being initiated.

These policy issues add an important final dimension to the overall image of the resource sectors of the United States and Canada that this chapter has presented. Resource-commodity production and trade have played a major role in the development of the two countries and continue to be a vital link between the two economies. Yet there are two types of concern always looming in the background and casting a shadow of uncertainty over the resource sectors. One is the possibility of depletion of the resource base. This is mostly a problem of the distant future because it has been possible to counteract the threat by increasing the efficiency of product use, by the development of technology to increase resource recovery, and by the discovery of substitute products. The other cause of uncertainty is implied by the above array of policy issues. This source of uncertainty seems clearly more serious for the immediate future because it represents a constant threat to the stability of world markets and the capacity for producing particular resource commodities.

Notes

1. All dollar values in this chapter are in U.S. dollars.

2. The value of primary production includes the value of mine output in the mining industry, the value of logs for industrial use (that is, excluding fuelwood) in the forest industry, and farm cash receipts in agriculture.

3. See Figure 2.2 for sources. Per capita production can be used as a measure of the relative importance of raw materials production in the two countries because the two economies are of similar size on a per capita basis. If per capita income in one country were significantly larger than in the other, this comparison would be much less meaningful. In a subsequent section of this chapter, the relative importance of the resource sectors in the two countries will be developed in some detail. It will be shown that value added in the primary mining, forest, and agricultural industries was 4.8 percent of gross national product in the United States in 1972 and 8.1 percent in Canada. It is misleading to talk in terms of value of production as a share of gross national product because some double-counting of intermediate inputs would be involved. This would lead to the value of production of all goods and services exceeding GNP and would make meaningful conclusions about individual sectors impossible.

4. The theory of "staple products" as an explanation of Canada's economic history was advanced primarily by Harold A. Innis.

5. The most notable assessment of the supply-demand situation for minerals at the time was the Paley Report, which attracted widespread attention to the changing resource position of the United States (see President's Materials Policy Commission, *Resources for Freedom*, 1952).

6. There are some difficulties in analyzing flows of resource commodities between countries. If only primary products are counted, a misleading picture may be created because some primary products will be contained in manufactured-goods or partially-manufactured-goods exports. Conversely, if secondary products are counted among resource-commodity exports, only part of the value can properly be

attributed to a resource sector. The rest is value that has been added by the labor, capital, and other inputs, such as fuel, that have gone into transforming the primary product into the secondary product. For purposes of trade analysis of the resource sectors, this chapter assumes that resource-commodity exports and imports include crude and fabricated commodities. U.S. and Canadian trade data distinguish between crude and fabricated mineral and forest-product commodities. These are also shown in Table 2.3. In the mineral sector, crude materials include the output of mines up to the concentrate stage and scrap materials. In the forest sector, logs for lumber and other building materials and pulpwood are the main crude materials. Fabricated raw materials are raw materials that have been transformed into a more finished form but are not yet end products. Some examples of fabricated mineral commodities are refined metals and alloys; steel in bars, rods, plates, and sheets; and refined petroleum products, such as gasoline. Fabricated forest products include lumber, veneer and plywood, wood pulp, and paperboard.

7. Calculated from Statistics Canada, *Summary of External Trade,* December, 1975 (Ottawa: Information Canada, 1976).

8. Ibid.

9. Use of both primary and secondary resource industries in this analysis is consistent with the inclusion of both crude and fabricated commodities in the trade data in this chapter.

10. Statistics Canada, *Fixed Capital Flows and Stocks, 1970-74* (Ottawa: Information Canada, 1975).

11. One recent such study is R. W. Boadway and J. M. Treddenick, *The Impact of the Mining Industries on the Canadian Economy* (Kingston, Ontario: Centre for Resource Studies, Queen's University, 1977).

12. See Chapter 5 by D. J. Daly.

13. Statistics Canada, *General Review of the Minerals Industries,* 1974 (Ottawa, 1976), pp. 8-9.

14. Estimated from U.S. Department of Commerce, Bureau of the Census, *Statistical Abstract of the United States,* 1974 (Washington, D.C.: U.S. Government Printing Office, 1974), pp. 659, 671-72.

15. Calculated from Statistics Canada, *Manufacturing Industries of Canada: National and Provincial Areas,* 1972 (Ottawa: Information Canada, 1975).

16. Statistics Canada, *Corporation Taxation Statistics,* 1974 (Ottawa, 1977), pp. 76-77.

17. Statistics Canada, *Consolidated Government Finance,* 1974 (Ottawa, 1977), pp. 80-90.

18. Ibid.

19. U.S. Department of Commerce, Bureau of the Census, *State Tax Collections in 1974* (Washington, D.C.: U.S. Government Printing Office, 1975), and U.S. Internal Revenue Service, Statistics Division, unpublished information.

20. It was a major factor, for example, in the decision of the government of Saskatchewan to take ownership of part of the potash industry in that province in 1975.

21. This point is considered in Chapter 5 within the context of the Canadian mineral industry.

22. Thomas Robert Malthus, *Essay on the Principle of Population* (1798), and Donella H. Meadows et al., *The Limits to Growth,* A Report for the Club of Rome's Project on the Predicament of Mankind (New York: Universe Books, 1972).

23. For a concise description of economic depletion, see John E. Tilton, *The Future of Non-Fuel Minerals* (Washington, D.C.: The Brookings Institution, 1977), Chapter 2.

24. Estimates by Professor Kalervo Ramkama of the University of Helsinki, cited in James F. McDivitt and Gerald Manners, *Men and Minerals* (Baltimore: The Johns Hopkins University Press for Resources for the Future, 1974), p. 11.

25. Ibid.

26. These definitions are from U.S. Department of the Interior, *United States Mineral Resources*, ed. Donald A. Brobst and Walden P. Pratt, Geological Survey Professional Paper No. 820 (Washington, D.C.: U.S. Government Printing Office, 1973), p. 3.

27. Figure 2.3 is based on work by V. E. McKelvey and Brobst and Pratt (op. cit.). Their analyses contain some additional breakdowns of conditional and undiscovered resources.

28. Brobst and Pratt, op. cit.

29. Ibid.

30. Federal and Provincial Mines Ministers, *Towards a Mineral Policy for Canada* (Ottawa: Information Canada, 1974).

31. National Commission on Supplies and Shortages, Government and the Nation's Resources (Washington, D.C.: U.S. Government Printing Office, 1976), p. 9.

32. For example, see A. G. Chenoweth, "Materials Conservation: A Technologist's Viewpoint," *Impact,* No. 16, 1976.

33. See Erik P. Eckholm, *Losing Ground: Environmental Stress and World Food Prospects* (New York: W. W. Norton and Company, 1976).

34. U.S. Department of Agriculture, Forest Service, *The Outlook for Timber in the United States,* Forest Service Report No. 20 (Washington, D.C.: U.S. Government Printing Office, 1974), pp. 8-9.

35. Glenn H. Manning and H. Rae Grinnell, *Forest Resources and Utilization in Canada to the Year 2000,* Canadian Forestry Service, Publication No. 1304 (Ottawa: Information Canada, 1971).

36. U.S. Department of Agriculture, Forest Service, op. cit., p. 10.

37. Ibid., p. 1.

38. Ibid.

39. Food and Agriculture Organization of the United Nations, *Production Yearbook,* 1975 (Rome, 1977), p. 45.

40. U.S. Department of Agriculture, Economic Research Service, *Cropland for Today and Tomorrow,* Agricultural Economic Report No. 291 (Washington, D.C., 1975), p. 6.

41. Statistics Canada, 1971 Census of Canada, *Agriculture* (Ottawa: Information Canada, 1973), Table 1.

42. U.S. Department of Agriculture, Economic Research Service, op. cit., p. 8.

43. M. L. Cotner, M. D. Skold, and O. Krause, *Farmland: Will There Be Enough?* (Washington, D.C.: U.S. Department of Agriculture, Economic Research Service, 1975), p. 13.

44. Statistics Canada, 1971 Census of Canada, *Agriculture,* op. cit., Table 2.

45. E. W. Manning and J. D. McCuaig, *Agricultural Land and Urban Centres* (Ottawa: Fisheries and Environment Canada, Lands Directorate, 1977), p. 4.

TABLE A.1

Raw Materials Production, United States and Canada, 1975

	Unit	Quantity Produced (unit of measure as indicated)		Value of Production (million U.S. dollars)		Shares of Value of Production	
		U.S.	Canada	U.S.	Canada	U.S.	Canada
Minerals:[a]							
Metals:							
Bauxite	thou. long tons ore	1,772	–	25	–	0.0	–
Chromium	–	–	–	–	–	–	–
Cobalt	sh. tons metal	–	1,493	–	12	–	0.1
Copper	thou. sh. tons metal	1,413	808	1,815	1,013	2.9	8.3
Gold	thou. troy oz. metal	1,050	1,654	170	266	0.3	2.2
Iron ore	mil. long tons ore	78.9	44.9	1,621	903	2.6	7.4
Lead	thou. sh. tons metal	621	385	267	153	0.4	1.3
Manganese	–	–	–	–	–	–	–
Mercury	76-lb. flasks metal	7,366	12,000	1	n.a.[b]	0.0	–
Molybdenum	mil. lb. metal	106.0	28.7	259	70	0.4	0.6
Nickel	thou. sh. tons metal	17.0	267.0	n.a.[b]	1,082	–	8.9
Platinum group	thou. troy oz. metal	19.0	399.2	n.a.[b]	56	–	0.5
Silver	mil. troy oz. metal	34.9	39.7	154	176	0.2	1.4
Tin	sh. tons metal	n.a.	352	n.a.[b]	2	–	0.0
Tungsten	thou. lb. metal	5,490	1,628	29	n.a.[b]	0.0	–
Uranium	sh. tons U_3O_8	12,100	6,082	281	n.a.[b]	0.5	–
Zinc	thou. sh. tons metal	469	1,163	366	858	0.6	7.0
Others				207	122	0.3	1.0
				5,196	4,712	8.3	38.7

Non-metals:							
Asbestos	thou. sh. tons	99	1,164	14	263	0.0	2.2
Phosphate rock	thou. sh. tons	48,816	—	1,122	—	1.8	—
Potash	thou. sh. tons K$_2$O	2,501	5,152	223	353	0.4	2.9
Others[c]				8,159	298	13.1	2.5
				9,518	92.3	15.3	7.6
Fuels:							
Coal	mil. sh. tons	655	28	12,671	576	20.3	4.7
Natural gas	bil. cu. ft.	20,109	3,090	11,718[d]	2,264[d]	18.8	18.6
Petroleum	mil (42-gal.) bbls.	3,052	521	23,116	3,691	37.1	30.3
				47,561	6,531	76.4	53.7
Total, minerals				62,275	12,167	100.0	100.0
Forest products:							
Industrial round-wood	mil. cu. ft.	9,965	3,478	13,788[e]	1,882	100.0	100.0
Agricultural products:[f]							
Crops:							
Wheat	mil. bu.	2,134	628	7,263	2,543	8.1	26.8
Rice	mil. cwt.	128	—	1,046	—	1.2	—
Corn	mil. bu.	5,767	143	8,907	153	9.9	1.6
Barley	mil. bu.	383	437	628	621	0.7	6.5
Soybeans	mil. bu.	1,521	13	7,076	45	7.9	0.5
Tobacco	mil. bu.	2,193	234	2,155	198	2.4	2.1
Cotton	mil. bales	8	—	2,069	—	2.3	—
Fruits and vegetables				8,918	475	10.0	5.0
Others				8,599	654	9.6	6.9
				46,661	4,689	52.1	49.3

TABLE A.1 (cont.)

Unit	Quantity Produced (unit of measure as indicated)		Value of Production (million U.S. dollars)		Shares of Value of Production	
	U.S.	Canada	U.S.	Canada	U.S.	Canada
Livestock:						
Cattle and calves	mil. lb.	24,849	2,395	17,482	1,818	19.5	19.1
Hogs	mil. lb.	11,503	1,094	7,948	886	8.9	9.3
Poultry and eggs				6,739	671	7.5	7.1
Dairy products	mil. lb. milk	115,000	17,675	9,866	1,348	11.0	14.2
Others				867	90	1.0	1.0
				42,902	4,814	47.9	50.7
Total, agricultural products				89,563	9,503	100.0	100.0

(Note: columns are Unit | Quantity U.S. | Quantity Canada | Value U.S. | Value Canada | Shares U.S. | Shares Canada)

aMine production.
bIndicates data withheld to avoid disclosing individual companies' confidential information; included in "metals: others" and in the totals.
cIncludes structural materials.
dIncludes natural gas by-products.
eEstimate.
fCash receipts from farming operations.

Sources: U.S. Department of the Interior, Bureau of Mines, *Minerals Yearbook*, Vol. I, 1975; U.S. Department of Commerce, *Statistical Abstract of the United States*, 1976 (Washington, D.C.: U.S. Government Printing Office, 1976), p. 647; U.S. Department of Agriculture, Forest Service, *The Demand and Price Situation for Forest Products*, 1974-75 (Washington, D.C.: U.S. Government Printing Office, 1975), p. 36; Food and Agriculture Organization of the United Nations, *Yearbook of Forest Products*, 1974 (Rome, 1976); Statistics Canada, *Quarterly Bulletin of Agricultural Statistics*, October-December, 1975 (Ottawa: Information Canada, 1976); Statistics Canada, *Canada's Mineral Production*, Preliminary Estimate, 1976 (Ottawa, 1977); Statistics Canada, *Canadian Forestry Statistics*, 1974 (Ottawa, 1976).

TABLE A.2

Trends in the Production of Selected Raw Materials,
United States and Canada, 1952-55 to 1972-75

	Production in the United States As Percentage of World Production		Production in Canada As Percentage of World Production		Ratio of Production in 1972-75 to Production in 1952-55		
	Average, 1952-55	Average, 1972-75	Average, 1952-55	Average, 1972-75	World	U.S.	Canada
Minerals:							
Metals:							
Bauxite[a]	13.0	3.4	—	—	4.9	1.3	—
Chromium[b]	2.8	—	—	—	2.6	—[c]	—
Copper[b]	33.2	22.9	10.2	12.2	1.7	1.7	3.0
Gold[a]	7.5	3.6	17.2	5.2	1.4	0.7	0.4
Iron ore	33.0	10.4	2.9	5.7	3.1	1.0	6.2
Lead[a]	17.7	19.9	9.9	11.4	1.6	1.8	1.8
Manganese	1.9	0.2	—	—	1.9	0.3	—
Mercury[a]	10.8	2.5	0.7	7.6	1.3	0.3	—[d]
Molybdenum[a]	91.0	69.7	—	18.3	2.6	2.0	65.7
Nickel[b]	1.1	2.8	80.2	42.7	3.3	8.4	1.8
Silver[b]	20.0	14.0	15.1	17.0	1.4	1.0	1.5
Tin[a]	—	0.04	0.1	0.2	0.9	—[d]	1.4
Tungsten[a]	25.7	14.5	3.6	6.6	1.1	0.6	2.0
Uranium	n.a.	49.5	n.a.	19.0	—	—	—
Zinc[b]	19.9	9.0	14.3	23.5	1.9	0.9	3.2
Non-metals:							
Asbestos[a]	3.8	3.3	66.0	44.2	2.8	2.5	1.7
Phosphate rock[a]	54.4	49.4	—	—	3.4	3.1	—
Potash[a]	27.2	14.2	—	27.7	2.6	1.4	—[d]

TABLE A.2 (cont.)

	Production in the United States As Percentage of World Production		Production in Canada As Percentage of World Production		Ratio of Production in 1972-75 to Production in 1952-55		
	Average, 1952-55	Average, 1972-75	Average, 1952-55	Average, 1972-75	World	U.S.	Canada
Fuels:							
Coal	22.5	17.6	0.7	0.7	1.6	1.3	1.6
Natural gas	90.0	47.8	1.2	6.0	4.5	2.4	22.5
Petroleum	46.5	16.4	1.8	2.9	3.9	1.4	6.4
Forest products:							
Industrial roundwood	31.5	24.3	10.0	10.0	1.6	1.3	1.6
Agricultural products:							
Wheat[b]	18.7	17.8	9.0	5.6	1.7	1.6	1.1
Rice[b]	1.4	1.5	–	–	1.8	1.9	–
Barley[b]	11.1	7.2	8.6	8.6	1.9	1.2	1.9
Corn[b]	54.4	46.2	0.4	1.0	2.0	1.7	4.8
Meat[b]	25.8	23.2	2.3	2.2	2.3	2.1	2.2
Milk[b]	21.9	18.1	3.0	2.7	1.2	1.0	1.0

[a]World production excludes China and the USSR.
[b]World production excludes the USSR.
[c]Not applicable because no production in 1972-75.
[d]Not applicable because no production in 1952-55.

Source: United Nations, Statistical Yearbook, 1957, 1976 (New York, 1958, 1977).

TABLE A.3(a)

Trade in Crude and Fabricated Resource Commodities, United States, 1975

	Exports			Imports		
	Value of Exports (mil. U.S. $)	% of Total Exports	% Exported to Canada	Value of Imports (mil. U.S. $)	% of Total Imports	% Imported from Canada
Mineral commodities:						
Metals:						
Crude	1,355.2	1.3	10.8	1,976.7	2.1	33.8
Fabricated	4,368.3	4.1	21.7	7,303.8	7.6	19.7
Non-metals:						
Crude	892.1	0.8	19.9	464.4	0.5	33.8
Fabricated	1,906.8	1.8	15.0	1,854.3	1.9	30.9
Fuels:						
Crude	3,483.1	3.3	19.7	20,797.6	21.6	21.3
Fabricated	981.8	0.9	18.2	5,678.0	5.9	6.3
Total, mineral commodities	12,987.3	12.2	18.7	38,074.8	39.6	20.0
Forest commodities:						
Crude	751.3	0.7	6.9	41.1	0.1	81.0
Fabricated	3,329.6	3.1	21.0	4,181.9	4.3	84.2
Total, forest commodities	4,080.9	3.8	18.4	4,223.0	4.4	84.2
Agricultural commodities	21,876.9	20.6	5.6	8,409.5	8.7	4.4
Total, resource commodities	38,945.1	36.7	11.3	50,707.3	52.7	22.8
Total, all commodities	106,156.7	100.0	20.2	96,140.4	100.0	22.9

Sources: U.S. Department of Commerce, Bureau of the Census, U.S. Imports: Commodity by Country, December, 1975, and U.S. Exports: Commodity by Country, December, 1975 (Washington, D.C.: U.S. Government Printing Office, 1976).

TABLE A.3(b)

Trade in Crude and Fabricated Resource Commodities, Canada, 1975

	Exports			Imports		
	Value of Exports (mil. U.S. $)	% of Total Exports	% Exported to U.S.	Value of Imports (mil. U.S. $)	% of Total Imports	% Imported from U.S.
Mineral commodities:						
Metals:						
Crude	2,198.2	7.0	33.3	459.1	1.3	57.5
Fabricated	2,638.7	8.4	61.7	1,957.4	5.7	59.6
Non-metals:						
Crude	769.5	2.4	51.6	177.3	0.5	85.6
Fabricated	160.1	0.5	77.8	355.2	1.0	66.7
Fuels:						
Crude	4,558.4	14.4	89.6	3,817.9	11.2	15.0
Fabricated	611.6	1.9	79.0	270.8	0.8	31.4
Total, mineral commodities	10,884.9	34.6	68.4	7,037.7	20.7	35.2
Forest commodities:						
Crude	59.4	0.2	60.8	64.0	0.2	99.2
Fabricated	4,911.0	15.6	66.6	634.1	1.9	87.6
Total, forest commodities	4,970.4	15.8	66.6	698.0	2.0	88.7
Agricultural commodities	3,743.2	11.9	13.0	2,645.4	7.8	55.2
Total, resource commodities	19,598.5	62.3	57.4	10,381.2	30.5	43.9
Total, all commodities	31,451.6	100.0	65.2	34,078.0	100.0	67.8

Source: Statistics Canada, Summary of External Trade, December, 1975 (Ottawa: Information Canada, 1976).

TABLE A.4

Trends in Resource-Commodity Trade, United States and Canada, 1956-75

UNITED STATES

Year	Resource-Commodity Exports As Percentage of Total U.S. Exports				Resource-Commodity Imports As Percentage of Total U.S. Imports			
	Mineral	Forest	Agricultural	Total	Mineral	Forest	Agricultural	Total
1956	17.0	2.3	20.4	39.7	29.3	12.7	27.0	69.0
1965	12.4	3.4	23.2	38.9	30.8	9.2	17.6	57.6
1975	12.2	3.8	20.6	36.7	39.6	4.4	8.7	52.7

Year	Resource-Commodity Exports to Canada As Percentage of All Resource-Commodity Exports				Resource-Commodity Imports from Canada As Percentage of All Resource-Commodity Imports			
	Mineral	Forest	Agricultural	Total	Mineral	Forest	Agricultural	Total
1956	27.8	28.5	8.5	17.9	18.7	81.7	4.6	24.8
1965	23.3	19.0	9.6	14.8	23.1	81.7	5.8	27.2
1975	18.7	18.4	5.6	11.3	20.0	84.2	4.4	22.8

TABLE A.4 (cont.)

CANADA

	Resource-Commodity Exports As Percentage of Total Canadian Exports				Resource-Commodity Imports As Percentage of Total Canadian Imports			
Year	Mineral	Forest	Agricultural	Total	Mineral	Forest	Agricultural	Total
1956	30.0	31.1	20.7	81.8	27.5	2.7	12.3	41.4
1965	41.4	24.0	18.1	83.5	14.4	2.3	11.2	27.8
1975	34.6	15.8	11.9	62.3	20.7	2.0	7.8	30.5

	Resource-Commodity Exports to the United States As Percentage of All Resource-Commodity Exports				Resource-Commodity Imports from the United States As Percentage of All Resource-Commodity Imports			
Year	Mineral	Forest	Agricultural	Total	Mineral	Forest	Agricultural	Total
1956	61.5	82.3	20.2	58.9	62.3	86.2	50.5	61.9
1965	56.7	75.6	16.7	53.5	33.6	85.9	55.0	46.5
1975	68.4	66.6	13.0	57.4	35.2	88.7	55.2	43.9

Sources: U.S. Department of Commerce, *United States Exports of Domestic and Foreign Merchandise*, December, 1956 (Washington, D.C.: U.S. Government Printing Office, 1957); U.S. Department of Commerce, *U.S. Exports: Commodity by Country*, December, 1965, December, 1975 (Washington, D.C.: U.S. Government Printing Office, 1966, 1976); U.S. Department of Commerce, *United States Imports of Merchandise for Consumption*, 1956, December, 1965 (Washington, D.C.: U.S. Government Printing Office, 1957, 1966); U.S. Department of Commerce, *U.S. Imports: Commodity by Country*, December, 1975; Dominion Bureau of Statistics, *Trade of Canada*, Vol. 1, 1956, and 1964-66 (Ottawa: Queen's Printer, 1958, 1970); Statistics Canada, *Summary of External Trade*, December, 1975 (Ottawa: Information Canada, 1976).

TABLE A.5

Value Added in Resource Industries, United States and Canada, 1963-72

	United States 1963 mil. $	% GNP	United States 1972 mil. $	% GNP	Canada 1963 mil. $	% GNP	Canada 1972 mil. $	% GNP	Average Annual Growth, 1963-72 U.S.	Canada
Primary industries:										
Agriculture	17,700	3.0	28,800	2.5	2,665	5.8	3,327	3.2	5.6	2.5
Forestry	521	0.1	1,163	0.1	749	1.6	814	.8	9.3	0.9
Mining	15,920	2.7	26,471	2.3	1,856	4.0	4,267	4.1	5.8	9.7
Total, primary resource industries	34,141	5.7	56,434	4.8	5,270	11.5	8,408	8.1	5.7	5.3
Secondary industries:										
Food manufacturing	18,100	3.0	28,928	2.5	1,4328	3.1	2,550	2.5	5.4	6.7
Forest-based manufacturing	10,896	1.8	22,208	1.9	1,753	3.8	3,326	3.2	8.2	7.4
Mineral manufacturing	18,782	3.6	29,051	2.5	1,991	4.3	3,353	3.2	5.0	6.0
Total, secondary resource industries	47,778	8.0	80,187	6.8	5,172	11.2	9,229	8.9	5.9	6.6
Primary and secondary industries:										
Agriculture and food manufacturing	35,800	6.0	57,728	4.9	4,093	8.9	5,877	5.7	5.5	4.1
Forestry and forest-based manufacturing	11,417	1.9	23,371	2.0	2,502	5.4	4,140	4.0	8.3	5.8
Mining and mineral manufacturing	34,702	5.8	55,522	4.7	3,847	8.4	7,620	7.3	5.4	7.9
Total, resource industries	81,919	13.8	136,621	11.7	10,442	22.7	17,637	17.0	5.8	6.0
Total, manufacturing industries	191,562	32.2	352,891	30.1	12,568	27.3	24,315	23.4	7.0	7.6
Gross national product	594,700	100.0	1,171,100	100.0	45,978	100.0	103,952	100.0	7.8	9.5

Sources: Statistics Canada, Manufacturing Industries of Canada: National and Provincial Areas, 1972 (Ottawa, 1974); Statistics Canada, Survey of Production, 1974 (Ottawa, 1976); Department of Finance, Economic Review, April, 1976 (Ottawa: Supply and Services Canada, 1976), p. 109; Dominion Bureau of Statistics, Manufacturing Industries of Canada, 1963 (Ottawa, 1966); Dominion Bureau of Statistics, Survey of Production, 1963 (Ottawa, 1966); U.S. Department of Commerce, Statistical Abstract of the United States, 1974 (Washington, D.C.: U.S. Government Printing Office, 1974), pp. 606, 666-67, 724-29; U.S. Department of Commerce, Business Statistics, 1975 (Washington D.C.: U.S. Government Printing Office, 1976), p. 1.

TABLE A.6

Employment in Resource Industries, United States and Canada, 1963-72

| | United States | | | | Canada | | | | Average Annual Growth 1963-72 | |
| | 1963 | | 1972 | | 1963 | | 1972 | | | |
	Thousands	% Civilian Labor Force	Thousands	% Civilian Labor Force	Thousands	% Civilian Labor Force	Thousands	% Civilian Labor Force	U.S.	Canada
Primary industries:										
Agriculture	4,687	6.5	3,475	4.0	649	9.6	484	5.4	-3.4	-3.3
Forestry	73	0.1	79	0.1	60	0.9	48	0.5	0.9	-2.7
Mining	635	0.9	621	0.7	96	1.4	107	1.2	-0.3	1.3
Total, primary resource industries	5,395	7.5	4,172	4.8	805	11.9	639	7.2	-2.9	-2.6
Secondary industries:										
Food manufacturing	1,438	2.0	1,348	1.6	182	2.7	190	2.1	-0.7	0.4
Forest-based manufacturing	1,078	1.5	1,235	1.4	189	2.8	224	2.5	1.5	1.9
Mineral manufacturing	1,279	1.8	1,278	1.5	156	2.3	183	2.0	0.0	1.8
Total, secondary resource industries	3,795	5.3	3,861	4.5	527	7.8	596	6.7	0.2	1.2

Primary and secondary industries:									
Agricultural and food manufacturing	6,125	8.5	4,820	5.6	831	12.3	674	7.6	-2.7	-2.4
Forestry and forest-based manufacturing	1,151	1.6	1,314	1.5	249	3.7	271	3.0	1.5	0.9
Mining and mineral manufacturing	1,914	2.7	1,899	2.2	252	3.7	290	3.2	-0.1	1.6
Total, resource industries	9,190	12.8	8,033	9.3	1,332	19.7	1,235	13.8	-1.5	-0.9
Total, manufacturing industries	16,958	23.6	18,919	21.9	1,425	21.1	1,676	18.8	1.2	1.8
Civilian labor force	71,833	100.0	86,542	100.0	6,748	100.0	8,920	100.0	2.1	3.2

Sources: Bank of Canada, *Review*, February, 1972, March, 1977; Statistics Canada, *General Review of the Mineral Industries, 1974* (Ottawa, 1976); Dominion Bureau of Statistics, *General Review of the Mineral Industries, 1963* (Ottawa, 1965); Statistics Canada, *Canadian Forestry Statistics*; Department of Finance, *Economic Review*, p. 139; U.S. Department of Commerce, *Statistical Abstract of the United States, 1974, op. cit.*, pp. 724-29; U.S. Department of Labor, *Handbook of Labor Statistics, 1973* (Washington, D.C.: U.S. Government Printing Office, 1973), pp. 27, 95.

TABLE A.7

Production of Primary Mineral Products, by Region, United States and Canada, 1972
(percentage shares)

UNITED STATES

	New England	Middle Atlantic	East North Central	West North Central	South Atlantic	East South Central	West South Central	Mountain	Pacific
Metals:									
Bauxite	—	—	—	—	wᵃ	w	90.5	—	w
Cobalt	—	w	—	—	—	—	—	—	—
Copper	0.1	0.2	4.0	0.7	—	0.7	w	94.1	w
Gold	—	w	—	28.2	—	—	w	68.2	0.8ᵇ
Iron ore	—	w	18.7ᵇ	63.3ᵇ	w	0.2	w	w	w
Lead	—	0.2	0.3	79.1	0.6ᵇ	—	—	19.2	0.6
Mercury	—	—	—	—	—	—	—	14.7	81.3ᵇ
Molybdenum	—	—	—	—	—	—	—	87.3ᵇ	w
Nickel	—	—	—	—	—	—	—	—	100.0
Silver	—	w	2.1ᵇ	5.6	w	0.2	w	90.7	1.1ᵇ
Tungsten	—	—	—	—	w	—	—	w	w
Uranium	—	—	—	w	—	—	w	88.2	w
Zinc	1.2	24.5	3.8	13.0	3.5ᵇ	21.6	w	30.8	1.6
Non-metals:									
Asbestos	w	—	—	—	w	—	—	w	64.9
Phosphate rock	—	—	—	—	83.5	5.3	—	11.2	—
Potash	—	—	w	—	w	—	—	85.4ᵇ	w
Fuels:									
Coal	—	16.8	18.3	1.1	35.1	23.8	0.5ᵇ	3.6ᵇ	0.6ᵇ
Petroleum	—	0.2	1.9	3.1ᵇ	0.1ᵇ	2.2ᵇ	72.7	9.5ᵇ	10.0
Natural gas	—	0.4	0.9	3.4	1.3	0.7	80.7	7.6	7.3

TABLE A.7 (cont.)

CANADA

	Atlantic Provinces	Quebec	Ontario	Prairie Provinces	British Columbia	Yukon and Northwest Territories
Metals:						
Bauxite	—	—	—	—	—	—
Cobalt	—	—	77.1	18.1	4.8	—
Copper	2.5	22.3	36.4	9.1	29.5	0.2
Gold	0.8	26.0	49.0	3.3	5.8	15.0
Iron ore	48.1	20.8	28.5	—	2.6	—
Lead	15.8	0.4	2.9	—	26.4	54.6
Mercury	—	—	—	—	100.0	—
Molybdenum	—	1.8	—	—	98.2	—
Nickel	—	0.1	72.5	26.2	0.6	0.6
Silver	10.0	7.9	43.7	2.5	15.5	20.2
Tungsten	—	—	—	13.7	28.5	71.5
Uranium	—	—	86.3	—	—	—
Zinc	16.1	13.0	32.2	5.0	10.7	23.0
Non-metals:						
Asbestos	5.3	76.2	2.1	—	10.1	6.3
Phosphate rock	—	—	—	—	—	—
Potash	—	—	—	100.0	—	—
Fuels:						
Coal	13.0	—	—	39.0	48.0	—
Petroleum	—	—	0.2	95.7	4.1	0.1
Natural gas	—	—	0.7	91.7	7.3	0.3

[a] "w" indicates that one or more states in the region produced the mineral, but that data for all were withheld.

[b] Data were withheld for at least one of the states in the region producing the mineral and disclosed for the rest.

Sources: U.S. Department of the Interior, Bureau of Mines, Minerals Yearbook, 1973, Vol. 1 (Washington D.C.: U.S. Government Printing Office, 1975); Statistics Canada, General Review of the Mineral Industries, 1974 (Ottawa, 1976).

3

Continuity and Change in the U.S. Decision-Making Process in Raw Materials

JOHN H. ASHWORTH

Introduction

Since the beginning of the 1970s, the production and distribution of raw materials have become subjects of intense public debate and scholarly analysis in the United States. Part of this attention has been caused by the "energy crisis" and by the sudden realization that it brought of the non-renewable nature of once-plentiful domestic minerals. Another contributing factor has been the surge of interest in the activities of transnational corporations.[1] These vertically integrated companies, primarily U.S.-based, play a dominant role in the production, extraction, and fabrication of fuels, ores, and metals. There has also been recent academic research concerning the role of non-governmental, non-official, and bureaucratic actors in governmental decision-making. The actions of governmental bureaucracies, functioning independently of their central governments or in accord with their own internal norms,[2] have proved to be important in establishing patterns of resource use and distribution. The examination of the raw materials decision-making process has taken on particular significance in the U.S.-Canadian relationship because of the interpenetration of the two economies, the vast number of informal ties across the border, and the importance of raw materials in the bilateral trading pattern.

This chapter examines the nature and powers of the governmental actors, private interest groups, and political alliances that collectively have determined, and will continue to shape, U.S. mineral policy. Two distinct questions will guide the presentation:

- What has been the U.S. decision-making process in raw materials—who participates, what are the limitations on the powers

67

of various public and private actors, and what principles guide the
participants' actions?
- How is the traditional decision-making pattern changing, and why?

While of intrinsic interest, these questions take on an even greater importance when examined in the larger context of U.S.-Canadian relations.
Therefore, following a review of the legal and historical background of
U.S. mineral policy, of the changing role of the major producing states,
and of the complex list of federal policy-setting bodies, two recent cases
where U.S. decision-making has affected Canadian interests are examined
briefly. The first case, the imposition and the subsequent revocation of
"anti-dumping" duties on Canadian lead, is a straightforward example of
the type of issues that have traditionally influenced U.S. mineral
policy: the protection of domestic industry from import competition, the
political importance of maintaining domestic mining employment, and the
divisions of opinion within the federal government over granting the requested protection. This case is also interesting because it demonstrates the
ability of Canadian officials and private interest groups to function effectively as domestic actors within the U.S. decision-making process—building alliances with U.S. bureaucrats and domestic interest
groups and defusing potentially volatile situations before they escalate into
diplomatic confrontations. The second case, the choice of a northern
natural gas pipeline, demonstrates the complexity of forming policy in the
1970s, with many federal and state agencies sharing the administrative
power and many other groups interceding in pursuit of a host of divergent,
and often contradictory, goals.

The chapter concludes with observations on the potential impact of current changes in the U.S. decision-making process on future relations with
Canada in raw materials issue-areas. Changes to be analyzed include the
growth in the United States of joint state-federal administration and recent
state initiatives toward the limitation of mineral production and toward
heavy taxation of the mineral industries. The growing tendency within
both the U.S. and the Canadian governments to seek a more coherent (and
centrally controlled) bilateral bargaining system is examined, and an attempt is made to assess the impact of this trend on the treatment of
Canadian-mineral issues within the U.S. decision-making system.

The Complexity of the System

The United States does not possess an integrated mechanism for coordinating decisions affecting raw materials supplies. This point was hammered home dramatically by the metal and mineral price surges of 1972-74

and by the simultaneous rise in fuel costs. The realization of this lack of central direction and the fear of future market disruptions spawned a number of major studies,[3] both governmental and private, which examined the issue of U.S. raw materials dependency and its implications for the national economy (and for the world economic system) in the 1970s and 1980s. Virtually all these reports noted that effective coordination of U.S. policies toward raw materials and raw materials producers was non-existent and suggested that extensive cooperation would be necessary if the nation were to take steps toward eliminating future market uncertainties.[4]

Yet saying that the United States does not have a coherent national raw materials policy does not answer the obvious question: How does it deal with raw materials issues? Raw materials worth tens of millions of dollars flow into and out of the United States every day. While the private markets are able to allocate most of these supplies rapidly and efficiently, there are still numerous cases that are perceived to require governmental intervention and regulation. This is particularly true where political and social objectives (employment maintenance, pollution abatement, and national self-sufficiency are obvious examples) are not accurately reflected in the market mechanism. How do we order all the discrete actions of U.S. state and federal decision-makers? The answer is that the United States has not one raw materials policy, but many. Specifically, it has at least as many raw materials policies as it has decision-making centers solving materials questions and administrative agencies implementing decisions. Many of these policies are contradictory. Collectively, the decision-making and administrative agencies form a loosely knit, enormously complex process for settling disputes, primarily, and, secondarily, for formulating policy.

Part of this complexity is due to the nature of all U.S. governmental decision-making. The size of the U.S. government, its inherent separation of powers, and its large use of independent agencies make centralized policy formation difficult. As Roger Swanson concisely stated the problem in the opening remarks of an article on U.S. organizations that deal with Canadian questions:

> The United States policy process is heterogeneous, not homogeneous. It is decentralized, not centralized. Instead of a highly efficient, monolithic planning-programming-budgeting system, there is a neo-feudal collection of loosely interconnected components, each having an organizational life—and sometimes death—all its own.[5]

This systemic complexity of the U.S. policy-formation process is made even more convoluted, in the case of raw materials, by the addition of a large number of purely domestic political and economic actors. Indeed, much of traditional U.S. decision-making in materials issue-areas can be understood only by investigating the web of domestic political relations within the regions of the United States that have been dependent on extractive resources for employment and income. As will be shown in the sections below on the producing states and on the major congressional committees, these political relations have been undergoing massive changes in the past few years, changes that will alter future decision-making patterns.

Finally, the complexity of the decision-making process has recently been increased by the introduction of new policy concerns and new bureaucratic actors. Included in the new concerns are a wide variety of issues, ranging from environmental protection to land-use planning, but they all have a common characteristic: they involve social externalities not adequately reflected in the market mechanism. Therefore, government usually intervenes in the form of regulation and rule-setting. But the perception of a need for regulation does not solve the jurisdictional question of which level of government should assume the authority, especially in a federal system such as that in the United States.

Constitutional Framework and Historical Context

Ownership of Land and Minerals

Throughout the history of the United States, raw materials have been considered to be private rather than public goods. Underground mineral rights are not automatically the property of the federal government, as in most major mineral-producing countries, or of the states and provinces, as in the case of Canada, but rather belong to the owner of the surface land under which the minerals are found. Indeed, much of the power of the federal government and the individual states over mineral development policy is derived not from their status as governmental regulators but from their private roles as massive landholders, particularly in the states located west of the Mississippi River.

The principle of private ownership of mineral rights has had a profound impact upon the development of U.S mineral industries. In many locations it has meant an extremely complex mineral ownership pattern, a condition that stymied early state and federal efforts to regulate production practices. The problem was most acute in the early days of oil and gas regulation, with the most spectacular example being the West Texas field. Thousands of wildcat drillers moved into that barren region in 1930-31, purchased land or mineral rights, and resolutely resisted any efforts by the state government to control the rate of production or the waste of natural gas. Faced with virtually complete non-compliance and severely depressed oil prices, the governor of Texas finally declared martial law and sent in troops to shut down the field.[6]

The fragmenting tendencies of private ownership have often been overcome by a second major principle of the U.S. mineral ownership system—the separability of mineral rights. Mineral rights underneath a piece of land can be severed from the surface ownership and sold or transferred. This has often led to concentrated mineral ownership, even in areas of small landholders, as producing companies and speculators amassed and sold packages of mineral rights. This principle has allowed producers to put together economical working units and was a source of little conflict as long as surface disruption was minimal, as generally was the case in oil and gas production or in underground mining. However, the separation of surface and subsurface rights has brought about tremendous conflict in recent years, with the dramatic upsurge in large-scale strip mining.

Problems created by the separability of mineral rights and by variations in ownership patterns are highly regional within the United States, being based largely on when or if the land was separated from the public domain. During the formative years of the new republic, the federal government owned virtually all the North American continent south of the 49th parallel (and all the mineral rights as well). To settle these massive territories and to raise revenue for its impoverished treasury, the federal government sold off this land as rapidly as possible, often at the minimal price of $1.25 per acre. In most areas of the United States east of the Mississippi River, land passed into private hands between 1790 and 1850, along with the rights to any minerals that might later be found and developed.[7]

The passage of the Mineral Land Act of 1846 marked the beginning of a second phase of U.S. policy toward land and minerals, one characterized by active governmental stimulation of mineral production. This law provided for the outright sale of federal mineral lands to private individuals or corporations for a minimum fee of $5.00 per acre. Companies that had previously leased mineral lands from the federal government were allowed to buy the lands they were working for only $2.50 per acre.[8] Three years later gold was discovered in California, and the age of exploitation of the mineral wealth of the western public lands was launched. For the next fifty years the principle prevailed that whoever located mineral resources on the public domain had the right to claim that land and its minerals for his own, provided that he paid a minimal fee and agreed to develop the land. This period also coincided with redoubled governmental efforts to distribute the rest of the public domain to settlers and private landholders. The Homestead Act was expanded in an effort to stimulate migration to the Northern Great Plains and to portions of the Southwest. Vast sections of the public lands were granted to corporations in order to stimulate the rapid development of east-west railroad lines. Between 1850 and 1923 the railroads received 91.2 million acres of federal lands.[9] Virtually all of these grants, the homesteading sales, and the mineral lands sales transferred the mineral rights as well as the land to the new owners.

In the last decade of the nineteenth century, the country suddenly realized that the public domain was rapidly shrinking, that to a large extent the nation's raw materials were in the hands of private firms, and that the rate of exploitation of minerals had become so prodigious that depletion was for the first time a serious possibility. Out of this realization arose the conservationist movement, and with it a further reorientation of federal mineral and land policy. Under the leadership of President Theodore Roosevelt, a vigorous campaign was waged to ensure that portions of the western mineral lands remained in federal hands. In 1906, when the Congress was hopelessly deadlocked over changing the laws governing the disposition of the public domain, Roosevelt withdrew nearly 67 million acres of coal lands from further development by executive order, followed later with the reservation of 3 million acres of oil lands. Successive presidents continued these withdrawals.[10]

These land reservations had an unexpected consequence — they brought about the severability of mineral rights on federal lands. Roosevelt's removal of the coal lands from future settlement had left many homesteaders in the western states in an intolerable position, since they had settled on land to which they could not gain legal title. The Congress and the President worked out a compromise on this specific issue: the settlers received title to the surface land for agriculture, but the federal government retained the rights to coal underlying the land.[11] This principle of the federal government's retention of mineral rights on land it sold was gradually expanded in the following years to other minerals besides coal and oil, and when the public lands were reopened to homesteading in 1916, all mineral rights were reserved to the federal government. The public domain was finally closed to sales and homesteading, except in Alaska, in 1935. Since that time all federal lands that have been opened to mineral operations have been leased rather than sold, with the federal government drawing royalties from the production.

Thus the United States has evolved a complex system of mineral ownership, largely private but with significant federal participation in the western states, in which it is both a prominent landowner and the holder of severed mineral rights under private lands (a status it shares with several states and with the major railroads). The regional asymmetry of land and mineral ownership patterns carries political significance because of the way it affects the distribution between the federal and the state governments of the power to regulate and tax mining activities. For example, the rules issued by the

Bureau of Land Management or by the Forest Service have a large political and economic impact in the western half of the country, where the federal government supervises vast stretches of mineral, grazing, and forest lands, while they have relatively little impact in the industrialized states of the Northeast and the Midwest.

The Power to Tax

The right to levy severance taxes on mineral production from private lands is reserved to the individual states in the U.S. system, and virtually all mineral-producing states have enacted such taxes.[12] For several of the southwestern and western states, these assessments on mineral output loom extremely large in the support of the state's educational system and of the general treasury. As will be discussed later, in the section on the producing states, this dependence for current expenditures on mineral tax revenue often has had a dramatic impact on a state's willingness to regulate an industry and on the willingness of state officials to press for protection for mineral industries threatened by import competition or by increased federal regulations.

The federal government's role in taxing the mineral industries is limited to two broad areas: it collects corporate income taxes from firms in the extractive industries, just as it does from companies in other fields; and it collects bonuses and royalties from mineral production on federal lands. Federal income taxes on mineral-producing firms have been a source of continuous contention since the end of World War II because of special exemptions granted by Congress or by administrative rulings favorable to the extractive industries (the percentage depletion allowance and the foreign tax credit are the most significant examples). While most of these exemptions have recently been eliminated or are being gradually phased out, the question of whether extractive industries should be taxed differently from manufacturing and service industries still remains unresolved. Bonuses for the right to lease federal mineral lands and offshore oil lands are obtained by auctioning off these rights to the highest bidders, with royalties being paid on a percentage basis for actual production. While the receipts for lease sales have been large in certain years (in August, 1976, oil companies paid more than $1 billion for oil-leasing rights off the Atlantic Coast), bonuses and royalties have never been a significant source of revenue for the federal treasury. This is due largely to the fact that most of the funds are already earmarked for specific uses. Under the Mineral Leasing Act of 1920, 37.5 percent of the royalty money from mineral leasing was returned to the states in which the production took place, 50 percent went to the Reclamation Fund (largely benefiting the same western states), and only 12.5 percent went to the general treasury. Under recently enacted

revisions the amount flowing from mineral leasing to the producing states
was increased to 50 percent. While the amount of revenue to the federal
treasury from mineral leasing is not significant to the federal treasury, it is
important to some of the states with large federal landholdings, such as
Wyoming and Nevada. These same states are also heavily dependent on
the irrigation activities provided by the Reclamation Fund.

The Power to Regulate

Until the last decade the power to determine the manner in which
minerals were extracted from private mineral reserves rested primarily with
the individual states or, in some cases, with local communities. The producing states had the right to set standards for production techniques,
water quality protection, and land reclamation on private and state lands
within their boundaries. The states were also the chief conservation agencies, which gave them the power to regulate extensively the rates of production of certain key industries (chiefly oil and gas). The federal government
was restricted, except in time of war, to several functions authorized by the
Constitution: the regulation of foreign trade, the maintenance of mineral
stockpiles for national defense, the regulation of facilities serving interstate
commerce (oil and gas pipelines, for example), and the leasing and
maintenance of federal lands and federal mineral rights. Other powers and
responsibilities, such as the prosecution of anti-trust activities and federal
control over natural gas pricing, were acquired by the federal government
by legal precedent or by judicial interpretation.

Within the past decade there have been two consistent trends that have
altered and blurred the division of regulatory responsibility for mineral
policy between state and federal authorities. The first has been the rise of a
host of new governmental objectives—environmental protection, safer
working conditions for miners, and coastal-zone management are but three
examples—at both the state and federal levels. Second, there has been an
increasing demand by the western states for more input into the regulation
of federal lands and federal mineral leasing. Whereas producing states were
once allied with both domestic producing industries and the Department of
the Interior in promoting mineral production, they are now equally concerned with alleviating the potential socio-economic impact of development
on federal lands. The states insist that if they are to suffer the adverse effects
of federal leasing (particularly of coal), they should have a decisive role in
controlling the federal process.

These two pressures have brought about significant changes in the
allocation of regulatory power in the past ten years. One response favored
by Congress has been to set federal standards and then to offer the power of
regulation to the states if they meet or exceed these standards.[13] This prac-

tice began in the late 1950s, with the 1959 Amendments to the Atomic Energy Act of 1954, but it became a major principle of regulation with the environmental legislation of the late 1960s and the 1970s. The Clean Air Act, the Federal Water Pollution Control Act, and the 1977 Federal Strip-Mining Act all employ this basic concept. For example, in the new strip-mining act signed by President Carter on August 3, 1977, a state "which wishes to assume exclusive jurisdiction over the regulation of surface coal mining and reclamation operations" can submit within eighteen months a state program that meets the guidelines of the act and then assume the regulatory powers.[14]

It is too soon to determine what the final balance of state versus federal regulatory power over raw materials will be or what impact it will have on the future course of U.S. mineral and fuel policy. One thing is certain: the new state role is markedly different from the pro-development stance taken by producing states prior to the late 1960s. In the next section, the traditional political alliance between state governments and the extractive industries is reviewed briefly and an attempt is made to pinpoint the changes that fractured that coalition.

The Changing Role of the Producing States

For many years the major mineral-producing states of Appalachia, the Southwest, and the Far West served as the political strongholds of the domestic mineral industry. These states and the domestic industry worked in concert in pursuit of two common objectives: the expansion of the level of production of minerals and the minimization of federal interference in the mineral extraction process. The only potential point of friction, the level of state taxation of production, has become a real issue mostly in the past ten years, as will be explained below.

Mining States

The states had differing reasons for this steadfast support of the mineral industry, with the crucial division being between those states dependent on mining industries (including coal) and those with significant oil and gas industries. The political power of the mining industries lay in their labor intensity—they provided jobs in areas where few alternative occupations existed. When the coal, lead and zinc, copper, or iron ore industries were depressed, the major producing states suffered massive unemployment. For example, when slumping coal production caused 2,400 marginal mines to close between 1950 and 1953, coal employment dropped from 400,000 to 214,000, with most of this hardship being concentrated in four Appalachian states.[15] Similarly, when import competition caused many western lead and zinc mines to cease operations, the small, isolated communities that had grown up to service the mines found themselves without a major employer.

A second characteristic of states dependent on coal or hardrock mining is that until a few years ago they used their power to assess taxes very sparingly. In part, this was due to the political power of the major producing companies in the state legislatures. Until recently, Montana has had no net-proceeds or net-profits tax on copper, despite numerous efforts to reform the law, because of the steadfast oppositon of the Anaconda Copper Company.[16] Until 1972 Kentucky had no severance tax on coal, one of its largest industries, and Tennessee instituted its first coal severance tax only in 1974.[17] Since these states derived little or no income from mining, they were unwilling to appropriate sufficient sums for the control of mining practices. This unwillingness was reinforced by the personnel of the state bureaus of mining, who often had experience in private industry and shared many of the industry's beliefs—including its distaste for active governmental supervision and taxation. When pressure began to rise in the early 1970s for stiff mineral taxation and strong reclamation laws, the demands for action came not from state mining supervisors, but from state legislatures and from the progressive sectors of the executive branches.

Oil and Gas States

In contrast to the mining states, the major oil- and gas-producing states have derived significant portions of their revenue from severance taxes since the end of World War II. Texas led in the shift to larger tax assessments, just as it did in all aspects of oil and gas regulation. In 1935 it assessed a minimal 2 percent on oil production, which netted the state treasury $9.7 million, or 11.5 percent of its total tax revenue. By 1949, as a result of sharply higher oil prices, increased production, and stiffer state taxes, revenue from the Texas oil and gas severance tax had soared to $102.7 million, or nearly one-third of total state revenue.[18] Other states, such as Louisiana, became even more dependent on oil-based revenue for current expenditures. It was common practice to "earmark" the severance tax income—that is, designate its use for certain state functions, primarily support for education. Since the severance tax was customarily calculated as a percentage of market price for each unit produced, any external changes that lowered either the rate of production or the market price decreased the state's ability to pay for current school expenses. This was particularly true for Texas, since it originally had more than 42 million acres of state lands that were reserved to support education and that contained major oil- and gas-producing fields.[19] To preserve this revenue and to maintain the support of the independent petroleum-producer associations, the state governments of the major oil states were in the vanguard of the political coalition pushing for oil import controls (which were eventually instituted in 1959 and not allowed to lapse until 1973).

The oil- and gas-producing states differed from the mining states in another significant respect: they had active governmental supervision of production practices and stiff penalties for violation of state regulations. By the mid-1950s, state laws dictated minimum standards for everything from well-spacing to natural gas utilization. These regulatory actions were accepted by the oil industry, after initial fierce opposition, because they increased the amount of oil any given field could produce in the long run, even though they might limit the short-term profits of any one operator. The state oil and gas regulatory agencies had ample operating funds, since they usually received a set portion of the severance tax proceeds, and were virtually autonomous within the state governmental structure. In Texas, state regulators gained further autonomy by their status as elected officials, with their own constituents and their own bases of political power.

Finally, the oil and gas regulatory agencies were different from state mining agencies in that they had the power to determine the levels of allowable production for each well in the state, setting them according to estimates of aggregate demand. This system, known as "market-demand prorationing," had originally been devised to control the massive surges in production in the late 1920s and the 1930s that threatened to destroy the domestic oil industry and the states dependent upon it. The system evolved rapidly under the skillful guidance of the most powerful state agency, the three-member Texas Railroad Commission (TRC), into a system for maintaining domestic oil prices in the face of rapidly growing supplies of inexpensive imports. As has been demonstrated elsewhere in considerable detail,[20] between 1945 and 1973 the Texas Railroad Commission expanded and contracted the output of Texas oil wells to ensure that domestic oil prices remained steady or rose slightly. To achieve that price stability, the TRC was willing to shut in virtually all of its state's prodigious production capacity. In 1958 there were months when Texas wells were open for only eight producing days.

By the mid-1950s the Texas Railroad Commission was one of the most powerful regulatory bodies in the United States, determining domestic oil availability according to its own internal norms and domestic political objectives. The federal government had no input into the TRC decision-making process, a fact made only too clear by the Suez crisis of 1956. With the sudden cessation in the flow of Middle Eastern oil, the United States and Europe were faced with a crude-oil shortage of one million barrels per day. At the time, Texas had a shut-in capacity of 900,000 barrels per day, but the TRC refused to increase Texas' production by more than 23,000 barrels per day. The shortage that followed forced a rise in the price of domestic crude oil, something Texas had been pressing for since 1953.

Once the price rise became universal, Texas belatedly increased its allowables, and the crisis was over. Both the executive and the legislative branches of the federal government were powerless in the face of Texas' action. Despite cries of outrage, the federal government had no legal power to force Texas to cooperate.

The late 1950s marked both the zenith of the power of the domestic oil and gas regulatory system and the nadir of state regulatory control of the mining process. But regardless of the level of state control, the political alliance between producing states and the domestic industry remained constant for most of the following decade. Then, in the middle and late 1960s, the friendly state-industry relationship began to unravel, with the most dramatic changes occurring in the mining states of Appalachia and the Far West. While there were many reasons for the growing estrangement — the most obvious being the resentment over the low industry tax contributions and the declining relative importance of the mineral industries to the state economies — the issue that came to symbolize the new relationship was strip mining. Underground mining, although dangerous and costly in terms of human health, had the twin virtues of employing a large number of workers and leaving the land's surface relatively undisturbed. The benefits, especially in terms of jobs, seemed to outweigh the drawbacks. But strip mining greatly altered the benefit/cost ratio, employing many fewer men per ton mined and leaving large areas of surface land devastated. Suddenly, states began to look upon the mining industries as curses rather than as blessings. The worry about environmental degradation was reinforced by the realization that price rises in the early 1970s had made mining highly profitable and that the state was not getting any part of the increased economic rent.

The mining states reacted by passing strip-mining laws and setting up state agencies to enforce them. They also enacted sizable severance taxes, despite industry warnings that such taxes would slow or halt planned mine expansions. The funds provided by the new severance taxes allowed several states to increase their enforcement of existing mining laws and to ensure compliance with reclamation standards. Congressmen from the Appalachian region and from the western states took the lead in pressing for a national strip-mining bill, despite the adamant opposition of the mining industry. As previously mentioned, western governors took an active role in securing a strong state role in the formation of federal leasing policy. The states were afraid, among other things, that the Department of the Interior was too development-minded and too pro-industry, a worry that would have appeared strange to many state officials only five years earlier.

The dramatic rise in the regulatory force and the taxing powers of the state agencies concerned with mining was mirrored by the striking loss of power of the state oil and gas agencies. The power to restrict production became irrelevant when domestic excess capacity disappeared and imports began to rise. The massive rise in world oil prices brought federal price controls, further decreasing the political impact of state regulatory decisions. With virtually all domestic wells producing at 100 percent of maximum-efficiency rates, the state agencies are reduced to doing the non-political tasks for which they were originally created — promoting conservation, ensuring engineering efficiency, and adjudicating local disputes. The creation of the new federal Department of Energy only ensured the continued migration of policy-setting power in energy from the state to the federal level.

In contrast to the dramatic changes in the mining states, the past five years have not seriously damaged the oil-industry–producing-state relationship. Both the industry and the states have opposed the extension of federal controls. The environmental issue has not caused the same estrangement that it did in coal-mining areas. The rise in world oil prices brought large increases in state revenue without any changes in the state rate of taxation. By 1975, Texas was receiving $664 million from its oil, gas, and sulfur taxes, with Louisiana close behind at $558 million.[21] While oil production is no longer as important to the newly diversified economies of the major producing states as it once was, it still provides many benefits, including substantial revenue and employment, with relatively few social or environmental costs.

Federal Actors and Institutions

The federal government has always played a decisive role in U.S. mineral resource policy because of its jurisdiction over foreign trade, interstate commerce, national defense, and the disposition of the public domain. Until World War I, however, the sale and use of federal lands were the predominant concern of officials responsible for national resource policies. With the closing of the public domain to further land sales, the rise of the Cold War, and growing U.S. dependence on foreign mineral and fuel supplies, more and more federal agencies became actively involved in the planning of raw materials policy. The purpose of this section is to catalogue these organizations briefly and to indicate how they work with other federal, state, or foreign agencies and with the mining industry.

The Foreign-Policy Network

Only those organizations that view U.S. raw materials policy in the context of its coordination with the structures and institutions of the international system and of its impact on bilateral relationships with other nations are dealt with here. The primary members of this network are the **Departments of State, Treasury, and Defense, the National Security Coun-**

cil, and the Office of the Special Trade Representative (STR). The actions of the foreign-policy network are closely monitored by the two congressional watchdog committees, the Senate Committee on Foreign Relations and the House Committee on Foreign Affairs.

The State Department forms the core of the foreign-policy network. In the international environment it serves as the point of contact between the governments (and nationals) of other countries and the U.S. decision-making process. In bilateral or multilateral negotiations the State Department normally plays a key role in all issue-areas, including raw materials supplies and U.S. private investment in extractive industries. Within the U.S. government, however, the State Department is often relegated to a secondary role, particularly when strong domestic interests are involved.

The position of the leaders of the foreign-policy network is often secondary in intragovernmental bargaining, for two reasons. First, those leaders lack a powerful domestic political-support group — a natural constituency for the department's policies. Second, the positions the State Department takes are often sympathetic to the problems of foreign producers, making the department suspect in the minds of U.S. politicians responsive to domestic pressures. In theory, the State Department provides analyses of the externalities of proposed actions: it spells out the implications of policy alternatives for foreign economies and for U.S relations with foreign countries. In practice, it tends not only to present the views and desires of foreign governments and producers but also to act as a domestic advocate for them. As Robert Dickerman has observed in an analysis of the varying approaches of U.S. departments to Canadian issues: "Lacking easy access to political judgment, State, legitimately the leading organization on external matters but lacking both power and legitimacy in domestic matters, instead tends to stress its own constituency's view: that of Canada."[22]

This perception of the State Department as being more concerned with the problems of foreign producers and amicable foreign relations than with the domestic ramifications of the policies it advocates was voiced by several U.S. decision-makers interviewed for this study.[23] It was not a belief shared by State Department officials at any level. Nonetheless, this perception does tend to lower the impact of State in issue-areas with strong domestic political components. This is doubly true in fields where other agencies are considered to have greater functional expertise, as is the case in raw materials.

As rising mineral prices and changes in world markets have focused attention on raw-materials-policy formulation, other members of the foreign-policy network have greatly expanded their divisions dealing with raw materials and energy, a rise in expertise that has been accompanied by demands for increased participation in the formulation of foreign-materials policy. In particular, the Department of the Treasury, under the guidance of several dynamic secretaries, has become a forceful actor in international relations (as in the case of the recent commodity-stabilization talks). This proliferation of expertise in international economic affairs and raw materials policy has eroded, and will continue to erode, State Department primacy in these areas.

The difficulty of maintaining a coherent foreign policy and centralized control over raw-materials-policy formulation has traditionally been a problem for the U.S. federal government when dealing with Canada. Because of physical proximity, common language, and frequency of contact, most U.S. federal agencies have in the past routinely bypassed State Department channels, both in the seeking of information and in the working out of informal agreements on policy. They contacted Canadian officials directly in Washington and in Ottawa, and their counterparts reciprocated the process. While much of the contact was by telephone, there has been a steady flow of official visitors across the border in each direction.[24] Officials of both governments met regularly at industrial conferences, regional gatherings, and bilateral talks. These close ties led at times to informal alliances between functionally similar agencies as they pressed for adoption of policies within their respective governments.

These frequent transgovernmental contacts often led to the neglect of normal diplomatic channels. Information was exchanged and policies coordinated without the intermediation of either the U.S. State Department or the Canadian Department of External Affairs. U.S. agencies, and even congressional committees, conducted their own foreign relations with portions of the Canadian bureaucracy, and the ability of the U.S. official foreign-policy system to coordinate policy suffered accordingly.

There have been numerous signs that the "special relationship" that the United States and Canada enjoyed in the period after World War II in many raw materials issue-areas is rapidly changing. As the control of the resource trade, the ownership of minerals, and the usage of raw materials have become politically more important within each country, the power to determine resource policy has migrated from career bureaucrats within specialized agencies to elected officials. While a full analysis of this trend is beyond the scope of this chapter, we return to an examination of future patterns of U.S.-Canadian relations in raw materials in the two case studies and in the concluding observations.

Domestic Resource-Policy Institutions

The second cluster of federal decision-centers is that concerned primarily with the domestic impacts of raw materials production and consumption.

For these institutions, foreign-policy considerations are largely exogenous factors that constrain policy options and make the achievement of domestic economic and political objectives more difficult.

Domestic raw materials policy has traditionally been determined by the Congress and administered by the Departments of the Interior and Agriculture. Until recently, that policy was based on two premises: (1) the United States needed a healthy and prosperous domestic mineral industry, and (2) active government encouragement of mining was necessary to maintain jobs in sparsely populated parts of the country. While this policy was supported by the major mineral-producing areas, it also was part of a larger partisan coalition. As Mayhew has carefully documented, mineral subsidies and other support programs were an integral part of the Democratic Party consensus in Congress in the fifteen post–World War II years that he surveyed.[25]

The many facets of U.S. raw materials policy touch upon a multitude of congressional committees. The armed services committees have traditionally dealt with the strategic stockpile and with the use of naval petroleum reserves, while the House Ways and Means Committee and the Senate Finance Committee have jurisdiction over most areas of trade policy. The agriculture committees play central roles in shaping policy whenever the welfare of the American farmer is involved. But most legislation dealing with raw materials inside the United States is handled by the House and Senate Committees on Interior and Insular Affairs.[26] It is here that the power of the major raw materials states of the West and the Southwest is concentrated, and it is also here that the plans of successive administrations designed to ensure raw materials security or to control the domestic mineral industry foundered.

The interior and insular affairs committees in both chambers of the U.S. Congress have always been the virtual preserves of states located west of the Mississippi River. The major reason for this regional concentration has been these committees' jurisdiction over the usage of the public domain. Indeed, until the legislative reorganization of 1946, these committees were simply called public land committees. As has already been noted, federal land ownership is concentrated in the western states and in Alaska. Over 400 million acres of public land tracts are located in the eleven Rocky Mountain and West Coast states, and they comprise the bulk of the area of most of the states. Nevada, for example, has 83 percent of its 70 million acres owned by the federal government; Arizona, 60 percent; and Utah, 71 percent; even populous California has 45 percent, or 45 million acres, of its land area controlled by federal agencies.[27] What is done with these vast blocks of land is of vital interest to those who live near them and draw their livelihood from using them. While western congressmen may have joined these low-prestige[28] committees out of interest in public lands and public works projects (primarily dams and irrigation systems), they have stayed to set mineral policy as well.

In the Eisenhower, Kennedy, and Johnson administrations, the actions of the congressional interior committees (and of the Public Works Committee as well) reflected the dominant concerns of these western congressmen and their constituents: the promotion of rapid growth, the development of natural resources to provide employment, the provision of federal funds for local infrastructure creation (particularly water systems and highways), the minimization of federal interference with private enterprise, and the promotion of the U.S. domestic mining industry (against import competition). In the period since 1970 the traditional pro-development bias of the interior committees has been erased. In large part this has been in response to the changing climate of opinion within the mining states. Now western congressmen, like their home-state governments, are more interested in controlling the adverse impacts of the process of growth and in limiting environmental degradation than they are in promoting the rapid expansion of mineral production. As already noted, they have also been instrumental in the drive to give states more regulatory power over the federal lands within their boundaries and more input into the federal decision-making process in leasing and land-use.

While the shifts in attitude toward the expansion of mineral extraction have been as dramatic among mining-state congressmen as they have been among mining-state governments, it is important to realize that these changes have not necessarily meant a lessening of support for existing raw materials producers when they are threatened by import competition. This support is a classical constituent service, as important for one-industry mining communities in the West as they are in New England communities dependent on the domestic shoe and fishing industries. As we will see in the lead-tariff case below, congressmen concerned about saving jobs can, and will, apply considerable pressure on U.S. raw-materials-policy formulation.

There has long been a close working relationship between the congressional policy-setting committees and the Department of Interior, the chief federal agency charged with administering federal lands, leasing policy, and mineral development. This department has traditionally been the federal government's reservoir of technical experts on mineral production and exploitation, particularly within the Bureau of Mines (BOM). In U.S. intragovernmental bargaining, the Department of the Interior and congressional interior committees traditionally served as spokesmen for U.S. domestic raw materials producers. This frequently put them in opposition to the State Department and other members of the foreign-policy network.

The disagreement was often not over facts but over the weighting of these facts in the determination of policy. Each sought to protect the interests of its constituents. As one high-ranking official put it: "It's a matter of degree: the State Department may be a little more interested in the position of foreign production, we [the Department of the Interior], pursuant to our legislative mandates, are more concerned with domestic production, and the Commerce Department may place more emphasis on the impact on domestic consumers."[29]

The same changes that strained relations between mining states and the domestic mineral industry also produced tensions between the Department of the Interior and key congressional committees. The crucial issue was western coal development—where should it take place, how quickly should it proceed, and who should control the process. In 1971 the Secretary of the Interior suspended further western coal leasing, but by that time large tracts had already been assembled by major oil companies, coal companies, and electrical utilities. For the next five years the Department of the Interior marked time, waiting for the development of a national consensus on land-use management and energy development. It also struggled to integrate its new responsibilities for environmental protection with the mandate to administer mineral development on the public lands. This has not been an easy union, and the first tentative plans announced by the Bureau of Land Management have satisfied neither the domestic mineral industry nor environmental spokesmen. What is clear is that decision-making in the future will be extremely complex, time-consuming, and incremental, with input from the states, other federal agencies, and the general public at each successive stage.

Federal Managers and Regulators

Much of the output of the U.S. governmental decision-making process comes not from politically responsive bodies, such as the Congress and the Office of the President, or from policy-formulating groups, such as the Economic Policy Group or the National Security Council, but from the myriad semi-autonomous agencies charged with implementing one or more congressional mandates. Although they are not raw-materials-policy-making bodies—and indeed often have very little knowledge of either raw materials issues or the foreign-relations problems of raw materials questions—their decisions affect both raw materials supplies and prices. Some such agencies exist because the Congress does not trust itself or the executive branch to reach an objective decision in a politically sensitive area. The creation of such an "apolitical" agency also removes the pressure on the Congress from powerful constituents while still providing an appeal process. The prime example of this type of institution is the International

Trade Commission (ITC — formerly the Tariff Commission), which since the 1950s has had the responsibility of hearing complaints from domestic producers that have been harmed by reciprocal trade agreements or by the unfair business practices of foreign producers. The ITC is a unique institution, deliberately bipartisan in composition and autonomous in its actions, created by Congress but independent of it and of the executive branch.

Other agencies administer the federal government's considerable ownership of raw materials and raw-materials-processing capacity. The Federal Preparedness Agency of the General Services Administration (GSA) not only provides guidance on stockpiling policy but also actually manages the acquisition and disposal of the supply of materials that the federal government has accumulated since the end of World War II.[30] While the general guidelines for stockpiling policy are determined by the National Security Council and while specific disposals must be authorized by Congress, the enormous size of the GSA's holdings means that the timing and magnitude of any action can greatly influence not only U.S. domestic producers but also the well-being of foreign suppliers. Still other institutions were designed to regulate specific industries or specific practices. The Federal Power Commission, for example, not only has regulated the rates and activities of interstate gas pipelines, but since 1954 has also set the well-head price of gas sold in interstate commerce. The crucial fact about all these administrative agencies is that they are responsive primarily to their legislative mandates and not to political pressures, changing supply conditions, or foreign-policy considerations. In order to change their actions, one would have to change their mandates, usually by amending the enabling legislation.

New Regulatory Agencies

Finally, the process of forming U.S. raw materials policy has become infinitely more complex in the 1970s with the addition of a variety of new objectives, including environmental protection, occupational safety, and land-use planning. These new national goals have, in turn, meant the development of a series of new federal agencies to bring these objectives into practice. Chief among these have been the Environmental Protection Agency (EPA), founded under the authority of the National Environmental Policy Act of 1970,[31] and the National Institute of Occupational Safety and Health (NIOSH). The formation of these new agencies at the federal level, plus a concomitant growth of their state and regional counterpart offices, has had a marked impact on the rate and pattern of U.S. raw materials development. With the advent of the EPA, some antiquated but regionally important metal smelters had to be shut down, since they could not meet the new air and quality standards. Several large domestic mining operations were delayed or finally abandoned (as in the Kaiparowitz case) because of environmental objections and increased government insistence on advance planning. At times the new requirements threaten to overwhelm the capacity of government to choose, since so many factors and policy objectives are introduced. In the case of the Federal Power Commission's deliberations on alternative northern natural gas routes, the initial Department of Interior/EPA environmental impact statement ran to more than 1,000 pages, and it was attacked as being incomplete.

Congressional preference for state implementation of federal standards for environmental quality, strip mining, coastal-zone management, and a host of new objectives has also ushered in an era of joint state-federal regulation of the extractive industries. Because of the narrowness of the mandates for each of these collaborations, it is difficult to predict the overall effect on the pattern of U.S. mineral resource development. The most that can be said is that these recent changes have led to the formation of new bureaucratic alliances, have facilitated the movement of information among different levels of government, and have led to a harmonization of state regulatory practices.

The major impact of these new federal and state agencies has been not to stymie decision-making, as some critics of the EPA charge, but rather to make it more complex and more subject to bureaucratic norms and values (rather than to electoral controls). In the international context it has made U.S. decision-making more susceptible to transnational and transgovernmental alliance formation. This is particularly true in the case of the United States and Canada because of the widespread recognition by environmentalists and officials concerned with environmental issues that they confront shared problems. The problems of air and water pollution do not respect national boundaries, and the alliances opposing them do not either.

Two Recent Cases of Policy Formation

In this section the working of the U.S. decision-making process in two cases that affected Canadian interests is examined. These cases have been chosen because they illustrate the continuing co-existence of the traditional political alliances that support the domestic mining industry with the new, complex resource management of the 1970s. The two cases are also interesting because they demonstrate the different approaches that the Canadian government can take to U.S. raw materials decision-making: working as a "quasi-domestic"[32] actor within the U.S. system or seeking to influence U.S. policy through bilateral diplomatic negotiations. In the case of lead and zinc, the autonomy of the process and the skill of the Canadian government participants in dealing with that process point to the advantages that

Canada enjoys in the U.S. federal system by virtue of its physical proximity and of the wealth of transgovernmental information contacts it maintains. In the case of northern natural gas we can see the new realities of more formal bilateral relationships and the problems and opportunities these will pose for both countries.

U.S. Duties on Canadian Lead, 1973-76

On February 5, 1973, the Bunker Hill Lead Company filed a complaint with the U.S. International Trade Commission,[33] charging that one Australian firm (Broken Hill) and two Canadian firms (Noranda and Cominco) were dumping, or selling their exports at less than fair value (LTFV). The terms "dumping" and "LTFV" as used in this case mean that a foreign producer is selling a product in the U.S. market for less than it sells that good in its country of origin (after a transportation differential is applied). This is illegal under section 201 of the 1921 Anti-Dumping Act. Dumping, in the eyes of the International Trade Commission and of many members of Congress, is a factual issue: a good is either sold at an unreasonably low price in the United States or it is not. The responsibility for handling such a complaint is divided between the Department of the Treasury and the ITC. The Treasury Department acts as a fact-finding unit for the ITC and determines whether dumping, as defined by the law, has taken place. If dumping has taken place, it is then the task of the ITC to determine whether the dumping action has resulted in injury to the domestic industry and to take the countermeasures it deems necessary. In the fall of 1973 the Treasury Department certified that foreign lead was indeed technically being sold for less in the United States than the home price plus the freight differential, although the amount of the differential was small. After this certification the ITC began an investigation on October 18, 1973, as it was required to do by law.[34]

Once the process of investigation was begun, the ITC was a totally autonomous agency. None of the steps that were to unfold during the process were subject to the approval of either the Congress or the executive branch, even though the outcome would affect domestic lead-producing areas and U.S. relations with major lead-exporting countries. The Canadian and Australian governments were not parties to the dispute, and they had no standing in the proceedings. Likewise, the State Department's Office of Canadian Affairs was not consulted before the investigation was begun and would not have had any standing to protest an ITC finding.

After initial staff investigations and the receipt of legal briefs and other background information, the ITC held hearings on December 4-6, 1973, for the case of Australian lead and on December 6-7 for the two Canadian firms. The hearings were uneventful and mostly technical in nature, but they did feature presentations by two U.S. senators and by aides to two other congressmen from lead-producing areas,[35] who testified in favor of increased duties. Those political leaders made the presentations because they were asked to by processors in their constituencies and because the closings of lead and zinc smelters in their sparsely populated districts were having a major impact on local employment and income. This testimony, however, did not resolve the question of injury, since it did not establish whether the unemployment and smelter closings were due to pricing action of the Canadian and Australian producers or to unrelated factors, such as added costs from new U.S. environmental controls. If foreign actions were found to be the root of the problem, then the law required the ITC to impose penalty duties on imports from the dumping companies.

On January 11, 1974, despite the opposition of U.S. lead consumers and of State Department and Treasury officials, the ITC voted 2-2 (with two abstentions) to find the Canadian and the Australian firms guilty of dumping. The law provides that a tie vote is sufficient to invoke the imposition of duties. This ITC decision was not expected by those following the cases and provided a number of problems for the foreign producers, U.S. consumers, and interested government officials in each country. U.S. Treasury officials were faced with the problems of what levels of duties to assess and how retroactive to make them. U.S. consumers did not know what new price they would face. Foreign producers could not have their U.S. prices raised by a penalty duty (which could be larger than that needed to neutralize dumping) and still remain competitive in the U.S. market. They also did not want to agree to the right of the U.S. government to interfere with their worldwide pricing patterns. The Australian firm, Broken Hill, decided to protest by stopping all shipments to the U.S. market (except occasional spot-market contracts). The Canadian firms adopted a different strategy: they lowered their Canadian prices, thereby creating a differential of between 2.25 and 3 cents per pound between their home price and the U.S. contract price.[36] Thus the initial result of the ITC decision was not protection for U.S. lead producers but a substantial benefit, in terms of lower prices, to Canadian lead consumers.

The U.S. political-bureaucratic combination that had brought about this decision was a classical one, representing a pattern of coalition that had been used on numerous occasions to change the flow of resources in the U.S. economy. It consisted of a declining U.S. domestic industry seeking protection from import competition, producing-state officials trying to maintain employment in their districts, and independent regulators responding to highly specific congressional mandates and injunctions.

The transnational coalition that was quickly formed to seek a reversal of the ITC finding was also a classical response to a protectionist action. Actively involved were the Canadian embassy's mineral counselor, U.S. Treasury Department commodity experts, the State Department Office of Canadian Affairs, the two Canadian firms, and their U.S. customers. Rather than lodging diplomatic protests, Canadian officials quietly pressed the point with U.S. officials that this action would only compound the problems facing U.S. consuming industries. Data and information to reinforce this assertion were passed from Canadian officials to their counterparts in various U.S. departments. The Canadian contention was also supported by a strong U.S. domestic demand for lead and by an upward movement of prices. The Canadian efforts, plus the changing U.S. market, triggered a favorable response in the Treasury Department, the agency charged both with collecting tariffs and duties and with overall monitoring of the U.S. economy. Treasury Secretary Shultz, in his position as chairman of the Cost-of-Living Council (the Nixon wage-price monitoring agency), publicly asked the ITC to reverse its decision, arguing that any additional duties would be inflationary.[37] This was an unprecedented action, since it constituted a public call by a powerful U.S. agency for the reconsideration of an ITC finding. Normally, ITC decisions were not reviewed by Treasury for a minimum of two years, and often longer. The ITC angrily refused the Shultz request, and the Treasury Department reluctantly acquiesced on April 17, 1974, by publishing the LTFV finding in the *Federal Register*.[38] But the foreign producers did not accept the finding, and the Treasury Department did not collect any penalty duties as long as Australian metal was not imported and Canadian domestic prices were lowered.

The Canadian government and the Canadian producers continued to work quietly for a reversal of the ITC finding. Canadian officials researched the legislative history of the 1974 Trade Act, as they do in all U.S. trade protection actions, and conferred frequently with company lawyers who were compiling a brief on the intent of the Congress which became the basis for the later successful appeal.[39] In October, 1974, the three foreign producers met in Washington with major U.S. consumers of lead to plot a common strategy for upsetting the ITC finding.[40] It was decided that an appeal would be launched by U.S. domestic consumers, since they would have more standing with the ITC, and that the Canadian and the Australian producers should stay out of the proceedings. This effort was actively encouraged by the U.S. Treasury Department, and a petition based on the legislative history of the new Trade Act was submitted to the Treasury by U.S. consuming companies in February, 1975. It was delayed for nearly a year, however, while the Treasury gathered data on foreign markets and foreign pricing to support the petition. Finally, on January 5, 1976, the Treasury Department submitted to the ITC the long-delayed appeal and its own supporting briefs.[41] On February 24-26, 1976, the ITC held hearings to reinvestigate its earlier findings. In mid-April, 1976, it voted unanimously to revoke its findings and thus remove the necessity for the countervailing duties (which had never been assessed). This finding was a major triumph for the Canadian producers and for the Canadian officials who helped to devise the strategy. Not only was the threat of duties removed, but the ITC agreed in principle that Canadian producers could, in future, establish a uniform price for the whole North American market, provided that U.S. domestic producers were not harmed by this action.[42] This meant that they could restore their domestic prices to U.S. levels without U.S. governmental sanctions.

The lead-dumping case was indicative of one facet of U.S. raw materials policy-making—the protection of producers from import competition by administrative action, with anti-dumping regulations being a favorite vehicle. In recent years Canadian producers have faced such actions in pig iron, sulfur, potash, and semi-fabricated metals. But the outcome of the lead-dumping case demonstrated the skill of Canadian corporations and Canadian officials in overcoming these obstacles. By relying on U.S. domestic actors and on alliances with sympathetic U.S. agencies, the Canadian government and the Canadian companies had gained a favorable decision from a generally protectionist agency that would have been difficult to win from the U.S. government by confrontation and high-level bilateral negotiation.

The Northern Natural Gas Pipeline

During the period 1973-77 the U.S. government struggled with the question of how to deliver Alaskan (and possibly Canadian) natural gas to customers in the Lower 48 U.S. states and in Canada. During this time three consortia of oil and gas companies, pipeline firms, and natural-gas-distributing utilities were competing with each other for the permission of the U.S. and Canadian governments to build the necessary transmission system. This section focuses on the complexity of the objectives facing the federal administrators, on the insistence of the Congress and of the various federal agencies on sharing in each phase of the selection process, and on the choice to move the final decision-making point to the hands of elected rather than appointed officials.

Because it meant the allocation of a scarce and highly prized benefit, the selection of a route for the natural gas pipeline was certain to be important, controversial, and political. In most countries such a choice would have been a cabinet-level decision from the start, initiated after formal diplomatic negotiations with the neighboring country and lengthy parliamentary debate. In the U.S. system the task initially fell upon an independent, non-partisan agency, the Federal Power Commission (FPC), which has six appointed commissioners, charged with the regulation of interstate pipelines. The FPC is a highly bureaucratic domestic organization, ponderous and meticulous in its deliberations. Having received the initial two proposals (from the Arctic Gas Consortium and from El Paso Natural Gas), the FPC began gathering data, soliciting briefs from interested parties, and developing staff studies, environmental impact statements, and economic-feasibility studies.

The new policy objectives of the 1970s, combined with the massive scale of the proposed projects, made the FPC review process cumbersome, complex, and time-consuming, taking nearly three years. Testimony was heard from 194 witnesses,[43] and the transcript ran to nearly 45,000 pages. The active participants reflected a new emphasis on public participation and state-federal cooperation. Intervenors representing nearly half of the states of the United States, environmental interest groups, and interested consumers of natural gas were all given permission to provide their evaluations of the alternative routes.[44]

The FPC was not, however, allowed to proceed alone in its considerations: the issues were too important, and the stakes, especially to consumers, too high. Congress expressed an interest in influencing the proceedings from the very outset: on March 22, 1974, twenty-two senators, led by Birch Bayh of Indiana, wrote to Interior Secretary Rogers Morton, urging immediate adoption of the Arctic Gas alternative.[45] Their constituents in the Midwest and in the north central states badly needed supplies of natural gas, and the Canadian route offered the best way of getting them rapidly.

Portions of the executive branch were also involved from the beginning. The National Environmental Policy Act of 1970 gave the Department of the Interior the task of granting permits for any rights-of-way across federally owned lands. Since virtually all Alaska is public land, Interior would have to approve the construction of any of the proposed alternatives.[46] Also, in January, 1974, before the FPC had received any proposals, President Nixon ordered the Department of the Interior to study alternative methods for getting Alaska's large natural gas supplies to market.[47] After the initial proposals were submitted, FPC and Interior specialists jointly undertook the onerous task of preparing the required environmental impact studies.

As 1974 and 1975 passed without any FPC decision, pressure grew within the U.S. political system for an imposed solution. On February 26, 1976, President Ford asked Congress to give him the right to decide, subject to congressional review, between the two alternatives then under consideration (the Alcan proposal had not yet been submitted).[48] After lengthy hearings there emerged a remarkably complex bill, known as S.5321, that passed the Senate unanimously on July 1, 1976, and cleared the House on September 30, 1976 (with major revisions). The final law, officially titled the Alaska Natural Gas Transportation Act of 1976,[49] gave the President the power to review the FPC decision and then reserved for the Congress the final judgment on the President's findings. The FPC was suddenly transformed, in the middle of its review process, from an autonomous regulatory body to an advisory committee.

Throughout these initial three years of administrative deliberations and legislative maneuvering, the selection process was treated as a U.S. domestic problem, with Canadian issues being treated as matters of foreign relations. In the 7,000-word text of the Alaska Natural Gas Transportation Act of 1976, Canada is mentioned only twice.[50] No Canadian officials testified at the FPC hearings. Rather, Canadian concerns were presented formally through diplomatic notes to the U.S. State Department, as well as by U.S. environmental intervenors and by U.S. and Canadian oil and gas corporations. Nonetheless, continuous informal, transgovernmental discussions ensured that federal, state, and provincial officials of each country were aware of the progress of decision-making within the other. There were also formal negotiations on a U.S.-Canadian treaty that would bind both sides not to interfere with oil and gas flowing to customers in the other country. A draft of this treaty was initialed by representatives of both nations in early 1976, final copies were signed the following January,[51] and the text was approved by the U.S. Senate in the summer of 1977.

On February 1, 1977, FPC Administrative Law Judge Nuhum Litt issued his long-awaited decision, a monumental 430-page document that favored the Arctic Gas proposal, rejected the Alcan system entirely, and rated the El Paso concept as feasible but distinctly inferior to the Arctic Gas system. Three months later, however, on May 2, 1977, the entire FPC issued an equivocal finding on the dispute: two commissioners favored the Alcan route, and two the Arctic Gas alternative.[52] This change was due in large measure to the new complexity of balancing development with environmental constraints. The Alcan proposal, hurriedly submitted two years after the others, won immediate endorsement in both countries from a wide variety of groups and officials concerned with minimizing ecological and social dislocations. Although the Alcan route was not markedly less expensive and did not provide immediate market access for Canadian gas, it did have the major advantage of generating the least opposition on both sides of the border. The Alcan proposal was the lowest common denominator among the contending forces seeking rapid development, environmental protection, and social impact alleviation.

After the FPC divided finding, the problem of working out an acceptable solution moved to the Office of the President. At this point the emphasis shifted from technical analysis to the integration of U.S. needs, with the outcome emerging from the Canadian decision-making process. The National Energy Board of Canada had given qualified approval to the Alcan route, but the Canadian government had made it clear that important issues of timing, financing, final route selection, and environmental impact alleviation would have to be resolved before construction would be allowed to begin.

In contrast to previous U.S.-Canadian pipeline efforts, the final route-selection process was not determined by the major oil- and gas-producing companies, in informal consultation with career mineral specialists in each federal government. Instead, a series of top-level diplomatic talks were begun in August, 1977, which eventually led to formal bargaining sessions in both Washington and Ottawa. Indicative of the importance of the sessions, the U.S. contingent was headed by the new Secretary of Energy, James Schlesinger, and the Canadian side was led by Privy Council President Allan MacEachen.[53] Both sets of negotiators were under considerable pressure to "win"—to extract the maximum number of concessions and to give up as few as possible. In this setting, transnational alliances and informal transgovernment contracts among lower-level officials were of little importance. The bargaining was extensive and detailed, with the Canadians dropping their insistence on a route closer to the untapped Canadian reserves of the MacKenzie Valley and easing the payment mechanisms of a $200 million socio-economic-impact-alleviation fund, while the United States agreed to help finance later development of Canadian reserves and to higher taxes in the Yukon territory on the pipeline right-of-way.[54] The final details and the indication of the choice of the Alcan route were made public jointly by President Carter and Prime Minister Trudeau at the White House, a procedure far different from informal announcements marking earlier major North American energy projects. Despite this top-level executive agreement, however, the process was not yet final in either country. In the United States the President's decision had to be submitted to the Congress for approval. Hearings were held to allow advocates of the other routes one last chance. Finally, the four years of deliberation and uncertainty ended on the U.S. side on November 2, 1977, when the House and the Senate both approved the President's choice.[55]

Observations and Conclusions

The U.S. Process

The formation of public policy in the United States has traditionally been complex and marked by a careful separation of functions among the branches of the central government and by a division of power among the individual states, the federal government, and a large number of semi-autonomous regulatory agencies. In the mineral resources area, this complexity is compounded by the separability of mineral rights, regional diversities in mineral ownership patterns, and widely varying levels of local mineral tax dependence. During the past ten years, concerns over environmental degradation, the socio-economic impact of rapid development, worker safety, and consumer protection have heightened the difficulty of formulating national policy. As new goals have led to federal legislation and regulation, they have also generated a countertrend of state demands for a sharing of federal regulatory powers and for increasing local roles in federal mineral-leasing and land-use decisions. This has resulted in contradictory policy objectives, delay, and confusion. An appointed regulatory agency is uniquely unsuited to determine outcomes in such a complex situation, especially when many of the major points of dispute involve the distribution of valuable goods (scarce, non-polluting natural gas) or jobs (in the construction of the pipeline) among competing political coalitions. Congress and the President have felt compelled to intervene in a number of cases, including the choice of a northern natural gas pipeline, and will do so increasingly in the future as raw materials decisions become matters of regional division and international confrontation.

Despite the new policy objectives and the insistence of elected officials on their right to determine controversial outcomes, independent agencies and regulatory bodies such as the FPC and the ITC will continue to make decisions affecting the price and supply of important raw materials within the United States. More important for this analysis, domestic regulatory agencies and ostensibly domestic federal departments increasingly are making decisions that affect the flow of raw materials in the international marketplace. There are many reasons for this growing importance of domestic agencies in international policy formation and execution, as Raymond Hopkins has ably noted, ranging from growing world interdependence to the specialization of skill that domestic departments naturally acquire in performing their domestic tasks.[56] Whatever the reasons, this internationalization of domestic policy-making will have a profound impact on the capability of the foreign-policy network to centralize decision-making, particularly in areas where bureaucratic control has already been weakened by transnational and transgovernmental ties, as in the case of U.S.-Canadian raw materials issues.

The movement toward state participation in federal regulation, combined with rapidly rising levels of severance taxation in the major mining states, will have broad implications for future U.S. policy formation. On the one hand, these trends have created new state agencies with the bureaucratic norms and the necessary funds (generated by new mineral production taxes) to control or even curtail the activities and the impact of domestic mining industries. These new state units share many goals and ideals with their federal counterparts and thus are prime candidates for new federal-state governmental alliances. Industry representatives charge that the resulting proliferation of rules, regulations, and taxes has made it virtually impossible to initiate a new large-scale mining operation in the United States. On the other hand, much of the future course of U.S. mineral development will depend on how the states decide to deal with their mineral-severance-tax income, particularly in the case of coal. If they decide to use this revenue for current expenditure, as the oil- and gas-producing states and major eastern coal states such as Kentucky have done, then they will rapidly become committed to increasing levels of mineral production. If they use it for environmental impact alleviation (as in the case of North Dakota) or set the revenue aside as a trust fund (as will be done in Montana), then the states may be more inclined to pursue a relatively restrictive policy toward mineral development.

The changes that have been occurring inside the U.S. mineral-policy system have as yet had little impact on the nature and the direction of U.S.-Canadian trade. For example, the drive by U.S. mining states to influence federal mineral-policy formation and to control the pace of mineral production has had few Canadian repercussions. For the next few years, state efforts will primarily affect the rate and the cost of western coal production, none of which moves across the border. However, Canada does import more than 16.5 million tons of coal from the United States annually from fields in the Appalachian states.[57] If the eastern states chose to follow the example of Montana and to enact a heavy severance tax, this could have a serious impact on the price of energy in eastern Canada and on the competitive position of Canadian heavy industries dependent on U.S. coal supplies.

The Canadian Connection

Canadian issues are often treated as "quasi-domestic" within the U.S. government, partly because of the perceptions of U.S. policy-makers and partly because Canada actively seeks this treatment. Particularly in cases where decision-making takes place in independent agencies or inside departmental bureaucracies, Canadian officials are extremely proficient at fathoming the intricacies of the U.S. process, building or encouraging bureaucratic alliances that favor Canadian producers, and limiting the degree of politicization of issues.

Part of the Canadian success is due to specialization. Besides Australia, Canada is the only country that has a commercial counselor in Washington who works full-time on mineral issues. Canada also has a legislative liaison

officer attached to its embassy who spends all his time following issues in
the U.S. Congress that are of interest to Canada. These specialized officials
provide a number of services that raw materials producers and consumers
in other countries do not receive from their governments. First, they serve
as an early-warning system, picking up and transmitting hints of issues as
they arise so that the Canadian position or positions can be hammered out
in advance. Second, they maintain a widespread net of informal contacts
with U.S. officials in most of the departments, congressional committees,
and independent regulatory agencies that might take an action affecting
Canadian raw materials. Not only does this network improve their
information-gathering; it also provides immediate access, rather than indirect contact through circuitous diplomatic channels, to the individuals
who actually make the decisions. Third, these specialized Canadian officials are able to provide advice to other Canadian government departments or to Canadian industry on the best strategy for achieving desired
outcomes. Being familiar with the workings of the U.S. regulatory agencies, they are able to assist in framing submissions from individual firms
and industrial groups. In the lead anti-dumping case, for example, the
mineral counselor and embassy legal staff worked with the smaller Canadian firms to formulate a common position and later helped to do the
research into the legislative history of the 1974 Trade Act that became the
basis for the successful appeal.

In providing all these services, the Canadian officials function not as
diplomatic envoys but essentially as U.S. domestic political actors. Indeed,
the tasks they undertake are those that political scientists have long noted
are performed by successful Washington interest-group lobbyists.[58] They
provide fast and accurate information both to busy U.S. decision-makers
and to their Canadian home constituents. They continually monitor the
positions of different decision-makers on issues important to their constituents and facilitate access to U.S. decision-makers whenever it is needed
by the leaders of groups they represent.

The skill of Canadian officials in representing their client groups and in
understanding the byzantine machinations of Washington's bureaucratic
politics, however impressive, can provide only a partial explanation of the
generally favorable treatment that Canadian raw materials issues have
received in the U.S. decision-making process. Much of the remaining
variance can be explained by transgovernmental contacts. U.S. officials, as
many authors have noted, have constant informal contact with their Canadian counterparts. They are linked by a common telephone system, and the
available evidence[59] is that they use it to contact their counterpart officials
as often as they do other members of their own government. These constant
contacts among officials not only transmit information, but lessen the need

for diplomatic contacts and for political decision-making.

In an examination of these transgovernmental ties, the interesting question that arises is not whether they are important today, but rather whether they will be less important in the future. There are several contradictory trends that will help determine the answer. The presence in Washington of specialized Canadian officials able to provide data and information will reduce the need for U.S. decision-makers to contact their counterparts in Ottawa. The rapid growth in expertise of Canadian officials in the past few years has also reduced the need for such contact in the opposite direction. As the acting director of the U.S. Bureau of Mines noted in a recent interview, there is less contact between his agency and Canadian federal officials today than there was two decades or even one decade ago. He ascribed this partly to the reduced pace of defense planning compared to the Korean War period and partly to the new professionalism of Canadian decision-makers in raw materials areas.[60] No longer do they turn to their U.S. counterparts for staff support on complex technical matters or for advice on procedures such as formulation of reserve estimates. Offsetting these two trends will be the growing attention given to international affairs by U.S. "domestic" departments and agencies and the interest of these agencies in transnational and transgovernmental ties.

One of the results of these trends may be an increase in the number of transgovernmental contacts, but a decrease in the formation of transgovernmental alliances. Contacts will be used to explain policy positions and to explore options rather than to develop common strategies. The final outcome of important bilateral raw materials decisions may be determined by formal bargaining rather than by informal agreement. The choice of an Alaskan natural-gas-pipeline system is a typical example of the new complexity, which requires high-level political management and bilateral negotiation.

It remains to be seen whether periodic cabinet-level diplomatic negotiations will become the norm for future U.S.-Canadian relations in natural resources. If so, this would signal a continued migration of decision-making in U.S. resource policy toward Canada, from middle-level civil servants to the Office of the President and the Congress. Such a shift would diminish the importance of informal transgovernmental contacts and would vitiate some of the advantages accruing to Canada from its specialized Washington officials and its ready access to U.S. federal bureaucrats. The discretionary power of federal officials in both governments to settle problems as they arise through informal contact and accommodation would be diminished, since issues would be held for resolution at the next high-level bilateral sessions. It is not clear whether the unity of foreign policy toward Canada that such centralization of U.S decision-making would bring would

98   JOHN H. ASHWORTH

offset the loss of day-to-day adjustment and compromise that the current
system provides. What is certain is that the next decade will bring massive
procedural and substantive changes as external relations begin to reflect
new policy concerns and new institutional realities within the domestic
political systems of each country.

Notes

1. I will adopt the terminology, refined by Nye and Keohane, of transnational
and transgovernmental actors, where *transgovernmental* is taken to mean "direct interaction between agencies (governmental subunits) of different governments where
these agencies act relatively autonomously from central governmental control" and
transnational "refers to interactions across the border in which at least one actor is
nongovernmental" (see Robert O. Keohane and Joseph S. Nye, Jr., "Introduction:
The Complex Politics of Canadian-American Interdependence," *International Organization* 28, No. 4 [Autumn, 1974]: 596; see also Nye and Keohane, *Transnational Relations and World Politics* [Cambridge: Harvard University Press, 1974], and *Power and
Interdependence: World Politics in Transition* [Boston: Little, Brown & Co., 1977]).

2. For the classic statement of the impact of bureaucratic politics on decision-
making, see Graham T. Allison, *The Essence of Decision: Explaining the Cuban Missile
Crisis* (Boston: Little, Brown & Co., 1971). See also Raymond F. Hopkins, "The
International Role of 'Domestic' Bureaucracy," *International Organization* 30, No. 3
(Summer, 1976): 406-32.

3. The following is a selected list of recent governmental publications on raw
materials policy: Council on International Economic Policy (CIEP), *Critical Imported Materials,* Special Report (Washington, D.C.: U.S. Government Printing Of-
fice, 1974); Office of Technology Assessment, *Requirements for Fulfilling a National
Materials Policy* (Washington, D.C.: U.S. Government Printing Office, 1974); U.S.
Congress Joint Committee on Defense Production, *Purpose and Organization of
Economic Stockpiling: Hearings before the Subcommittee on Materials Availability*
(Washington, D.C.: U.S. Government Printing Office, 1976); National Commis-
sion on Supplies and Shortages, *Government and the Nation's Resources* (Washington,
D.C.: U.S. Government Printing Office, 1976). Four private publications on the
subject should also be noted: Eugene N. Cameron, ed., *The Mineral Position of the
United States: 1975-2000* (Madison: University of Wisconsin Press for the Society of
Economic Geologists Foundation, 1973); Jeffrey S. Carroll, *Survey of Existing
Literature of Nine Key Non-Fuel Minerals* (Washington, D.C.: National Planning
Association, 1976); the special February 20, 1976, issue of *Science* (Vol. 191, No.
4227) devoted to material resources and problems; the International Economic
Studies Institute, *Raw Materials and Foreign Policy* (Washington, D.C., 1977).

4. Some analysts, however, have questioned sharply whether a coherent raw
materials policy would necessarily be a good thing, since it would conflict with many
other existing policies (see the argument by Leonard Fishman, quoted in National
Commission on Supplies and Shortages, *Government and the Nation's Resources,* op cit.,
pp. 110-11).

5. Roger F. Swanson, "The United States Canadian Constellation, I: Washington, D.C.," *International Journal* 27, No. 2 (Spring, 1972): 185.

6. For a summary of the events leading to the formation of the state-centered system for controlling U.S. domestic oil production, see John H. Ashworth, "The Movement to Closure: The Politics of U.S. Petroleum Trade Policy, 1945-1960" (Ph.D. diss., Harvard University, 1977), Chap. 3.

7. Much of the following analysis is based on Roy M. Robbins, *Our Landed Heritage: The Public Domain, 1776-1970* (Lincoln: University of Nebraska Press, 1976).

8. Ibid., pp. 150-51.

9. Ibid., pp. 223-24, for a listing of these grants.

10. For a detailed account of the controversy over mineral policy in the Roosevelt administration, see Todd Alan Linsermayer, "The Separation of Surface Mineral Estates in Public Land Disposition," Bureau of Land Management internal paper, April, 1964.

11. Ibid., pp. 9-12.

12. An excellent current compilation of mineral-taxing systems of most of the major raw-materials-producing states is found in Thomas F. Stinson, *State Taxation of Mineral Deposits Production* (Washington, D.C.: Office of Research and Development, U.S. Environmental Protection Agency, 1977).

13. A valuable summary of federal legislation that specifies regulatory roles for state governments is to be found in John Watson and Douglas Larson, *Precedents and Proposals for State Involvement in Federal Energy Decisions,* Special Report (Lakewood, Colorado: Western Interstate Nuclear Board, 1977).

14. Ibid., p. 4.

15. U.S. Congress, House Committee on Ways and Means, *Hearings on Trade Agreements Extension,* Part 2, 84th Cong., 1st Sess., p. 1457.

16. For a controversial discussion of the problems facing Montana, including mineral taxation, see K. Ross Toole, *The Rape of the Great Plains: Northwest America, Cattle and Coal* (Boston: Little, Brown & Co., 1976).

17. Stinson, op. cit., pp. 24, 41. For a penetrating analysis of the power of the coal industry in Kentucky, see Marc K. Landy, *The Politics of Environmental Reform: Controlling Kentucky Strip Mining* (Washington, D.C.: Resources for the Future, 1975).

18. Texas Legislative Council, *A Survey of Taxation in Texas,* Part I (Austin, 1950), p. 39.

19. Caleb Perry Patterson, Sam B. McAllister, and George C. Hester, *State and Local Government in Texas,* 3rd ed. (New York: MacMillan Co., 1961), p. 198.

20. See Ashworth, op. cit., pp. 364-76.

21. Stinson, op cit., pp. 25-26, 41.

22. C. Robert Dickerman, "Transgovernmental Challenge and Response in Scandinavia and North America," *International Organization* 30, No. 2 (Spring, 1976): 232.

23. This was voiced most strongly by congressional staff members and Department of the Interior spokesmen.

24. For a summary of these visits as tabulated by Canadian officials in 1969, see Dickerman, op. cit., p. 227.

100 JOHN H. ASHWORTH

25. David R. Mayhew, *Party Loyalty Among Congressmen: The Difference Between Democrats and Republicans, 1947-1962* (Cambridge: Harvard University Press, 1966), p. 130.

26. In the 1977 congressional reorganization, the senate committee was broken into two new committees: the Committee on Energy and Natural Resources, headed by Senator Jackson, and the Committee on Environment and Public Works, headed by Senator Randolph. For purposes of continuity and symmetry, the senate side will be referred to collectively as Interior and Insular Affairs unless one of the new committees is specified in the text.

27. See Marion Clawson and Burnell Held, *The Federal Lands: Their Use and Management* (Baltimore: The Johns Hopkins Press for Resources for the Future, 1957), pp. 401-02. These figures have been updated to reflect government sales and purchases since the publication of the Clawson and Held book.

28. George Goodwin ranked committees for the 81st through the 90th Congresses according to whether congressmen requested to join them or leave them when the opportunity presented itself. The House Interior and Insular Affairs Committee ranked 15th out of 19 committees, while its senate counterpart was 8th out of 15 (see George Goodwin, *The Little Legislatures: The Committees of Congress* [Amherst: University of Massachusetts Press, 1970], pp. 114-15).

29. Interview with Dr. John Morgan, Acting Director of the Bureau of Mines, March 30, 1977.

30. For a history of the acquisition of that stockpile, see Glenn H. Snyder, *Stockpiling Strategic Materials: Politics and National Defense* (San Francisco: Chandler Publishing Company, 1966).

31. 42 U.S. *Code* 4331.

32. Dickerman, op. cit., p. 232.

33. In the first round of the proceedings, the ITC was known by its traditional name—the U.S. Tariff Commission. For consistency, its current name is used throughout the text.

34. These were Tariff Commission investigations AA1921-134 and AA1921-135.

35. Speaking for increased duties were Senators Wallace Bennett of Utah and James McClure of Idaho. Congressmen represented at the hearings were Steven D. Symms of Idaho and Thomas A. Foley of Washington. The text of these presentations can be found in U.S. Tariff Commission, *Hearings on Primary Lead Metal from Australia*, December 4, 1973, p. 8ff.

36. *Metals Week* 45, No. 15 (April 15, 1974): 3, 45, and No. 16 (April 22, 1974): 3.

37. *Metals Week* 45, No. 13 (April 1, 1974): 9.

38. *Metals Week* 45, No. 16, op. cit., p. 3.

39. Interview with Canadian embassy officials, March 31, 1977. The text of this legislative history was incorporated in the final report of three ITC commissioners (see *Primary Lead Metal from Australia and Canada: Determination of No Likelihood to Injury*... [U.S. International Trade Commission Publication 772, April, 1976], p. 6).

40. *Metals Week* 45, No. 44 (November 4, 1974): 2.

41. U.S. Tariff Commission, *Hearings* . . . , op. cit., Appendix C.

42. *Metals Week* 47, No. 17 (April 26, 1976): 1.

43. For a list of the participants and "intervenors," see Federal Power Commission, *Initial Decision on Competing Applications for an Alaskan Transportation Project, Docket No. CP75-96 et al.* (Washington, D.C.: Federal Power Commission, 1977), pp. 1-6.

44. Ibid., p. 8, fn. 2.

45. Richard Corrigan, "Energy Report/El Paso, Arctic Firms Compete for Alaska Transportation Rights," *National Journal,* August 3, 1974, p. 1159.

46. Ibid.

47. Ibid.

48. *New York Times,* February 27, 1976.

49. P.L. 94-586, October 22, 1976. The full text of the law can be found in Appendix D to the FPC's *Initial Decision on Proposed Alaska Natural Gas Transportation Systems* or in 90 *Stat* 2903.

50. P.L. 94-586, sections 5(d), 7(d).

51. *Energy Users' Report,* No. 190, March 31, 1977, p. 11.

52. *New York Times,* May 3, 1977.

53. *The Energy Daily* 5, No. 168 (August 29, 1977): 1-2.

54. *The Energy Daily* 5, No. 173 (September 6, 1977): 1-2; *The Oil and Gas Journal,* September 12, 1977, p. 73.

55. *New York Times,* November 3, 1977.

56. Raymond Hopkins, "The International Role of 'Domestic' Bureaucracy," *International Organization* 30, No. 3 (Summer, 1976): 414-18.

57. Bureau of Mines, *Bituminous Coal and Lignite Distribution in Calendar Year 1976* (Washington, D.C.: U.S. Department of Interior, 1977). This figure understates the total shipment, since it does not include anthracite, coke, or prepared briquets, which in 1975 amounted to more than 1.2 million tons.

58. See Raymond Bauer, Ithiel Pool, and Lewis Dexter, *American Business and Public Policy* (New York: Atherton Press, 1963), and Lewis A. Dexter, *How Organizations Are Represented in Washington* (Indianapolis: Bobbs-Merrill, 1966).

59. Dickerman, op. cit., p. 229.

60. Interview with Dr. John Morgan.

4

U.S. Resource Policy: Canadian Connections

JACOB KAPLAN

The Growth of Interdependence

Before World War II, Canada's economic relations with the United States were remarkably limited, given the 3,200-mile border shared by the two countries. Great Britain was Canada's largest market, absorbing 40 percent of its exports in 1938. One-third of Canadian exports went to the United States and accounted for about 15 percent of U.S. imports. U.S. imports of crude raw materials from Canada amounted to only $36 million, including $24 million worth of nickel. As the United States contemplated the security of its supply of imported raw materials on the eve of the war, the only mineral resource it could depend upon from its large northern neighbor was nickel.[1] Indeed, Canada was a net importer of coal and petroleum from the United States. The book value of all U.S. direct investment in Canada was a modest $2 billion, only 15-20 percent of it in the mining, smelting, and petroleum industries.

At the time, Canada was a thinly populated agricultural country with a large but undeveloped resource potential and little industry. Its eleven million people produced a GNP of $5 billion and exported nearly $900 million of goods annually, primarily agricultural and forestry products. The United States was essentially self-sufficient in the basic raw materials its industrialized economy required and spent relatively small amounts on imports of a limited number of critical materials that had never been discovered in significant quantities within its borders. It had a population of 132 million, a GNP of about $100 billion, and annual exports totaling more than $3 billion.

The postwar period saw a radical change in these magnitudes, as the U.S. and the Canadian economies were transformed by an era of rapid economic growth and price inflation, both internally and in the rest of the world. The less developed Canadian economy grew much more rapidly than did the U.S. economy. By the end of the third quarter of the century,

103

the prewar disparity in the size of the two economies had been greatly reduced, although the U.S. economy remained much the larger. At nearly $7,000 in 1975, per capita Canadian GNP was about on a par with that of the United States. Canada's population had increased to 23 million and its exports to $35 billion per year, the former being one-ninth, the latter one-third, the size of comparable figures for the United States.

Both countries increased aggregate production at more rapid rates than either had previously recorded. In the process their economic inter-dependence increased. Canada replaced Great Britain as the single leading market for U.S. exports. The United States, in turn, became Canada's principal market, absorbing three-fifths of all Canadian exports and two-thirds of its exports of mineral and forest materials. By 1970 Canada had become the source of one-quarter of all U.S. imports and one-half of its raw materials imports. The list of materials imported from Canada has become extensive: in 1975, Canada supplied 15 percent of U.S. imports of petroleum (50 percent in 1970), virtually all imported uranium and natural gas, 85 percent of forest products, 73 percent of nickel, 51 percent of zinc, 49 percent of iron ore, 48 percent of copper, 37 percent of mercury, 30 percent of lead, 23 percent of tungsten, and 15 percent of tantulum.[2] The capital for developing Canadian raw materials production was supplied predominantly from the United States, and the book value of U.S. direct investment in such production multiplied 26 times.

The extent of this interdependence, despite the prosperity that has accompanied it, has given rise to concern in Canada. To some, the large equity interest of U.S. corporations in Canadian manufacturing and raw materials production seems a threat to Canadian political and economic independence. The high concentration of trade with the United States could put Canada at the mercy of the U.S. business cycle. Some feel that Canada's exhaustible natural resources are being depleted for the benefit of the U.S. economy and to the detriment of future generations of Canadians. The Canadian government has been under pressure to control and contain these trends. The United States, on the other hand, tends to feel that the extent and the character of this interdependence have been the result of a natural economic process and have conferred comparable benefits on both parties. It prefers that the process should be reinforced rather than constrained.

With the very desirability of interdependence called into question, current and future policy issues may be better understood in the light of some historic perspective. On the Canadian side, the coincidence of sharply rising exports of raw materials to the United States and a high rate of economic growth over a protracted period suggests that careful analysis is required before major changes in the policies that facilitated such exports are introduced.

On the U.S. side, it has become necessary to re-examine the policies that indirectly — if not directly — affected the production of Canadian materials and their export to the United States. Not only the motivations, but also the manifestations, of these policies need to be understood, as well as the role of government policy in bringing about the observable results.

The Evolution of U.S. Raw Materials and Foreign Economic Policies[3]

Incredible though it may seem to many contemporary foreign observers, the historical record offers no evidence of a deliberate U.S. government policy designed to assure expanding industries in the United States of ever-increasing supplies of raw materials at reasonable prices. *A fortiori*, a specific policy toward Canadian resources eludes identification.

The United States did, however, develop a view of how the postwar international economy should operate; raw materials problems were expected to fall into place within an overall system. The essence of the U.S. view was a global arrangement for multilateral trade and payments, with all foreign business treated alike irrespective of nationality and with restrictions progressively eliminated as rapidly as an expanding world economy would permit. Such an economic system was regarded as a building block for a comprehensive structure to promote peace and a viable international order.

During the early years after World War II, the United States successfully incorporated its vision into a series of international arrangements. The United Nations and its specialized agencies were brought into being, with the International Monetary Fund (IMF), the International Bank for Reconstruction and Development (IBRD), and the General Agreement on Tariffs and Trade (GATT)[4] as the focal operating economic institutions.

While these arrangements did not single out raw materials production and trade for special attention, the reason was not obliviousness to the possibility of a recurrence of the problems that had beset the raw materials sector in the interwar period. An expanding world economy, with trade and capital unhampered by restrictions, was expected to alleviate such problems as might arise. Only token recognition was accorded the possibility that persistent overproduction and unemployment might require commodity agreements in the case of some basic materials.

The Approach to International Raw Materials Policy

In its posture toward international raw materials, the United States was inevitably conditioned by its own experience, although it was motivated primarily by the idealistic values that form the underpinnings for traditional international trade theory. Unlike Europe and Japan, the United States had a relatively large domestic raw materials base, so that concern about the reliability of imported supplies was minimal. On the other hand, it had protested against international cartel arrangements for some materials without much effect in the 1920s and had obtained access for its entrepreneurs to Middle East and Dutch East Indies oil in 1928 only after energetic diplomatic intervention. The United States had also objected to the restrictions placed on its foreign economic activity by preferential arrangements established by colonial powers.

Accordingly, when the time came for a statement of postwar aims, the 1941 Atlantic Charter called for "access on equal terms to the trade and raw materials of the world." Proclaimed as the fourth point of an eight-point U.S.-U.K. declaration of intentions, the phrase concerning raw materials was directed primarily at Eastern Hemisphere nations that had long been worried about the national-security implications of their dependence on imports for many basic materials.[5] At the time, Churchill was preoccupied with deterring Japan's entry into the war, as well as with forging an alliance with the United States; Roosevelt's concerns were for an altruistic statement of long-range goals that would blunt the fears of U.S. isolationists. Together, Churchill and Roosevelt promised, *inter alia,* that in the postwar world neither the have-not nations nor anyone else would be denied essential raw materials.

Whatever the purpose and however simplistic the formulation, equal access became, in fact, the essence of U.S. raw materials foreign policy for more than a quarter of a century thereafter. The United States steadfastly resisted the notion that special arrangements might better serve the interests of producers and consumers of any commodity other than a few foodstuffs. Thirty-five years were to elapse before the United States joined an international agreement affecting the market for a non-agricultural commodity—the International Tin Agreement in 1976.

"Access on equal terms" came to mean more than freedom to purchase available supplies. The concept was meant to include freedom for private business to invest abroad and to be treated on terms as favorable as those offered to domestic investors. That policy was an important part of a generalized belief in the procreative power of invested capital that dominated all aspects of U.S. economic policy in the postwar period. Capital investment was regarded as the key to unlocking economic growth; economic growth, in turn, was perceived as the cornerstone of a stable world order. Government capital was provided to speed economic reconstruction in Western Europe and Japan and, later, to less developed countries. However, such government capital was to play only a pump-priming role, accelerating the economic-growth process to the point where private capital could and would take over.

The Role of Private Capital

Private capital was considered more likely to be used effectively in speeding growth and, in any event, was more readily available. U.S. investors were urged to invest in Europe as the Marshall Plan came to an end. Official aid to developing countries included bilateral and multilateral loans and grants for expanding the production and export of raw materials. It was accompanied by tax incentives for private investors and by other forms of government risk sharing, together with efforts to persuade recipients to create a more hospitable and profitable environment for potential private investors. Because raw materials projects were relatively quick to generate foreign exchange, the limited supply of government capital was largely reserved for other projects, even in the case of countries otherwise considered to be in need of grants or loans repayable on very soft terms.

After World War II, ample U.S. capital and technology were available for the exploration and development of mineral production around the globe. Mineral output expanded at an unprecedented rate to meet steeply accelerating demands for reconstruction and industrialization throughout the non-Communist world. Moreover, these demands were satisfied at prices that by and large kept pace with the prices of manufactured goods over the years, although without any real increase.

Trade Negotiation Goals

At the end of World War II the United States initiated a series of multilateral negotiations aimed at reducing tariffs under the auspices of the GATT and was reasonably successful in reducing its own foreign-trade barriers in return for concessions by other countries. Even in the high-tariff era, most raw materials had entered the United States free of duty, and tariff barriers were generally not a major trade barrier for raw materials in their primary state. Early in the postwar period the emphasis in international trade negotiations was on eliminating quantitative restrictions and on bargaining down tariff barriers on processed raw materials and manufactured products, where the levels were particularly high. In the 1960s, attention was increasingly directed to the special problems of agricultural trade; more recently, non-tariff barriers have been pushed to the forefront. Barriers to free trade in primary raw materials were of less concern, since the burgeoning demand of industrialized countries served to keep their markets open, and protectionist pressures from higher-cost domestic producers of materials were dampened by competitive pressures on the prices of the manufactured goods in which they were incorporated.

The United States regarded these results as the fruits of its striving for a global system of multilateral trade and payments as free from restrictions as possible. Within such a system, raw materials — like all other goods and services — flowed much more freely, and impressive increases were registered in the volume of international trade. As government intervention abated, raw materials problems tended to fall into place.

The pursuit of such an international economic system enabled U.S. foreign policy to focus its primary efforts on building a stable international order and on dealing with specific political and military threats.[6] It also permitted U.S. domestic policy to concentrate on managing the business cycle and, later, to coordinate such management with that of other industrialized countries. Relatively little attention was paid to micro-economic issues. With increasingly few exceptions, market forces controlled production and international trade in raw materials and manufactured products for a full two decades after World War II, as U.S. economic and military strength underwrote its vision of an effective international economic system.

Policy Lapses

The pursuit of a free global trading system was marked by some lapses from grace to deal with specific problems that compelled government intervention. The postwar behavior of Stalinist Russia created a new wave of strategic concerns that forced a reorientation of U.S. foreign policy and led to increased government management of foreign trade. Moreover, by the end of the 1950s, persistent balance of payments deficits became a matter of growing concern and led to measures to contain their size. In a few cases, restrictions were introduced to temporarily protect domestic industries that had suffered substantial injury from imports. Nevertheless, while such national considerations were used to impose or increase trade barriers in a number of cases that raised outcries, they did not significantly impede a large expansion in the general level of U.S. imports.

On the whole, these lapses concerned a relatively small volume of trade in raw materials or were limited in time. Controls established by the United States and its allies over exports to the Soviet bloc primarily restricted the export of high-technology manufactures. The lengthy U.S. embargo on trade with Communist China, North Korea, and Cuba did cover raw materials and agricultural products, as well as manufactures. During the Korean War, an international materials conference was organized to allocate raw materials, as had been done during World War II. International machinery was created to share petroleum supplies during the 1956 Suez crisis and again in the face of the Middle East export restrictions that resulted from Arab-Israeli hostilities in 1973-74. The United States used import quotas to protect domestic producers of petroleum between 1959 and 1974 and to protect employment in lead and zinc mines between 1958 and 1965. Strategic stockpiles of critical materials were maintained after World War II and augmented in the 1950s, although the goals were changed from time to time — in part, at least, with an eye on the impact on current market prices of subsequent sales or purchases.

While these and other lapses were significant, the general thrust of both U.S. government policy and U.S. official behavior was to let the market match raw materials supply and demand with a minimum of interference. For the first two postwar decades the U.S. government was able to keep internal protectionist forces under close check with the help of a relatively prosperous economy and a currency whose foreign exchange value was unquestioned. The result was a policy that gave every appearance of the absence of specific goals in the presence of eminently satisfactory results.

Implications for U.S.-Canadian Relations

U.S. policy fostered the expanded interdependence with Canada described in the first section of this chapter. Canada shared and supported U.S. aspirations for a global system of free multilateral trade and payments and a stable international order. Indeed, it sought a more comprehensive approach to tariff reduction in the postwar world than U.S. political realities would permit. Few countries were more disappointed by the failure of the U.S. Congress to ratify the International Trade Organization (ITO) charter. Canada played a leading role in fashioning the concept of the GATT and provided the first chairman of its contracting parties.[7] Soon after the GATT was completed, Canada severed its commitment to the Imperial Preference system, while participating actively and constructively in the IMF and in the other specialized agencies of the United Nations. It cooperated with U.S. efforts in international forums to induce others to apply non-discriminatory treatment to foreign investment. Relations with U.S. diplomatic representatives to multilateral organizations were generally close and harmonious, and many senior Canadian economic officials developed cooperative working relations with their counterparts in Washington.

Policy Conflicts

Nevertheless, discrepancies in size, global responsibilities, and national interest did give rise to differences in emphasis and to policy conflicts. Canada was less than enthusiastic about U.S. support for European integration, with its attendant acceptance of discrimination against North American exports. It preferred to develop Article 2 (non-military aspects) of NATO but met with little cooperation from its neighbor to the south. Canada felt that the U.S. tariff structure discouraged the processing of Canadian raw materials prior to export; the United States contended that a relatively high Canadian tariff on manufactures had forced U.S. firms to invest in manufacturing facilities in Canada that were unlikely to achieve competitive scale. While the United States joined Canada in an international wheat agreement, its attitude toward such agreements for other commodities was less forthcoming than that of Canada. U.S. anti-trust policy was more restrictive, and Canada came to resent what it regarded as extraterritorial attempts to enforce that policy. Canada was less apprehensive than the United States about trade with Communist countries and objected particularly to U.S. limitations on exports to China and Cuba as they applied to U.S. affiliates in Canada. Yet until the Vietnam War none of these differences appeared to damage what was essentially a common attitude about major international political and economic issues and the objectives of foreign policy.

Approaches to Bilateral Issues

On bilateral economic matters Canada negotiated vigorously, and the United States was not ungenerous in making concessions, recognizing Canada's special interest in expanding its manufacturing industries. For both Lend-Lease and Marshall Plan procurement, Canada was treated as a source eligible for the expenditure of U.S. government funds. Until tied procurement was introduced in 1959, the U.S. bilateral foreign aid program procured substantial quantities of Canadian commodities — primarily, though not exclusively, raw materials. The defense agreements inevitably involved Canadian purchases of major weapon systems from the United States, but offsetting U.S. procurement from Canada was arranged, sometimes in amounts ranging up to 200 percent of the U.S.-dollar cost of Canadian purchases. At least in its early years, the automotive trade agreement of 1965 drastically reduced a large U.S. bilateral trade surplus in automotive products, from $589 million in 1964 to $97 million in 1969. All these efforts led to an increasing proportion of manufactures within Canada's expanding volume of exports to the United States. By 1975, U.S. imports of machinery and vehicles from Canada totaled more that $7.2 billion, one-third of all its purchases from Canada. In 1955 such imports totaled $125 million, only 5 percent of the total.

The instances in which the United States did resort to trade and payments restrictions could have been particularly damaging to Canada and its raw materials industries, but on the whole Canada gained exemption from their application. Except for the short-lived import surcharge of 1971 and the tying of aid expenditures, U.S. balance of payments protective measures were not applied to Canada. Overland imports of petroleum were first omitted from the U.S. quota sytem and then covered in a 1967 agreement under which Canadian exporting companies were to limit their shipments. Without an enforcement mechanism, however, the limitations were ineffective. The zinc quotas had a more significant impact on Canadian exports. As for the international raw-materials-allocation machinery in the early 1950s, Canada was an active participant. As far as its strategic stockpiling program was concerned, the United States regarded Canada as a secure source of supply, analogous to domestic production. Accordingly, iron ore has never been stockpiled, and the strategic inventory of nickel and copper has been eliminated, while stocks of lead and zinc are relatively minor. A much larger strategic stockpile is maintained for materials — chromium, tin, cobalt, and manganese — whose principal sources are distant and may be less secure in times of emergency.

Nevertheless, difficulties arose as Canada became increasingly uncomfortable about its growing economic interdependence with the United States. To the U.S. government that development represented little more than a statistical event. Its importance was noted, but the prevailing view was that nothing much needed to be done about it. In the much smaller Canadian economy and polity, however, this interdependence stimulated an increasing preoccupation with preserving economic independence and with defining and maintaining a national identity. Measures taken by the United States to control its expanding balance of payments deficits in the second half of the 1960s and distaste for the Vietnam conflict further helped sharpen Canadian opposition to growing interdependence. These preoccupations led Canada to pursue policies for the 1970s that looked toward less dependence on U.S. direct investment for the expansion of both its manufacturing and its raw materials industries and for a greater diversity in both its sources of capital and its export markets.

A New Era in Raw Materials Policy

At the beginning of the 1970s the United States became newly conscious of its imports of raw materials from overseas sources. Earlier qualms about such imports concerned dependence on production under the control of Communist governments and the security of shipping lanes. The new insecurities were less related to military contingencies: development in many Third World countries raised doubts about the continuing reliability of these countries as suppliers of raw materials; in the United States, environmental preoccupations and the depletion of lower-cost resources increased the demand for some imported minerals; and concern about the future world supply of raw materials was stimulated by the 1972 Club of Rome report. If shortages of raw materials in general seemed too nebulous, the emergence of a strident OPEC in the early 1970s was specific enough to command attention, and the potential for similar difficulties with other materials had to be addressed. Much more than the UN resolutions following the creation of the United Nations Conference on Trade and Development (UNCTAD) in 1964 and the rhetoric of the New International Economic Order first proclaimed in 1974, the behavior of many foreign states raised doubts about the realism of a policy based on progressive liberalization of global trade and payments. With government intervention on the increase, reliance on the outcome of open trading systems no longer offered sufficient assurance of satisfactory results.

Then for the first time in its peacetime history, the United States began to grope for an affirmative raw materials foreign policy designed to assure reliable supplies at reasonable prices. External conditions were propelling U.S. policy-makers toward materials-supply issues and toward considering the foreign-policy implications of current and prospective raw materials needs. Nevertheless, a U.S. policy with respect to raw materials from foreign suppliers has yet to evolve. In large measure, such a policy could affect individual suppliers or potential suppliers as the United States seeks not only to augment the external availability of materials it may wish to import but also to ensure that its sources of supply remain reliable in the face of economic and political contingencies. In this context, Canada transcends its statistical importance in the international accounts of the United States.

U.S. Perceptions of Canada

The major role of resources in U.S. economic relations with Canada is the product of the free-market policy to which both governments have adhered. It reflects the needs of the U.S. economy, the relative availability and the cost of raw materials produced in the two countries, the availability and the cost of capital in the two countries, and the low-risk premium attached by the U.S. capital market to investments in Canada. Nevertheless, if the United States wishes its access to Canadian raw materials to continue to grow over succeeding decades, it has become clear that ways must be found to cope with Canadian resistance to greater dependence on the U.S. economy.

To date, Canada remains a preferred source of supply, although U.S. importers are still essentially free to purchase from the lowest-cost supplier. In the event of a military contingency, Canada's advantages are apparent — geographic proximity, the absence of a need for ocean-borne shipping, continuing cooperation in hemispheric defense planning, and a long history of military alliance and friendly political relations. To U.S. investors and importers, a common language and mutual respect for the sanctity of contractual obligations add significantly to Canada's attractiveness as a source of supply.

Nevertheless, such U.S. concerns about dependence on foreign sources of supply as the possibility of export restrictions or sharp price increases imposed by a cartel of producing countries could conceivably extend to Canada. These concerns include fears of expropriation of raw-materials-producing properties once they have been developed and brought into production, the imposition of large export taxes, and the embargoing of shipments for political purposes. To date, the United States has assumed, and with good reason, that in any military contingency Canada would be a friend and ally and that it could depend on continued access to Canadian raw materials. However, economic and political contingencies may develop where Canadian behavior woud be less assured.

Of course, the possibilities for U.S. retaliation are great, given the extent and the nature of Canadian dependence on the U.S. economy. But retaliation is a particularly difficult and undesirable path for the United States to travel as it seeks a more secure and stable international political structure and a freer international economic system. Retaliation sets bad precedents, it embarks nations on a course of mutual disadvantage that is difficult to reverse, and it is bound to be costly by material and other measures. Strengthening the process of mutual concern and accommodation and coping with the objections to which interdependence has given rise in Canada offer a more constructive path.

The future thus depends less on specific prescriptions for resolving particular problems than on the way interdependence is managed and on the attitudes and understanding brought to bear in individual situations. Growing interdependence has given rise to problems in the past and present and will assuredly continue to do so. The nature and prospective evolution of that interdependence guarantee the reappearance of issues concerning raw materials. A policy of reducing interdependence by means of governmental restrictions would be costly to both countries, yet such a policy could become inevitable if the conflicts accompanying interdependence cannot be managed acceptably. Both countries have reached a stage of affluence that permits considerable economic sacrifice in the pursuit of other objectives. Nevertheless, the historical record since World War II concerning the resolution of differences of view and interest is a propitious one in an imperfect world. The management of interdependence to date has not been bad.

In order to understand better both the significance of what has gone before and the potential for better accommodation, a more detailed examination of individual problems is necessary. The preceding general review is supplemented in the following pages by a closer inspection of two policy areas: (1) the impact of U.S. macro-economic policies (including balance of payments management) on Canada and their transmission through the raw materials sector and (2) U.S. foreign-investment policy and its effect on Canadian raw materials production and trade. In both cases, four questions are of principal concern: (1) What has motivated U.S. behavior? (2) How have U.S. actions affected Canada? (3) Has this impact been taken into account in framing U.S. policies and behavior? (4) Have actions affecting Canadian interests been discussed with the Canadian government?

Economic-Policy Harmonization

It has already been noted that by the 1970s Canada was selling more than three-fifths of all its exports to the U.S. market, including two-thirds of all exported mineral and forest materials. Primary and secondary production of these resources, predominantly for export, is equivalent to more than one-tenth of Canadian GNP. An important linkage thus exists between U.S. demand for raw materials and the state of the Canadian economy. Moreover, Canada's economic growth has been financed to a substantial extent by U.S. capital flows. Canada's prosperity in general, and the development of its resources in particular, have depended on free access to the U.S. capital market (especially to finance large projects) and are affected by the cost of such capital. For Canada's economic policy-makers — and its raw materials producers — U.S. policies that influence the level of internal demand or that propose to limit the outflow of capital for balance of payments purposes have been of critical importance.

Business Cycle Linkages

Canada's dependence on the state of the U.S. economy extends, of course, well beyond the raw materials sector proper, and that dependence is becoming more diverse as Canadian exports of manufactures to the United States increase. Readers of the annual reports of the Bank of Canada are familiar with the regular inclusion of charts in which superimposed U.S. and Canadian trends for major economic indicators move pretty much in tandem. Since Canada is still by far the smaller partner, Canadian policy-makers must respond to U.S. developments.

The dates of business cycle peaks and troughs are almost identical for both countries, but their amplitude has usually been less in Canada.[8] Like Canada, the United States has pursued active macro-economic policies with a view to reducing such business cycle fluctuations. The greater success achieved by the Canadian authorities reflects, to some extent, their skill and effectiveness. However, the greater stability of the Canadian economy has been attributable in part to the tendency of its imports to respond more sharply than domestic production to changes in domestic demand. Moreover, for the first twenty-five years after World War II, many other industrialized countries were also less vulnerable to recession than the United States, and such declines as they experienced were not closely synchronized with the U.S. experience. Nevertheless, Canadian monetary and fiscal policy-makers must be attentive to changes in the U.S. economic climate and in U.S. macro-economic policies.

Canadian exports of raw materials have suffered during U.S. recessions and benefited from the considerable extent to which U.S. economic policy has been successful in offsetting reductions in internal demand. The demand for raw materials responds more than proportionately to variations in the level of economic activity, creating a particularly strong transmission effect on the Canadian economy. With recession widely synchronized in the industrialized world since the quadrupling of international oil prices by OPEC, the problems for Canadian macro-economic policy have been magnified.

Despite the importance of a healthy U.S. economy to Canada's well-being, only minimal formal bilateral machinery for coordinating economic policies was established in the 1960s, and even that has fallen into disuse in the 1970s. To be sure, consultations in the International Monetary Fund (IMF) and in the Organisation for Economic Co-operation and Development (OECD, formerly OEEC) have become increasingly institutionalized. Moreover, the Canadian embassy in Washington has always been well staffed and active, particularly in economic matters, and a wide variety of close working relationships have developed among individuals with comparable responsibilities in the two governments.

In part, at least, to reduce the impact of changes in the U.S. economy, Canada has resorted to a floating exchange rate for much of the past four decades. Canada's foreign trade has paid a certain price for that policy, since exchange rate fluctuations have frequently resulted from capital movements. After a period of tight exchange controls, Canada introduced a floating rate in 1950, returning to a regime that had worked reasonably effectively in the 1930s.[9] Although the failure to maintain a par value for its currency put Canada technically in violation of the Articles of Agreement of the IMF, the United States acquiesced, along with other IMF members.

U.S. Balance of Payments Pressures

At the beginning of 1961 a new U.S. government took office, determined to reduce the rate of unemployment without exacerbating a balance of payments deficit that had persisted for a decade. With economic expansion, pressure on the U.S. balance of payments position increased, particularly since U.S. interest rates were relatively low and government policy was one of reluctance to see them rise lest the economic recovery be aborted.

In mid-1963 the U.S. government proposed an interest equalization tax, which was enacted a year later. The immediate effect of the announcement was to produce a sharp curtailment in new foreign issues on the U.S. capital market. Canada protested that it would bear much of the burden of this effort to protect the U.S. balance of payments, although the flow of U.S. capital to Canada had been proceeding normally without producing any particular drain on U.S. foreign exchange reserves. Canada's protest resulted in its being exempted from the tax, on the understanding that the Canadian authorities would take appropriate measures to assure that the net flow of funds was not in excess of what was needed to balance Canada's current-account deficit.

Early in 1965 the United States announced new balance of payments restrictions. Canada was again exempted. Despite these exemptions and the discount of its currency against the U.S. dollar, Canada's official holdings of dollars declined from the end of 1962 to 1967 as Canadian output and imports rose rapidly and the inflow of capital was moderated. It was a period of substantial growth and prosperity for both economies.

The Vietnam inflation of 1967 led, in November of that year, to still tighter rules for U.S. capital outflows at a time when Canada was experiencing more inflation and a reduced growth rate. By March of the following year the United States had again exempted Canada in return for Canada's agreement to invest any increased U.S. dollar reserves in nonliquid U.S. government bonds.

Thus, until the 1970s Canada was generally able to adjust to trends in the U.S. economy and to gain special exemptions from U.S. policies that would have had a heavy impact on its economy, particularly those concerned with balance of payments management. During 1969 and 1970, stagflation in the United States had its counterpart in increased unemployment in Canada. Another surge in Canada's foreign reserves occurred, and in mid-1970 Canadian authorities decided to let the Canadian dollar float again.

At this point the U.S. balance of payments problem was reaching unmanageable proportions. U.S. suggestions of countervailing action by other industrialized countries that were experiencing much larger accumulations of dollars than Canada generally met with unacceptable counterproposals for the United States to deflate its own economy. In a much more modest way, the United States included Canada in its efforts to persuade other countries to help it out of its balance of payments difficulties. It proposed modifications in the automotive agreement and increases in Canadian expenditures for U.S. military material and in the customs-free allowance for Canadian travelers to the United States.

Canada, facing its own economic problems, responded modestly and reluctantly to these proposals.

Finally, the United States was forced to stop converting dollars into gold in August, 1971. At the same time, it imposed a temporary 10 percent surcharge on dutiable imports and decided against permitting Canada an exemption comparable to that offered after earlier measures to protect the U.S. balance of payments. In December, 1971, the United States agreed to devalue the dollar and to lift the surcharge.

Both the U.S. and the Canadian economies recovered in 1972 from prolonged high unemployment. By the beginning of 1973, however, the United States was again forced to devalue the dollar. Both economies experienced high growth and inflation during 1973, followed by prolonged stagflation.

In the 1972-74 period, Canada's exchange rate policy was essentially neutral. After doubling between 1969 and 1971, Canadian foreign exchange reserves fluctuated only minimally during the next three years. Intervention was frequent on both sides of the market, although generally it was not aimed at a particular rate of exchange. Since the Canadian-dollar float was relatively "clean," there was no cause for the United States or the IMF to take a critical view of Canadian exchange rate policy.

In the period since early 1974, international exchange rates and balance of payments variations have primarily reflected the after-effects of the quadrupling of petroleum prices by OPEC. To a somewhat lesser extent, so too have the appearance and the persistence of inflationary pressures, together with high unemployment, in both economies. For a while, employment and output held up better in Canada than in the United States, in large part because Canada was less dependent on OPEC for energy, it could better insulate its economy from the effects of energy shortages, and it benefited from the related boom in other raw materials prices in 1974. By 1976-77, however, the Canadian economy was suffering from the synchronized recession in the industrialized world, although it was helped to some extent by the modest recovery in the United States. Once again, the need for successfully coordinating economic policies had been brought to the fore.

The Effectiveness of Harmonization

The preceding summary account of some three decades of economic coexistence between two neighboring economies of disparate size points to a reasonably successful record of mutual accommodation. The nadir reached in 1970-71 is being succeeded by an improved relationship as both countries struggle with the economic after-effects of sharply higher oil prices.

Trade between the two countries increased substantially in the postwar period. Despite some retreats and threats, the barriers to a free flow of goods, services, and capital were low enough to facilitate that growth, although tariffs in both countries inhibited a larger exchange of manufactured products. By their own historical standards, both economies maintained high rates of growth in output over this period, with the Canadian economy growing at a significantly faster rate. Thus, between 1960 and 1974 real Canadian GNP rose at an annual rate of 5.3 percent, compared to 3.9 percent for the United States. Within this relatively favorable climate the production and export of raw materials from Canada expanded significantly, sometimes in fits and starts as the level of U.S. economic activity fluctuated.

Canada could hardly insulate its own economic evolution from that of the larger neighbor with which it had become so intertwined. For the most part, it maintained some flexibility in managing its domestic economy through a floating exchange rate. Nevertheless, the sharp declines in raw materials demand that resulted from U.S. recessions were reflected in reduced output, employment, and income in Canadian raw materials industries, moderated to some extent when demand for such products in other markets remained strong. Given the stresses that continue to plague the world economy, the Canadian raw materials industry — and the Canadian economy as a whole — may be more dependent than in the past on better economic-policy coordination with the United States.

Foreign-Investment Issues

The U.S. economy emerged from World War II with a strong economy and war-devastated trading partners. By 1948 its holdings of foreign exchange reserves exceeded those of the rest of the world combined. Europe and Japan needed imports of agricultural products, raw materials, and equipment but could not export enough to pay for them. Private U.S. business was reluctant to invest in their war-shattered economies, and the U.S. government sought to fill the gap through loans and grants. By 1952 the Marshall Plan had accomplished its purpose. The U.S. balance of payments was registering a small deficit, but it would take the rest of the decade before foreign exchange reserves were built to the point where Europe could dismantle its trade and foreign exchange restrictions. Up to that point, private U.S. capital was reluctant to venture overseas.

Canadian Capital Needs

Canada joined the United States in helping to finance European reconstruction. Rich in natural resources and with a relatively low-cost supply of skilled labor, Canada was ripe for accelerated development in the postwar period, and it attracted U.S. capital on a large scale. Canada's savings were insufficient to take advantage of its domestic investment opportunities. Furthermore, many Canadians found it preferable to place their savings in investments abroad, primarily in the United States. As a result, Canada's gross foreign liabilities rose from $8.2 billion in 1945 to about $46.9 billion at the end of 1969, representing mainly additions to foreign direct investment in Canada.[10] In the 1962-64 period, foreign direct investment was equal to 56 percent of net capital formation in Canada, slackening to 41 percent in the second half of the 1960s. As shown in Table 4.1, U.S. direct investment in Canada ballooned during the postwar period.

By the 1970s Canada accounted for one-quarter of all U.S. foreign direct investment and for a full half of all such investment in mining and smelting, up from 30 percent in 1950. This occurred without specific U.S. government subsidies or other direct support. The U.S. government did promote such investment in Europe during the 1950s and used a variety of risk-sharing and tax incentives to promote investment in developing countries throughout the postwar period.[11] Investment in Canada benefited only from tax payments on foreign petroleum production being treated as eligible for full credit against U.S. income tax liability rather than as royalties deductible from pre-tax income.

The flow of U.S. capital to Canada resulted from a favorable investment climate and the operation of market forces. For all practical purposes, a common capital market has existed between the two countries, and capital has been able to move back and forth with relatively few restrictions. Tariff protection accorded to manufactured products encouraged the establish-

TABLE 4.1

U.S. Private Long-Term Direct Investment in Canada, 1936-75
(book value at year-end — million dollars)

Year	Total	Mining and Smelting	Petroleum
1936	1,952	239	108
1943	2,378	384	161
1957	8,637	856	2,016
1966	15,713	2,089	3,608
1975	31,155	3,058	6,209

Source: U.S. Department of Commerce, *Survey of Current Business,* various issues. Figures for 1966 and thereafter are not strictly comparable to those for earlier years as a result of statistical revisions explained in the October, 1975, issue.

ment of manufacturing facilities in Canada, and the absence of significant
U.S. import restrictions supported U.S. investment in developing Canadian raw materials production. In the 1960s U.S. capital flows to Canada
benefited from restrictions on capital movements to other developed countries from which Canada was exempted. As the investment climate for exploring and developing mineral production deteriorated in the less
developed countries in the late 1960s, the attractiveness of Canadian
resources to U.S. investors was further enhanced.

The expansion of petroleum production in western Canada prompted investment in further exploration and development, a process encouraged by
the exemption of petroleum exported overland to the United States from
Canada from the oil import restrictions established by the United States in
1959. An intergovernmental agreement in 1967 set ascending annual limits
on the volume of Canadian shipments to the United States, but no enforcement mechanism was provided, and there were complaints about
shipments in excess of the agreed limitations.[12] Given U.S. preference, for
reasons of national security, for oil from Canadian rather than from
Eastern Hemisphere sources, investment in developing Canadian
petroleum resources was not seriously hampered by such limitations.

Canadian Reactions to Foreign Ownership

A significant segment of the Canadian polity has come to object to the
high concentration of U.S. ownership of, and control over the development
of, Canadian resources. As early as the mid-1950s the Royal Commission
on Canada's Economic Prospects (the Gordon Commission) registered concern about the large role of foreign investment (mostly U.S.) in the Canadian economy. Later to become finance minister, the chairman of that
commission, Walter Gordon, revived this theme in his budget message of
1963,[13] although his specific proposals were subsequently substantially
modified or abandoned. A 1972 task force report (the Gray Report)[14] led to
the passage of the Foreign Investment Review Act (FIRA) in 1973, which
provided for the review of foreign investment in the form of acquisitions
and new ventures on the basis of their contribution of significant benefits to
the Canadian economy. About the same time, the Canada Development
Corporation was established to promote Canadian ownership of Canadian
industry, and one of its major actions to date has been the acquisition of a
bloc of shares in Texasgulf, an important mining company based in the
United States but with significant assets in Canada.

The introduction of FIRA stirred the U.S. business community and produced a flurry of enquiries and consultations on the part of the U.S.
government. Nevertheless, U.S. official reaction has been more moderate
than in the case of restrictions imposed by other countries on foreign invest-

ment, in part because the actions of the board established under the act appear to be fair, even-handed, and non-discriminatory. Relative to recent treatment of U.S. direct investment by many other countries concerned about foreign ownership, Canadian behavior has to date been exemplary from a U.S. government viewpoint.

Outlook

The outflow of U.S. capital to Canada has continued. It responds, as in the past, to the relatively low risk attached to investment in Canada, the need of the Canadian economy for more development capital than its own savings will provide, and the interest of Canadians in using part of their capital to make foreign investments of their own. However, portfolio investment has assumed a larger role relative to direct investment than was the case in the earlier postwar period. Thus, in 1975 Canada floated a record $3.2 billion in bonds in the U.S. capital market, a substantially larger sum than the $2.75 billion increase in U.S. direct investment in Canada.

The future of U.S. investment in the development of Canadian raw materials production and the growth of the Canadian economy as a whole are more clouded than they were a few years ago. On the political front, the election in Quebec of a party dedicated to achieving some form of independence for that province and uncertainties about the evolution of confederation and about the division and use of federal and provincial powers have added a new dimension to the evaluation of risks in investing in Canada. On the economic front, higher costs for wages and tax payments in recent years have affected adversely the comparative attractiveness of Canada as an investment location.

Quite apart from these recent uncertainties, other trends have appeared in Canada that may affect prospects for U.S. investment. The role of U.S. capital could well diminish if, as appears to be a policy goal, Canadian GNP and savings grow and Canadians become increasingly able to finance internally the investment needs of their economy. Moreover, the flow of raw materials to the United States could be inhibited if Canada decides to conserve so-called non-renewable resources for its own future internal needs, to limit growth in its exports of such materials, and to diversify their marketing.

Controversy persists as to whether such decisions are better made by market forces than by governments and whether the immediate and the long-term interests of the Canadian economy would be well served by such policies. The United States would undoubtedly feel aggrieved and might suffer some economic damage in the short run. It has welcomed Canada's efforts to expand its economic links with the rest of the world, although it would not wish to see Canada pursue the "third option" at the expense of U.S. interests. Stringent Canadian controls and a wave of expropriations could provoke the United States to take measures that would have an adverse effect on Canada. Furthermore, such Canadian actions might also push the United States into seeking accommodation with other potential sources of supply that could prove to be both lower in cost and equally reliable.

Summary

U.S. dependence on a secure and reliable flow of raw materials from Canada expanded tremendously during the post–World War II period despite the absence of deliberate U.S. government policy to that end. Its growth was promoted by more general U.S. policies that supported free access to raw materials and a free multilateral system of trade and payments, policies that were in accord with the views of the Canadian government. Increased dependence was therefore largely based on the natural endowments and economic development of the two countries, relative production costs, and propinquity. Both countries prospered as economic interdependence increased, and the disparities between the two countries were significantly reduced.

Considerations of national security, domestic employment, and balance of payments protection produced a number of departures in U.S. practice from the principles of general U.S. policies, departures that have implications for Canada's raw materials sector. Their practical significance was, however, limited. Consideration was given to the impact of such policies on the Canadian economy; and on the whole, the United States was conciliatory, although often only after protest and debate. Significant U.S. concessions were made in the course of bilateral discussions and negotiations on trade matters. Although a low point was reached in the early 1970s, a unique and special relationship has developed over the past three decades, founded on compatibilities of interest and views and good working relationships between diplomatic and governmental personnel.

Nevertheless, Canada has become increasingly uncomfortable with its role as a supplier of raw materials to the United States, with the large role of U.S. direct investment in its raw materials and other industries, and with its dependence on the U.S. market. Environmental concerns, native claims, and the possible depletion of its natural endowment add further impediments to the development of Canada's raw materials production for export to the United States. The United States, for its part, has developed a heightened consciousness about its imports of raw materials. Its concerns now extend beyond previous planning for military contingencies to the possibility of export restrictions, price increases imposed by a cartel of producing countries, expropriations of raw-materials-producing properties, excessive taxation, and political embargoes. Although Canada has been treated as a particularly secure and reliable supplier, these new concerns could conceivably extend to it.

The future of U.S.-Canadian interdependence will rest heavily on the attitudes and understanding of both governments. The new concerns in both societies suggest that their economic relations—with respect to raw materials and other matters—will be increasingly subject to governmental management. Resource needs and a less propitious environment in the Third World have given the United States a powerful impetus for improving and intensifying relations with its northern neighbor. At a minimum, a heightened awareness is needed of the particular impact of U.S. policies and actions on Canada. Reinstituting formal intergovernmental consultations at the cabinet level would appear to be in the interest of both governments.

The foregoing propositions derive from an examination of the record over the years since the end of World War II. The problems that have arisen and the way they have been resolved foreshadow difficulties that can be expected to recur. They also indicate the scope for better anticipation of issues and for concerting their resolution in a constructive fashion.

Notes

1. A. Maffry, "Strategic Materials in U.S. Trade," *Survey of Current Business,* December, 1940.

2. U.S. Department of Commerce, Bureau of the Census, *U.S. Imports: Commodity by Country,* December, 1975 (Washington, D.C.: U.S. Government Printing Office, 1976).

3. This section is based on the author's contribution to an earlier volume on U.S. attitudes and behavior concerning foreign materials (see International Economic Studies Institute, *Raw Materials and Foreign Policy* [Washington, D.C., 1977], Chaps. 1-3).

4. Although the U.S. Senate refused to ratify the charter for the International Trade Organization, the GATT structure has served the essential purposes envisioned for the ITO.

5. Subordinates clashed over the implications of this statement for the future of the Imperial Preference system erected in 1932. A qualifying phrase, "with due respect for their existing obligations," was added out of deference to Britain's contention that it could not unilaterally modify these arrangements without a new Commonwealth conference. Foreign-trade experts, including the U.S. Secretary of State, falsely concluded that Roosevelt had made a major substantive concession by

124   JACOB KAPLAN

agreeing to the phrase. Subsequent U.S.-U.K. controversy demonstrated that the suspicions were misplaced.

6. To be sure, a substantial portion of the large U.S. government foreign-affairs establishment was engaged in the pursuit of freer trade, investment, and payment policies, both at home and abroad. However, not since the days of Cordell Hull has a U.S. Secretary of State personally been much preoccupied with such matters.

7. The Hon. Dana Wilgress. As Canada's Ambassador to NATO and the OEEC, he was a potent influence for protecting the prerogatives of the GATT.

8. See D. J. Daly in M. Bronfenbrenner, *Is the Business Cycle Obsolete?* (New York: Wiley Interscience, 1970).

9. A.F.W. Plumptre, *Exchange Rate Policy: Experience with Canada's Floating Rate,* Princeton Essays in International Finance No. 81 (Princeton, New Jersey: Department of Economics, International Finance Section, Princeton University, 1970).

10. Statistics Canada, *Canada's International Investment Position, 1926 to 1967* (Ottawa: Information Canada, 1971).

11. *Raw Materials and Foreign Policy,* op. cit., pp. 30-34.

12. See U.S. Cabinet Task Force on Oil Import Control, *The Oil Import Question* (Washington, D.C.: U.S. Government Printing Office, 1970).

13. Canadian-American Committee, *Recent Canadian and U.S. Government Actions Affecting U.S. Investment in Canada* (Washington, D.C., and Montreal, 1964).

14. *Foreign Direct Investment in Canada* (Ottawa: Government of Canada, 1972).

5

Mineral Resources in the Canadian Economy: Macro-Economic Implications

D. J. DALY

Historically, Canada has been a major exporter of primary products, and primary products continue to be more important in exports and the domestic economy than is the case in other high-income industrialized countries. A major share of these exports go to the United States. This chapter emphasizes the overall impact of minerals on the Canadian economy. Studies of individual minerals will be covered in a later volume.

This chapter consists of five sections, the first of which is a short introduction. The second section provides some perspective on the extent of minerals in the Canadian economy, including comparisons with the United States, Northwest Europe, and Japan. The third section assesses some of the implications and effects of minerals on the Canadian economy, looking initially at the positive aspects. However, there has been a growing degree of public and professional concern about some features of economic growth and about some aspects of the extent of Canada's dependence on foreign markets and of foreign ownership of Canadian minerals. The sources of these concerns are discussed in the fourth section, which includes some data for testing the validity of these concerns. The concluding section considers future trends and options.

This chapter has two primary purposes. One is to explore some of the concerns about the extent of Canadian dependence on the mining industry, some of which border on being fallacious when the available evidence is ex-

This chapter is an outgrowth of a broader study financed by Energy, Mines and Resources Canada, which provided data, departmental studies, and comments on an early draft. Assistance and comments on an early draft have also been provided by Carl Beigie and other members of the C. D. Howe Research Institute staff, William Diebold, Jr., C. J. Cajka, Rolands Muiznieks, George Miller, and other authors in the volume. The analysis and conclusions are the responsibility of the author.

amined. The second is to evaluate policy options in a realistic way. The emphasis in the analysis is on the degree to which the mineral industry contributes to high real incomes (per capita and per person employed) on a current and sustainable basis in Canada. In assessing the contribution of the mineral industry to Canadian real incomes and the role of the industry in the country's policy options, some evidence on Canada's comparative advantage in relation to its major markets will be introduced.

Introduction

The major periods of Canadian history since the country's initial discovery by explorers from Europe and subsequent settlement have been marked by the development and export of a variety of staple products. Initially, the major product was furs, but then came fish, forest products, and some agricultural products (especially grain). These developments have been described by such important Canadian economists and historians as Harold A. Innis and W. A. Mackintosh; and the staple theory of economic growth, initially developed in a Canadian context, has subsequently influenced analysis and policy in other countries, especially in some of the early stages of economic development.[1]

Exports of primary staples continue to be important for Canada, although shipments of motor vehicles and parts have become the largest single export category since about 1967, after the U.S.-Canadian automotive agreement of 1965 came into effect. Currently, exports of mineral products (such as ores and concentrates) share the role of a staple export with such product groups as agriculture (wheat, animals, and other edible products) and forest products (lumber, woodprint, and newsprint). The importance of natural resources in general, and minerals in particular, in the Canadian economy is widely known, and Chapter 2 of this volume has provided perspective on this importance for both Canada and the United States. It was pointed out there that by the early 1970s mining had replaced agriculture as the largest primary industry in Canada as measured by value added and that the combination of the mining and the manufacturing of minerals has become the largest resource industry.

In the light of the historical and current importance of the mineral sector, it may be helpful to mention the source and nature of the major current concerns. One of these grows out of the economic-growth debate, revolving around the possibility of a check to economic growth arising from possible natural resource scarcity. Although this possibility has historical roots, the renewed concern dates from the early 1970s. A second aspect of the economic-growth debate is that growth has some adverse side effects on the quality of the environment through pollution. These two areas of concern have been widely discussed in North America and elsewhere. A third area of concern stems from a perception that the mining industry has been receiving an undesirably large share of the returns from the sale of natural resources and that the system of taxation relating to mining should be modified. Other commentators are particularly concerned that a high proportion of these returns go to foreign owners, an area of concern among some nationalists. These concerns are sometimes difficult to identify or to assess quantitatively, but some relevant material will be provided later to help put them into perspective.

Extent of Mining in the Canadian Economy

This section provides some descriptive highlights of the size of mining in the Canadian economy, with some comparisons with other countries to provide an international perspective.

It is a widely recognized fact that, in relation to population, Canada is more favorably endowed with natural resources than any other high-income country in the non-Communist world. This is supported by Table 5.1, in which production is used as a proxy for resource endowments and which provides comparisons of Canada with the United States, Northwest Europe, and Japan. This table includes countries comprising more than 80 percent of Canadian exports and imports and all the market economies of the industrialized countries in the Northern Hemisphere. As these countries are markedly different in size of employment and population, they are all put on a per-person-employed basis for comparability. As prices of individual minerals vary among countries and could be valued in different currencies, they are all valued at U.S. prices in the base period. The expanded list of minerals contains about 93 percent of mineral production in both Canada and the United States in 1970.

Mineral production has been used as a proxy for mineral resource endowment in Table 5.1, since suitable data on the latter were not available. To some degree the availability of mineral products and resources in Canada reflects the country's large land area. One recent study shows a high correlation between land area and the number and value of minerals produced in thirty major developed and centrally planned countries.[2] In terms of land area, Canada is smaller than the USSR, but larger than such other countries as the United States and China. The relatively low level of population density in Canada is a factor in the higher levels of mineral production in relation to total employment reflected in Table 5.1

It is clear from Table 5.1 that Canada is more actively involved in mineral production than is any other country or region shown—twice the extent of the United States, about eight times that of Northwest Europe, and about fifty times that of Japan (the least well-endowed with natural resources of any of the industrialized countries). The basis of comparison is total employment in the various countries, which takes account of the differences in labor force size and emphasizes the differences in resources available per person employed.

Additional documentation concerning the relatively greater importance of mining and minerals to the Canadian economy than to the U.S. economy is provided in Table 5.2. As one would expect, these indicators show a greater relative emphasis on minerals in Canada than in the United States. The share of total mining and mineral-manufacturing activity is about 50 percent greater in Canada than in the United States for such indicators as value added, employment, and wages and salaries.

There are two interesting contrasts among the various indicators for Canada in Table 5.2 that merit comment. First, the share of wages and salaries and value added is larger than the share of employment. This reflects the fact that hourly earnings are higher in mining than in other industries in Canada — considerably higher than in some larger industries, such as retail trade, finance, and services. Second, the share of the mining sector in investment is higher than the shares in employment and income, reflecting the fact that mining is a very capital-intensive industry. For example, in 1970 the gross and net capital stock per employee in mining were, respectively, 4.6 and 5.0 times the corresponding levels in manufacturing in Canada.

It might be noted that one indicator frequently used for the mining industry has not been referred to above. That is the gross value of mineral production in relation to gross national product. All data on the gross value of production in the mining and manufacturing industries include interindustry purchases and sales, while the gross-national-product measure excludes such sales. The extent of these interindustry purchases and sales is quantitatively quite large, which introduces serious problems regarding lack of comparability between the numerator and the denominator of measures so constructed. The measures in Table 5.2 provide unbiased estimates of the direct impact of mining on the economy, but they exclude the indirect effects on supplying industries. Measures of these indirect effects will be included and discussed in the next section.

Positive Macro-Economic Implications for Canada

This section considers initially how mineral products fit into the broader picture of comparative advantage in the Canadian economy, with special emphasis on comparisons with the United States. Subsequently, the im-

TABLE 5.1
Mineral Production per Person Employed, 1960 and 1970
(relatives, United States = 100)

| | Value in U.S. Dollars of Mineral Production per Person Employed | |
	Denison List	Expanded List
United States	100	100
Canada (1970)	181	222
Northwest Europe (1960)	26	26
Japan (1970)	3.7	n.a.

Sources: United States and Europe: Edward S. Denison and Jean-Paul Poullier, *Why Growth Rates Differ* (Washington: The Brookings Institution, 1967), Table 14-2, p. 184; Japan: Denison and William K. Chung, *How Japan's Economy Grew So Fast* (Washington: The Brookings Institution, 1976), Appendix 0, p. 258; Canada: Dorothy Walters, *Canadian Income Levels and Growth: An International Perspective* (Ottawa: Queen's Printer, 1968), Table 64, updated to 1970 with sources as described on pp. 233-34. The United States provides the basis for comparison in both 1960 for Northwest Europe and 1970 for Canada.

TABLE 5.2
Indicators of the Importance of Resource Industries
in the Economies of the United States and Canada, 1972

| | Value Added As Percentage of GNP | | Employment As Percentage of Labor Force | | Wages and Salaries As Percentage of Total | | Capital Stock As Percentage of Total | |
	U.S.	Canada	U.S.	Canada	U.S.	Canada	U.S.	Canada
Mining	2.3	4.1	0.7	1.2	1.0	1.8	9.1	8.8
Mineral manufacturing	2.5	3.2	1.5	2.0	2.2	3.0	5.5	5.8
	4.8	7.3	2.2	3.2	3.2	4.8	14.6	14.6

Source: Chapter 2, Table 2.6.

plications of the mining industry for employment at the national level are considered, followed by a brief comment on the regional aspects of employment.

Comparative Advantage and Relative Prices

The concept of comparative advantage has played a central part in the theory of international trade since it was first introduced by David Ricardo in his *Principles of Political Economy,* initially published in 1817.[3] A key theme in the explanation of the direction of trade flows is differences in the relative prices of various products among countries. Essentially, a country exports products for which its prices are relatively low and imports products for which it tends to be a high-cost producer. This exchange encourages specialization in different products in different countries, and the people in both countries end up with higher real incomes with international trade between them than if trade did not take place.

These differences in relative prices can come about for two reasons. One reason is variations among countries in the relative supplies, or relative prices, of the basic input factors of production (essentially labor, capital, and land). The second reason is different production conditions for different industries in the various countries, an emphasis that goes back to David Ricardo.[4]

Applying the theory of comparative advantage to Canada, it is clear that Canada has important advantages in the production of minerals because of the comparatively greater supply of natural resources relative to the size of the domestic economy. In addition, there are dramatic differences in the levels of output per person by industry. In mining, for example, the levels of output per person in Canada were more than 60 percent higher than in the United States in 1970.[5] This comparison is important when such a large part of both mineral exports and total exports from Canada go to the United States.

At the same time, Canada has some serious comparative disadvantages in manufacturing production and international trade relative to the United States. In 1974, for example, the levels of output per worker in Canadian manufacturing were about 25 percent lower than in the United States, and the differences were even greater during the 1950s and 1960s. These differences cannot be explained by lower levels of capital stock per person employed in manufacturing in the two countries, as Canada is quite capital-intensive, even relative to the United States, especially in construction facilities.[6] Furthermore, Canadian firms generally appear to be well informed of U.S. practices and techniques, and this is facilitated by the significant degree of U.S. ownership and control. Canadian plants have also been slower to adopt new products and new processing than have those of some other major countries, a tendency that can perpetuate the persistence of lower levels of manufacturing performance.[7]

These differences in comparative advantage are not immutable and partly reflect economic policies in different countries. For example, the emphasis on mineral exports in Canada partly reflects the low tariff and non-tariff barriers in other countries for such exports in relatively unprocessed form and the early encouragement of the industry by tax and transportation policies in Canada. In contrast, exports of manufactured products have been discouraged by high effective tariff rates in Canada (and the lower levels of productivity thus encouraged) and high tariff and non-tariff barriers to imports of manufactured products in other countries.

On the wages side, Canada historically has had a lower level of average hourly compensation than the United States — about 20 percent less in the mid-1960s. However, during the 1970s this ratio has been reversed, and the level of average hourly compensation in 1976 was about 7 percent higher than the U.S. national average. Regionally, hourly earnings in Ontario and Quebec were still below those in the northeastern states but well above those in the southeastern states. When one combines the emergence of higher hourly earnings with lower levels of output per man and per man-hour, one observes a tendency for prices of a wide range of manufactured products to be higher in Canada than in the United States.[8] The policy implications arising from prospects in mining, manufacturing, and additional processing are considered further in the last section of this chapter.

The persisting comparative advantages to Canada in minerals are reflected in the exports of crude and fabricated minerals (on both a gross and a net-of-imports basis); the high-cost, low-productivity position of manufacturing is reflected in a continuing large net deficit in manufacturing end products. As long as anything close to the recent pattern prevails in levels of wage rates, productivity differences, and costs of manufactured products, a large export surplus in mineral products is necessary to help provide a basic equilibrium in the Canadian balance of payments (including both current and capital transactions).[9]

This specialization also contributes to higher standards of living for Canadians. It involves the exchange of resources that are available in relative abundance in Canada, and that are produced efficiently by international standards, for products that are produced in Canada relatively inefficiently, and therefore at high cost, by international standards. This process illustrates the benefits of trade based upon comparative advantages.

Employment Effects

Thus far the discussion has emphasized, from an international perspective, the positive benefits of the mining industry in terms of its contribution to an efficient use of resources and to high living standards within Canada. The question of the level of resource utilization and the levels of employment and unemployment have not been considered, and this is the next major topic in this section.

It is frequently suggested that the contribution of mining to employment in Canada is small. That sort of conclusion is reached from data such as those in Table 5.2, in which employment in mining and in mineral manufacturing is shown as amounting to 1.2 and 2.0 percent of the labor force, respectively. However, these figures measure only the direct employment effect. The mining industry is a high-paying industry; moreover, its purchases of capital equipment, coal, power, transportation, and so forth have multiplier effects in a series of backward linkages. These linkages have been estimated using input-output tables for Canada that trace an increase in investment or exports in the mining industry back through the various supplying industries (both within Canada and abroad through import leakages). Several such studies have been made, and a few examples serve to illustrate the main results and conclusions.[10]

A number of studies distinguish between the impact on employment of the construction phase and the effects of increased exports during the subsequent production phase of an ongoing mine. In one, the impact of an equivalent investment expenditure was estimated for two different industries, mining and oil-well drilling and manufacturing.[11] In the construction phase, 3,600 man-years of employment were generated by the mining industry, compared with 1,800 man-years for an equivalent initial expenditure in manufacturing. This difference presumably reflects the high construction component of mineral investment; investment in manufacturing has a higher share of expenditures on machinery and equipment, which has a larger import component.

Other studies have dealt with the direct and indirect effects on employment of the production phase of mining. Bucovetsky estimated the employment multiplier of the mining sector as 2, which implies one indirect job existed in backward-linked industries for every direct job in mining. The coal-mining industry taken separately had a ratio of 2.44. Seven manufacturing industries were studied, with ratios ranging from 1.77 for appliances to 3.08 for manufacturing, with an unweighted average of the individual manufacturing ratios of 2.32. His study, however, did not allow for induced effects through consumption and other final demand influences.[12]

The study by Stahl and McCulla included the employment effects induced by consumer spending attributable to direct job creation. At the extraction stage of mining, the ratio was 2.64 for both metal ores and concentrates and non-metallic minerals and 3.28 for iron ores and concentrates. For six commodity groups in manufacturing not related to mining, the ratios ranged from 2.32 for printing and publishing to 5.64 for pulp and paper products, with an unweighted average ratio of 3.89.[13]

The general conclusion from the above examples (and from other studies using similar input-output techniques) is that the impact on employment of the construction phase of mining is appreciably higher than for manufacturing, while the employment multipliers of an ongoing mineral operation are somewhat lower than in manufacturing. The relative impacts of the effects of alternative mining and manufacturing construction and machinery and equipment expenditure on total employment are not as different as would be suggested by comparisons of the direct employment levels alone in the two types of industries.

Another important favorable feature of employment in the mining industry is that earnings are above the average in manufacturing, and much above those in agriculture, in the same localities. However, mining earnings are below those in construction; and with the marked increases in money and real earnings in manufacturing during the 1970s, the differential in relation to manufacturing has narrowed. It should also be noted that living costs are frequently higher in outlying mining communities than in urban areas. Labor turnover also contributes to high costs in mining from the viewpoint of the mining company.

A different type of concern is sometimes raised in relation to the degree of cyclical volatility in employment and prices in mining. Cyclical changes in the mineral industries are related fairly closely and directly to demands in foreign markets. This inevitably means that the United States has a great deal of influence on the Canadian mining industry. There is no question that prices of primary products tend to move more frequently and with a greater amplitude than prices of manufactured products. It is also true that mining undergoes a greater degree of instability on a year-to-year basis than the average for all industries (as measured by real domestic product and by employment and output per worker).[14] The general argument that overall economic activity in Canada is highly unstable because of the share of exports going to the United States is frequently overstated, however. For one thing, exports of mineral products to Japan and to Western Europe (excluding the United Kingdom) have been growing somewhat more rapidly than exports to the United States for some years. Furthermore, during all the postwar recessions in the United States except that of 1973-75, economic activity in the other industrialized countries was expanding.[15] Declines in mineral exports and total exports to the United States were partly offset by increased sales in other markets.

Even more significant is the fact that the magnitudes of the declines in domestic activity during business cycle recessions in Canada have normally been smaller than those taking place almost simultaneously in the United

States. This tendency has been apparent during almost every recession in the present century. Both the increased quantitative size of the built-in stabilizers in Canada and the degree of stabilization from housing investment are important factors in the moderate extent of the postwar recessions.

A key reason for the smaller declines in economic activity in Canada than in the United States during the current century is that a significant part of the decline in demand in Canada (for both final demand and inventory investment) falls on foreign suppliers rather than on domestic producers. To some extent this reflects the tendency for imports to provide an important source of supply for such cyclically volatile expenditure sectors as machinery and equipment investment and consumer spending on durable goods. In addition, however, imports of a wide range of manufactured products drop more sharply during recessions than does domestic production of a comparable range of items. The reverse development occurs during business cycle expansions, with imports increasing more rapidly than domestic production of comparable items.[16] This means that domestic production in manufacturing is less volatile over both business cycle expansions and recessions than are associated domestic expenditures.

A key implication of these studies is that the open nature of the Canadian economy contributes to its greater stability, rather than greater instability. This is the opposite conclusion from one made by those who consider only one or a few export industries (such as mining) and conclude that the Canadian economy must be inherently more unstable than that of the United States.

Although this chapter emphasizes the national and more aggregative implications of the mining industry, one regional aspect might be briefly noted. During the earlier decades of the present century, when the primary industries (agriculture, mining, and forestry in particular) accounted for a relatively larger share of the Canadian economy than they do now, the population and the labor force were relatively more widely dispersed geographically. Manufacturing and the service industries are much more highly concentrated in the major population centers, and the more rapid growth of these industries has encouraged a concentration of population in major metropolitan areas. With a greater degree of public and government discussion of the costs of urban growth and of regional disparities, the mining industry is one of the few industries that are both located away from population concentrations and internationally competitive. Mining thus has some positive regional features that are being covered more fully in Chapters 8 and 9 in this volume.

In summary, the mining industry makes a number of important and positive contributions to the performance of the Canadian economy. It is clearly an industry in which Canada has a comparative advantage, both in terms of a greater supply relative to domestic employment than any of Canada's major markets, and as measured by the levels of output per person compared to the United States. The exchange of such products, of which Canada is a low-cost producer, for other products whose domestic production is high-cost and low in productivity by world standards is important both for the balance of payments and for domestic living standards. The mining industry plays a major role in the efficient use of resources domestically and in relation to international markets. In addition, the secondary effects of mining (during both the construction and the production phases) on domestic employment (taking account of the secondary and indirect effects rather than just the direct employment side) are not radically different from those of manufacturing — much larger during the construction phase, and somewhat smaller during production. Economic developments in foreign markets affect both prices and production in the mining industry, but close examination of a wider range of indicators suggests that the Canadian economy is less, rather than more, volatile over business cycles because of its open nature, especially in relation to the United States. The mining industry is also a high-wage industry and provides employment and income away from major population concentrations, a point worth noting in view of the degree of public discussion of the costs of urban growth and the extent of regional disparities in income and employment oportunities.

Public-Policy Concerns

Interests and concerns of the public, government, and media commentators change and evolve over time. Old topics and issues take on a different perspective from new viewpoints, and the changes at times almost seem like fads. A number of concerns about the Canadian economy have emerged during the 1970s, some of them reflecting comparable discussions in the United States, Northwest Europe, and Japan. One of these concerns has arisen in the context of an economic-growth debate and has had two dimensions: the possible check to economic growth from a potential scarcity of natural resources and the environmental costs of economic growth. Another issue has been the question of the taxation of profits in the mining industry, which has been further complicated by federal-provincial controversies concerning the sharing of taxes from natural resources. There has also been an increase in economic nationalism within Canada and in concern about the degree of foreign ownership and control.

All these issues and concerns have some bearing on the mining industry in one form or another. This section summarizes the broader issues (giving the pros and cons of the discussion, where appropriate) and provides some evidence on the issues wherever possible. In each section, the discussion explores the ramifications for the mining industry.

Natural Resource Scarcity

For about two decades after the cessation of the commodity price boom of the Korean War period, prices of internationally traded primary products were relatively weak compared to those of manufactured products. During this period the terms of trade between primary and manufactured products were a major concern of the developing countries.

Two developments in the early 1970s contributed to a radically different concern for some analysts—namely, that continued rapid economic expansion was leading inevitably to shortages of natural resources, with serious long-term implications for economic growth as experienced since the Industrial Revolution.

One development was the widespread publicity given to a computer simulation of long-term economic growth entitled *The Limits to Growth,* published in 1972.[17] This was an application of a systems model initially developed by Jay Forrester at MIT to long-term projections of population, real income, natural resource supplies and uses, and associated pollution. The study predicted a high risk of the collapse of the economic system.

The second development was the emergence of significant price increases in almost all the industrialized market economies, with particularly sharp price increases in natural resource products, of which the price increases in petroleum initiated by the OPEC cartel in 1973-1974 were the most dramatic. These two developments, occurring close together, initiated renewed discussion about natural resources and economic growth that created an unusually high degree of both professional and public interest.

The Limits to Growth led to active public and professional discussion and to the emphasis on, and the use of, a "world model" to study a variety of longer-term variables and relationships. The book's concern about the possibility of natural resources' acting as a check on economic growth was not a new idea, since this concept had been a central part of Malthus' concern that food supply would act as a limit on economic growth by checking population growth. A number of the critics of *The Limits to Growth* pointed out that the methodology was a computerized variation of the earlier Malthusian views.[18] A further criticism was that the study did not adequately incorporate the effects of any developing scarcity on the price system and subsequent responses by the participants. Pressure of demand against a limited supply would lead to a relative price increase for a scarce commodity. The higher price would act as a restraint on demand from industrial users and the final consumer and would encourage an increased supply and the development of substitute materials by the incentives of higher profits and prices to the producer.

These concepts had also been discussed in the context of natural resources. The first edition of Anthony Scott's *Natural Resources: The Economics of Conservation* was published in 1955, and Barnett and Morse's outstanding study, *Scarcity and Growth*, was published in 1963,[19] but neither was referred to in *The Limits to Growth*.

One way of testing the hypothesis that natural resources are scarce is to compare their prices with those of other factors, such as labor, over time. This has been done by William Nordhaus,[20] and his results follow in Table 5.3. The prices of most primary products have declined compared to wages during the present century in the United States, as illustrated in Table 5.3 by the ratio of the prices of eleven important minerals to the price of labor. Even when the changes to 1974 are included, prices are relatively lower than in 1960 for all minerals except coal, zinc, and petroleum. In discussing the implications of these past changes for the future, Nordhaus comments: "This indicates that there has been a continuous decline in

TABLE 5.3

Prices of Important Minerals
Relative to Labor Costs, United States, 1900-74
(1970 = 100)

	1900	1920	1940	1950	1960	1970	1974
Coal	459	451	189	208	111	100	182
Copper	785	226	121	99	82	100	101
Iron	620	287	144	112	120	100	99
Phosphorus	n.a.	n.a.	n.a.	130	120	100	n.a.
Molybdenum	n.a.	n.a.	n.a.	142	108	100	n.a.
Lead	788	388	204	228	114	100	110
Zinc	794	400	272	256	126	100	179
Sulphur	n.a.	n.a.	n.a.	215	145	100	97
Aluminum	3,150	859	287	166	134	100	90
Gold	n.a.	n.a.	595	258	143	100	92
Crude petroleum	1,034	726	198	213	135	100	164

Source: Values are the price per ton of the mineral divided by the hourly wage rate in manufacturing. Data are from *Historical Statistics, Long Term Economic Growth, Statistical Abstract.* Reproduced from William Nordhaus, "Resources As a Constraint on Growth," *American Economic Review, Proceedings,* June, 1974, p. 24. 1974 data added from same sources.

resource prices for the entire century. Unless all minerals suddenly hit a kink in the cost curve at the same time, it seems unreasonable to foresee a drastic turnup of the cost of minerals relative to wages in the near future."[21]

In light of the traditional similarity between broad economic developments in the United States and Canada, it is probable that comparable developments also took place in Canada.

Even if mineral prices were to increase much more than the above analysis would suggest, there is still a substantial adjustment on the supply side potentially available. Known reserves are only a small fraction of the crustal abundance of the major minerals, and increases in relative prices of such minerals would permit the development of lower-grade ores or those farther from present major markets.[22] There is also active discussion currently under way about the extent of mineral resources on the ocean bed and the jurisdiction over such resources.

It should also be borne in mind that an increased supply of scrap from metals as a by-product of economic growth could lead to more reclaimed materials. Some European countries are already using a larger share of scrap and reclaimed metals than the United States.[23] A comparable change would emerge if prices of minerals were to increase significantly more than wages and the general price level.

In summary, although the possibility that economic growth could be checked by a scarcity of natural resources has been discussed for more than a century and a half, it seems unlikely that mineral resources could act as such a constraint in the foreseeable future in light of recoverable reserves and the likely response of producers and consumers to higher mineral prices. Minerals are too small a share of gross national product (GNP), and there are too many substitutes available, for either their supplies or their prices to act as a major check or drag on the growth rate in the foreseeable future. Although minerals in a particular mine or region can become exhausted, this does not seem to be a general or imminent development.

Some discussion developed in Canada about public policies on the assumption that a scarcity of natural resources was a serious and near-term development. Those holding to this view suggested that in negotiations with other countries Canada use the availability of natural resources to obtain concessions on other issues. This does not appear to have been done. The implications of the analysis in this section are that mineral resources are not really scarce on a world basis and that other supply sources of high-quality and low-cost minerals exist. Thus Canadian mines could be vulnerable to competition from other sources of supply, especially in view of higher taxation and tighter pollution regulations in Canada.

A rather different concern about economic growth is that it can involve costs and side effects that are undesirable and not usually reflected in the traditional measures of economic growth. This range of issues will be considered next.

Environmental Quality

Some, but not all, of the discussants concerned about the supply of natural resources as a check to growth are also concerned about the adverse side effects of economic growth, especially on the quality of the environment — the pollution of air, water, and land, and noise pollution. This is particularly relevant for mining because of the amount of waste from the industry (in the form of overburden, rock, tailings, and water associated with mining, and gases and acids from smelting and refining). The interests of this second group are primarily focused on welfare, especially that of the consumer. As an illustration of this area of concern, the contribution of E. J. Mishan in *The Costs of Economic Growth,* published in 1967, will be emphasized.[24] This book was an outgrowth of an extended interest in the economics of welfare. The book followed up the distinction between costs borne by the producer (and reflected in prices to buyers) and the side effects of costs that fall on third parties (other than the producers and consumers of the output) through the effects of production on the air through smoke or noise or of the discharge of industrial waste into rivers and lakes. These costs fall on the general public in the vicinity or downstream from the polluting plant. At times the study almost rejects the successes of an industrial society. The book contains no estimates of the costs of these side effects, the gains from economic growth, or any references to literature on such costs and benefits.

The basic recognition of the side effects noted above has had a long history in economics. The distinction between private and social costs, illustrated by the effects of smoke from a factory on third parties, was made by Pigou as far back as 1912.[25]

One issue that the current debate has raised is whether existing measures of output (usually GNP in real terms on a per capita basis) are satisfactory measures of economic growth for welfare purposes. Existing measures of GNP in real terms were designed initially to measure shorter-term variations in demand for demand analysis by business and government. It is not too difficult to adjust these measures to make them quite appropriate for the analysis of long-term economic growth (as has been done by Denison and others in such analysis). However, the additional steps to make these output measures into measures of economic welfare would make them *less* satisfactory measures of output. Such measures of welfare have been made, and the occasional preparation of such special independent measures is desirable.

If measures of welfare are prepared, how do they differ in level and rate

of change from existing real output measures? Such measures have been
made by Nordhaus and Tobin for the United States and by Usher for
Canada. Their estimate of a "disamenity correction" for the costs of urban
life and urban growth amounted to about 10 percent of personal consumption, as now measured, in 1965. At the same time, additions to measured
consumption to allow for imputations for leisure and non-market activities
raised the level of consumption to three or four times the level as now
measured. Over time, the rate of growth of their preferred measure of per
capita economic welfare was 1.1 percent from 1929 to 1965, compared to
1.7 percent for per capita net national product. "The progress indicated by
conventional national accounts is not just a myth that evaporates when a
welfare-oriented measure is subsituted."[26] (For the 1945-65 period, their
preferred measure of per capita welfare increased by 1.1 percent, even
higher than the 0.9 percent increase in per capita GNP.) Similar estimates
were developed by Dan Usher for Canada, with comparable conclusions.
He made an imputation for the increase in life expectancy since the late
1920s, and this was a major factor in a higher level and faster increase from
this source than from the existing measures of real output on a per capita
basis.[27]

Many observers would agree that more attention to the environment is
needed and that Mishan and others were effective in making an impact on
public attitudes in the early 1970s. It is not so obvious what the appropriate
steps would be to devise socially acceptable measures to reduce costs to the
public and to achieve a better balance of benefits and costs to society. A
promising route appears to be to put more of these costs back on the producers and consumers of products that tend to produce particularly high
amounts of pollution. It may also involve the use of taxes and subsidies by
government, but these should be based on careful estimates of costs and
benefits as part of evolving the new levels of taxes and subsidies. There are
clearly less expensive ways of correcting for the costs to economic welfare
from environmental side effects than by checking economic growth. A
number of observers have pointed out that the problems of human waste,
animal waste, sewage, and pure water were much greater before the Industrial Revolution than recently, and conditions that still prevail in many
low-income countries are more serious than those that currently prevail in
North America.[28]

This discussion of the environment is particularly relevant for a discussion of mining, as mining is the largest single contributor to solid wastes in
Canada, as shown in Table 5.4.[29] The waste quantities of minerals are
about two-thirds of total waste in Canada and are larger than the total of *all*
wastes in the United States on a per capita basis. On a per capita basis,
mineral wastes in Canada are about four times the level in the United

TABLE 5.4

Waste Quantities in the United States and Canada

Type of Waste	United States		Canada	
	Pounds Per Capita per Day	%	Pounds Per Capita per Day	%
Household, commercial, and municipal	6.4	7.2	4.3	2.5
Industrial	2.8	3.1	2.8	1.6
Agricultural (excluding animals)	14.0	15.7	14.0	8.2
Agricultural (animal)	38.0	42.6	38.0	22.3
Mineral	28.0	31.4	111.3	65.3
	89.2	100.0	170.4	100.0

Source: Thurlow and Associates, "A Preliminary Overview of the Solid Waste Problem in Canada," Solid Waste Management Report EPS 6-EP-73-1, February, 1973, from R. H. Clark, "Solid Wastes and Resource Recovery in Canada," paper presented to the Royal Society of Canada, Queen's University, Kingston, Ontario, 1975.

States. Most mines and smelters are located in remote areas and thus may not be as visible to as many people as if they were adjacent to highly populated areas.

Increased public concern about the environment during the 1970s has led to more restrictive legislation and to more aggressive enforcement of environmental standards. Radioactive wastes from uranium mines and lead from a refining operation in Toronto are recent examples that have had wide publicity. Pressures for higher environmental standards have affected not only the mining, smelting, and refining industries, but other primary industries such as pulp and paper, and such food-processing industries as meat packing. Such measures can lead to an improved physical environment without necessarily checking overall economic growth, and more of these costs will now fall on the producers in those industries and on the related consumers, rather than on some or all of the general public. These costs could be relatively large for some individual firms or industries, even though they may not be large in relation to either GNP or the overall gains from economic growth. For example, the costs of installing and operating modern plants to control the wastes of mining and milling operations can easily amount to one-quarter or more of the total costs of operating a mineral-processing plant. This is well above expenditures on pollution control and conservation in British Columbia from 1965 to 1970.[30]

An illustration of the possible conflict between an untouched rural hinterland, on the one hand, and vigorous urban and industrial development, on the other, is provided by the problems of supply and costs of sand, gravel, and crushed stone for the central Ontario region. This region covers an area of about 100 miles surrounding Toronto down to the U.S. border. Costs of transportation rise sharply with distance, and supply can become a problem, especially when 90 percent of the rural municipalities have restrictive bylaws of one form or another relating to aggregate extraction operations. One study recommended the interim use of an area for mineral resource extraction and its eventual use as a park, recreation area, or a site for residential subdivision or industrial development.[31]

The discussion of environmental quality and the costs of economic growth has not modified the general conclusion that significant growth in per capita measures of welfare has occurred. However, increased public concern about environmental standards has had a significant impact on the mining and smelting industries in Canada, especially in light of the very significant quantities of waste produced in mining, particularly when ore grades are low. The raising of environmental standards could eventually increase costs to the mining and smelting industries, to industrial users, and to final consumers, which presumably puts the costs of pollution where they belong. As a result, however, some mines may close, and other possible mineral developments may not go ahead, especially when mineral inventories are high and operating rates are low.

It should also be borne in mind that the developing countries have thus far been showing less concern for the quality of the environment than the developed countries. Some of the low-income countries would welcome the export earnings from new mining developments, and this could influence the location of future mine locations outside, and in competition with, Canada.

Taxation and Economic Rent

The two previous sections summarized the economic-growth debate, a discussion that has been taking place in the United States and many other parts of the world and that is particularly relevant for the mining industry in Canada. This section and the next raise other issues that have had relatively more consideration, in the context of mining, in Canada than in other countries.

A key aspect of economic rent and the associated discussion of taxation in relation to the Canadian mining industry is the significant variations in the quality of mineral deposits within Canada and in comparison with alternative sources of supply outside Canada. These variations (concentration and size of deposit, ease of access, and the availability of water for sluicing, rinsing, and flotation) influence the corresponding costs of finding, mining, and processing minerals of diverse quality. This contributes to an element of resource "rent" that is related principally to the quality of the mineral, the ease with which it can be mined, and its location. A recent development in a number of countries is an attempt by the countries in which mines are located to obtain a larger share of such economic rents from the mineral companies, both domestic and foreign-owned.[32] Mining taxation has been an important topic in the discussion of tax reform and tax changes beginning in the 1960s in Canada.

It has been a theme in economics for many decades that government policy should not normally encourage or discourage individual industries on either the consumption or the production side. This is normally described as neutrality in the tax system, and sometimes as Pareto optimality, after the Italian economist who initially stated it in its general form. This basic rationale was accepted by the Canadian Royal Commission on Taxation (frequently referred to as the Carter Commission after its chairman) in its report. In the context of mineral taxation, the Carter Commission followed the analysis of a staff study by M. W. Bucovetsky and recommended the elimination of many of the federal tax privileges conferred on depletable resource industries, the analysis having concluded that the mining and the petroleum industries were experiencing lower effective rates of taxation than other industries such as manufacturing. The commission did not get into an important related source of non-neutrality — namely, tariffs and non-tariff barriers to trade, topics of particular interest to manufacturing.

In the discussion of the Carter report and the federal government's subsequent White Paper on Taxation, the government proposed to modify the previous taxation system for mining, but to nothing like the degree that had been recommended by the Royal Commission on Taxation. The mining industry and a number of provincial governments made strong representations against the initial recommendations.[33]

The next stage in the discussion was a series of studies by Eric Kierans, some for individual provincial governments, which contained new material on the effective tax rate in mining compared to other industries.[34] Table 5.5 contains more recent data along the lines he initially developed. The ratios of taxable income to reported profits increased appreciably in the early 1970s, compared to the late 1960s. In metal mining, for example, the ratio increased from 13 percent in 1965-68 to 35 percent in 1972-74. Further recent changes have included the dropping of the three-year, tax-free holiday for new mines beginning in early 1975; the withdrawal of automatic percentage depletion since 1976; and tax changes in a number of provinces. There has been a great deal of tax uncertainty in the industry. Kierans' analysis and recommendations seemed to have more impact on the

TABLE 5.5

Comparison of Profits before Taxes and Taxable Income,
Selected Industries, Aggregated for 1972-74 and 1965-68
(million dollars)

	(1) Reported Profits, 1972-74	(2) Taxable Income, 1972-74	(3) (2) as % of (1)	(4) % in 1965-68
Metal mining	3,123	1,098.1	35	13
Mineral fuels	1,986	1,172.2	59	5.7
Other mining	568	304.5	54	32
Manufacturing	19,637	14,130.7	72	63
Wholesale trade	4,687	4,264.6	91	87
Retail trade	4,769	2,513.9	53	90

Source: Statistics Canada, Corporations and Labour Unions Returns Act, Part 1, Corporations, 1973, 1974 (Ottawa: Information Canada, 1976, 1977), Tables 4, 8. 1965-68 estimates from Eric Kierans, "Contributions of the Tax System to Canada's Unemployment and Ownership Problems," in John Chant, ed., Canadian Perspectives in Economics (Toronto: Collier-Macmillan Canada, 1972), Table 2.

provincial governments than the Carter Commission eventually had on federal government legislation. Some provinces increased their shares of mineral and petroleum revenues, and some of the issues of taxation of mining and petroleum erupted into federal-provincial conflict and negotiation. The situation was further complicated by the sharp increases in petroleum prices, and Canada introduced price differentials between the foreign buyer, the domestic producer, and the domestic consumer, with the domestic price to the consumer eventually moving up in steps toward the world price.

The preceding discussion has related to the policy of making the effective rate of corporation-profits tax in the mining industry broadly comparable to that paid in manufacturing and other industries. However, this would help achieve total neutrality only if other sources of non-neutrality were also removed. At present, employment in Canadian manufacturing is encouraged to a significant extent by the Canadian tariff, which is an important source of high costs to the consumer and of lower levels of output in relation to labor and capital in domestic manufacturing. A completely neutral system of taxes and tariffs would require the removal of both the favorable tax treatment of mining and the tariff protection provided to domestic manufacturing. As long as the tariffs remain, a second-best neutrality could be achieved by lower taxes on mining.[35]

Some evidence concerning total tariff and non-tariff protection is relevant. In 1970 it was estimated that such protection to the mining industry was 13.64 percent (with metals at 9.44 and mineral fuels much higher at 17.68), while for all manufacturing it was 12.44.[36] Since then, additional tax changes by the two levels of government combined would further increase effective mineral taxation rates, especially on petroleum companies. Thus it is by no means clear that mineral taxation is now too low in relation to manufacturing industries (in spite of the differences in effective rates of corporate-profits taxes shown in Table 5.5) as long as present levels of tariffs persist. The mining industry has been expressing concern about the increases in federal and provincial taxes and in environmental controls since 1970 and about continuing federal-provincial tax conflicts.[37] The expanding mining capacity and lower mineral taxation in developing countries and the persisting slack in industrial countries have shifted concerns from shortages to surpluses in mineral resources. The implication is that both taxes and tariffs should be adjusted, rather than either one in isolation from related policies in other fields.

The discussion of economic rent and the argument that mineral industries in Canada have not been bearing a reasonable share of taxation has had an important impact on federal and provincial taxation since 1971, with increased mineral taxes developing in a variety of forms. The analysis here suggests that total tariff and non-tariff rates were not too different between mining and manufacturing in 1970, but increases in mineral taxes since may slow further mineral development.

Foreign Ownership and Control

A further area of concern about mining is the degree of foreign ownership and control; this is symptomatic of the increased degree of nationalism that has been observed in Canada (as elsewhere) in recent years.[38] Economic nationalists usually prefer additional domestic processing of minerals to having them exported primarily in crude form.[39] This area will be explored further in the last section. Another area of concern sometimes expressed is that the major benefits from foreign ownership and control accrue to the foreign investor, rather than to domestic income and the balance of payments.

Considerable evidence is available to test this hypothesis. In 1976, materials, labor, and other expenses amounted to 67 percent of sales in the mining industry.[40] A recent study has found that the indirect import multiplier for mining from the 1966 input-output tables was .08, well below the average of .18 for all industries and values of between .22 and .35 for various mineral-related sectors of domestic manufacturing.[41] (The term in-

146   D. J. DALY

direct import multiplier refers to the impact on imports associated with the
expansion of various economic activities.) In commenting on these results,
the author of the study observes: "The indirect import multipliers for the
primary industries are significantly lower than for the other industry
groups. The implications for the balance of payments current account are
obvious. Production in the primary industries, especially for export, will
have a generally favourable impact on the current account."[42]

Some perspective on profits and their distribution in the mining industry
might also be helpful. In 1974, base profits (which include depreciation and
depletion and are before taxes) were about 36 percent of sales.[43] In the
same year materials, salaries, and wages were 51 percent of sales of foreign-
owned, but only 40 percent of sales of Canadian-owned, mining companies. Profit ratios were smaller on all measures in 1974 for foreign-owned
than for Canadian-owned mining companies (profits before and after tax in
relation to total equity, profits before tax in relation to capital
employed) — usually about two-thirds the Canadian level for all three ratios
in 1974. Only part of profits after tax are paid out in dividends — 51 percent
for Canadian-owned mining firms, but only 27 percent for foreign-owned
firms.[44] The balance of net profits and the depreciation and depletion
reserves are left in the firm for reinvestment in a variety of asset forms.

Dividends as a percentage of product sales were 2.6 percent for foreign-
owned firms compared to 11.2 percent for Canadian-owned firms with
assets of $25 million and over; the corresponding percentages for firms with
assets of between $10 million and $25 million were 5.9 and 11.7 percent,
respectively. These two asset-size groups comprise 98 percent of the sales of
all mining firms with assets of more than $5 million.[45] In other words, both
profits and dividends were markedly smaller for foreign than for Canadian
mining firms in 1974 in relation to all measures of sales and assets.
However, dividends are not the only form of payment by the subsidiary to
the parent, as payments for management fees, machinery, and materials
are normally also made.

It is of interest that sales were equal to 58 percent of total assets for
foreign-owned companies but only 44 percent for Canadian-owned companies.[46] Sales of products were also relatively larger in relation to salaries
and wages for foreign-owned companies than for Canadian-owned companies in the two largest asset-size groups.[47] This suggests that for these
years sales were relatively larger in relation to both employees and total
assets (the main factor inputs in value added) for foreign-owned than for
Canadian-owned companies. In terms of contributing to output, foreign-
owned firms apparently outperformed Canadian-owned firms (as
measured by output in relation to measures of labor and capital input) and
paid out relatively less in the form of dividends.

In 1974, 64.5 percent of Canadian mineral industry sales were by foreign-owned firms, and 58 percent of Canadian mining assets and equity were accounted for by foreign-owned firms.[48] It seems clear that, because of the risky nature of exploration and development and the capital-intensive nature of mineral production, foreign investment has been an essential step in getting the mining industry and mineral exports to their present size. It would seem that Canadian real incomes per capita are higher because of foreign investment in mining, even after allowing for dividends paid out and the indirect impact of mining on imports of other goods and services directly and indirectly. Direct investment in mining is analogous to trade in that both participating countries gain, rather than there being a zero-sum game in which one party gains and the other loses.

It would appear that foreign-owned mining firms tend to be more productive than domestically owned firms; to pay out relatively more for materials, salaries and wages; to have relatively lower profit rates; and to pay out relatively less in dividends. Some of these differences may reflect transfer-pricing differences or differences in the distribution of foreign-owned and domestically owned firms at a finer level of detail, but these possibilities have not yet been explored systematically. Furthermore, the indirect effects on imports are relatively less for mining than for manufacturing. On the basis of this review of the evidence, there seems to be little reason to believe that foreign ownership and control in the mining industry have been unfavorable to the attainment of such domestic goals and objectives as increased employment opportunities, improved real incomes, and a healthy balance of payments.

Mining-Industry Options and Future Trends

Earlier parts of this chapter emphasized the size of the Canadian mining industry and the implications thereof, with some comparisons with the United States. This section puts the discussion of mining and mineral trade into a longer-term world perspective before considering future trends.

World Trends in Mining and Mineral Trade

Historical studies of economic growth in the major industrialized countries indicate that mining has tended to decline in importance as a share of the individual industrialized economies, measured by employment and national income by industry. Mining in the United States reached its peak share of the economy in 1930; the major countries in Europe experienced a declining share much earlier (Germany in 1907, Austria in 1910, Belgium in 1920, and Great Britain in 1921, for example). In Canada mining reached its peak share in 1911.[49]

A number of factors have contributed to this decline in the share of mining in these industrialized countries.[50] As economic growth has evolved in the postwar period, the most rapidly expanding industries have been in the service sectors, which do not require large quantities of metal and other mineral inputs. Technological change has sometimes involved the substitution of new materials, such as plastics, for metals and minerals. Furthermore, increased use of reclaimed metal from scrap has been taking place. Further economic growth and increased sensitivity to the quality of the environment could accentuate this trend. In addition, some mines in the major industrialized countries have been closed because they were higher-cost than alternative sources of supply.

A similar decline in the share of metal exports in world trade has gone on since 1913. From 1929 to 1959, world manufacturing production tripled, international trade in manufactured products more than doubled, and total metal exports increased by about 75 percent.[51] The slower growth in international trade in primary products has been widespread, with the important exception of petroleum products. The more rapid growth in manufactured-product exports than in metals exports has continued since 1959.

International trade in manufactured products has been expanding more rapidly than world manufacturing production since about 1950.[52] This trend reflects reductions in tariff and non-tariff barriers to trade under GATT, both on a multilateral basis and on a regional basis through such developments as the European Common Market (which is in the process of expanding to encompass a free-trade area larger than the United States in terms of population). These reductions in trade barriers have been associated with increased specialization, increased productivity in manufacturing, and an increased flow of manufactured products in what has been called intra-industry trade.[53]

This decline in the relative share of mineral exports on a world basis has been going on for more than two decades, and exports of ores and minerals (excluding fuel and fabricated metals) have amounted to only about 3 percent of world exports in recent years. The decline in the share of mining employment and output in the economies of the major industrialized countries has been going on much longer. Neither of these developments has received very much attention in Canada.[54]

One of the dilemmas Canadians have to face is that one of their strongest areas of comparative advantage in recent decades, mining, has not been growing on a world basis in line with total output and employment. At the same time, international trade in manufactured products has been growing more rapidly than domestic production and consumption of manufactured products. However, Canada is a high-cost, low-productivity producer of most manufactured products and has serious comparative disadvantages in this field.

There has been some concern in Canada that the heavy reliance on natural resources as a source of foreign exchange to pay for imports can be only a short-term strategy. Canada's natural resources may not continue to be as important in domestic and world trade as they have been in the past because of shifts in demand and the development of new low-cost sources of supply elsewhere. This is quite a different assessment from the view that a scarcity of minerals could act as a check on economic growth, a point of view considered previously.

Labor Supply and Turnover

Labor supply and turnover are topics that began to be of concern to those in the Canadian mining industry only during the 1970s; a number of studies have been made recently by individual companies, the mining association, federal and provincial government agencies interested in mining, and some scholars (usually based in schools of business and commerce). Their concerns are that there may be an inadequate number of workers for the Canadian mining industry and that the costs of recruiting and retaining workers for the mines will be high.

Traditionally, many Canadian industries have experienced a significant degree of labor turnover. Such turnover is normally lower for males of prime working age and higher for young people and women. Some data on labor turnover for the major working categories in mining are shown in Table 5.6. The turnover rate among unskilled workers is substantially higher than for skilled workers; it is lowest among technical and management staff. The original study provided data for different-sized mines, by age, by province, by distance from major city, and in relation to community facilities.[55] In 1973, employee turnover was 1.7 times the average for all Canadian industries.

An intensive study of turnover in a major smelter in the interior of British Columbia estimated that changes in turnover and subsequent repercussions throughout the plant increased the cost of operations by approximately $3-4 million per year.[56] In relation to the annual wage bill for hourly rated employees, this would amount to 15-25 percent, a very significant factor in labor costs. The costs would be relatively less in a recession, when turnover typically drops.[57]

The mining industry has also been experiencing job vacancy rates well above the average for all industries during the 1970s.[58] The Mining Association of Canada estimated that lost production might have amounted to 8 percent of 1974 output, or $320 million, an estimate that has been widely quoted subsequently.[59]

TABLE 5.6
Labor Turnover, by Category, Canada, 1973
(percentages)

Category	Mean Turnover, All Mines, Weighted by Size of Mine
Unskilled labor	77.5
Skilled miners	40.5
Office workers	33.0
Technical staff	34.4
Management staff	25.0

Source: Mining Association of Canada, *Labour Turnover and Shortages in the Canadian Mining Industry: Principal Statistics of the Problem* (Ottawa, 1974).

Mining has traditionally been a high-wage industry. Annual wages in mining were about 10 percent higher than in construction in the late 1950s and early 1960s, but by the early 1970s mining wages had slipped to about 10 percent lower than construction wages. Mining wages continued about 10 percent higher than in durable manufacturing in the late 1960s and early 1970s.[60] It is possible that the differential is not regarded as adequate to cover the disamenities present in the mining industry. For example, occupational fatality rates were 1.34 per 1,000 employees in mining, compared to .12 in manufacturing and public administration.[61] There is also evidence that community-stress symptoms are more frequent: there is a feeling of isolation; significant pollution of the environment has been present but is receiving increased consideration; and costs of food and services are frequently higher.[62]

In order to make mining more attractive and to reduce turnover, mining firms and governments are giving more attention to community facilities. More community amenities encourage greater labor stability, but the relationship is not strong.[63] Miners express dissatisfaction with such factors as the level of company concern with employee welfare, individual appreciation and recognition, and inadequate communication with management. More emphasis on these internal aspects of management seems desirable if mining companies hope to recruit and retain workers of the number and quality they desire.[64]

One interesting experiment under way is that of Gulf Minerals Canada Limited. The company runs a staff shuttle system from Saskatoon to Rabbit Lake in northern Saskatchewan, with intermediate stops. This practice replaces a mining community with air-travel commuting.

Share of Canadian Mineral Exports to the United States

The United States continues to be Canada's most important export market for non-fuel mineral industry exports. The U.S. share of Canada's total exports was about 37 percent in 1926, ranged close to 60 percent from the mid-1950s to the early 1970s, and increased further to between 65 and 70 percent in the mid-1970s. Although there has been an increased share of exports to Japan and the European Economic Community since 1950 (reflecting their more rapid economic growth), these have been more than offset by a relative decline in exports to the United Kingdom since the latter part of the 1950s.[65]

In 1972, while he was Minister of External Affairs, Mitchell Sharp released a statement on Canadian foreign policy that recommended an increased emphasis on international trade with the European Common Market and Japan, as opposed to increased economic integration with the United States, primarily because of the expressed public concern about potential U.S. political influence. This apparently continues to be the emphasis of the current Liberal government, as reflected in several widely publicized trips by Prime Minister Trudeau to Europe and Japan and travel in both directions by working delegations from Canada and Japan.

This emphasis on a relative shift in trade away from the United States has been questioned within Canada. One line of criticism is that the modern theory of federalism distinguishes a number of channels of communication and influence between countries and that increased economic integration need not lead to increased political integration either in theory or in actual experience.[66] The federal government has indicated a desire for increased exports of manufactured products. However, the Economic Council of Canada has pointed out that total exports to European countries and Japan are even more heavily concentrated in renewable and non-renewable natural resources than are exports to the United States.[67] Canadians thus seem to have another choice — exports to the United States involve relatively more shipments of manufactured products than to other industrialized countries, and an increased emphasis on exports to Japan and Western Europe would further increase the share of exports of primary products.

Comparative Advantage and Export Composition

Canada's comparative advantage in mineral production and exports and comparative disadvantage in manufacturing production were introduced earlier in this chapter. It was pointed out that minerals were relatively more plentiful in Canada than in any industrialized country examined and that output of mineral products per person employed in mining was more than 60 percent higher in Canada than in the United States in 1970. In contrast, the levels of output per man and per man-hour in Canadian manufacturing were more than 20 percent lower than in the United States in the 1970s, while average hourly earnings were more than 10 percent higher in Canadian than in U.S. manufacturing by late 1977 (reversing the historic pattern of 20 percent or more lower than the United States as recently as a decade ago). These areas of comparative advantage reflect differences in factor supplies, productivities, and costs and are influenced by government policies both in Canada and elsewhere. These factors change over time and are not immutable, but change only slowly. As long as these long-standing productivity differentials between Canada and the United States persist, any attempt to shift resources from mining to manufacturing will involve a relative decline in real income to Canadians that would be associated with analogous changes in money costs and prices and the price of the U.S. dollar in Canada. Although certain limited groups could benefit from such a change, this would be offset by declines in potential national income in real terms.

There are a number of reasons for the persistence of a lower level of manufacturing output per man and per man-hour in Canada than in the United States, and a number of policy routes are open to narrow the current differentials. These include commercial policy, science policy, education and selection of middle and senior management, and openness to change, but these issues would divert us from our major areas of interest here.[68] This discussion emphasizes the effective use of labor, capital, and natural resources for a given level of employment.

There is also some feeling that the share of mineral exports in crude forms is too high and that increased employment could be achieved domestically from a greater degree of processing, including both smelting and refining and semi-fabricated manufacturing. One recent study, for example, provided data on the employment and national income created by the additional processing of $1 million worth of ore through the system, showing larger increases with additional processing and fabrication compared to production at the primary stages.[69] The study considered only the employment aspects of economic policy, however, and ignored efficiency and resource allocation considerations. It did not consider Canada's comparative advantage, but the evidence in this chapter emphasized that a shift of labor and capital resources from mining to manufacturing would lower, not raise, Canadian national income and would affect resource allocation adversely. It seems preferable to increase employment by appropriate long-term use of fiscal and monetary policy, rather than to encourage production and employment by selective measures in industries where Canada is already an inefficient producer by world standards.

There has been an increase in the proportion of exports in crude form. For example, only about 15 percent of Canadian nonferrous mineral exports were in crude form in 1950, but this figure had approached 40 percent by the early 1970s.[70] Between 1960 and 1975 there was a significant decline in the proportion of copper, lead, and zinc production in western Canada that was refined in Canada. Over this period, increases in refining capacity did not keep pace with the marked increase in mineral production. On the other hand, new refining capacity in eastern Canada permitted an increased share of mineral production to be processed in that region.[71] However, there may not be a sound basis on the cost and economic side for such a development in western Canada. This possibility can be illustrated for copper smelting and refining in British Columbia, where a significant portion of recent mining development has taken place on the basis of long-term supply contracts and long-term debt financing from Japan but limited managerial or technological involvement. It is of interest that Japan is now the second-largest Canadian export market after the United States.

There are significant economies of scale in the smelting and refining of copper, and a facility of minimum efficient size is substantially larger than the average size of most of the recent new mines. Some of the new mines have been developed on the basis of long-term contracts with Japanese interests, which already have established processing facilities but need more raw material for processing. Japan has also been interested in securing a variety of mineral suppliers. Sales of by-products are a partial offset to the costs of processing. The Japanese firms have their processing plants at tidewater, and the raw ore can be unloaded at the dock and the by-products piped to an adjacent chemical plant, which can use the sulphur gases for basic chemicals, such as fertilizers for rice production. In addition, the processing developed by the Mitsubishi group of firms is highly automated and computerized. Both the construction and the production costs of the Mitsubishi process smelter are lower than the more conventional flash and reverberatory processes, with more effective control of pollution, together with lower energy and labor requirements. The associated tankhouse for refining involves a lower investment cost, substantially smaller labor requirements, reduced land-area needs at the site, and lower metal inventories. The new copper smelter and electrolytic refinery being constructed by Texasgulf Canada at Timmins in northern Ontario are based on the Mitsubishi technology in both the smelter and the refinery design.[72]

In this example, the analysis of comparative costs favors processing of Canadian copper in Japan rather than in western Canada. There may be some economic gains to Canada from additional mineral processing in other fields, but it would be unwise to assume this as a general rule without more consideration of costs and benefits.

Future Problem Areas in Canadian Mining

Although this chapter has suggested that mining has played a net positive role in determining the real incomes of Canadians and the Canadian balance of payments, there are a number of factors that could influence the rate of future development, some of which have been raised in other parts of this volume and this chapter. These are summarized briefly here.

The whole area of labor turnover, labor shortages, and labor management relations in the mining industry seems likely to need, and to receive, more attention in the future than in the past. A number of studies have recently been completed, and a further pickup in world demand could lead to an intensification of business and government concern in this area.

Taxation, economic rents, and conflicts between the federal government and the provinces have become important issues, as discussed by Garth Stevenson in Chapter 6 of this volume. The changes in taxation and increased emphasis on reducing the adverse environmental effects of mining have introduced a new degree of uncertainty into longer-term mineral development.

Although Canada is relatively well-endowed with mineral resources compared to other industrialized countries, the developing countries in South America, Africa, and Asia also have large reserves and potential, and Canadians cannot afford to be complacent about the quality and the cost of mineral development domestically relative to alternative sources of supply. Japan, for example, is concerned about interruptions to supply caused by strikes on Canadian railways, on Vancouver docks, or at the mines and has other sources of supply in Australia, Brazil, and elsewhere and plans for further expansions, frequently on a joint venture basis. Canada's share of world trade in asbestos, nickel, and aluminum has dropped sharply in the past two or three decades, and further changes in other metals and minerals might easily occur.

Rates of return were markedly lower in metal mines from 1971 to 1975 — about 30 percent less than from 1962 to 1970. In comparison with after-tax rates of return in manufacturing, returns on metal mines were about 70 percent higher from 1966 to 1970; but during the following five years they were about 17 percent lower.[73] For 1974-76 the average return on shareholders' equity was about 11.5 percent for metal mining, 14 percent for total manufacturing, and about 10 percent for such safe investments as government bonds. The average mining investment was providing a smaller return than manufacturing, and not much more than government bonds.[74] These lower rates of return in mining than in manufacturing do not seem to reflect the higher risks associated with individual new mineral developments. Since most Canadian mining companies believe they cannot pass along the tax increases of recent years to foreign buyers, some feel the lower returns partially reflect the higher taxes on the mineral industry. This can slow and check the development of new mines and encourage "high grading" in existing mines (which concentrates on high-grade ores and reduces interest in, and use of, lower grades previously mined). This drop in the rate of return in some important mining sectors partly reflects the lower level of world economic activity during the most widespread and severe business cycle recession of the postwar period. However, longer-term factors that may have contributed to the lower profits would include the decline in the relative importance of mineral trade, the emergence of new sources of supply, the increased costs of mineral development, the increased costs of pollution control, higher taxes, and the costs of recruiting and retaining labor.

Growth Prospects

As recently as 1974, federal and provincial ministers responsible for mineral policy were quite optimistic about the future of Canadian mineral production and exports during the remainder of this century. By late 1976 this optimism had been scaled down considerably.[75]

These changes have been reflected in lower levels of drilling by mining companies, which were down to about 60 percent of the 1962 high by 1971, with declines being relatively greater for exploratory than for developmental drilling. Monthly seasonally adjusted data for drilling activity continued at an irregularly lower level during the 1970s, although more than seasonal increases occurred during 1977.[76] Exploration expenditures in Ontario averaged about $23 million in the 1967-71 period, but were down to $16.3 million in 1973 and $14.2 million in 1976. No discovery leading to the probable construction of a new mine has been made in Ontario since 1971, and discovery costs per mine have exhibited an upward trend for at least the past twenty-five years.[77]

These developments and other factors highlighted in previous pages suggest that further increases in mineral production and exports over the balance of the present century are likely to be at much lower rates than previously. The increases are expected to continue to be less than the growth of real income in industrialized countries.

In recent years Canadian mining has been experiencing slower growth in world demand for mineral products, increased relative costs of labor and other materials, actual declines in levels of output (in relation to total inputs) from existing mines, high costs of labor turnover and labor shortages, and increased real costs of development of new mine sites. The policy environment within Canada has also become more adverse — increased federal taxes, still-unresolved conflicts on mineral taxation between the federal government and the provinces, and tighter environmental standards. The federal government and some provinces have been encouraging additional processing and manufacturing within Canada rather than the continued export of minerals in relatively unprocessed forms. The analysis in this chapter has suggested that moves in the direction of reducing the historic emphasis on crude exports and encouraging more manufacturing would be contrary to Canada's existing comparative advantage and would reduce, rather than increase, potential real incomes in Canada. A diversion of trade from the United States to Japan and Western Europe would probably further increase Canadian exports in unprocessed form.

A resolution of some of these contradictory goals and policies and the creation of a more stable environment of taxation and environmental standards would be of assistance in clarifying the environment for decision-making pertinent to the Canadian mining industry. A continuation of recent trends in the areas of taxation and environmental standards in the industry could check or reverse the growth in the mineral industry, a sector that has contributed to high real incomes and that has made a positive net balance of payments impact because of its significant comparative advantage in Canada in relation to its major trading partners, including the United States.

The Mineral Industry in a Balanced Economy

The opening pages of this chapter discussed the importance of export staples in Canada's historical development, and it has been pointed out that the mineral industry continues to make a more important contribution to investment and exports than is suggested by the extent of direct employment in the mining industry. Mineral production is relatively more important in Canada than in other high-income countries such as the United States, Japan, or Northwest Europe. It is clearly a sector in which Canada has a comparative advantage relative to the United States and to many other countries, in terms of both availability of mineral resources and levels of output in relation to labor and capital inputs.

The combination of government policies and corporate decisions at the end of the 1960s could be described as creating an environment in which current expenditures by individuals and governments were being partially supported and financed by the sale of non-renewable assets abroad. This was a continuation of a strategy that had been followed for decades, and historically it had served Canadians well. It led to high standards of living in Canada, and the persistent real-income gaps in relation to the United

States have become narrower in the 1970s with this strategy. The mining industry has played a major role in Canadian balance of payments viability and present living standards.

However, there are grounds for asking whether this strategy is the most appropriate policy for the future. Two adverse developments, noted earlier in this chapter, are the declining share of mineral products in world trade and the increased role of some developing countries in world mineral exports. These developments suggest that while Canada should not count on the mineral industry excessively for growth in the longer term, it would not be advisable to penalize the industry significantly, especially when this has been an area in which we have had a comparative advantage. If Canada had not had the mining industry and other natural resource industries to fall back on, it would have had to face much earlier the major issues it is now confronting.

One cannot consider the possibilities of a more balanced Canadian economy without considering secondary manufacturing, which is quantitatively a much larger part of the domestic economy than mining, both directly and indirectly. The preference for more secondary manufacturing and the unease about mining may reflect the view that secondary manufacturing deserves a higher status as a measure of the level of economic development achieved than does primary industry. This view is reflected in the frequent, somewhat derogatory, description of Canada as a hewer of wood and drawer of water. How might an industrial strategy of an enlarged manufacturing sector and a smaller natural resource sector to achieve a more balanced Canadian economy be implemented?

At the risk of oversimplification, there seem to be two main routes government policy could take in order to achieve such an objective. One route would be to discourage the development and the export of mineral products. The increased taxation of mineral industries in Canada during the 1970s illustrates a shift in the direction of a policy that could achieve such a result. Unfortunately, this policy would handicap the development of an industrial sector where Canada has a comparative advantage relative to other countries. An alternative strategy would be to introduce measures that would further narrow the persisting gaps in productivity between manufacturing industries in Canada and the United States and thus encourage a wider range of manufacturing industries to be more competitive in world markets. This strategy would promote a more balanced Canadian economy by encouraging a more efficient secondary manufacturing sector, thereby reducing the comparative disadvantage this sector has been experiencing for decades. This would lower the prices of manufactured products to the consumer and increase national income.

There seems little rationale for a policy encouraging high-cost production of secondary manufacturing products, since such costs must eventually be borne by the Canadian consumer and the taxpayer. But lowering costs will require major adjustments to increase real productivity levels in manufacturing to bring costs more into line with foreign alternative sources of supply, and such changes would not occur easily or quickly. It would appear that a necessary, but not a sufficient, part of such a strategy would be further reductions in tariff and non-tariff barriers to trade in manufactured products, both in Canada and in its major trading partners. A fuller discussion of that range of issues would take us beyond the confines of mineral resources in a U.S.-Canadian context. Even so, this chapter should help to put the mineral industry into the broader perspective of the kinds of major economic-policy problems now being debated in Canada.

Notes

1. For early statements by W. A. Mackintosh and H. A. Innis, see their articles reprinted in W. T. Easterbrook and M. H. Watkins, eds., *Approaches to Canadian Economic History* (Toronto: McClelland & Stewart, 1967), pp. 1-19. For further discussion of the staple approach, see the selections from A.R.M. Lower, M. H. Watkins, G. W. Bertram, and W. T. Easterbrook and the introduction by the editors in the same volume.

2. G.J.S. Govett and M. H. Govett, "The Inequality of the Distribution of World Mineral Supplies," *Canadian Mining and Metallurgical Bulletin,* August 1977, Figures 6, 8, and discussion on pp. 6-12.

3. David Ricardo, *Principles of Political Economy and Taxation,* with an introduction by William Fellner (Homewood, Illinois: Richard D. Irwin, 1963).

4. For a fuller discussion and a longer bibliography on the earlier literature, see D. J. Daly, "Canada's Comparative Advantages," paper presented to the Canadian Economics Association, Laval University, May 31, 1976. For evidence on the extent of differences in both the relative prices of factor inputs and relative commodity prices in different countries, see D. J. Daly, "Uses of International Price and Output Data," in D. J. Daly, ed., *International Comparisons of Prices and Output* (New York: Columbia University Press, 1972).

5. The comparison is based on an analysis using outputs of 22 major industrial products relative to employment in the mining industry in each country. It is thus comparable to the productivity comparisons for manufacturing in other studies referred to later in this chapter. The weights for the 22 products are based on the shares in the gross value of total output of the individual mineral products in the United States, using average U.S. prices. This is equivalent to a base-weighted quantity index. The coverage amounts to 92.6 percent of U.S. mineral production and 93.3 percent of Canadian production. Specifically, the 22 products are coal,

natural gas, crude petroleum, iron ore, copper, uranium, zinc, lead, gold, silver, china clays, lime, phosphate rock, salt, sulphur, pyrites, potassium salts, asbestos, nickel, cement, sand and gravel, and stone. (See Dorothy Walters, *Canadian Income Levels and Growth: An International Perspective* [Ottawa: Queen's Printer, 1968], pp. 233-34.) Sources are Bureau of Mines, *Minerals Yearbook*, 1973 (Washington, D.C.: U.S. Government Printing Office, 1974) 1:45, 88-89, and Energy, Mines and Resources Canada, *Canadian Minerals Yearbook*, 1971 (Ottawa: Information Canada, 1972), pp. 483-84, 547.

6. The comparisons of estimates of output per man-hour for manufacturing are based on updated estimates from E. C. West, *Canada-United States Price and Productivity Differences in Manufacturing Industries, 1963* (Ottawa: Information Canada, 1971). See Walters, op. cit., pp. 81, 83, for capital-stock comparisons. Results almost identical to those in the text are given in James G. Frank, *Assessing Trends in Canada's Competitive Position* (Ottawa: The Conference Board in Canada, 1977), p. 69.

7. For a fuller discussion of the evidence and analysis relating to Canadian manufacturing, see D. J. Daly and S. Globerman, *Tariff and Science Policies: Applications of a Model of Nationalism* (Toronto: University of Toronto Press, 1976), pp. 1-67.

8. See Daly and Globerman, op. cit., especially pages 18-61, for comparisons of prices, real wages, and productivities between the two countries.

9. It might be noted that alterations in the exchange rate (such as took place from the summer of 1975 to early 1978) do not change the general picture regarding comparative advantages. Prices of both exports of primary products and imports of manufactured products are largely determined and quoted in U.S. dollars. A depreciation in the Canadian dollar is reflected in a comparable increase in unit values of both exports and imports in Canadian currency, and the relative positions of various industries in the previous comparisons of price and productivity levels are still relevant and valid. The depreciation would raise the price and profit positions of both exporting and import-competing firms, the extent depending on the pricing policies of firms in the domestic market.

10. For a descriptive summary of a number of studies that appears fairly complete, see Natural Resource Institute, *Economic Linkages of the Canadian Mining Industry* (Kingston: Centre for Resource Studies, Queen's University, forthcoming), Chap. 2, "The National Economic Impact of the Mining Industry."

11. J. E. Stahl and D. J. McCulla, *The Canadian Mineral Industry and Economic Development* (Ottawa: Energy, Mines and Resources Canada, 1975), and D. J. McCulla and J. E. Stahl, *Quantitative Impact of Minerals on Canadian Economic Development: A Partial Analysis* (Ottawa: Energy, Mines and Resources Canada, 1977).

12. M. W. Bucovetsky, "A Study of the Role of the Resource Industries in the Canadian Economy," Working Paper No. 7301 (Toronto: Institute for the Quantitative Analysis of Social and Economic Policy, University of Toronto, 1973).

13. Stahl and McCulla, op. cit.

14. Economic Council of Canada, *Toward More Stable Growth in Construction* (Ottawa: Information Canada, 1974), pp. 108-09 and the charts and tables on those pages.

15. Geoffrey H. Moore, "The State of the International Business Cycle," *Business*

Economics, September, 1974, pp. 21-29, and Philip A. Klein, *Business Cycles in the Postwar World: Some Reflections on Recent Research* (Washington, D.C.: American Enterprise Institute for Public Policy Research, 1976).

16. The facts and analysis relating to the differences in business cycles between Canada and the United States have been examined in a series of studies by Gideon Rosenbluth, Ted Chambers, W. A. Beckett, and Derek White, applying the methods of business cycle analysis developed by the National Bureau of Economic Research. For further discussion and additional references see Derek White, *Business Cycles in Canada* (Ottawa: Queen's Printer, 1967), and D. J. Daly, "Business Cycles in Canada: Their Postwar Persistence," in Martin Bronfenbrenner, ed., *Is the Business Cycle Obsolete?* (New York: John Wiley and Sons, 1969), pp. 45-65.

17. Donella H. Meadows *et al., The Limits to Growth: A Report for the Club of Rome's Project on the Predicament of Mankind* (New York: New American Library, 1972).

18. Although the number of critical assessments is large, the following are illustrative: Christopher Freeman, "Malthus with a Computer," and K.L.R. Pavitt, "Malthus and Other Economists," in H.S.D. Cole *et al., Thinking about The Future: A Critique of the Limits to Growth* (Toronto: Clarke, Irwin & Company, 1973), pp. 5-13, 137-58; Carl Kaysen, "The Computer That Printed Out W*O*L*F*," *Foreign Affairs* 50 (1972): 660-68; William Nordhaus and James Tobin, "World Dynamics: Measurement Without Data," *Economic Journal*, 1974, pp. 1156-83; Robert Solow in Andrew Weintraub, Eli Schwartz, and J. Richard Aranson, eds., *The Economic Growth Controversy* (White Plains, N.Y.: International Arts and Sciences Press, 1973).

19. Anthony Scott, *Natural Resources: The Economics of Conservation*, 2nd ed. (Toronto: McClelland & Stewart for the Carleton Library, 1974), and H. J. Barnett and Chandler Morse, *Scarcity and Growth* (Baltimore: The Johns Hopkins Press for Resources for the Future, 1963). The latter study considered the contributions of the classical economists and of the conservation movement to this topic and examined the statistical evidence accumulated in previous Resources for the Future studies. This excellent study has not had the attention it deserves in the discussion of this topic that emerged a decade or more after its initial publication.

20. William Nordhaus, "Resources As a Constraint on Growth," *American Economic Review, Proceedings*, May, 1974, pp. 22-26.

21. Ibid., p. 24.

22. Ibid., p. 23; Nathan Rosenburg, "Innovative Responses to Materials Shortages," *American Economic Review, Proceedings*, June, 1973, pp. 111-18; David B. Brooks and P. W. Andrews, "Mineral Resources, Economic Growth, and World Population," *Science* 5 (July, 1974): 13-19; British-North American Committee, *Mineral Development in the Eighties: Prospects and Problems* (Montreal and Washington, D.C., 1976), pp. 3-6.

23. Ingo Walter, *A Discussion of the International Economic Dimensions of Secondary Materials Recovery* (Washington, D.C.: International Economic Studies Institute, 1975), tables on pp. 6, 12-13, and related discussion.

24. E. J. Mishan, *The Costs of Economic Growth* (Harmondsworth, Middlesex, England: Penguin Books, 1967).

25. A. C. Pigou, *Wealth and Welfare* (London: Macmillan & Co., 1912), p. 159.

The similar distinctions and example are retained in the later editions (see A. C. Pigou, *The Economics of Welfare*, 4th ed. [London: Macmillan & Co., 1932], p. 184).

26. Quotation and data are from William D. Nordhaus and James Tobin, "Is Growth Obsolete?," in National Bureau of Economic Research, *Economic Growth*, Fiftieth Anniversary Colloquium (New York: National Bureau of Economic Research, 1972) 5: 14-17.

27. Dan Usher, "The Measurement of Economic Growth," Discussion Paper No. 131 (Kingston: Queen's University Press, 1973). Some, but not all, chapters from this study have been published.

28. For a range of views that are highly criticial of the "no-growth" school or present a more balanced assessment, see some of the following surveys and studies: Wilfred Beckerman, *In Defence of Economic Growth* (London: J. Cape, 1974); J. H. Dales, *Pollution, Property and Prices* (Toronto: University of Toronto Press, 1968); D. N. Dewees, C. K. Everson, and W. A. Sims, *Economic Analysis of Environmental Policies* (Toronto: University of Toronto Press, 1975); Robert Dorfman and Nancy S. Dorfman, eds., *Economics of the Environment*, 2nd ed. (New York: W. W. Norton and Co., 1977); Harry G. Johnson, *Man and His Environment* (Montreal and Washington, D.C.: British-North American Committee, 1973); Allen V. Kneese and Charles L. Schultze, *Pollution Prices and Public Policy* (Washington, D.C.: The Brookings Institution, 1975); Milton Moss, ed., *The Measurement of Economic and Social Performance* (New York: Columbia University Press, 1973); Dennis M. Paproski, *Environmental Management in a Canadian Context*, Discussion Paper No. 73 (Ottawa: Economic Council of Canada, 1977).

29. R. H. Clark, "Solid Wastes and Resource Recovery in Canada," paper presented to the Royal Society of Canada, Queen's University, Kingston, Ontario, 1975.

30. Examples of such costs in both future investments and past expenditures in the provinces are found in George W. Poling, "Treatment of Mineral Industry Effluents in British Columbia," in James B. Stephenson, ed., *The Practical Application of Economic Incentives to the Control of Pollution: The Case of British Columbia* (Vancouver: University of British Columbia Press, 1977), p. 79, and Peter N. Nemetz, "Mining and Milling in British Columbia," in Stephenson, op. cit., p. 120.

31. Proctor and Redfern Limited, *Toward the Year 2000: A Study of Mineral Aggregates in Central Ontario*, report to the Ontario Ministry of Natural Resources (Toronto, 1974).

32. Helen Hughes, "Economic Rents, the Distribution of Gains from Mineral Exploitation, and Mineral Development Policy," *World Development* 3 (1975): 811-25.

33. M. W. Bucovetsky, "The Mining Industry and the Great Tax Reform Debate," in A. Paul Pross, ed., *Pressure Group Behaviour in Canadian Politics* (Toronto: McGraw-Hill Ryerson, 1974), pp. 87-114.

34. Eric Kierans, "Contributions of the Tax System to Canada's Unemployment and Ownership Problems," in John Chant, ed., *Canadian Perspectives in Economics* (Toronto: Collier-Macmillan Canada, 1972), Table 2.

35. D. J. Daly, *A Submission by the International Nickel Company of Canada Limited on the Proposals for Tax Reform* (Toronto: International Nickel Company of Canada

Limited, 1970), Appendix D1. For a fuller discussion of theory and evidence applied to Canada, see J. R. Melvin, *The Tax Structure and Foreign Trade: A Theoretical Analysis* (Ottawa: Information Canada, 1975).

36. Economic Council of Canada, *Looking Outward: A New Trade Strategy for Canada* (Ottawa: Information Canada, 1975), p. 17. A further study by Boadway and Treddenick used input-output methods to analyze the effects of removing both taxes and tariffs and concluded that the 1966 tax structure discriminated against, rather than encouraged, the mining industry and that the mining industry would expand relatively if both taxes and tariffs were removed. However, their study assumed no changes in manufacturing output in relation to inputs with the removal of tariffs. This is inconsistent with the experience of the auto industry in Canada with the U.S.-Canadian automotive agreement.

37. For example, Peter M. Watt, "Are We Overtaxing Our Resources?," *C. J. M. Bulletin*, September, 1977, pp. 116-23.

38. J. Alex Murray and Lawrence Le Duc, *A Cross-Sectional Analysis of Canadian Public Attitudes Toward U.S. Equity Investment in Canada*, Working Paper No. 2 (Toronto: Ontario Economic Council, 1975).

39. For a fuller discussion of the symptoms of economic nationalism and its costs and potential beneficiaries, see Harry G. Johnson, "A Theoretical Model of Economic Nationalism in New and Developing States," *Political Science Quarterly*, 1965, pp. 1969-85, reprinted in Harry G. Johnson, ed., *Economic Nationalism in Old and New States* (Chicago: University of Chicago Press, 1967). This model has been tested empirically for tariff and science policies in Canada in D. J. Daly and S. Globerman, *Tariff and Science Policies*, op. cit.

40. Statistics Canada, *Industrial Corporations: Financial Statistics*, 4th Quarter, 1976 (Ottawa, 1977), pp. 34-35.

41. D. J. McCulla, *Minerals in Canadian Economic Development: Recent Quantitative Analysis* (Ottawa: Energy, Mines and Resources Canada, 1976), Table 1, p. 14.

42. Ibid., p. 9.

43. Statistics Canada, op. cit. Base profit reflects net income of a corporation before income taxes and extraordinary items and before recording transactions that, to a greater or a lesser extent, can be altered at the discretion of corporate management (p. 14). These adjustments include depreciation, depletion, amortization, interest and dividend income, and all exploration and development charged to current expenses. The possible extent of "transfer pricing" of exports from wholly or partially owned Canadian subsidiaries on transactions with the parent is hard to assess. During the 1960s a number of independent pieces of evidence suggested that minerals were being exported at prices less than their prices for sale within Canada. A decision by a U.S. court that this practice was dumping and subject to countervailing duties was a factor in the sharp reduction in this practice by the early 1970s.

44. *Annual Report of the Minister of Industry, Trade and Commerce under the Corporation and Labour Unions Returns Act*, Part I, *Corporations* (Ottawa: Statistics Canada, 1977), pp. 40-41.

45. Ibid., calculated from details provided on pp. 168-69.

46. Ibid., p. 41.

47. Ibid., pp. 168-69, lines 34, 41.

48. Ibid., calculated from Statement 10 A, p. 40.

49. Colin Clark, *The Conditions of Economic Progress* (London: Macmillan & Co., 1957), Table III, pp. 510-20; Simon Kuznets, *Modern Economic Growth: Rate, Structure, and Spread* (New Haven: Yale University Press, 1966), Table 3.5, pp. 131-32; Simon Kuznets, *Economic Growth of Nations* (Cambridge: Belknap Press for Harvard University Press, 1971), Table 39, pp. 259-60, 159, 162.

50. Alfred Maizels, *Industrial Growth and World Trade* (Cambridge: Cambridge University Press, 1963), adapted from pp. 235-36.

51. Ibid., Table 9.1, p. 233.

52. Ibid., Table 4.1, p. 80.

53. Economic Council of Canada, *Looking Outward*, op. cit. pp. 68-70, and Herbert G. Grubel and P. J. Lloyd, *Intra-Industry Trade: The Theory and Measurement of International Trade in Differentiated Products* (New York: John Wiley and Sons, 1975).

54. These topics are discussed in a Canadian context in *Mineral Industry Trends and Economic Opportunities*, Mineral Policy Series (Ottawa: Energy, Mines and Resources Canada, 1976), pp. 18-24, and especially Figures 11 and 12, p. 19.

55. The Mining Association of Canada, "Labour Turnover and Shortages in the Canadian Mining Industry: An Analysis of the Principal Statistics," mimeographed (Ottawa, 1974).

56. L. T. Pinfield *et al.*, "Manpower Planning in Northern B.C.," paper presented at the Conference of the Canadian Association for Administrative Sciences, 1974.

57. Information provided orally by Cal Hoyt.

58. Robert B. Elver, "Human Resources and Resource Industries," *The Canadian Business Review*, Autumn, 1975, p. 27, which contains a chart on job vacancy rates per 1,000 jobs. Mining had about 23 per 1,000 in 1974, compared to the average of all industries of about 11 per 1,000. For additional evidence and discussion of the causes of turnover and labor shortages, see Aluminum Company of Canada, Ltd., *Report of the Task Force on Employee Turnover, 1973* (Kitimat, B.C., 1973); J. A. Mac-Millan, "Is Mining Industry Manpower Stability Possible?," *Canadian Institute of Mining Bulletin*, January, 1975, pp. 75-77; O. Fisher, "The Labour Shortage in Mining," talk presented at the Canadian Institute of Mining and Metallurgy, Toronto, May, 1975; Thomas F. Cawsey and Peter R. Richardson, *Labour Turnover in the Mining Industries: A Summary of Current Practices* (London, Ontario: Research and Publications Division, School of Business Administration, University of Western Ontario, 1975); *Women in Mining: The Progress and the Problems*, Mineral Policy Series MR 152 (Ottawa: Energy, Mines and Resources Canada, 1976); John Desmarais, "Labour/Management Relations and the Mineral Industry: An Overview," mimeographed (Ottawa: Energy, Mines and Resources Canada, 1976); George C. Hoyt, "Miners and Mining Towns in British Columbia," *Industrial Relations*, forthcoming. My thanks to Cal Hoyt and Sandor Derrick for making some of these studies available to me and for advice on this section.

59. The Mining Association of Canada, "Labour Turnover and Shortages in the Canadian Mining Industry," op. cit., pp. 9-11.

60. *Mineral Industry Trends and Economic Opportunities*, op. cit., p. 29.

61. Energy, Mines and Resources Canada, *Mining Communities*, Mineral Policy

Series (Ottawa, 1976), p. 11, relating to the 1965-74 period, inclusive.

62. Ibid., pp. 3-11.

63. William C. Wedley, "Resource Town Labour Turnover: The Impact of the Community," mimeographed (Burnaby, British Columbia: Simon Fraser University, 1976).

64. George C. Hoyt, "Miners and Mining Towns in British Columbia," op. cit.

65. Data compiled from *Trade of Canada* by Energy, Mines and Resources Canada in *Canadian Minerals Yearbook,* various issues, and forwarded by C. J. Cajka. However, the levels and share of exports to the United States do not correspond to the presentation in Figure 17, p. 23, in *Mineral Industry Trends and Economic Opportunities,* op. cit.

66. Naomi Black, "Absorptive Systems Are Impossible: The Canadian-American Relationship As a Disparate Dyad," in W. Andrew Axline *et al.,* eds., *Continental Community? Independence and Integration in North America* (Toronto: Mc-Clelland & Stewart, 1974); Peyton V. Lyon, *Canada-United States Free Trade and Canadian Independence* (Ottawa: Information Canada for the Economic Council of Canada, 1975).

67. Economic Council of Canada, *Looking Outward,* op. cit., Appendix C, pp. 203-06; Harry H. Postner, *The Factor Content of Canadian International Trade: An Input-Output Analysis* (Ottawa: Information Canada, 1976).

68. For additional evidence, analysis, and policy discussion, see D. J. Daly and S. Globerman, op. cit., and Economic Council of Canada, *Looking Outward,* op. cit.

69. *Mineral Industry and Economic Opportunities,* op. cit., Table 12, p. 43, and related discussion on pp. 35-45.

70. Ibid., Figure 14, p. 21. These issues are discussed in Louis Silver, *HRI Observations,* No. 6, *The Pursuit of Further Processing of Canada's Natural Resources* (Montreal: C. D. Howe Research Institute, 1975).

71. Joseph Lajzerowicz and Peter Reilly-Roe, "The Technology and Economics of Alternative Control Mechanisms in the Smelting and Refining Industries," in James B. Stephenson, ed., *The Practical Application of Economic Incentives to the Control of Pollution: The Case of British Columbia* (Vancouver: University of British Columbia Press for the B.C. Institute for Economic Policy Analysis, 1977), pp. 160-62.

72. T. Iwasaki, "A Summary Review of the Japanese Copper Smelting Industry," mimeographed (Toronto: Collier, Norris and Quinlan, 1972); Mitsubishi Metal Corporation, *Guide to Non-Ferrous Metals Smelting and Refining Technologies* (Tokyo, n.d.); Izumi Sukekawa, "Some Topics of Mitsubishi Continuous Copper Smelting Process and No. 3 Jumbo Tankhouse System," paper presented at the Pacific Northwest Metals and Minerals Conference, Seattle, Washington, May 4-6, 1977. Information and advice on the Japanese material from J. Iwasaki and F. M. Aimone are appreciated.

73. *Mineral Industry Trends and Economic Opportunities,* op. cit., pp. 24-27.

74. Mineral Resources Branch, *The Ontario Metal Mining Industry: Present and Future* (Toronto: Division of Mines, Ontario Ministry of Natural Resources, 1977), p. 18.

75. *Mineral Industry Trends and Economic Opportunities,* op. cit., pp. 1, 15-32.

76. Mineral Report 23, *Canadian Mineral Yearbook,* 1973 (Ottawa: Energy, Mines and Resources Canada, 1973), pp. 616-17. Monthly data from the Canadian Diamond Drilling Association have been seasonally adjusted by the author.

77. Mineral Resources Branch, *The Ontario Metal Mining Industry,* op. cit., pp. 6-7.

6

The Process of Making Mineral Resource Policy in Canada

GARTH STEVENSON

Introduction

A simplified, but for some purposes useful, model of mineral resource policy-making in Canada would view it as a series of relationships among three actors: provincial government, federal government, and private sector. Each can be viewed as an organization that, like all other organizations, seeks power, control, and expansion at the expense of other organizations. An additional, and fundamental, conflict of interest among the three actors is financial, with each wishing to maximize its share of the profits or "rents" from resource extraction at the expense of the others. This conflict can be minimized if resource prices are low and rents too negligible to be worth fighting about, but it can never disappear entirely. Alliances between two of the actors against the third are bound to be temporary, since they are only tactical devices to contain the more immediate of two permanent threats to the financial interest of each actor.

The model, however, is obviously an oversimplification in several respects. The private sector is varied and diverse in its interests. The provincial governments also differ among themselves, with some being heavily dependent on mineral resources for their revenues and for the health of the provincial economy, while for others resources are a fairly minor consideration. With regard to energy resources, although not to others, there are important conflicts of interest between provinces that import them and those that export them, to which the federal government may respond either by supporting the importers, as it did by delaying the increase in the price of oil and by supporting Polysar's plans to expand in Ontario rather than Alberta, or else by adopting a compromise position. An additional source of interprovincial conflict is the desire of each province to attract investment, growth, and employment at the expense of other provinces. Both the federal government and the private sector should, in principle, be neutral in regard to this type of conflict, but it is not clear that either is completely

167

neutral in practice. Interprovincial conflicts, like federal-provincial or government-private sector conflicts, can be temporarily ameliorated but never entirely resolved.

An additional complication arises from the fact that no government is a homogeneous single actor.[1] Each can better be viewed as a collection of organizational structures, with its own objectives, priorities, and external constituency to which it responds. Here too is a source of conflict that can be ameliorated but never resolved. Each department or agency strives to maximize its power and jurisdiction at the expense of others. In addition, each has specific objectives and priorities that conflict with those of others. The desire of departments responsible for fiscal policy to increase taxation conflicts with the tendency of mines and resources departments to support the private sector, to take only one example.

The outline of the policy-making process in the following pages begins with a description of the legal and constitutional framework within which the two levels of government operate. A subsequent section deals with the participants in policy-making at the provincial level, their differing objectives and priorities, and the political process by which policy emerges from their interactions. The scene then shifts to the federal level; and the participants, the objectives, and the processes at this level are described in a similar manner. The participation of the private sector and its relations with both levels of government are considered subsequently. Another section is devoted to federal-provincial relations, both formal and informal, insofar as these relate to mineral resource policy. The final section evaluates the process of policy-making as a whole and examines the feasibility of making it more "rational."

The Legal and Constitutional Framework

The politics of mineral resource development in Canada cannot be understood without some knowledge of the legal and constitutional framework within which development takes place.[2] This framework is very different from that existing in most other mineral-producing countries, a fact that has important consequences not only for domestic resource politics, but for Canada's external relations as an exporter of minerals. A number of major mining countries have federal institutions, since federalism is almost a necessity in countries of large geographical extent, and the larger a country's territory is, the more likely it is to have the resource base for a significant mining industry. In most federations, however, the central government is the legal owner of mineral resources (except to the extent that they are in private hands) and can dispose of these resources with little or no restraint or influence by subnational levels of government. Only Australia shares with Canada the not always enviable distinction of being an exception to this rule.[3]

The basic constitutional provision concerning mineral resources is section 109 of the British North America Act (BNA), which provides that "All Lands, Mines, Minerals and Royalties" belonging to the original provinces at the time of Confederation remain in provincial hands. The terms on which British Columbia, Prince Edward Island, and Newfoundland subsequently entered the federation contained similar provisions. Manitoba, Saskatchewan, and Alberta, on the other hand, were formed out of federal territories, and the federal government retained the mineral rights for some time after they achieved provincial status. In 1930, however, control over lands and resources was ceded to these provinces as well, placing them in the same constitutional position as the other provinces.[4]

Confederation took place at a time when minerals were of little significance in the Canadian economy, so that section 109 did not seem incompatible with the intention of giving the federal government the major responsibility for economic affairs. Apparently the few resources that the provinces were known to possess were viewed at the time as "matters of a merely local or private nature," to quote from another section of the act, and possibly as a much-needed source of revenue for provinces that had lost their right to levy customs and excise taxes as a result of Confederation. The significance of section 109 was fundamentally altered by the twentieth-century growth of the mining industry, the territorial expansion of Ontario and Quebec to their present boundaries, and the transfer of control over resources to the Prairie provinces.

Provincial Powers

The impact of provincial jurisdiction on the mining industry has been affected by certain principles of resource law inherited from the United Kingdom, notably the presumption of crown ownership and the separability of mineral rights from surface ownership of the land. The principle of crown ownership—which, in the light of section 109, means provincial ownership of most Canadian mineral resources—has been interpreted with varying degrees of rigor in different provinces and at different times. Ontario, for example, formally cedes its ownership of an ore body to the private operator when it grants the right to open a mine, while in some other provinces the mineral is held to be crown property until it leaves the ground. Nova Scotia law until recently held that gypsum was not a mineral and was therefore not owned by the Crown, an enactment recalling Bagehot's observation that Parliament could do anything but turn a man into a woman. Certain mineral rights in western Canada were long ago alienated into private hands, particularly those of the Hudson's Bay Company and the Canadian Pacific Railway.

Perhaps the chief significance of crown ownership in practical terms is the fact that it has been considered to imply some special rights of the provinces in regard to the taxation of mining enterprises, over and above the normal taxation to which all business enterprises are subject. This has led to major conflicts with the federal government as the other major beneficiary of taxation, most notably, although by no means exclusively, in the past few years. More generally, crown ownership is available as an ideological weapon for use against the federal government, against the private sector, or against provincial governments whose political opponents perceive them as being too generous to the private sector. Almost any federal intervention in resource policy can be branded as an attempt to deprive the provinces of their property, while the mining firms and their numerous friends in provincial capitals can at times be placed on the defensive by appeals to protect the public domain against the encroachment of private greed. The Constitution and the political culture thus ensure that the Canadian version of the almost universal demand in recent years for community control over mineral resources is at least as likely to be "economic provincialism" as "economic nationalism." The provincial governments, rather than the federal government, tend to be the vehicles and the beneficiaries of this widespread sentiment, yet it is the federal government that is expected to develop and express a Canadian position with respect to international resource issues, as well as to defend a national interest the very existence of which is implicitly denied by much of the rhetoric emanating from the provincial capitals.

The Constitution thus gives the provinces the right to determine who may develop and extract the mineral resources within their boundaries and under what terms and conditions development shall take place. It also gives them the right—and, from one point of view, the obligation—to derive considerable revenues from the mining industry, insofar as economic and political conditions allow them to do so. This is so not only for minerals occurring under crown land, but also for most of those occurring under privately owned land, since land ownership normally carries with it only surface rights.

Federal Powers

The federal government, however, has its own rights and responsibilities with respect to mineral resources, although not all of these have yet been clearly defined in relation to those of the provinces. In the Yukon and the Northwest Territories it exercises proprietary rights similar to those that the provincial governments enjoy within their own boundaries. Although the federal territories presently account for only about 3 percent of the value of Canadian mineral production, it is reasonable to assume that this proportion will increase, since they comprise more than one-third of Canada's land area and are now more accessible to exploration and development than they were in the past.

Federal proprietary rights also extend to offshore minerals, although this has not yet been clearly established in relation to the coasts of Newfoundland (including Labrador), the only province that was an independent dominion under the Statute of Westminster before it became a part of Canada. With this possible exception, federal ownership has been clearly established by the Supreme Court's opinion on the offshore minerals reference.[5]

In addition to these proprietary rights of the Crown, the federal government has certain legislative powers under the BNA Act that are relevant to mineral resource policy. The most important of these are "the regulation of trade and commerce" and "the raising of money by any mode or system of taxation." The former is the basis for federally imposed restrictions on the export of certain commodities, such as natural gas, and also ensures that a province cannot impede interprovincial trade by monopolizing its resources for local use. The unrestricted federal taxing power, which contrasts with the restriction of the provinces to direct taxation for provincial purposes, means that tax revenues extracted from the mining industry must, in fact, be shared between the two levels of government. The trade and commerce and the taxation powers together provide the basis for federal control over the tariff and, more generally, for federal responsibility in commercial dealings with other states.

The federal Parliament also has the power to assume jurisdiction over "works" by declaring them to be "for the general advantage of Canada" either before or after they come into existence. This power appears in the BNA Act as one of three exceptions to the general rule of provincial jurisdiction over "local works and undertakings." Its chief significance, at least to date, for mineral resource policy lies in the fact that the Atomic Energy Control Act of 1946 declared all existing and future uranium mines to be works for the general advantage of Canada. Thus a federal agency, the Atomic Energy Control Board, could be given the power under the same statute to make regulations with respect to uranium mining and prospecting anywhere in Canada and to regulate the production, import, export, transportation, refining, possession, ownership, use, or sale of uranium and other "prescribed substances." This statute remains in force today, although a few years ago the government of Ontario (one of the two provinces where uranium is mined) suggested that uranium should be restored to provincial jurisdiction. The Atomic Energy Control Act does not alter the fact that uranium, like other minerals, is considered to be a provincially owned resource if it occurs on the territory of a province. Provinces can thus impose royalties or mining taxes on miners of uranium just as they would on miners of any other mineral. They do not, however, have the regulatory powers over uranium mining that they have over other forms of mining, and the industry is, in practice, quite closely controlled by the federal government.

Although uranium is the only one of the mineral resource industries that Parliament has chosen to regard as "for the general advantage of Canada," there is no legal reason why any other type of resource extraction could not be brought under federal jurisdiction in the same way. The possibility that this might be the ultimate fate of the petroleum industry has recently caused some alarm in the province of Alberta. The government of that province has responded to the perceived threat by demanding that the declaratory power (section 92-10-c) be deleted from the BNA Act before Alberta will agree to any "repatriation" of control over the amendment of Canada's Constitution. Resort to section 92-10-c would certainly increase Ottawa's influence over the petroleum industry, but it would not interfere with Alberta's royalty revenues. In any event, it should be noted that Ottawa already controls the export of petroleum through the National Energy Board and sets the domestic price of crude oil after consultation with both the consuming and the producing provinces.

The Conduct of External Relations

Given the increasing importance of mineral resources in international affairs, it is worth considering whether the constitutional division of authority over mineral resources might have an impact on Canada's external relations. Because the BNA Act was designed as the constitution of a dependent state, it contains no explicit reference to foreign policy, apart from the now-obsolete section 132, which gives Ottawa power to ensure that Canada performs any obligations arising from British Empire treaties. The courts have since ruled that no such power exists with regard to treaties entered into by Canada itself, unless the subject matter of the treaty falls under federal jurisdiction. It is probably true, nonetheless, that almost any conceivable international agreement concerning minerals could be implemented by Ottawa under its "trade and commerce" power. At the same time, certain types of agreements would have political ramifications that might make Ottawa reluctant to enter into them without the approval of the provinces. Although Canada's refusal to join such cartels as the Council of Copper Exporting Countries (CIPEC) and the Association of Iron Ore Exporters (AIEC) appears to have motives unrelated to federalism, it is also true that federal efforts to control the export price or volume of important metallic minerals might be resented or resisted by the provinces. Export controls and administered prices for oil and gas have admittedly been implemented, but arguably this was possible only because Ontario and Quebec, as importers and non-producers of these commodities, supported the federal initiatives. Copper and iron, on the other hand, are produced in both Ontario and Quebec.

Policy-Making: The Provincial Level

Since all provinces have the same constitutional rights and responsibilities and since all except Prince Edward Island are significant producers of minerals, there has been little variation, at least until recently, in the machinery by which mineral resource policy is made and implemented. "Policy" was typically embodied in a mining act devoted mainly to specifying the terms and conditions under which the rights to explore for minerals, and to extract them from the ground, could be granted by the Crown to private operators. The language of these acts for the most part suggests an industry of small entrepreneurs and primitive technology, especially at the stage of exploration, rather than one dominated by a handful of giant corporations as is increasingly the case. In some provinces, such as Quebec, the mining act also specified the rates of mining taxation, but the increased emphasis on this aspect of policy in recent years has led all but the three Maritime provinces to provide for the taxation of mining enterprises in separate statutes.

Administrative Arrangements

Administrative arrangements for the implementation of mining legislation vary to some extent from province to province. In Alberta, New Brunswick, and Ontario, mineral and forest resources are the responsibility of the same department of government, although in Ontario this has been the case only since 1972. Forestry is of slight importance in Alberta, but in the other two provinces it is a significant sector of the economy, particularly in New Brunswick. British Columbia, Nova Scotia, and Saskatchewan have departments exclusively devoted to mineral resources. Newfoundland's Department of Mines and Energy, Quebec's Department of Natural Resources, and Manitoba's Department of Mines, Resources and Environmental Management are each responsible for both minerals and water resources, but not for forestry, which is handled in another department. Manitoba's department is unique, as its name suggests, in having responsibility for both the development of the mining industry and the protection of the environment, two objectives that may not always be compatible.

In New Brunswick and Manitoba all minerals are the responsibility of a division headed by an assistant deputy minister. In Ontario the head of the division of mines is called the executive director, and Alberta uses the term "director" for the head of its mineral division. Quebec has separate divisions for mines, water, and energy resources, although its energy resources, apart from hydro-electricity, are negligible. In British Columbia and Saskatchewan the mineral resource departments are divided into two branches, one for mining and one for petroleum. Newfoundland's department has a petroleum branch and an energy branch, each headed by an assistant deputy minister. In British Columbia the heads of the branches have the unusual title of associate deputy minister, while Saskatchewan, like Alberta, refers to them as directors.

In all provinces the breakdown into branches or divisions is based mainly on types of resources, producing a departmental structure well-adapted to close liaison with the private sector but having little capability for independent policy initiatives or for taking a holistic view of the provincial interest with respect to natural resources. Alberta appears to be an exception, with a division responsible for "finance"—in other words, for taxation and royalties—while another division has responsibility for "economic planning." Although divisions with these types of responsibilities may also have dealings with the private sector, their role is not to provide services to the private sector as do the other divisions, and their personnel are more likely to be aware that provincial interests and private sector interests do not always coincide.

As suggested above, mineral resources were until recently not highly "political," if politics implies controversy over objectives and a high degree of public interest. This fact shaped the pattern of policy-making and policy implementation in important ways. Since the problems to be resolved were considered mainly technical rather than political or economic, officials were recruited on the basis of practical knowledge of the mining industry or of expertise in such fields as mining engineering or geology. Almost by definition such expertise implies experience in the private sector, and personnel with such experience tend to work closely with acquaintances and former colleagues in the private sector on the basis of shared objectives and assumptions. The corollary of this circulation of personnel between the private sector and the mineral resource bureaucracy was the tendency of the latter to form a specialized group not easily assimilable into the larger provincial bureaucracy and lacking horizontal contacts with other ministries. Both factors together produced a clientelistic relationship between private and public sectors, with mineral resource officials both viewing themselves and being viewed by others as suppliers of services to the mining industry and as spokesmen for the industry within the councils of government.

Perhaps partly for this reason and partly because they account for a relatively small, and in recent years declining, proportion of provincial government expenditure, ministries of mines or resources and the politicians who preside over them do not rank particularly high in prestige, influence, or importance. Apart from René Lévesque, it would be difficult to cite a past or present resources minister in any province east of Manitoba whose name would merit inclusion in a general political history of the province in question. Even Lévesque owed his early fame to hydro-electricity and not to mineral policy, although the latter also fell within his jurisdiction as a member of the government headed by Jean Lesage.

Politically strong ministers have normally not been placed in charge of natural resources, presumably because it is assumed that their talents could be put to better use in departments whose operations inspire more interest on the part of the electorate, such as education, labor, and health, or in departments that have a broader impact on more than one area of policy. In turn, of course, the absence of strong ministers has weakened the resource departments and prevented them from having much effect on government policies and priorities, as suggested by their declining share of provincial budgets. This did not, however, cause them much concern as long as they were able to pursue their own objectives without interference from other departments, as was generally the case until recently.

New Approaches to Policy-Making Machinery

These conditions began to change as growing controversy surrounded the resource industries, and particularly mining, from about 1970 onward. Since the trend is well-known and by no means unique to Canada, it requires little comment or description in the present context. Resource industries were becoming associated in the public mind with environmental destruction, foreign ownership, economic subservience to the United States, the inequities of the tax system, and even unemployment (since they were alleged to provide fewer jobs per unit of capital investment than other sectors of the economy). Partly in response to these sentiments, some provincial governments perceived a need to reshape the departments responsible for mining into effective policy-making organizations, or else to create new organizations which supplemented and in part superseded them. In addition, other departments, such as provincial treasuries and newly created departments of the environment, began to have a significant impact on mineral resource policy.

Ontario established its Ministry of Natural Resources in 1972 as part of a general reorganization of the provincial bureaucracy and cabinet structure. The former Ministry of Mines and Northern Affairs was absorbed into the new ministry. A Mines Division consisting of operational sections with specific functional responsibilities assumed jurisdiction over the mineral industries. A further change took place in 1974, when a Mineral Resources Branch was inserted between the Mines Division and the operational sections for the explicit purpose of giving the ministry a capacity for "policymaking" and economic analysis. The ministry's annual report listed thirteen functions of the mineral resources branch. Included were research into mineral markets, commodities, and the behavior of multinational corporations; determining the extent of Ontario's resources and their position in relation to world supply and demand; analysis of existing programs and policies and development of new ones; and liaison with the federal government on mineral resource problems. The branch consists mainly of a small team of economists who have produced a considerable output of studies and reports, most of them available to the public. Information is exchanged with the private sector, with the federal government, and with foreign governments, particularly the U.S. Bureau of Mines and the governments of Michigan and Minnesota. Although the establishment of this branch was a step forward in that it gave the ministry some capacity for economic analysis, it should be noted that the branch is subordinate to the Mines Division and tends, like the latter, to express a viewpoint very similar to that of the private sector. Providing for economic analysis to be performed in a separate division reporting directly to the deputy minister, as in Alberta, would seem likely to produce a more balanced evaluation of the province's interests.

Another alternative, and the one most conducive to independence from the private sector, is to locate the economic-analysis and policy-planning unit entirely outside the department. Manitoba, for example, prefers to concentrate such functions in agencies that report directly to the cabinet. Both the small size of the province and the former NDP government's emphasis on "planning" are conducive to this approach. It is significant, for example, that the controversial and much publicized *Report on Natural Resources Policy in Manitoba* was prepared by Eric Kierans and his research assistants with practically no participation by the Department of Mines, Resources and Environmental Management.[6]

Saskatchewan is perhaps the most striking case of a province in which the Mineral Resources Department was effectively relegated to the sidelines by new policy-making machinery that emerged in response to new priorities. Although the province was governed by the CCF/NDP from 1944 until 1964, its resource policy in this period did not differ noticeably from that of other provinces. Times were changing, however, when the NDP returned to office after seven years in opposition, and Premier Blakeney's government embarked on a major effort to maximize the province's return from its resources by a combination of higher taxes and extension of the public sector at the expense of the private sector. The department was neither particularly sympathetic to these goals nor particularly well-adapted to pursuing them. The result was the formation of two new organizations, the Energy Secretariat and the Potash Secretariat, which reported to the cabinet and had no organizational ties to the department. The Energy Secretariat, however, is now in the process of being grafted onto the department, which is also for the first time headed by a deputy minister who did not come up through the departmental ranks and who has no experience in the mining or petroleum industries. As for the Potash Secretariat, it was never viewed as a permanent organization and will presumably disappear once the government's objective of taking over more than half the potash-mining capacity has been achieved.

It is not only in Saskatchewan, however, that the traditional resource bureaucracies have had their hegemony over mineral policy challenged by other organizations with different goals and priorities. As might be expected, the "old guard" of mining officials have not been sympathetic to what has been the most striking, and almost universal, trend of provincial resource policy in recent years — namely, the increase in levels of taxation imposed on the mining and petroleum industries. The impulse in this direction came from provincial treasuries and from cabinets, but the mines and resources departments and their friends in the private sector had little power to resist it.

Provincial Taxation of Mining

The traditional form of provincial mining tax has been based on the profit or net income of a mine and was levied until recently at very low rates. "Royalties," a term normally used for imposts levied on the basis of a fixed amount per unit of output, have always been collected from oil and gas producers but have been less commonly used to collect revenues from mining. Royalties are not, strictly speaking, taxes, but rather payments to the Crown in return for the removal of the Crown's non-renewable property. Because of the fluctuating prices of metals, they would have little relationship to ability to pay if imposed on that sector of the industry and would also encourage the industry to mine only the richest and most accessible deposits. Hence the tax on profit or net income has been more widely used. Until the 1970s the return from all types of resource taxes and royalties, except for those on petroleum, typically made no net contribution to general government revenues, since they were equaled or exceeded by the operating expenditures of the departments that serviced the resource industries.

After 1973, the year that saw both the publication of the Kierans report and the beginnings of the "energy crisis," all this changed very rapidly.

Alberta and Saskatchewan devised more complex systems of royalties to capture the benefits of rising oil prices. Ontario replaced its 15 percent mining-profits tax with a progressive tax at rates of up to 40 percent. Quebec, which already had a progressive tax, increased the maximum rate from a nominal 7 percent, which had been in effect for forty years, to 30 percent. Newfoundland retained fixed rates but increased them substantially. British Columbia increased royalties on coal to six times their previous level and experimented with royalties on metals at rates set by order-in-council, an experiment terminated by the restored Social Credit dynasty in 1976. Saskatchewan developed new systems of taxation for potash and uranium, while Manitoba increased the rate of its mining tax and supplemented it with a system of "basic" and "incremental" royalties, the latter being imposed on profits in excess of a "profit base" determined by the government. Even Nova Scotia, the only province that had traditionally imposed royalties rather than a profits tax on its mining industry, doubled the rate of royalties on coal and various other commodities.[7]

These innovations for the most part did not originate in the mines and resources departments of the various provinces, which were typically opposed to the view that the mining industry should be regarded as a potential major source of provincial government revenues. Given the close ties between these departments and the private sector, it is not surprising that they repeated privately, and even publicly, the private sector's arguments against increased taxation.[8] The weakness of the mines and resources departments in relation to political leaders and other sectors of the bureaucracy was revealed by their failure in almost every province to prevent important changes in resource taxation from taking place.

Particularly in the western provinces, much of the impetus for increased resource taxation came from the cabinets and from the premiers' offices. All the western provinces except Alberta had NDP governments between 1972 and 1975. All except Manitoba were important producers of energy commodities whose prices were rising rapidly, a fact of which politicians and the public were well aware. Resource taxation thus appeared as a possible solution to the problem posed by the seemingly irresistible and continuous rise in the costs of health and education that all the provinces were facing. A similar conclusion was reached, not only in the western provinces but elsewhere, by officials in the provincial treasury departments.

Participants in the Policy-Making Process

In all the provinces the treasury has become the most important and powerful department, staffed by officials who tend to comprise an elite within the provincial bureaucracy. This fact is a consequence of the evolution of federal-provincial fiscal arrangements over the past two decades, which has required highly qualified officials both to devise and implement increasingly complex and sophisticated systems of provincial taxation and to present the province's case in periodic renegotiations of the federal-provincial agreements.[9] Ontario has perhaps gone farthest in building its treasury department (known as TEIGA, or the Ministry of Treasury, Economics and Intergovernmental Affairs) into a powerful central mechanism for coordinating all aspects of government activity and managing the province's economy; but the other provinces, particularly Quebec, Alberta, and Saskatchewan, have not been far behind. Thus in any bureaucratic struggle between the treasury and the mines or resources department, the result is almost a foregone conclusion.

Mining taxation in Ontario was traditionally imposed and collected by the Mines Department, later the Ministry of Natural Resources, rather than by the Treasury. This practice was criticized in the 1960s by the Ontario Committee on Taxation, a body established to recommend changes in the province's tax system, on the grounds that there was a natural conflict between the objective of stimulating and serving the mining industry, on the one hand, and that of collecting revenue from it, on the other.[10] As in other metal-mining provinces, such as Manitoba and Quebec, the mining tax was not really viewed as a source of revenue, but more as a means of encouraging local processing and creating jobs. Reductions of the tax could be earned by smelting the ore in Canada, a policy whose antecedents in Ontario date back to 1907.

The Ontario Ministry of Natural Resources produced in 1973 a violent attack on Manitoba's Kierans report, and particularly on the latter's contention that economic rents resulting from high resource prices should accrue to the Crown rather than to private operators.[11] Nonetheless, in April, 1974, the Minister of TEIGA, John White, announced in his budget speech that a new progressive mining tax would replace the old flat rate of 15 percent, an innovation that he supported by arguing that "it is only fair that we secure for the people a higher return from our natural resources."[12] The new tax went into effect immediately, although the legislation imposing it was not adopted until a year later. The final form of the tax represented a negotiated compromise between TEIGA and the Ministry of Natural Resources. According to one official, the two departments "went through about fifteen different versions" of the tax before arriving at the compromise. The Natural Resources officials saw themselves as fighting for the industry against TEIGA's appetite for money and against what they viewed as a dangerous climate of opinion which required a "political" response from the government and which they attributed to irresponsible agitation by Eric Kierans and the NDP. In the end they succeeded to a considerable extent — aided, no doubt, by the highly conservative nature of the

Ontario government. Assessment and collection of the tax remained in the hands of the Ministry of Natural Resources, and the increase in the tax itself was largely offset by increases in the processing incentives. The new tax, while not welcomed by the mining industry, was one it could live with, and it was innovative enough to satisfy the Liberal opposition in the legislature, although not the NDP.

Manitoba's Department of Mines, Resources and Environmental Management also had a certain amount of success in resisting the winds of change, despite the fact that the department's own minister, Sidney Green, was reputedly the leader of the cabinet's left wing. In Saskatchewan, and temporarily in British Columbia, the resistance to change was much weaker and less successful. Saskatchewan's Mineral Resources Department was hardly involved at all in the establishment of new tax regimes for oil, potash, and uranium. The Saskatchewan Department of Finance did not even seek the views of the Mineral Resources Department, although it did consult directly with the private sector.

Although provincial treasuries and finance departments have provided the strongest and most successful threat to the monopoly that mines and resources departments previously enjoyed over mineral policies, there have been other competitors as well. Departments of the environment have been established in every province except Newfoundland, Quebec, and Manitoba, and the mining industry has been a principal target of environmentalists. Manitoba and Saskatchewan have departments of northern affairs, and Ontario announced its intention to establish one in early 1977. (The "nouveau Quebec" division in Quebec's Department of Natural Resources serves the same purpose.) In Saskatchewan the attorney-general has played a major role in mineral policy, partly because he is considered the second most powerful man in the governing party, but mainly because the province's controversial initiatives in mineral policy have involved it in a series of legal disputes with private interests and with the federal government. In Alberta the Minister and Department of Intergovernmental Affairs have been important for somewhat similar reasons. Quebec is the only other province with such a department, but mineral resource policies have contributed little to federal-provincial conflict in Quebec's case.

A final set of participants in the making of provincial mineral resource policy that must be mentioned are the various crown corporations and other quasi-independent agencies that the provinces have established in recent years as a means of intervening directly in various aspects of the mining and petroleum industries. Some of these agencies, particularly those concerned only with exploration, have played a modest role in support of the private sector, while others have entered into competition with it or attempted to supplant it. Among the earliest of the former type were

Quebec's SOQUEM, established to explore for minerals in 1965, and SOQUIP, which appeared four years later and was supposed to explore for petroleum.[13] Manitoba Mineral Resources Limited, similar to SOQUEM, dates from 1971, and the Saskatchewan Mining Development Corporation from 1974. All these agencies are empowered to enter into joint ventures with private firms. Alberta Energy Company, established in 1973, is involved in the development of the tar sands but does not engage in exploration. Saskatchewan Oil and Gas Corporation and Saskatchewan Potash Corporation, both established by the present NDP government, are provincial crown corporations of a type more threatening to the private sector. The former may eventually become the major producer of oil in the province, although the government is clearly in no hurry to see this happen. The latter was established with the explicit objective of bringing more than half of the potash-mining industry under government ownership, and this is well on the way to being achieved. If a province's mineral resource industries were predominantly in the public sector, a mines or resources department, at least of the type that has traditionally existed in Canadian provinces, would be practically superfluous. Saskatchewan is the only province that shows any signs of moving in this direction.

Policy-Making: The Federal Level

Federal involvement in mineral resource policy has been continuous since Confederation, but has always been less direct, less extensive, and less important than that of the provinces. The Geological Survey of Canada was formed as early as 1842. With the acquisition of the Hudson's Bay Company territories in 1869, the federal government became the proprietor of lands and resources in a territory comprising more than half of Canada's present area, and the Department of the Interior was established to exercise the responsibilities of ownership. Little development of mineral resources took place in the federal territories, however, and the department was mainly concerned with the disposal of agricultural land to settlers. Federal ownership of mineral resources was reduced by extending the boundaries of Ontario and Quebec, both of which reached their present limits in 1912, and by ceding public lands and resources to the Prairie provinces in 1930. After 1930 the Department of the Interior was dismantled, and a new Department of Mines and Resources was established. It exercised both the remaining proprietary rights of the federal government, now confined to areas north of the sixtieth parallel, and a broader but less clearly defined interest in the Canadian mining industry, of which the Geological Survey was one manifestation. Growing interest in the North after World War II led to the establishment of the Department of Northern Affairs and

National Resources, an event that left the older department, now known as Mines and Technical Surveys, in a position of minimal importance.[14]

Department of Energy, Mines and Resources

In 1966, however, the Department of Energy, Mines and Resources was established as part of a general reorganization of government departments. This occurred at a time of considerable, although misguided, optimism concerning offshore petroleum resources, which the federal government believed, and the Supreme Court later confirmed, were under federal jurisdiction. It was also a time when resource issues were taking on international ramifications that could not safely be left to the provinces, a fact that had recently been demonstrated by the fiasco of the Columbia River Treaty.[15]

Establishment of the new department was supported by all parties in Parliament, but there was some discussion of the division of responsibilities between it and the Department of Indian Affairs and Northern Development. Although the latter's name would no longer include reference to resources, the department would continue to act on the federal government's behalf as proprietor of resources north of the sixtieth parallel, while the new department, in addition to its responsibilities inherited from Mines and Technical Surveys, would act as proprietor of resources on the continental shelf. This division of authority was criticized, as it deserved to be, by the official Opposition in 1966, but the disappointing results of offshore exploration have made it of little practical significance, at least so far. There remains, however, a division of authority in another sense, although one more easily justified. Indian Affairs and Northern Development exercises powers analogous to those of a provincial department of natural resources in the Northwest Territories and the Yukon. Thus decisions concerning minerals in these areas must involve both departments, and the relations between them tend to resemble those between the federal government and a province. Energy, Mines and Resources cannot impose its will with respect to territorial resources any more than it can with respect to provincial resources, and relations between the two departments are by no means without friction.

Most of the personnel of Energy, Mines and Resources are located in the units inherited from Mines and Technical Surveys, which are now grouped under an assistant deputy minister in what is called the Science and Technology sector. This part of the department performs services for the mining industry such as mapping, surveying, and various kinds of research. Policy-making, insofar as it exists, takes place in two other sectors known as Energy Policy and Mineral Development, each headed by an assistant deputy minister. Energy Policy, the larger, older, and better-known of the two, is concerned with oil, gas, coal, electricity, and uranium.

Mineral Development deals with metals and miscellaneous minerals such as potash and asbestos.

Although on paper the Energy Policy and the Mineral Development sectors look much the same, the nature of federal concern with the two sets of commodities is quite different. The various energy sources are to some extent interchangeable, a fact that both justifies and facilitates treating "energy policy" in a holistic manner. An additional rationale for energy policy is the problem of scarcity, which suggests such responses as conserving supplies, limiting the growth of consumption, and exploring alternatives to traditional sources of energy. These tasks are only indirectly related to the management of mineral resources, but the Energy Policy sector is concerned with all of them.

The Mineral Development sector deals with commodities that are not interchangeable with one another, not in short supply, and of little apparent concern to the general public, except in the localities where they are produced. The direct responsibility for encouraging and regulating the production of these commodities is divided between the provincial governments and the Department of Indian Affairs and Northern Development. The rationale for the Mineral Development sector's existence, therefore, must be found mainly in the external ramifications of Canada's position as a major exporter of these commodities and the need for an integrated Canadian approach in dealings with foreign markets and foreign competitors. The validity of this argument for federal involvement is accepted, at least up to a point, by the provinces, on whose cooperation the Mineral Development sector largely depends. At the same time, these international aspects of mineral resource policy demand the involvement of other federal departments, particularly External Affairs and Industry, Trade and Commerce. The federal government itself thus speaks with a multiplicity of voices.

Like its provincial counterparts, Energy, Mines and Resources has a large proportion of personnel with experience in the mining and the petroleum industries. This is true of the Science and Technology sector, for fairly obvious reasons, but it is equally true of the two "policy" sectors, whose senior personnel pride themselves on their knowledge of the private sector and their close working relationships with it. There is thus some tendency for officials in other federal departments to view Energy, Mines and Resources as the voice of the mining and petroleum industries within the councils of government, in much the same way as provincial departments of mines are viewed by other segments of provincial bureaucracies.

Involvement of Other Departments

The list of other federal departments involved in various aspects of mineral resource policy is a surprisingly long one, particularly in view of the constitutional limitations on federal powers in this area. The explanation for the large number of participants lies in the fact that the federal government plays a number of different roles, each of which involves a different set of departments and agencies, not to mention different branches and divisions within departments. Indian Affairs and Northern Development is involved because the federal government owns the resources north of the sixtieth parallel. Industry, Trade and Commerce and External Affairs are involved because of the external aspects of resource policy, including trade, foreign investment, and more recent concerns such as UNCTAD and the law of the sea. The Department of the Environment assesses the environmental impact of all new resource projects and developments that receive federal assistance. The Department of Regional Economic Expansion (DREE) has become an important participant, since it now has a broad concern with economic development in all ten provinces, and not just in the traditionally impoverished regions. A large proportion of the specific projects whose costs are shared by the federal government and provincial governments under DREE's general agreements with the provinces are related to the development of mineral resources. Even the Department of Justice has become involved in legal challenges to some of Saskatchewan's resource legislation, either as a co-plaintiff or an interested observer.

The Department of Finance is involved in mineral resource policy in two entirely different ways. The first of these is through its Resource Programmes division, which must scrutinize all proposals for federal spending on the development of natural resources, both renewable and non-renewable. These terms of reference automatically involve it in virtually all resource developments in the northern territories, all of those in the provinces that are assisted by DREE, all in which the federal government is a direct participant, such as the Syncrude project, not to mention transportation projects associated with resource development. The division also represents Finance in more general discussions of resource policy, such as those associated with the three-phase "mineral policy for Canada" that has been devised in consultation with the provinces since 1973. Its main work, however, is in connection with specific projects, and it is represented on all the interdepartmental committees or "working groups" that consider whether a project should be approved. The other departments most frequently represented on such committees, apart from Energy, Mines and Resources, are DREE and Indian Affairs and Northern Development. Less frequent participants, depending on the nature of the project, include Transport, Public Works, and External Affairs.

The second area of involvement by Finance is that of resource taxation, which is among the many responsibilities of the Tax Policy and Federal-

Provincial Relations Branch. At the federal level, as well as at the provincial level, the taxation of the mining and petroleum industries underwent fundamental changes in the early 1970s. These began with the (Carter) Royal Commission on Taxation, some of whose recommendations were implemented in extensive amendments to the federal Income Tax Act in 1972. Carter was very critical of the mining and petroleum taxation then in force, arguing that these industries did not contribute their fair share of tax revenues.[16] The amendments that followed included termination of the three-year tax exemption for new mines (first introduced as an emergency measure during the Depression) and the substitution of earned for automatic depletion allowances, which was originally to have been delayed until 1977 but actually came into force in 1974.

The 1972 tax legislation also provided an additional abatement of corporation tax to the provinces after 1976, to replace the traditional system whereby provincial mining taxes and royalties had been deductible as business expenses from the income liable to federal corporation tax. In 1973 the Department of Finance became concerned that the upward trend of resource taxation in the western provinces was eroding the federal tax base. As a result, the federal budget of May, 1974, provided for non-deductibility to take effect immediately, unleashing a storm of protest from the provinces far in excess of that provoked by the income tax legislation two years previously. The federal NDP, largely under pressure from its allies in Saskatchewan, voted against the budget, abandoning the minority government it had upheld for two years. In the July election that followed, the Liberals were returned with a majority, and non-deductibility was reintroduced in a new budget in November. In the following year's budget the pill was sweetened slightly by the introduction of a "resource allowance" whereby 25 percent of profits could be deducted.

These tax changes, like most others, were the result of initiatives within the Department of Finance. The reasons for them were related to fiscal policy and the desire for greater revenues, not to resource policy as such. Non-deductibility was introduced in 1974 because of the belief that the new provincial royalties were, in effect, subverting the federal-provincial agreement on the division of corporation taxes. Energy, Mines and Resources (EMR), which had little interest or expertise on taxation matters, was apparently not consulted and generally opposed the changes. It is interesting to note that EMR subsequently established a Financial and Corporate Analysis Division in the Mineral Development sector and a Financial and Corporate Analysis Advisor in the Energy sector so that it might have some input into future decisions on resource taxation.

The international aspects of mineral policy involve a different set of actors in Ottawa than do the domestic aspects, apart from Energy, Mines and

Resources, which naturally participates in both. Industry, Trade and Commerce and External Affairs are the other departments most heavily involved in the international aspects. The former participates mainly through its rather oddly-named Office of General Relations, which includes a General Trade Policy Branch, responsible for commercial policy, and a Commodity Branch, responsible for commodity agreements such as those the developing countries are attempting to promote through UNCTAD. Although this department is usually identified with the secondary-manufacturing sector of the economy, the practice in multilateral trade negotiations of bargaining concessions in one area against concessions in another means that it cannot ignore the importance of the mineral sector in Canada's external trade. The fact that mining, smelting, and processing operations are often integrated is another reason for its interest, as is the importance of the mineral industries as sources of energy and raw materials for Canadian industry.

Industry, Trade and Commerce administers the Export Permits Act, which gives the government the power to control the export of materials and commodities. Uranium falls under this act, although in this case the department invariably acts on the advice of the Atomic Energy Control Board. In other cases it acts unilaterally. In one recent instance the act was used to terminate the sale to an Eastern European country of a mineral used in the manufacture of lasers. The exporter happened to be a firm in which a large share of the equity was held by a provincial government, and the province protested against the decision, which was also unwelcome to External Affairs because of the possible impact on Canadian relations with the country in question. The decision, however, was not reversed.

Industry, Trade and Commerce generally expresses rather conservative viewpoints that reflect those of its constituency in the business community. It was the main center of opposition to Canadian participation in Third World resource cartels such as CIPEC and the Iron Ore Producers' Association, an idea that had some supporters in other federal departments. Industry, Trade and Commerce also wanted the federal government to oppose the takeover of potash mines by the government of Saskatchewan, despite the fact that the province was unquestionably within its legal rights. On this occasion the department was not successful in winning support for its point of view.

External Affairs participates in mineral resource policy through several of its divisions, the most important being the Commercial Policy Division. The Transportation, Communications and Energy Division is involved in decisions concerning petroleum and pipelines. Questions involving the export of uranium and other nuclear materials, which has become highly controversial in recent years, also fall under this division's area of concern. The Federal-Provincial Relations Division of External Affairs may become involved when provincial resource policies have an international impact, and will be considered below in the section on intergovernmental relations. Saskatchewan's nationalization of potash provided an instance in which the division seized the opportunity to play a role that benefited both federal and provincial interests.

Other Federal-Level Participants

The federal government, like the provinces, has not confined its concern with mineral resources to expression through departmental structures. Regulatory agencies play an important part in certain aspects of policy, particularly the Atomic Energy Control Board and the National Energy Board. The Foreign Investment Review Agency might also be cited, although it has not to date played a particularly important part with respect to the resource industries. The federal government also participates directly in mineral resource extraction through crown corporations and other agencies. Eldorado Nuclear Limited has existed since 1944 and mines uranium in Saskatchewan. Cape Breton Development Corporation operates coal mines in Nova Scotia and is the major coal producer there. Petro-Canada Limited was established as a national petroleum company in 1975, and the following year it purchased all the shares of Atlantic Richfield Canada Limited, thereby becoming a producer of both oil and natural gas. Petro-Canada has also acquired the federal government's 45 percent interest in Panarctic Oils, a public-private consortium formed in 1967, and its 15 percent share of Syncrude Canada, whose other shareholders are the governments of Ontario and Alberta and three major oil companies. The Canada Development Corporation holds about one-third of the equity in Texasgulf, which has important metal-mining operations in Ontario and elsewhere. The federal government is also a participant in Nanisivik Mines Limited, which is developing a lead-zinc mine on Baffin Island. It might be noted that the federal agencies listed above report to Parliament through several different ministers.

Despite the range and complexity of federal involvement in the mineral resource industries, it is noteworthy how few mechanisms exist for the development and implementation of coordinated policy in this area. There is, for example, no cabinet committee on resources, and there do not seem to be any interdepartmental standing committees at the official level that deal with resources, with the exception of the Advisory Committee on Northern Development, whose responsibilities include a wide variety of economic and social questions. Interdepartmental liaison depends for the most part on informal contacts, exchanges of memoranda, or *ad hoc* bodies of short duration, such as the working groups that consider federal funding of specific resource projects.

The Role of the Private Sector

It is now well-known, at least to political scientists, that interest groups and other non-governmental actors play important roles in Canadian policy-making.[17] The mineral resource industry is no exception to this generalization. No account of the policy-making process can be complete if it neglects the participation and involvement of the private sector at both levels of government.[18]

Although "the private sector" has been referred to several times in the preceding pages, no attempt has been made to define the concept, which in fact obscures the heterogeneity of what is included. Of basic importance is the distinction between the petroleum (oil and gas) industry, on the one hand, and the mining industry, on the other, which is reflected in the existence of separate associations of interest groups for the two sectors. The two have very different characteristics: petroleum is concentrated in the far west, is overwhelmingly foreign-controlled, is a major item of interprovincial trade, is constantly and increasingly in demand, and is subject to price and export controls by the federal government. Metal mining is concentrated mainly in the Laurentian Shield, has a significant Canadian-owned element, accounts for little interprovincial trade, faces problems of fluctuating price and demand, and operates in a more free-market situation. Thus it is not surprising that their interests are divergent enough to require separate associations.

Within both sectors there are further elements of heterogeneity: between large, medium-sized, and small firms; between fully integrated firms that process or refine their products and those that only extract them; and between Canadian-owned and foreign-owned firms (although a few are difficult to classify). In addition to the mining and petroleum-extracting firms themselves, there are a number of contracting firms that supply them with services and expertise and that should also be considered part of the industry. A final distinction is between genuinely private firms and those totally or partially owned by one level of government or the other. This distinction has consequences for intra-industry politics, as suggested by the odd fact that Petro-Canada has been refused admission to the Canadian Petroleum Association, although firms controlled by the British and the French governments are members in good standing.

Industry Associations

The private sector is represented by a number of associations or interest groups. In the petroleum industry the Canadian Petroleum Association represents the larger firms, while the Independent Petroleum Association of Canada represents the smaller ones.[19] In the mining industry the Mining Association of Canada (MAC) ostensibly and to a large degree in fact represents everyone, apart from the coal-mining firms, which have their own association. There are also provincial mining associations having no organizational links with the MAC, although they represent the same members. In Quebec the asbestos producers have an association separate from that of the metal producers.

Although provincial and national associations represent the same member firms, the individuals who serve on their governing bodies differ. Since head offices are concentrated in Ontario and Quebec, provincial associations in the other provinces tend to consist of individuals relatively low in rank and authority, usually managers of local operations rather than senior executives. Both types of associations are primarily intended to serve as means of contact with government, but in recent years have devoted increasing attention to public relations, largely in an effort to counteract what they view as a climate of public opinion hostile to the resource industries.

Most formal contacts between industry and government seem to be through the associations, although some are made by individual firms. In some cases the distinction is unreal, since the same individual may at different times make representations on behalf of both the firm that employs him and the association of whose governing body he is a member. As might be expected, it is the largest firms that are most likely to make individual contacts and to have their executives elected to positions in the associations. A few of the larger firms have made special efforts to equip themselves for more effective relations with government: Inco, for example, has a Director of Government Relations and a Department of Public Affairs.

More than most industries, mining and petroleum are identified with attitudes of "rugged individualism," fundamentalist notions of "free enterprise," and an ideological aversion to government intervention in the marketplace. This image has a considerable basis in reality, but the reality is changing; and younger managers, more remote from the colorful origins of their industries but more aware of their industries' contemporary needs, recognize, at least privately, that the state is often an ally and supporter rather than an antagonist. Governments have always, in fact, assisted the mining and petroleum industries (for example, by providing geological surveys and infrastructure), but the variety of ways in which they do so has increased, and the need for their assistance against foreign competitors, who are usually receiving extensive support from their governments, is increasingly, although sometimes grudgingly, appreciated. At the same time the capacity, and the inclination, of governments to take policy actions inimical to these industries, through taxation, expropriation, environmental standards, price and export controls, or restrictions on foreign ownership, has also increased. This fact is recognized and leads to a certain ambivalence in dealings with governments, both federal and provincial.

Relations at Provincial and Federal Levels

The views of the mining industry on federalism and the industry's orientation toward the two levels of government appear to have changed considerably in the past few years, although it is possible that the change will prove to be temporary rather than permanent. Until a few years ago, relations with the provinces — or, more precisely, with their departments of mines and resources — were invariably intimate and friendly. Relations with the federal government were less extensive; it was viewed as being more remote and probably less sympathetic. At the time of the Carter Commission report and the subsequent federal White Paper on Taxation, the provincial governments — particularly those of western Canada, which depended heavily on the resource industries — fulfilled the expectations of the private sector by lobbying vigorously against tax reforms that would be detrimental to these industries.[20]

Unfortunately for mining and petroleum firms, the provinces soon began to behave in a less benign manner. The formation of NDP governments in three western provinces between 1969 and 1972 was a harbinger of worse news to come, and the replacement of the Social Credit government in Alberta by Peter Lougheed's more vigorous and interventionist Progressive Conservative party was probably viewed by the petroleum industry with only slightly greater enthusiasm.[21] The provinces now borrowed a leaf from the federal book by increasing their own resource taxes. Tighter environmental standards in some provinces, the Kierans report in Manitoba, and the takeover of potash mines in Saskatchewan completed the disillusionment of the private sector.

As a result of these events, the mineral resource industries appear to have discarded some of the pro-provincial bias that distinguished them in earlier years. Both publicly and privately, industry spokesmen have appealed to Ottawa to rescue them from high provincial taxes and royalties and to make the burden of taxation on their industries more uniform across Canada. They do not, however, explain how they expect the federal government to do this under existing constitutional rules; and the federal government's major initiative in this direction, the decision to make royalties nondeductible in 1974, is widely viewed as having worsened the situation and as having failed to change the behavior of the provinces. Whether federal support for legal challenges to Saskatchewan's oil and potash taxes will reap any benefits for the private sector remains to be seen.

Despite its disillusionment with the provinces, the private sector has not replaced its pro-provincial bias with a pro-federal bias. Some provincial governments, such as those of Newfoundland and, since the defeat of the NDP, British Columbia, are still perceived as highly sympathetic to the resource industries. Governments in provinces dependent on mining or petroleum for their prosperity share a common interest with the private sector, regardless of their philosophical views, and thus inevitably act as spokesmen for the resource industries in certain circumstances. Most important of all, the federal government is perceived as being preoccupied with the problems of the urbanized Quebec-to-Windsor corridor and thus as basically uninterested in the resource industries of the hinterlands. The federal government is often accused of not recognizing the importance of mineral resources and of ranking them too low on its scale of priorities. In addition, certain federal initiatives of recent years are resented by the private sector, particularly the establishment of Petro-Canada. Thus Ottawa is blamed both for intervening and for not intervening in the affairs of the resource industries.

Channels for Governmental Access

Access to both levels of government is available through a variety of formal and informal means. At the provincial level the multitude of informal and personal contacts with officials in the mines and resources departments are still of the greatest importance, although their usefulness has been lessened by the declining influence of these departments in policy-making. Formal submissions are also made on certain occasions, both by provincial mining associations and by individual firms. The dependence of bureaucracies on information supplied by the mining companies provides an important avenue of influence, more than counterbalancing the dependence of the companies on favors granted by the Crown. The growing tendency of bureaucracies to produce reports, studies, forecasts, and various kinds of "research" has increased their dependence on information supplied by the private sector. Even the devising of taxes and royalties to be imposed on the resource industries requires the cooperation of the potential taxpayers themselves in supplying information about their profits, prices, expenses, and the level of taxation that they can bear without being forced to suspend operations. Thus the practice of discussing potential tax and royalty changes with the industry before announcing them in the provincial legislature is practically universal. Usually the industry is happy to cooperate in these discussions and to supply information, presumably of a sort that does not overstate its ability to endure higher taxes. The Saskatchewan potash producers failed to cooperate in designing new taxes for themselves in 1975, and this fact contributed to the provincial government's decision to take over some of the mines itself.

At the federal level the division of policy-making authority among several departments has led the mining and petroleum industries to seek multiple points of access. Informal and personal contacts exist with officials in Energy, Mines and Resources, which is also the target of many submissions and representations. In addition, the minister of that department meets occasionally with the National Advisory Council on the Mining Industry, a body representing the private sector. The Council, however, has met only rarely under the present minister, Mr. Gillespie, and seems to be no longer a significant means of access, if it ever was.

Mining and petroleum firms also make frequent representations to the Tax Policy Division of the Department of Finance, either individually or through their associations. The Resource Programmes division of the same department has fewer dealings with the private sector. Industry, Trade and Commerce and, to a lesser extent, External Affairs provide opportunities for the private sector to express its views on international aspects of resource policy. The uranium industry interacts extensively with the Atomic Energy Control Board.

Despite frequent public lamentations by the resource industries about government policy at both levels, it would be difficult to support the proposition that they lack opportunities to make their views known and to influence government policy. There are grounds for suspecting, as some officials do, that the private sector is, in fact, less dissatisfied with federal and provincial resource policies than its public statements would suggest. Many of the difficulties of the resource industries are of external origin and will require more, rather than less, intervention by Canadian governments, particularly the federal government, if they are to be resolved. Probably the greatest obstacle to this is the fragmentation of policy-making authority both between governments and within governments, which makes it difficult for coherent and successful policies to emerge.

Intergovernmental Relations

Machinery for intergovernmental relations tends to arise and multiply in response to situations where the decisions and activities of one government have consequences for other governments, creating potential conflict between them. Although the area of mineral resource policy would seem to fit this description, little institutional machinery for the resolution or avoidance of intergovernmental conflict has developed, a fact that has recently been lamented in a lengthy monograph.[22] Presumably this institutional lag reflects to a large degree the recent origin of the circumstances that have made mineral resource policy an area of contention. It is also, however, in part a result of the fragmentation of decision-making authority within each level of government. If a single strong department in each of the governments had overall responsibility for mineral resource policy, consultation, coordination, and even conflict resolution might be relatively simple, but this is not in fact the case.

At the official level, relations appear to be reasonably satisfactory, although not particularly intimate, between the provincial resources or mines departments and the federal department of Energy, Mines and Resources. The similar background and professional expertise of officials at both levels, as well as the shared objective of promoting the expansion and development of the mining industry, make it unlikely that much conflict will develop. There is a certain amount of informal and more or less continuous interaction between officials at the two levels, but to a large extent the provincial departments can still perform their usual tasks virtually without reference to the federal government. The federal department seems to be perceived by some provincial officials as larger and more lavishly funded than it needs to be, but perhaps inferior to provincial departments in efficiency of operation. It is not, however, considered threatening or unfriendly.

Conference of the Provincial Ministers of Mines

An important opportunity for contacts among senior officials and their political superiors is the annual Conference of the Provincial Ministers of Mines, an institution first established in 1947. The fact that the federal minister is not formally a member of the conference suggests how limited the role of the federal government in mineral resource policy was a generation ago. Nevertheless, the federal minister or a representative of his department always attends the annual meeting as an observer. In 1977 the federal department was represented at the conference by an assistant deputy minister.

The conference is not really, and was not intended to be, a conflict-resolving mechanism. Its chief purpose is to exchange ideas and information through personal contacts among those involved in mineral-resource-policy implementation. Its annual meetings, which have been extensively described elsewhere,[23] are attended not only by the ministers but by large numbers of departmental officials and some representatives of the private sector. The chief reason the conference does not contribute significantly to conflict resolution is not the anomalous status of the federal representatives, but the lack of representation of departments other than those directly responsible for mines and resources. It is in these other departments, particularly the provincial treasuries and the federal Department of Finance, that most of the recent conflict over mineral resource policy has arisen. Good relations among mines and resource departments are not enough to avoid or resolve conflict when these departments do not have a monopoly over mineral resource policy.

There are, of course, other instances of collaboration and harmony in addition to those involving the mines and resources departments exclusively. For example, the Atomic Energy Control Board and the department officials in provinces that produce uranium appear to work together with considerable success. The Department of Regional Economic Expansion is also perceived favorably by provincial officials and seems to have developed effective mechanisms for consultation and coordination of policies. The fact that the federal government, through DREE, makes funds available to assist in developing provincial resources counteracts to a large extent the unfavorable impression created in the provinces by certain other aspects of federal mineral resource policy.

Department of External Affairs and the Provinces

Mention should also be made in this context of the Department of External Affairs. Quebec's attempt in the 1960s to develop an international personality and to challenge the federal monopoly over diplomatic activities had long-term consequences for all the provinces and for areas of policy far removed from the educational and cultural affairs that provoked the original confrontation. One aspect of the federal response to Quebec's offensive was a policy of encouraging provincial representation on Canadian delegations to international conferences. Thus some officials from provincial mines and resources departments have served on the Canadian delegation to the Law of the Sea Conference and have assisted in formulating a Canadian position with respect to offshore and deep-ocean mineral resources. The department also solicits views from the provinces on international questions affecting their resource industries, such as the proposal for an international buffer stock of copper at UNCTAD IV. In that instance, incidentally, none of the copper-producing provinces responded when the department requested their comments.

Another legacy of the 1960s is the Federal-Provincial Relations Division in the Department of External Affairs, intended to operate in situations where Canada's external relations have an impact on provincial governments, or vice versa. When the United States protested against the takeover of potash mines by the Saskatchewan government, it was this division, in consultation with Saskatchewan, that drafted the Canadian response. More generally, the division provided welcome support for Saskatchewan, not only against the United States but against other actors in Ottawa who were highly unsympathetic with the Saskatchewan government's potash policy. Since the province appreciated the support and since the division had an interest in demonstrating its usefulness to the provinces and in discouraging direct dealings between provinces and foreign governments, there was a community of interest between them that the U.S. protest led both to discover.

Canadian Ministerial Conference on Mineral Policy

A concerted effort to harmonize federal and provincial mineral resource policies has been made by the Canadian Ministerial Conference on Mineral Policy, which was established in 1972 at the suggestion of the federal government. This body resembles the Conference of the Provincial Ministers of Mines in that only mines and resources departments are directly represented, but, at least at the federal level, other departments have been involved in formulating positions. The Canadian Ministerial Conference has occupied itself with formulating what is described as "a mineral policy for Canada," now in its third phase. The first two phases were criticized on the alleged grounds that only meaningless generalities were arrived at, but the federal government considered it something of a triumph that all eleven ministers were able to agree in 1974 on the statement of objectives that represented the outcome of the second phase.[24] The third phase, now in progress, is supposed to devise policies for individual mineral commodities, but there are some grounds for suspecting that the provinces have lost interest in the exercise and that the third phase is proving to be much more of a unilateral effort by the federal government than were the first two phases. At least one province, Ontario, is now conducting its own review of mineral policy on a commodity-by-commodity basis, apparently quite unrelated to the similar exercise proceeding concurrently in Ottawa.

Taxation Conflicts

Federal-provincial conflict over mineral resources has been most evident in the area of taxation. The federal tax reforms of 1972, the increase in provincial royalties and taxes between 1973 and 1975, and the federal budgets of 1974 that terminated the deductibility of provincial royalties from taxable income were all initiatives that the other level of government viewed as threatening. Intergovernmental conflict over finance tends to have aspects of a zero-sum game and not to be amenable to solutions on the basis of shared professional standards or appeals to some overriding common interest.[25] Only a solution negotiated at the highest level, or what Simeon has called "federal-provincial diplomacy," can bring such confrontations to an end, and even then it is unlikely that all parties will be satisfied with the outcome.[26]

The controversies over taxation underline the relative weakness of Energy, Mines and Resources at the federal level and of the mines and resources departments at the provincial level. All the changes in taxation

that provoked conflict with the other level of government originated outside
these departments, or were even opposed by them. The departments were
apprehensive about the impact of these changes on the private sector; in
addition, they invariably deplored the intergovernmental conflict that resulted. They were not successful (or at best partially successful) in counterbalancing the pressure for change from the Department of Finance
and the provincial treasuries. The desire of the resource departments for
accommodation and their friendly relations with one another were also not
enough to resolve the intergovernmental conflicts, which quickly escalated
to the ministerial and even prime ministerial levels and thus could be
resolved only at those levels.

Interprovincial Relations

Apart from the Conference of the Provincial Ministers of Mines, interprovincial relations have been less extensive and less institutionalized than
have federal-provincial relations. With the exception of oil and gas, there is
not much trade in minerals among the provinces, and this fact has lessened
the impact that one province's policies can have on another province. The
conflict between Ontario and Alberta over the price of natural gas in
1973-74 was thus one of the few instances of interprovincial conflict.

A more typical impetus to interprovincial relations in recent years has
been the perception of common interests, often in opposition to the federal
government. New Brunswick, Nova Scotia, and Prince Edward Island
adopted a common position on the question of offshore mineral rights in the
1960s and adhered to it for more than a decade, despite changes of government in two of the three provinces. As a result they were able to negotiate a
better bargain with Ottawa than the weakness of their legal position would
have suggested. More recently, Saskatchewan and Alberta have discovered
a mutual interest as producers of oil, which sets them apart from the rest of
the country, and have collaborated extensively with each other. Efforts
have been made to build a common front of the four western provinces
against federal intrusions into mineral resource policy, but Manitoba's
position as an importer of energy and its generally pro-federal stance have
largely frustrated these efforts. Newfoundland, on the other hand, supported the oil-producing provinces in their confrontation with Ottawa in
1974 and has recently denounced its neighbors in the Atlantic region for
agreeing to a compromise with Ottawa on offshore minerals. As a result,
Saskatchewan, Alberta, and Newfoundland have begun to interact quite
extensively with one another on questions related to mineral resources. A
more long-standing interprovincial relationship resulting from ownership
of similar mineral resources is that of Quebec and Ontario, but the election
of the Parti Québécois to govern Quebec may prove to be an obstacle to
further collaboration.

Conclusions: An Overview of Policy-Making

From the preceding pages it should be apparent that the question of who makes mineral resource policy in Canada admits of no simple answer. The complexity of the policy-making process reflects in part the division of authority under the BNA Act, but in particular it reflects the diversity of interests involved in mineral resource policy, each of which finds expression through some part of the bureaucratic machinery involved in policy-making. The political scientist's preference, shared by many politicians, for neat, tidy, and "rational" structures and processes of policy-making assumes a homogeneity of interest and a concentration of power that do not exist in Canada, and are not likely to.

It seems to be only in recent years that the word "policy" has been widely used to describe the ways in which Canadian governments manage the country's endowment of mineral resources. In earlier times governments may, in fact, have been making mineral resource policy, just as Molière's bourgeois gentleman spoke prose all his life without being aware of it, but what they did was apparently not viewed as "policy-making," nor is it so viewed in retrospect by many of those involved in making policy today. The reasons why policy was not believed to exist are not mysterious. The subject of mineral resources ranked exceedingly low in political salience and thus received little attention from cabinets and legislatures. The role of the state in mineral resource management, while not lacking in importance, was largely entrusted to a small body of officials whose training and expertise were in the technical side of the mining industry, rather than in politics, economics, or public administration. Between this group and the private sector no major difference of opinion existed concerning the proper objectives of governments in relation to mining or the means of arriving at these objectives. Since there was no major conflict or controversy, there were no "politics" and thus no "policy." If it existed, as in a sense it obviously did, it was taken for granted.

This picture of the not-too-distant past is, admittedly, an oversimplification, and there were, in certain times and places, quite noticeable deviations from it.[27] Yet it is worth mentioning in order to contrast it with the situation today, in which mineral resource policy has become far more controversial, more complex, and more difficult to describe. The implicit questions to which this chapter seeks to respond — what is mineral resource policy and how is it made — would probably not have been asked twenty or even ten years ago, but the very circumstances that have made it possible to ask them have made it difficult to answer them with certainty. The fact that the federal government is now rather self-consciously engaged in the exercise of developing "a mineral resource policy for Canada" testifies to a certain dissatisfaction with the adequacy of recent policy-making, while the fact that the feasibility of the exercise appears to be viewed with widespread skepticism in the provinces, the private sector, and certain elements of the federal government itself suggests that the difficulty of defining policy is widely appreciated. Over and above the conflict between federal and provincial jurisdictions, which pervades this aspect of Canadian life even more than most others, there is the fact that new objectives and the growing political salience of the subject have made the policy-making process more complex within each level of government. Departments that deal with mineral resources have expanded and changed, while the heterogeneity of objectives and the impact of mineral resource policy on other areas of policy (and vice versa) have multiplied the number of bureaucratic actors that must be taken into account. Interaction between the public and the private sectors has also become more complex, and the boundary between them has been blurred by a variety of government interventions in the marketplace.

The growth and development of the resource industries have altered the distribution of power among participants and thus the range of possible outcomes in all the types of conflicts: public-private, intergovernmental, and interdepartmental. To some extent the private sector's bargaining power may be lessened once an extractive industry becomes mature and established, since its creative role has in a sense already been performed. On the other hand, the replacement of small, struggling entrepreneurs by giant, integrated corporations whose operations transcend national boundaries has strengthened the private sector in its dealings with government. The development of the resource industries has redistributed powers among Canadian governments and regions as well. In the early decades of this century Ontario and Quebec used the resources of the Laurentian Shield to expand their power in relation to that of the federal government, and today the energy resources of western Canada are causing another shift in power and placing new strains on Canadian federalism to which federal institutions have not yet found an adequate response. Finally, the distribution of power among departments and other governmental structures has been affected by the growing size and importance of the resource industries and the multiplicity of their ramifications for other areas of policy. Fiscal, environmental, diplomatic, and other concerns have produced new bureaucratic actors or strengthened the ability of old ones to challenge the traditional priorities of mines and resources departments.

At a time when the power to influence events is being redistributed in all these dimensions, the policy-making process inevitably appears confused, unpredictable, and "irrational." Given these facts, it appears unlikely that Canadian mineral resource policy can be made more coherent or more conducive to the pursuit of an assumed "national interest" than it is at present.

Notes

1. This theme is treated extensively in Graham Allison, *Essence of Decision* (Boston: Little, Brown and Company, 1972). This book was apparently responsible for popularizing the term "bureaucratic politics" as well as the now-celebrated aphorism, "Where you stand depends on where you sit."

2. For a fuller discussion see Gerald V. Laforest, *Natural Resources and Public Property under the Canadian Constitution* (Toronto: University of Toronto Press, 1969).

3. For the consequences in Australia see Garth Stevenson, *Mineral Resources and Australian Federalism* (Canberra: Centre for Research on Federal Financial Relations, 1977).

4. The transfer is discussed in Chester Martin, *"Dominion Lands" Policy* (Toronto: McClelland & Stewart, 1973), which also contains some information on the administration of Prairie resources by Ottawa before 1930.

5. *Reference re Ownership of Offshore Mineral Rights* (1968) 65 DLR (2d) 353.

6. Eric Kierans, *Report on Natural Resources Policy in Manitoba* (Winnipeg: Queen's Printer, 1973).

7. Provincial taxes and royalties as of February, 1976, are summarized in Jean-Paul Drolet, *Mining Legislation and the Role of Responsible Authorities* (Ottawa: Energy, Mines and Resources Canada, 1976).

8. See, for example, W. P. Gramm *et al., The Impact of Taxation and Environmental Controls on the Ontario Mining Industry* (Toronto: Ministry of Natural Resources, 1975).

9. This is an important difference between the situation in Canada and the situation in Australia as described in Stevenson, op. cit. Because the Australian states have depended more on federal grants than on revenues raised by their own taxation since 1942, their treasury departments have atrophied. As a result, it was the federal government in that country that had to take steps to collect resource rents for the public sector, despite the fact that the resources belong to the states.

10. Ontario Committee on Taxation, *Report* (Toronto: Queen's Printer, 1967) 3: 342-43.

11. G. Anders, "Rent, Communal Property, and Economic Nationalism: A Case Study," mimeographed (Toronto: Ministry of Natural Resources, n.d.). This document describes the Kierans proposals as "essentially Marxist in origin," a curious charge to lay against a former president of the Montreal Stock Exchange.

12. Ontario, 29th Legislature, Fourth Session, pp. 1017-18.

13. SOQUEM and SOQUIP are discussed in Pierre Fournier, *The Quebec Establishment* (Montreal: Black Rose Books, 1976), pp. 188-95. Fournier argues that they have supported, rather than competed with, the private sector.

14. Pierre Sevigny, a minister in the Diefenbaker government, complained in his memoirs that this insignificant department seemed always to be reserved for French Canadian ministers, while positions of real importance were occupied by anglophones (see Pierre Sevigny, *This Game of Politics* [Toronto: McClelland & Stewart, 1965], p. 225).

15. The Columbia River Treaty was signed by Prime Minister Diefenbaker and

President Eisenhower in January, 1961, but implementation was delayed because the Social Credit government of British Columbia insisted that Canada's share of the power to be generated should be exported to the United States. This demand was contrary to long-established federal policy, but Ottawa's ability to resist was weakened in 1962, when the British Columbia government purchased control of B.C. Electric, the province's principal utility. In 1963 the federal Liberals formed a minority government dependent on Social Credit support, and in 1964 a protocol was added to the treaty which reflected complete acceptance of the provincial government's position. Since that time the federal government has ceased to oppose long-term commitments for the export of power, a change in policy that has permitted other provinces to launch export-oriented power projects such as Churchill Falls. No satisfactory account of the Columbia affair has been published, but see *The Columbia River Treaty Protocol and Related Documents* (Ottawa: Queen's Printer, 1964).

16. Royal Commission on Taxation, *Report* (Ottawa: Queen's Printer, 1967), pp. 295-380.

17. This fact is demonstrated in Robert Presthus, *Elite Accommodation in Canadian Politics* (Toronto: Macmillan Company of Canada, 1973).

18. Further examination of private sector involvement is scheduled for the final volume in this project. An interesting issue, worthy of more research than was possible in this survey, is whether there are systematic differences between foreign- and domestic-owned firms in terms of their participation and involvement in Canadian policy-making processes. Little comparative research on this subject is available at this time.

19. For an account of their activities see Glyn Berry, "The Oil Lobby and the Energy Crisis," *Canadian Public Administration* 17 (Winter, 1974): 4.

20. M. W. Bucovetsky, "The Mining Industry and the Great Tax Reform Debate," in Paul Pross, ed., *Pressure Group Behaviour in Canadian Politics* (Toronto: McGraw-Hill Ryerson, 1975).

21. For a useful discussion of the Lougheed government and its economic policies, see Larry Pratt, "The State and Province-Building: Alberta's Development Strategy, 1971-1976," in Leo Panitch, ed., *The Canadian State* (Toronto: University of Toronto Press, 1977).

22. R. M. Burns, *Conflict and Its Resolution in the Administration of Mineral Resources* (Kingston: Centre for Resource Studies, Queen's University, 1976).

23. The conference is described in Burns, op. cit.

24. Energy, Mines and Resources Canada, *Towards a Mineral Policy for Canada: Opportunities for Choice* (Ottawa: Information Canada, 1974).

25. Economic and fiscal aspects of the federal-provincial controversy over mineral resource taxation are discussed in Anthony Scott, ed., *Natural Resource Revenues: A Test of Federalism* (Vancouver: University of British Columbia Press, 1976).

26. Richard Simeon, *Federal-Provincial Diplomacy* (Toronto: University of Toronto Press, 1972). The book is a study of federal-provincial negotiations in three issue-areas between 1963 and 1971.

27. For example, Ontario in the early twentieth century, where the expansion of the urban middle class, together with a rapid development of resource industries in the northern hinterland, produced an effective demand for "nationalist" or "provincialist" resource policies (see H. V. Nelles, *The Politics of Development* [Toronto: Macmillan Company of Canada, 1974], which is devoted to a discussion of Ontario's resource policies in that period).

7

The Evolution of Canadian Federal Mineral Policies

DONALD J. PATTON

Introduction: Tensions and Contradictions

And the princes said unto them, Let them live; but let them be hewers of wood and drawers of water unto all the congregation; as the princes had promised them.
—Joshua 9:21

At the federal level, Canada's mineral policies, particularly as they relate to the United States, reflect a continuing struggle to find the best approach for developing the country's rich endowment of resources to the maximum benefit of Canadians. In the initial phases of the Canadian mineral industry's growth, the struggle was to promote the rapid development of resources as an engine for economic expansion. Thus emphasis was placed upon attracting sufficient capital investment to undertake risky exploration and development activities and upon finding markets for the output of these activities.

Over time, however, the task of devising an appropriate approach to national mineral policies has become increasingly complex. Concerns have grown—and have found strong political expression—that the Canadian economy has become far too dependent upon the resource sector, thereby giving rise to an economic structure lacking the proper mix of activities required in a truly advanced industrial nation. There have also been growing concerns that the Canadian mineral industry has been shaped excessively by foreign, particularly U.S., influences to the point that Canada has been placed in the permanent role of resource hinterland, serving as a hewer of wood and drawer of water to satisfy the appetites of the dominant economic powers in the industrialized world.

These concerns figure prominently in the contemporary political reality of Canada and have given rise to widespread support for greater government activism in policies relating to trade and investment in the mineral sector. But the translation of this support into the design and implementation of a concrete and internally consistent national mineral policy has been frustrated by the interaction of three influences on the Canadian mineral-policy process.

The first of these influences is federal-provincial conflicts arising from the constitutional division of powers with respect to resources. These conflicts and tensions are reviewed in detail in Chapters 6, 8, and 9 of this volume. With the exception of the Yukon and the Northwest Territories, where regulation of mineral exploitation is the responsibility of the federal government, control over the development of Canada's mineral resources rests with the provinces. International and interprovincial trade in mineral resources, however, is a federal matter. Given the critical role of resources in the economic performance of most of the provinces, it is an exceptionally difficult task to achieve agreement on national mineral policies whenever the pursuit of such policies is viewed by one or more of the provinces to be detrimental to provincial interests and objectives.

A second influence consists of differences in policy objectives among the various regions of Canada. While all regions have come to seek more balanced economic structures with relatively less dependency on the resource sector, the ability to generate alternative sources of growth varies widely across regions. The struggle to design a national mineral policy has thus been played out within the context of a lack of a clear consensus on what the objectives of such a policy ought to be.

Finally, the third influence reflects an ambiguity within Canada concerning the proper role of market forces in any national approach to mineral policy. Many Canadians believe that the notion of world mineral markets' operating in a manner that provides maximum benefit for Canada is a myth. They point to the dominant role that multinational firms play in shaping these markets and to the biases they perceive in the way institutional factors influence trade and investment in favor of resource-importing nations. Other Canadians, supported by the arguments of industry spokesmen — many of whom are employees of foreign-owned firms — perceive very limited opportunity for effective activism by governments in a world where numerous sources of mineral supplies exist and where capital and management are free to move to alternative supply areas in the face of any serious attempt by a particular government to make terms of access to resources located within its jurisdiction more restrictive.

Federal mineral policies reflect these tensions and influences, and as objectives and constraints vary over time because of changing perceptions and market opportunities, these policies appear to evolve along uncertain, and often contradictory, paths. This chapter traces this evolution, focusing particularly upon policies regarding taxation, developmental expenditures, and international trade. In keeping with the other chapters of this volume, attention is confined largely to the post–World War II period. The concentration on Canadian federal mineral policies is not a denial of the importance of provincial policies, since the latter have had a profound influence on federal policies in general and on the bilateral relationship in particular. But federal mineral policies, which in theory reflect national objectives, provide a framework within which provincial policies and influences can be addressed.

The Objectives of Canadian Mineral Policy

Government policies, both federal and provincial, have long been an important factor shaping the environment within which firms in the mineral sector operate. Direct intervention in industry operations peaked during World War II but gradually subsided until the outbreak of the Korean War, during which mechanisms for direct control were re-established. Peacetime experience was characterized by fairly limited but gradually increasing government activism in industry affairs. This activism accelerated in the early 1970s as a result of growing concern that depletable Canadian resources were being mismanaged, with maximum benefits being foregone, excessive foreign ownership and control being tolerated, and harmful environmental damage going unchecked.

Despite the important role of government policies in the mineral industry, one seeks in vain for a detailed "master strategy" to guide the formation of policies for the mineral sector — except, of course, during a time of national emergency, such as World War II or, to a lesser extent, the Korean War. As in other policy areas, the development of a specific overall Canadian mineral policy has been constrained by the limited planning role in the economy of both the federal and the provincial governments. Therefore, mineral policies in Canada have tended to reflect a practicable "ad hocary" within the constraints of often conflicting statutory jurisdictions, varying regional pressures and desires, and changing international opportunities and challenges.

In general, this *ad hoc* approach to policy resulted in laws, regulations, practices, programs, and agreements supportive of the mineral industry and its development. Growth was the dominant policy objective.

Not until the late 1960s and early 1970s did the concept of a national mineral policy begin to emerge in Canada as a replacement for ad hocary.[1] This was a period of growing optimism concerning Canada's economic prospects. Rising commodity prices and a strengthening of Canada's balance of trade position gave rise to a sense that new policy options were opening up for the country. In particular, it was felt that Canada had stronger bargaining power in international trade relations, enabling it to obtain greater returns for Canadians from resource exports, and that Canada, in formulating its mineral policies, could replace a policy of maximum growth with the objective of achieving more balanced development.

It was in this context that the federal government's most explicit policy statement to date regarding the mineral industry — "Proposal for a Flexible Mineral Policy" — was approved at a joint federal-provincial conference in December, 1974.[2] A brief review of this proposed mineral policy casts light on both the traditional *de facto* objectives of Canadian mineral policies as well as on more recent, and possibly unattainable, policy goals.

As stated in this proposal, the overriding goal of Canadian mineral policy has long been, and will continue to be, to achieve "optimum benefit for Canada from present and future use of minerals."[3] In pursuit of this goal, the objectives that are spelled out reflect how perceptions have evolved as to how best to achieve optimum benefits for Canada.

The primary stated objectives are to promote diversification of industrial activity through resource upgrading prior to export and the development of manufacturing industries based on mineral processing. In cases where further processing is not feasible, the policy objective is to seek greater financial returns for Canada from mineral exports.

A number of related subobjectives are also spelled out that could modify the process of attaining the primary objectives. These include conservation of minerals for future use, increased Canadian ownership and control in the mineral industry, the fostering of more balanced regional growth, and minimization of adverse environmental impacts. Moreover, this policy framework is intended to serve the objective of ensuring an adequate supply of minerals, from either domestic or foreign sources, to meet the needs of the Canadian economy. This combination of objectives creates difficult trade-offs (for example, between conservation for future use and development of resource-based manufacturing activities) and the potential for conflict between the United States and Canada.

This policy statement is characterized more by strong wording than by convincing evidence that traditional barriers to forging a national mineral policy can be overcome. The means for achieving stated objectives are not clearly explained; neither is the process whereby potential conflicts among various objectives are to be resolved. Indeed, the statement arises out of the past inability of the federal government to persuade provincial mines ministers to choose among options and to adopt and pursue an agreed course of action toward the achievement of a national goal.

In the past, provincial jurisdictional powers have consistently frustrated federal attempts to formulate a national mineral policy. In the early 1960s, for example, federal efforts to achieve the relatively simple goal of standardizing terminology used in provincial mining legislation floundered because of the inability of the provinces to agree on basic definitions. Issues regarding lease conditions, tax matters, the provision of infrastructure facilities, and government involvement in ownership have generated insuperable obstacles to agreement among federal and provincial mines ministers on policy objectives.

Federal-provincial approval in 1974 of the "Proposal for a Flexible Mineral Policy" may have heralded the beginning of a new era in Canadian mineral policy, in which federal and provincial initiatives will consciously reflect integrated decisions aimed at achieving specific objectives within a carefully constructed framework of broad national policy. More likely is a blend of planning and ad hocary. Indeed, *ad hoc* approaches may be the most effective strategy for Canada to adopt.

Ad hocary has, in the past, been directed in a general way toward a number of broadly defined objectives that will no doubt continue to be dominant. In the next section of this chapter we turn to the policy instruments that have been employed in pursuit of these objectives. Attention is focused on those instruments aimed at achieving three goals of particular importance to the U.S.-Canadian mineral relationship: increasing investment in, and output of, the mining industry; diversifying export markets and investment ties; and increasing the degree of domestic processing of resources prior to export. Before turning to policy instruments, the objective of further processing merits elaboration.

Resource Upgrading Prior to Export

The objective of building an industrial structure based on the processing and further manufacturing of raw materials has long played an important role in Canadian mineral policy. As far back as just prior to World War I, a controversy raged over whether the International Nickel Company of Canada, Limited, should establish a refinery in the Sudbury region of Ontario or in a competing location in the northeastern United States. The head of the federal Department of Mines joined the debate surrounding this decision and, in arguing the merits of the Canadian location for the refinery, presented the essence of the case for further processing:

> Whenever we speak of our mineral wealth, we grow eloquent in describing our vast nickel resources . . . but really, of what particular and social benefit are these deposits to our country? We mine the ore, smelt it into matte and send it as such out of the country. If we want nickel or nickel steel, we have to import it. The employment of an inconsiderable number of men is all we get out of these splendid deposits.[4]

Another typical expression of the desire to see resources undergo processing in Canada prior to export came in 1956 from the Hon. George A. Drew, Leader of the Progressive Conservative Opposition, when he criticized the government's policy of exporting unprocessed raw materials, particularly to the United States. He presented before the House of Commons his party's position on the need for a "national development policy which will develop our natural resources for the maximum benefit of all parts of Canada and encourage more processing in Canada."[5] He expressed a concern, shared by an increasing number of Canadians, that the increasing dependence of the Canadian economy on the U.S. economy was casting Canada in the limited role of supplier of raw materials:

> Are we going to be hewers and diggers in large measure for a great and friendly neighbour who will then sell the finished products back to us after the most profitable employment has been created for their own people, or are we going to make the processed and finished articles that we need here in Canada . . . to use the materials and resources that providence has entrusted to our care?[6]

A year later, the author of a study prepared for the Royal Commission on Canada's Economic Prospects echoed this sentiment when he wrote of his "concern" about the low level of processing of Canadian mineral exports.[7]

It was not until 1973, however, that an explicit policy on further processing was enunciated by the Hon. Alastair Gillespie, Minister of Industry, Trade and Commerce. The Minister used the occasion of the release of a government report showing an actual drop in the degree of processing of Canadian mineral exports to express forcibly his government's concern over the exportation of unprocessed minerals and announced a policy of encouraging further processing where it would be internationally competitive: "The objective of a policy on processing before export would be to process surplus natural resources prior to export, wherever such processing would be internationally competitive and compatible with the development of a sound industrial structure. At the same time it would be necessary to ensure that indigenous natural resources were made available domestically at competitive prices."[8] Further processing would not be forced upon all raw materials exporters, but positive, cooperative action would be applied in those cases that appeared promising.

This policy statement stemmed from a recognition that, while the absolute amount of processing had been increasing, since 1960 the proportion of total Canadian exports of copper, lead, and zinc leaving the country in metal form had shown a steady decline. For example, between 1960 and 1974, copper exported in metal form dropped from 87 percent of total copper exports to 44 percent, and lead exported in metal form, from 71 percent to 24 percent of lead exports.[9] In other words, growth in resource exports in this period resulted primarily from increased exports of unprocessed, or little-processed, minerals.

This decline in the proportion of Canadian minerals exported in processed form was accounted for, in part, by a sharp increase in mineral exports to Japan, particularly from the West. Mineral projects developed in Canada and directed at the Japanese market have involved the export of ores and concentrates, with negligible shipments in metallic form. In contrast to the situation with respect to Japan, the percentage of copper, lead, and zinc exported to the United States as metal is relatively high and either improved or remained constant from 1960 to 1974.

A 1978 study sponsored by the Department of Energy, Mines and Resources attempted to measure the gains to Canada from further fabrication of raw materials before export. The report estimated the additional economic activity that would result from further processing of those minerals that would be prime candidates for such upgrading—namely, iron, copper, nickel, zinc, and asbestos. The authors of the report concluded that "at the initial stage [of production] the number of man-years per million dollars of output is smallest. The higher the level of fabrication the higher the labour requirement in general." Total GDP effects "are highest in the final stages of fabrication for all [minerals studied]."[10]

A practical historical example of the advantages of having upgrading capacity in Canada is provided by the aluminum industry. During World War II the Canadian aluminum-smelting industry increased its output sixfold. While half of this was exported to the United States, the ready availability in Canada of this strategic metal, in both ingot and fabricated forms, gave strong impetus to the development of the aircraft industry, which ultimately accounted for 85 percent of all aluminum used in Canada.[11]

Tariff escalation in relation to the degree of fabrication has frequently been cited as a major impediment to further processing in Canada. A GATT study confirmed the existence of significant tariff escalation for ferrous and non-ferrous metals in a number of developed countries, including Canada. The results of the study for non-ferrous metals are summarized in Table 7.1, where it can be seen that the United States imposes a tariff against ores and metal waste while Japan and the European Community allow essentially free entry of the raw material. Japan, however, imposes substantial tariffs on the entry of the unwrought metals and semi-manufactured items. At the final stage of processing—metal manufactures—the European Community retains the lowest level of tariff, while the

TABLE 7.1
*Tariff Averages for Non-Ferrous Metals
at Different Levels of Processing, 1973*
(percentages)

		United States	Canada	Japan	EC
Ores and metal waste	Aª	4.1	2.7	0.3	—
(including ferrous)	B	1.2	—	—	—
Unwrought metals	A	5.0	2.8	7.9	2.5
	B	2.1	0.5	5.6	1.0
Semi-manufactures	A	8.0	5.4	11.9	6.5
	B	4.3	4.0	10.9	7.6
Metal manufactures	A	10.0	11.9	10.9	7.9
(including ferrous)	B	8.7	11.1	9.3	8.4

ª "A" is a simple unweighted average of tariff items within each category, and "B" is an average tariff calculated by weighting the tariff item by the volume of imports in each category.

Source: Senate, *Proceedings of the Standing Senate Committee on Foreign Affairs: Twenty-Third Proceedings Respecting Canadian Relations with the United States,* February 24, 1976, pp. 23:29-33. This publication used the GATT study referred to in the text as its source.

United States, Canada, and Japan provide their national metal-manufacturing industries with substantial levels of nominal tariff protection.

It would appear that tariff escalation is a major obstacle to the further processing of Canadian metal exports, particularly given the effective tariff protection that is provided for the higher stages of processing.

The Instruments of Canadian Federal Mineral Policy

Taxation

Until fairly recently the mineral industry in Canada was accorded favorable tax treatment in comparison with other Canadian industries. Some tax incentives were put in place during the depression years; others originated during wartime, when it was deemed essential to increase the supply of strategic materials.

In the 1930s and during World War II, the mining industry was given such important tax benefits as a three-year tax holiday on income from new metal mines, introduced in 1936; an exemption from the Excess Profits Tax of 1940 for income derived from base metals and strategic-mineral mines; and an exemption from tax for income accruing to prospectors from the sale of mining properties.

When defending additional tax advantages for prospectors before the House of Commons in 1943, the Minister of Finance, the Hon. J. L. Ilsley, justified the added incentives by referring to the strategic role played by the mining industry in the war effort: "The government wishes to encourage the search for new base metal and strategic mineral deposits, which continue to be urgently required for war purposes."[12]

Favorable tax treatment of the mining industry continued throughout the 1940s, and this sector was spared the increased war taxes imposed on non-strategic industries following the outbreak of the Korean War in 1950.

Throughout the 1950s, mining-industry representatives expressed satisfaction with the favorable treatment accorded them by federal tax legislation. Typical of such statements was a submission by the Canadian Metal Mining Association to the Royal Commission on Canada's Economic Prospects, which expressed pride in the achievements of the mining industry and described federal tax legislation as "incentive legislation of the highest value. . . . It has proved an important factor in stimulating mining expansion and in securing development capital."[13]

Gold mining was given especially generous tax treatment during the postwar period because this industry had been one of the few bright spots in the depression-ridden economy of the 1930s. When the three-year tax exemption for new metal mines was introduced in 1936, it was with gold in mind that the Minister of Finance presented his "constructive government policy" of tax relief to increase mineral production and employment.[14] Later, in 1946, when both the cost structure and the price of gold in terms of Canadian dollars had turned against the gold-mining industry, the industry was once again provided special assistance by the federal government.

For most of the postwar period, mining was one of the least-taxed sectors of the Canadian economy. A 1963 report by the Department of Mines and Technical Surveys appropriately claimed that federal tax legislation "provides substantial direct encouragement to the Canadian mining industry [and has] played an important part in promoting its growth."[15] Moreover, the report recommended that Canada's favorable tax treatment be used as a model by developing countries.

Others were more critical, however, and as early as 1957 the *Final Report* of the Royal Commission on Canada's Economic Prospects foresaw the eventual removal of favorable tax treatment for the mining industry: "As the industry grows, stabilizes, and matures, it may well be unnecessary to accord it special treatment through subsidies and tax concessions in excess of those extended to any other Canadian industries."[16]

Canadian tax legislation applying to the mineral industry came under close scrutiny by the federal government, beginning with the Carter Royal Commission on Taxation in 1962 and continuing through the Benson White Paper in 1969 and the implementation of the revised Income Tax Act in 1972. This period of intensive examination revealed a changing attitude regarding the appropriate federal policy approach to the mining industry.

The final report of the Carter Royal Commission on Taxation, published in 1967, recommended basic reforms in the entire Canadian tax system and proposed markedly different tax policies for the mineral industry. The Commission criticized existing tax policies for their "non-neutral" effects on the pattern of investment and output in the industry. Non-neutrality in the tax system was to be tolerated only if other policies clearly discriminated against an industry, if the industry faced natural or market disadvantages, or if the sector in question was of such importance to the development of the country that it deserved special treatment to foster national economic development. While the mineral industry put forward each of these arguments in support of continuing non-neutral mineral tax policies, its claims were rejected in both the preliminary studies and the final report of the Carter Commission.

The concept of tax neutrality has had a powerful attraction as a policy guideline since at least the early 1960s, and it, along with the concept of "equality," underlay the system for tax reform recommended by the Carter Commission. As was pointed out later in the tax debate, the Commission's analysis was incomplete, since other national policies were already having non-neutral effects on the economy. For instance, the tariff structure, by providing protection for domestic manufacturing industries, had a non-neutral impact on the overall pattern of investment and output in the Canadian economy. Thus it could be argued that a non-neutral tax system that favored mining over manufacturing was needed to offset these tariff distortions and to restore balance to the nation's economic structure.[17]

Rejecting the carefully thought-out logic of the Carter Commission regarding the overriding need for "equity" and "neutrality" in the Canadian tax structure, the Minister of Finance, the Hon. Edgar J. Benson, proposed in a 1969 White Paper that special rules be applied to the mineral sector to offset the exceptional "riskiness" of the industry, on the one hand, and to provide a tangible recognition of the special contribution that mining had made to regional development, on the other. In his White Paper, *Proposals for Tax Reform*, he argued that, while past concessions had been overly generous, special concessions for the mining industry were still needed.

Tax incentives for exploration and development were to be maintained, but at the same time it was to be ensured that "the really profitable projects bear a fair share of the burden of taxation."[18]

To accomplish this dual objective, the White Paper proposed a number of tax changes:

- To encourage exploration and development by non-principal operators, a portion of exploration and development costs could be deducted from any taxable income earned, rather than from mining income alone.
- The costs of acquiring mineral rights were to be included in the definition of exploration and development costs and hence might be fully deducted from taxable income in the year incurred.
- The cost of mining machinery and buildings directly needed for production from new mines was to be fully deducted from income derived from that mine before any taxes would be owing.

The White Paper presented these three changes as the special concessions needed to support this risky, but high-growth, sector.

To increase the tax burden on highly profitable mines, however, the long-standing three-year tax holiday for new mines was to be rescinded. Describing this exemption as "too generous," the White Paper noted that, when combined with other deductions, "many more than three years are effectively exempt and taxpayers can recover much more than their investment without becoming taxable."[19]

Despite a recommendation by the Carter Commission to the contrary, the White Paper recommended that mineral exploration and development be given an extra boost through the retention of the depletion allowance. It recognized the weakness of the existing depletion allowance allowing firms to deduct up to one-third of pre-tax income without any commitment on their part for new exploration and development and proposed that depletion allowances instead be conditional upon such expenditures. Accordingly, for every three dollars of eligible expenditures, one dollar of depletion allowance could be deducted from net production profits, up to a limit of one-third of these profits. This proposed depletion allowance, which bore little resemblance to the traditional deduction for depletion, was, in reality, a financial incentive to increase mineral exploration and development in Canada.

Following release of the White Paper, lengthy hearings were held by two parliamentary committees, which arrived at different conclusions concerning the desirability of the proposed tax changes. The House of Commons Standing Committee on Finance, Trade and Economic Affairs was essentially in favor of the White Paper's proposals, while the Senate Standing Committee on Banking, Trade and Commerce, reflecting a more conservative sentiment, was in substantial disagreement with the White Paper on a number of points.[20] Nevertheless, the revised Income Tax Act, which came into effect in 1972, differed only slightly from the recommendations of the White Paper.

In the revised Income Tax Act, the three-year tax exemption for new mines was finally eliminated, but the immediate deduction for tax purposes of capital expenditures on new mines was expanded to include community and transportation facilities and new machinery and equipment for existing mines. The percentage depletion allowance was replaced by earned depletion, and eligible expenditures were broadened to include capital expenditures for the expansion of existing mines. Tax deductions were allowed for expenditures on exploration and development and for the cost of acquiring mineral properties. Income from the sale of mineral properties was taxable, and income accruing to prospectors and their financial backers was made subject to capital gains tax. The general corporate tax rate was to drop one percentage point each year, from 50 percent to 46 percent, with the actual federal tax rate dropping to 21 percent, leaving 25 percent of taxable income for revenue to the province.

The 1972 tax changes also supported the government's long-standing policy of further processing prior to export. Expenditures on facilities to process Canadian ores up to the prime-metal stage and investments by custom processors of mineral ores were defined as "eligible expenditures" to increase a firm's depletion allowance. An additional incentive was provided by including income from the further processing of Canadian minerals and the custom processing of imported minerals in "resource profits." As earned depletion cannot exceed 25 percent of resource profits, it is in the interest of the taxpayer seeking the maximum deduction to include as many revenue items as possible before deducting depletion.

Additional tax changes followed the passage of the revised Income Tax Act. For example, in 1973, in response to U.S. legislation creating the Domestic International Sales Corporation (DISC), the Canadian corporate tax rate was lowered to 40 percent on income from manufacturing, which included the processing of minerals beyond the prime-metal stage. A number of additional tax changes were also introduced in the budget speeches of 1974 and 1975 with the aim of stabilizing federal tax revenues in the face of increased provincial taxes and royalties.

In summary, it can be seen that for most of the postwar period the mining industry supported a lighter tax burden than the other sectors of the Canadian economy, reflecting a general acknowledgement that the industry faced exceptional business risks. A generous three-year tax holiday, the rapid write-off of capital expenditures, and a depletion allowance were deemed necessary to encourage private investment in an industry that had brought needed industrial activity to the North and to other less developed regions of the country. Gold mining was particularly well-regarded and received especially favorable treatment. As Canadian mineral ores and concentrates were competitive in international markets and accounted for a large share of Canadian exports, all levels of government were favorably disposed toward the industry and consciously used tax incentives to support its development.

Despite being a radical conceptual departure from previous tax legislation, the Income Tax Act of 1972 showed that the federal government still considered the mining industry to be in need of special assistance and encouragement; and while highly profitable mines were to carry an increased tax burden, exploration and development were encouraged through earned depletion, and further processing of Canadian ores was to be supported.

It is noteworthy that, in the years leading up to the tax reform, the mining industry was not earning unusually high profits; it was receiving approximately the same return on investment as the average of all other industries in Canada. Within the mining group, however, metal mines earned significantly more than mineral-fuel and other mining. Table 7.2 gives three after-tax measures of profitability for the mineral industry, and for all industries, for the years 1962-69.

On a company-by-company basis, none of the major mining firms earned consistently high returns over the years 1960-74. A recent study of the profitability of the largest Canadian mining companies during this period concluded that, "while most firms enjoy[ed] a healthy rate of return of between eleven and sixteen percent, none of these firms has realized abnormally high profits on average over the last fifteen years."[21]

International comparisons of tax legislation provide one perspective on the tax burden faced by the Canadian industry subsequent to the 1972 tax changes. A comparative tax study concluded that, as of May 25, 1975, Canadian federal tax legislation was more favorable for mining companies than that of the United States and many other industrial countries.[22] In this study, Canada ranked third in terms of tax incentives to the mining industry, behind Japan and France, while the United States ranked eighth. To the extent that international tax comparisons of this type are valid, it can be concluded that U.S. companies carry a federal tax burden substantially greater than that borne by their competitors in the Canadian mining industry.[23]

Taxes levied by certain Canadian provinces, however, render international comparisons of federal tax rates questionable. Combined Canadian federal and provincial taxes in 1975 varied widely among provinces. A

TABLE 7.2
Profitability Measures, 1962-69
(percentages)

Industry	Total Capital	Return on Invested Capital	Net Worth
Mining	9.00	10.01	13.00
Metal mining	12.19	12.85	14.64
Mineral fuel	4.91	5.50	9.84
Other mining	9.74	10.90	11.67
Mineral-based-manufacturing	7.33	8.75	8.92
Primary-metal	7.89	9.16	10.92
All mineral industries	8.15	9.25	11.04
All industries	8.38	10.34	10.36

Source: S. P. Malhotra, *Return on Capital Analysis in the Canadian Mineral Industry,* MR 118 rev. (Ottawa: Department of Energy, Mines and Resources, 1973), Tables 2, 4, and 6, pp. 30-32.

typical mining company in Quebec, for example, might have paid a total of 40 percent of net income, while in Manitoba the total federal and provincial tax burden was on the order of 50 percent. In Ontario and British Columbia the relevant figures were 65 percent and 73 percent, respectively. Except in Quebec, the combined effective tax burden in each of these provinces was undoubtedly substantially greater in 1975 than it had been in 1971.[24]

Indeed, in some provinces the combined tax burden imposed by the two levels of government had reached the point of being confiscatory, or nearly so, in 1975. There has subsequently been a recognition of the inability of firms to function in such an environment, caused by feuding by the two levels of government over their share of the tax spoils; and a variety of corrective measures have been taken to resolve, or at least to ease significantly, this problem.

In the context of the bilateral relationship, Canadian tax policies are of interest insofar as they affect the supply and price of Canadian ores, concentrates, and primary metals available for U.S. refineries and end-users. The level of exploration activity is an early indicator of changing company strategies, and it appears safe to conclude that the combined federal and provincial tax burden did have an effect on the location and level of mineral exploration activity in Canada. While total exploration expenditures in

1972 fell to almost one-half the 1970 level, this decline appears to have reflected adverse market conditions rather than the 1972 federal tax revisions. This interpretation is borne out by the fact that, between 1972 and 1974, despite increased sales by the mining industry, British Columbia and Ontario experienced declining levels of exploration, while exploration rose steadily in the Yukon and Northwest Territories. Consequently, it was not federal taxation that affected industry exploration; rather, high provincial royalties and taxes redirected exploration to areas of lower provincial taxation — such as Quebec — and to the territories that are solely under the federal tax regime. Canadian mining companies did, however, increase their exploration outside Canada, from 20 percent of the total in 1971 to 60 percent in 1975. [25]

Federal Developmental Expenditures

The Canadian government generally does not provide operating subsidies to the mineral industry. [26] The government, however, has carried out detailed assessments of Canada's mineral resource base, has financed pure and applied mineral-related research, and in 1961 brought in a special program, Roads to Resources, to open up potentially rich resource areas. [27] The principal form of financial assistance to the industry has been the provision of infrastructural support for mining ventures in remote regions.

A wartime example of support for a mining venture in Canada involved both the U.S. and Canadian governments' contributing directly to the development of the large iron ore deposits at Steep Rock Lake in northwestern Ontario. In the face of widespread concern over the adequacy and assured supply of strategic materials, in 1943 the U.S. Reconstruction Finance Corporation loaned $5 million to Steep Rock Iron Mines Limited, a company under the control of Canadian-born industrialist Cyrus Eaton. For its part, the Canadian government paid a subsidy to Canadian National Railways of 20 cents a ton on the first 5 million tons of ore transported from the mine to the head of Lake Superior and also loaned the railroad $2.5 million to build additional track and additional docking facilities for shipment of the ore through the Great Lakes. [28]

The decision by both the U.S. and Canadian governments to assist this challenging venture was no doubt based on each country's expecting to receive a share of the ore mined. The Canadian government seemed confident that, despite Steep Rock's being mined by a U.S.-owned company with financial assistance from the U.S. government, the iron ore deposit would be "a means of protecting Canada against a possible shortage of iron ore to meet war requirements." [29] Under questioning from the Opposition in the House of Commons, however, the Minister of Trade and Commerce, the Hon. C. D. Howe, was forced to admit that, while the underwriting agreement contained a stipulation that Canadian mills would have first call on the ore produced, there was no such agreement between the government and Cyrus Eaton or Steep Rock Iron.[30]

More recently, the Canadian government has provided transportation links, power stations, and townsites for three important mining developments in the Far North. In return for financial assistance to the Pine Point, Anvil, and Nanisivik mines, the federal government has increasingly sought a voice in the design and implementation of mining projects, culminating in direct government ownership in the Nanisivik mine on Baffin Island.

An example of untied government assistance is provided by the large-scale lead-zinc mine in the Northwest Territories owned by Pine Point Mines Limited, a mining consortium controlled by a Canadian company, Cominco Ltd. The development of this open-pit mine required the construction of a railroad to transport the ore to southern British Columbia for smelting. Despite the fact that Canadian Pacific owned Cominco and indirectly controlled Pine Point Mines, in 1961 the federal government agreed to finance the construction of a railroad from central Alberta to the mine site on the south shore of Great Slave Lake. The infrastructural support also included the construction of a road and a power plant and a grant for townsite development. Over $100 million was spent by the federal government; the company was required to ensure shipments of at least 215,000 tons of ore concentrate annually and to pay up to $20 million to Canadian National Railways over a twenty-year period.[31]

In another case, in return for $23 million of infrastructural support, the federal government also imposed certain obligations on Anvil Mining Corporation Limited in the development of its lead-zinc mine in the Yukon. In an agreement signed in 1967, the U.S.-controlled company, which was financed by Japanese debt capital, was required to employ native workers and to study the possibility of constructing a smelter at the mine site. If on-site smelting appeared profitable, the federal government would provide additional financial assistance for its construction. If such smelting were not feasible, the lead-zinc concentrate was to be smelted elsewhere in Canada to the extent possible. This could take place, however, only upon expiry of the eight-year purchase contracts for concentrate that had already been signed with Japanese smelters.[32]

Another example of increased control by government in return for infrastructural support is provided by Nanisivik Mines Ltd. on Baffin Island, where in 1974 the federal government took an equity share in the venture itself, as discussed more fully later in this chapter.

Financial support to industry to reduce regional disparities in income and employment is provided by the federal Department of Regional Economic Expansion (DREE). DREE has given the Canadian mineral industry $200 million to assess the mineral resource potential of selected regions and to encourage mineral processors and fabricators to locate in regions outside the industrial areas of the country.[33] However, direct financial assistance to Canadian industry, including the mineral industry, may become a source of conflict in U.S.-Canadian relations through the application of U.S. countervailing duties to any resulting exports.[34] Countervailing duties in the United States have not been applied against any of the products emanating from the mineral projects receiving this support, but conflict could develop between U.S. trade policy and Canadian regional development programs if financial assistance were to be given to a major mineral-processing unit exporting to the United States.

Commercial Policy

Multilateral Trade Negotiations. The mineral industry in Canada relies heavily on export markets, particularly in the United States, for sales of its ores, concentrates, metals, and fabricated products. Since World War II, Canada has sought freer access to foreign markets for its mineral products through active participation in each of the multilateral trade negotiations held under the auspices of the General Agreement on Tariffs and Trade (GATT).

In the early postwar rounds of trade talks in Geneva in 1946; at Annecy, France, in 1949; and at Torquay, England, in 1950 and 1951, the Imperial Preference System was an irritant to the United States but was valued in Canada as a trading arrangement worth preserving. Cabinet ministers and Opposition members frequently reaffirmed their support of the preferential system, which strengthened Canada's links with the Commonwealth.[35]

In at least one instance, however, Canadian trade negotiators judged it desirable to sacrifice the Imperial Preference System in favor of freer access to the U.S. market. At Torquay in 1950, U.S. trade negotiators were able to convince their Canadian and British counterparts to suspend the preferential tariff arrangement between their two countries for tinplate in exchange for a lowering of U.S. tariffs on a number of unrelated products. Tinplate from the United Kingdom had previously entered Canada duty-free, while that originating in the United States faced a tariff of 17.5 percent. The agreement stipulated that all tinplate entering Canada would face a 15 percent duty, in return for which Canada would receive "very important concessions in the U.S. tariff."[36]

During the early postwar period the structure of Canadian export trade shifted toward increased concentration on the U.S. market. Whereas in the prewar years one-half of Canada's total exports and almost two-thirds of its foreign shipments of copper, lead, and zinc had been destined for the United Kingdom, by 1950, balance of payments problems, exchange controls, and the post–World War II dollar shortage had limited Europe's capacity to import. As a result, Canadian trade policy centered on increasing exports to the United States and on purchasing more from Europe. In the words of the Hon. C. D. Howe, Minister of Trade and Commerce: "I have on many occasions explained that Canada's trade policy is to sell more to the United States and buy more from the United Kingdom and other European countries."[37]

As a result of the 1951 Torquay trade conference, Canadian exports to the United States faced lower tariffs, and the Canadian agreement with the United States was heralded as "the most important single agreement at Torquay." Among the concessions granted by the United States were lowered specific duties on aluminum and alloys, lead and zinc ores, and metals.[38] A subsequent round of trade negotiations at Geneva in 1956 further reduced U.S. tariffs on aluminum, steel, ferro-silicon, and manufactured products made from aluminum, iron, and steel. As a result, the Minister of Trade and Commerce was able to announce that "the agreement concluded between Canada and the United States is one of the major agreements resulting from this conference."[39]

The tariff concessions won from the United States at that time did not have the expected beneficial effects on Canadian exports. It was widely felt that, while Canada had lived up to its agreements in the GATT, the United States had instead launched a "commercial war of nerves against importers."[40] The U.S. tariff structure continued to allow raw materials to enter at very low — even zero — rates but applied substantially higher tariffs on processed and fabricated imported products. An indication of the problems this created for Canadian exporters is provided by the following U.S. tariff rates on aluminum and aluminum products agreed to at Geneva in 1956: aluminum in crude form, 1.25 cents per pound; sheets and bars, 2.5 cents per pound; wire and cable, 15 percent; household ware, 17 percent plus 3.5 cents per pound; and other aluminum articles, 19 percent.[41]

The Kennedy Round of tariff negotiations was completed in 1967, and a Canadian parliamentary committee assessing the outcome of this, until then the most important round of postwar trade negotiations, concluded that it "appeared to provide considerable potential benefit for Canada's export trade and the Canadian economy."[42] Reductions in U.S. tariff rates were negotiated for a number of minerals, metals, and metal products. For example, the tariff rate on specialty steel was reduced from 12 percent to 8 percent and on ordinary steel, from 9 percent to 6 percent. The tariff on cement was eliminated from a previous level of $2.25 per 100 pounds, and that on aluminum ingot was lowered from 1.25 cents to one cent per pound. Cadmium and bismuth entered duty-free, and the tariffs on copper, molybdenum, and magnesium were cut by one-half. Fabricated metal products still faced higher tariffs than ores, concentrates, and metals, as illustrated by the pre– and post–Kennedy Round rates on articles produced from tinplate (from 12 percent to 6 percent); asbestos (9 percent to 4.5 percent); iron and steel (19 percent to 9.5 percent); copper (1.275 cents per pound plus 15 percent to 0.64 cents per pound plus 11 percent); aluminum (19 percent to 9.5 percent); nickel (18 percent to 9 percent); and lead (11.25 percent to 5.5 percent).[43]

In contrast to the Kennedy Round, Canadian negotiating strategy at the Tokyo Round of trade negotiations, begun in 1973, included an attempt to gain general acceptance for a negotiating formula that would support Canada's policy objective of further processing prior to export through the reduction of tariff escalation abroad. This was the "sector approach," whereby products were to be related vertically rather than horizontally and negotiations were to focus on the trade barriers facing a particular commodity in all its forms, from the raw state through to manufactured items.[44]

The sector approach did not find general acceptance as a formula for trade liberalization. Essential support from the United States was not forthcoming, since U.S. negotiators regarded Canada's sector approach as a potential obstacle to across-the-board tariff cuts and saw it as a second choice, having merit only if the major trading nations were unable to agree on a more generalized approach.

During the postwar period the multilateral trade framework has provided Canadian negotiators with a means of increasing access to foreign markets for Canadian mineral products. While Canadian negotiating strategy at the first six rounds of postwar trade talks did not single out the mineral sector for special attention, the results of these negotiations led to lower tariffs facing Canadian mineral exports, particularly in the United States. By the Tokyo Round, however, a federal mineral policy had been made more explicit, and the sector approach was selected to support the prime policy objective of upgrading Canadian mineral resources prior to export.

Mineral Trade Issues with the United States. During the postwar period, U.S. non-tariff barriers have produced strains in the U.S.-Canadian resource-trading relationship. An example of this was the imposition by the United States during the late 1950s and the 1960s of quotas on the importation of lead and zinc.

The publication in 1952 of *Resources for Freedom,* the report of the Presi-

dent's Materials Policy Commission (commonly referred to as the Paley
Report), changed public and official attitudes toward the need for assured
sources of strategic and critical raw materials; and in 1954 the formation of
a "supplemental stockpile" greatly increased purchases by the U.S. government of specified minerals. From 1954 to 1957, lead and zinc stockpiles
were increased from approximately .7 million to 1.2 million tons each, with
Canadian companies shipping a substantial proportion of these and other
stockpiled minerals.[45] U.S. stockpiling authorities dealt with Canadian
companies; and since better-than-market prices were being paid, these
companies readily expanded their production to meet demand. In June,
1958, however, stockpile objectives for lead and zinc were reduced to less
than one-fifth the level of immediately preceding years.[46] The U.S. government's decision to stop new purchases and to sell much of the existing stockpiles of lead and zinc came on top of depressed market conditions
and had an adverse effect on both U.S. and Canadian suppliers.

The U.S. lead and zinc industry—including, as it did, a number of
small, high-cost producers—was facing a long-run decline in international
competitiveness; as a result, it had sought relief from import competition in
1950, 1951, 1953, and 1957. The conditions facing the industry in 1958
and a U.S. Tariff Commission finding that the industry was being injured
by imports tipped the scales in favor of protectionism; in September, 1958,
the President applied quotas to imported lead and zinc. Consequently, in
addition to facing tariffs on ores and concentrates, countries exporting to
the United States were limited to 80 percent of their average annual imports during the 1953-57 period. Since Canadian companies had been exporting to the United States steadily over the base period, the quota for
Canada was less onerous than that imposed on less-established supplying
countries. Nevertheless, Canadian exports to the United States were immediately reduced by 17 percent for lead and 15 percent for zinc.[47]

The Canadian industry pleaded its case against the quotas before the
U.S. Tariff Commission, but the Canadian government chose not to
challenge this decision in the multilateral forum of the GATT. Instead, in
November, 1959, the Canadian GATT representative stated his government's position, which recognized that the imposition of "temporary"
quotas was permitted under Article 19 of the GATT, and indicated that, as
a consequence, the Canadian government would not seek compensation or
take retaliatory action.[48] Despite the fact that the quotas persisted, Canada
continued to accept the U.S. contention that the quotas were temporary,
and the Prime Minister of Canada, John G. Diefenbaker, expressed his
hope that the quotas would be lifted. In a speech before the Economics
Club of Detroit in 1959, he said that "the lifting of the quotas on the import
of Canadian oil to the United States earlier in the year was widely welcomed and Canadians hope that similar action will be taken against import

restrictions on lead and zinc."[49]

The U.S. lead and zinc quotas also affected Peru, Mexico, and Chile and thereby advanced the time when Canada would be forced to develop another aspect of its mineral policy — that is, participation in international commodity arrangements. By 1958, when the United States imposed lead and zinc quotas, a meeting of lead- and zinc-producing countries had already taken place under the auspices of the United Nations. This meeting, and three subsequent ones, led to the formation in 1960 of the International Lead and Zinc Study Group. Canada participated actively in these meetings and joined the voluntary arrangement by producing countries to restrict production of lead and zinc as a means of sharing the burden of reduced U.S. imports.

There were additional points of concern and irritation between the United States and Canada. In July, 1958, a U.S. tariff was re-established on copper imports from all sources, with the exception of Cuba; similarly, Cuban nickel from a mine owned by the U.S. government was seen by Canadians as having an unfair advantage in the U.S. market. In addition, Canadian magnesium producers struggled against a 50 percent *ad valorem* U.S. tariff, which was five times the rate charged by Canada and Great Britain, and Canadian gold producers sought relief from their cost-price squeeze by arguing for a U.S. increase in the official price of gold.

Since August, 1971, Canadian mineral exporters have faced additional problems arising from the application of U.S. anti-dumping duties on, and from anti-trust actions against, potash, sulphur, lead, pig iron, and aluminum.[50] While the official Canadian response has stiffened since the lead and zinc quotas, the Canadian dependence on the United States implied in the overall trading relationship has reduced the desirability and the likely effectiveness of an aggressive Canadian stance on bilateral trade disputes in the mineral sector.

Export Controls. The Export Permits Branch was created in April, 1941, to help allocate Canadian supplies available for export markets and to streamline the mass of paperwork created by the war effort. The branch, with advice and counsel from the metals controller, screened out non-essential exports and directed the bulk of Canadian metal shipments to the United Kingdom and the United States, in conformity with declared government policy.

Following the war, the reconstruction effort in Europe generated a strong demand for Canadian minerals, and it became evident that exports would still have to be controlled in order to ensure adequate supplies for domestic users. Furthermore, in the face of continued international tension during the Cold War period, the export of strategic materials had to be controlled in cases where the export sale might be detrimental to Canadian and allied interests. In addition, the uncontrolled re-export of U.S. goods from

Canada had become an irritant in U.S.-Canadian relations, creating
another rationale for an export-control mechanism in Canada. These needs
were reflected in the passage of the Export and Import Permits Act in 1947.

Except for a slight modification in 1954 to incorporate provisions for
Canadian anti-dumping legislation, the act remained essentially unchanged until 1974. In that year it was amended as part of the government's
policy of trying to promote further processing and to improve the benefits
Canada receives for its resource exports. This amendment provides a
potentially powerful commercial-policy instrument. Whereas export controls had been permitted in the past for reasons of defense, implementation
of intergovernmental agreements, and assurance of adequate supplies for
domestic users, the amendment meant that export controls could
henceforth be used

> to ensure that any action taken to promote the further processing in Canada
> of a natural resource that is produced in Canada is not rendered ineffective by
> reason of the unrestricted exportation of that natural resource

and

> to limit or keep under surveillance the export of any raw or processed material
> that is produced in Canada in circumstances of surplus supply and depressed
> prices and that is not a produce of agriculture.[51]

Export controls had already been applied to copper ores, concentrates,
and products prior to 1974, but as a device for selective price stabilization
in Canada rather than as an instrument of national economic policy.[52]
With the 1974 amendment, authority was created, in the form of a reserve
power, to employ export controls to further Canada's prime mineral-policy
objective and to attempt to increase export prices in specified cases.

In presenting these amendments in the Senate, the Hon. Charles
McElman gave a clear statement of the government's policy on the application of export restrictions. These were to be considered only where such
processing was internationally competitive and where more positive
measures had already been tried and had failed. He stated that

> the government's general approach is to focus on constructive cooperative
> tools, such as multilateral trade negotiations, taxation policy, existing pro-
> grams of industrial support, consultation with industry and the foreign invest-
> ment review process. . . . In general it is expected, and it is the government's
> hope, that export restrictions will not be necessary to encourage increased
> upgrading of resources in Canada.[53]

Nevertheless, federal government officials now had a potentially powerful bargaining lever to apply not only in multilateral and bilateral trade negotiations but also in discussions with top executives of the large international mining companies operating in Canada.

The second part of the amendment was a response to the situation facing the world potash industry at the time. Overproduction had led to a drop in world potash prices, from $40 per ton in 1965 to approximately $22 per ton in 1969.[54] This had had an adverse effect on the U.S. potash industry, and it was feared in Canada that the United States might take steps to limit the importation of potash from Saskatchewan by, for example, the use of anti-dumping measures. Consequently, the government of Saskatchewan, purporting to act under the provincial Mineral Resources Act, developed a prorationing scheme that limited production in that province and succeeded in increasing the international price of potash. Prior to the passing of the Mineral Resources Act in 1965, concern had been expressed by Saskatchewan's premier, among others, that it infringed on federal powers over trade and commerce that had been granted in the British North America Act of 1867.

The federal government did not challenge the constitutionality of the provincial measures until a private potash producer, Central Canada Potash Co. Limited (owned 51 percent by Noranda Mines Limited and 49 percent by C. F. Industries Inc. of Chicago, Illinois), launched a suit against the Saskatchewan government, attacking the Potash Conservation Regulations of 1969. The decision of Saskatchewan's Queen's Bench in 1974 was "that the real purpose of the [legislation] was to restrict and limit the export of potash to the United States as well as to control and impede the flow of trade between Saskatchewan and other Canadian provinces." As a consequence of this decision, the company was awarded $1.5 million in damages.[55]

The Saskatchewan Court of Appeal reversed this decision in 1977, claiming that the real intent of the legislation had, in fact, been to protect the potash industry in Saskatchewan and that the prorationing scheme had not been introduced with the intent of controlling or restricting international or interprovincial trade.[56]

In a subsequent action that grew out of the conflict between the potash companies and the Saskatchewan government, the federal government found itself defending the actions of the provincial government. The government of Saskatchewan announced, in November, 1975, that it would act to acquire a portion of the potash industry—an action that brought a note of protest from the U.S. embassy in Ottawa to the Canadian Secretary of State for External Affairs. Expressing concern over the "major potential for damage to U.S. interests and to U.S.-Canadian relations inherent in the action," the aide-mémoire also aired a suspicion on the part of the U.S. government that "the province intends to realize additional benefits through control of the supply and price conditions for potash."[57] By way of response, the federal government defended the steps that the province had taken and the methods it intended to use in carrying out its acquisition policy, having been assured by the province that adequate compensation would be paid and that continuing supplies at fair prices would be forthcoming. It was a mistake, the note concluded, to suggest that the policy of the Saskatchewan government was comparable to the cartelization actions of OPEC.[58]

The 1974 amendment to the Export and Import Permits Act provides a vehicle whereby, should the need be perceived to have arisen, the export level and price of any resource can be brought under a review and control mechanism. With reference to potash, the amendment was a visible sign to the provinces that control over international trade was a matter of federal concern.[59]

This discussion has focused on the potential use of export controls for developmental purposes. Export controls can also be employed to achieve strategic and safeguarding objectives, as has been the case with Canadian uranium shipments. The special case of nuclear safeguarding is examined fully in Chapter 10 of Volume II of this series.

Framework Agreements with Europe and Japan. By 1972, international conditions were such that it appeared that Canada might finally be able to lessen the degree of its economic, political, and cultural dependence on the United States and to strengthen its relationships with the rest of the world. This choice was what the Secretary of State for External Affairs, the Hon. Mitchell Sharp, called the "Third Option." Pursuant to this policy, Canada has sought to encourage international trade and investment with other countries, leading to the signing in 1976 of bilateral cooperation agreements with the European Community and with Japan.

In the 1976 "Framework Agreement" between Canada and the European Community, reference is made to further processing of resources. Despite the vague wording of the relevant section, Canada's intent is clear. Specifically, the agreement states that the contracting parties shall "in accordance with their respective policies and objectives . . . take fully into account their respective interests and needs regarding access to and further processing of raw materials."[60]

Explicit recognition of Canada's interest in further processing was, however, one of the stumbling blocks in the negotiations leading up to the signing of the agreement. The European negotiators apparently were at first unwilling to take special cognizance of this desire and agreed to do so only when the Canadians agreed to non-discriminatory access to natural resources.[61]

Canada's interest in further processing is a constant, underlying theme in the agreement. When terms such as "new markets" are used, they refer, in part, to the substitution of finished products for the export of unprocessed materials. The Joint Cooperation Committee that was established under the authority of the agreement is to foster "mutual economic cooperation" in developing European and Canadian industries, creating new employment opportunities, and contributing to the development of the respective economies. The agreement's reference to new employment opportunities can be interpreted as a *de facto* recognition by the Europeans of Canada's interest in resource upgrading through the construction and operation of new smelting, refining, and metal-manufacturing facilities in Canada.

The inclusion of these advantageous clauses is not sufficient, of course, to ensure the implementation of a mutually beneficial policy regarding further processing. Canadian wishes must, and will, be matched against the interest that Europeans have in protecting and fostering their own transformation industries.

The economic cooperation agreement signed between Canada and Japan in October, 1976, also reflects Canada's interest in further processing.[62] When the problem of "market access" is raised early in the agreement, it is in the context of "minimizing fluctuations in patterns of supply and demand."[63] This can be seen as a reference to Canada's desire to increase exports of processed raw materials and allows for the interpretation that, if Canada is successful in doing so, steady supplies for Japan will result. Reference to "greater employment opportunities" stemming from industrial and economic development also implies further processing. Moreover, a clear statement is made to the effect that the two governments will "encourage and facilitate . . . cooperation in the development and marketing of resources and processed and manufactured goods."[64] On the occasion of the first meeting of the Canada/Japan Joint Economic Committee, formed under the auspices of the agreement, the Secretary of State for External Affairs restated Canada's position on further processing but at the same time reassured Japanese delegates that Canada's trade policy does not link increased acceptance of processed exports from Canada to continued Japanese access to raw materials.[65]

International Mineral Commodity Arrangements. The present worldwide interest in intergovernmental commodity arrangements brings to the fore a Canadian trade-policy issue that some fear could increase stress and add conflict to the bilateral relationship. It has been speculated that, at meetings of the GATT and UNCTAD, the United States and Canada might find themselves adopting widely differing strategies with respect to producer cartels and commodity agreements. As Canada ranks third in the production of non-energy minerals and is among the top world producers of such minerals as asbestos, potash, sulphur, nickel, zinc, lead, copper, and iron ore, there have been suggestions that Canadian policy-makers will, or should, support international agreements aimed at restricting supply and increasing returns to producing nations.

Canada is not philosophically opposed to participating in various types of international commodity arrangements. Indeed, it provided much-needed technical expertise in the formative stages of the 1956 International Tin Agreement and was a charter member of the 1960 International Lead-Zinc Study Group. Moreover, the Canadian Export and Import Permits Act contains provision for export restrictions should Canada choose to participate in an international commodity agreement.

But the official Canadian position on commodity arrangements, which was spelled out in 1974 by Mitchell Sharp at the Sixth Special Session of the U.N. General Assembly on Raw Materials and Development, makes it clear that Canadian policy is to support only those arrangements that involve both producing and consuming countries: "We support international commodity arrangements in which both exporters and importers are represented. . . . Canada recognizes the right of resource-owning states to dispose of their natural resources in the interest of their own economic development and of the well-being of their people."[66]

Canadian officials have been at the center of discussions on international commodity agreements, particularly in 1976, when the Secretary of State for External Affairs, the Hon. Allan J. MacEachen, served as one of the co-chairmen of the Conference on International Economic Cooperation. The North-South Conference, as it was widely known, brought together rich and poor nations for eighteen months of negotiations centered on the role of commodities in international trade. Also in 1976, the UNCTAD IV Conference in Nairobi, Kenya, unanimously adopted UNCTAD Resolution 93(IV), an Integrated Programme for Commodities, and laid out a two-year program for negotiating commodity agreements for eighteen specified products.[67] Two of these products — copper and iron ore — are produced and exported in substantial quantities from Canada, while a third, tin, affects Canada as a consuming nation.

The existing producers' association for copper — the Council of Copper Exporting Countries (CIPEC), comprising Chile, Peru, Zambia, and Zaire — has invited Canada and the other major copper-producing nations to join the cartel. Canada did attend a CIPEC meeting in June, 1974, as an observer, and since the membership of CIPEC may change to include consuming nations, Canada could be under increased pressure to participate actively in this international commodity agreement. In UNCTAD, Canada has proposed the formation of a consultative producer-consumer body on copper as a means of increasing knowledge about the possible effects on international trade of an expanded copper agreement.[68]

Canada's policy of fostering cooperation between producers and consumers also accounts for its refusal to follow the lead set by Sweden and Australia—that is, participation as a full member in the Association of Iron Ore Exporters (AIEC). In 1974, AIEC members accounted for 48 percent of world iron ore exports, and a decision by Canada to join this producers' group would substantially increase the percentage of world iron ore production under its control.

Changes in the Fifth International Tin Agreement, negotiated in 1975, provided another example of Canadian adherence to stated federal policy on intergovernmental commodity agreements. During the negotiations the seven producing members of the International Tin Council sought to have the consuming countries finance buffer stocks. Canada agreed to mandatory financing by consuming countries, but since the other major industrialized nations (the United States, West Germany, and Japan) would not accept this proposal, Canada instead supported a plan whereby the consuming countries would contribute voluntarily to buffer-stock financing. In contrast to the United States, Canada has been active in the Tin Agreement since its inception in 1956, while the Fifth Agreement was the first such accord signed by the United States.[69]

While a divergence between U.S. and Canadian policies on international commodity agreements is a potential source of tension in the bilateral relationship, U.S. dislike of such agreements appears to be lessening, and there is little reason to expect that Canada will join any producer-only arrangements seeking to limit world exports and to raise prices. An international trading system made up of producer cartels would have little attraction for Canada, itself dependent on the importation of such commodities as bauxite, chrome, manganese, and phosphate for domestic industry. It is also unlikely that Canada would support artificially high prices, thereby encouraging substitution and working directly against the interests of consumers. In addition, commodity arrangements that seek to raise prices internationally have had an uneven record of success in the face of internal disunity and shifting patterns of demand and supply.

Uranium has been one exception to the general rule guiding Canadian participation in international producers' arrangements. Between 1972 and 1975 the Canadian government was an active member in a uranium producers' agreement that operated out of Paris and included the governments of Australia, France, and South Africa and the large British mining corporation, Rio Tinto Zinc Limited, parent company of Rio Algom Mines Limited of Toronto. This "Club of Five" set minimum floor prices for export sales of uranium "yellow cake" and allocated contracts to each of its members on a rotating basis. The existence of the agreement, and Canada's active participation in it, was brought to public attention during U.S. congressional hearings in 1976 and 1977.[70]

Active Canadian participation in a "secret" producers' agreement raises doubts about the veracity of federal policy statements on intergovernmental commodity agreements. Upon examination, however, the uranium producers' agreement can be seen as arising from a set of conditions unlikely to be duplicated with non-fuel minerals. The development of the uranium industry in Canada, as elsewhere, has been greatly affected by government policies put in place for the control of strategic weapons, the construction of nuclear power stations, and safeguards on the international shipment of nuclear fuel and waste products. In Canada both the legislative mechanism, in the form of the Atomic Energy Control Act, and the precedent of direct government ownership in the industry by a crown corporation, Eldorado Nuclear Limited, created a unique set of circumstances favorable to government participation in an international restrictive agreement.[71]

This agreement was essentially a reaction to U.S. protectionist and strategic trade measures. In the face of a U.S. embargo, begun in 1966, on the importation of foreign uranium, which effectively closed 70 percent of the world market to non-U.S. producers, Canadian and other governments were faced with excess productive capacity that threatened Canadian mining communities, particularly in Ontario and Saskatchewan. From this vantage point, Canadian support of the uranium agreement can be seen as a necessary response to unwarranted U.S. actions, followed by a refusal by U.S. authorities to heed numerous Canadian protestations. Before the House of Commons in October, 1977, the Minister of Energy, Mines and Resources, Alastair Gillespie, invited government critics to consider the dilemma with which Canadian policy-makers were confronted as a result of the U.S. embargo: "[After consulting] the notes between the Canadian government and the U.S. government complaining bitterly about the embargo imposed by the United States on Canada and the rest of the world, . . . [one can] understand why we had to take action to protect Canadian industry."[72]

In the context of the bilateral relationship, it is important to note that Canadian federal government officials claimed that, in contrast to the treatment of purchasers elsewhere, U.S. and Canadian customers were to be protected from paying artificially high prices. If true, the uranium agreement would differ from the commodity agreements under study by

UNCTAD, where a major goal would be higher import prices for the industrialized nations, particularly the United States. In fact, U.S. and Canadian public utilities and other purchasers did pay the higher "world price," and it was the complaints of one of these producers, Westinghouse Electric Corporation, that brought the agreement to the attention of the public. In Canada, Ontario Hydro paid the higher price for uranium it purchased in 1974, a transaction reported to have netted the seller, Gulf Minerals Canada Limited, a profit of $50 million on a contract valued at $98 million.[73]

Finally, the Canadian government claimed that it had sought the participation of both producing and consuming nations when the agreement was first organized and that consuming nations were unwilling to join the agreement; in the face of impending economic difficulties, federal officials were forced to settle for their second choice, a producers' arrangement. As the Minister of Energy, Mines and Resources explained: "We tried to get a producer and consumer arrangement but unfortunately we were not able to get consumers alongside at that time so the arrangement became a producers' arrangement. Subsequently, that is to say in 1975, it was possible to disband the producers' arrangement and [to substitute] a producer-consumer dialogue through the formation of the Uranium Institute."[74]

It appears that the uranium agreement during the 1972-75 period was an exceptional, temporary measure to protect the interests of Canadian producers in the face of U.S. trade restrictions and that the Canadian position on producer-consumer commodity arrangements remains intact.

Government Ownership

The federal government has, until fairly recently, refrained from taking an active direct role in mineral development in Canada. In 1974, for the first time since the Korean War, the Canadian government participated directly in the development of a mine with the aims of stimulating activity north of the sixtieth parallel and capturing greater benefits for Canada.[75] The equity participation taken by the Department of Indian Affairs and Northern Development in Nanisivik Mines has been heralded as a new model for resource development in the Canadian North. As such it merits a brief review.

In July, 1974, an agreement was signed by the Minister of Indian Affairs and Northern Development and the president of Mineral Resources International Limited stipulating the terms and conditions under which Nanisivik Mines was to develop a lead and zinc deposit at Strathcona Sound on Baffin Island, north of the Arctic Circle.[76] The federal government provided $16.7 million in financial support for the construction of an airport, roads, a dock, and a townsite and in return received an 18 percent

equity share in the operating company, Nanisivik Mines, and the right to
nominate two members to the company's board of directors.[77] The mine
started operating in November, 1976, and, after an initial period of adjustment, reached capacity output.

Government approval and support for Arctic mineral development is
conditional upon investors' meeting at least some of the federal
government's mineral-policy and northern-development-policy objectives.
Greater Canadian participation in the mining industry is an objective of
the flexible mineral policy, and a favorable aspect of the Nanisivik project
was its largely Canadian ownership and control even before this was
strengthened by the government's equity participation. Had the mine been
a solely U.S. venture approved by the Foreign Investment Review Agency,
the project would probably not have received such generous financial support and equity investment by the federal government.

Further processing of Canadian minerals prior to export was not insisted
upon, since Canadian smelting capacity in the south was not available and
the mine's small output did not warrant the construction of such facilities. A
consideration weighing in favor of support for this project was the possibility of developing Canadian expertise in the construction of ice-strength-
ened ore carriers in harmony with Canada's Oceans Policy of 1973.

The most important factor favoring federal government investment in
Nanisivik Mines, however, was that it responded to one of the objectives of
Canada's policy for northern development, announced in 1972. *Canada's
North 1970-1980* calls for government support of "non-renewable resource
projects of recognized benefit to northern residents and Canadians generally."[78] For all these reasons, particularly the latter, financial assistance
from the government was forthcoming to ensure the development of a mine
that, it was believed, would not otherwise have been developed.

Joint ventures based on the Nanisivik experience are expected to provide
the model for mineral developments in the Yukon and the Northwest Territories. A representative of the Minister of Indian Affairs and Northern
Development indicated that, by means of active joint-venture partnerships
with industry, the federal government has sufficient leverage to implement
its stated or implied policies for mineral and northern development. At
least three other ore deposits in the Northwest Territories are candidates for
development using mixed public-private funding.[79]

Direct government participation in the industry also takes place through
the Canada Development Corporation (CDC), a government-backed,
private company responsible for increasing the number and the importance
of Canadian-controlled and Canadian-managed corporations. Former
Finance Minister and present-day economic nationalist Walter Gordon
first brought the concept forward in 1963, but it was not until 1971 that the

CDC was created by an act of Parliament.

The prime objective of the CDC is to increase Canadian ownership and control of industry while operating at a profit in the interests of its shareholders. A CDC corporate policy statement refers to the corporation's interest in "long range development and large projects, particularly those which involve an upgrading of resources."[80] In 1973 the CDC made its largest single investment when it purchased, for $271 million, a 30.3 percent interest in Texasgulf Inc., a U.S. corporation headquartered in Texas. Texasgulf deals in natural resources and has extensive holdings in Canada, including one of the world's largest producing mines for zinc and silver, at Kidd Creek, Ontario.

The acquisition of a major equity interest in Texasgulf by a Canadian crown corporation was vociferously protested in the United States, and in Texas courts the board of directors of Texasgulf fought what they labeled an "unfriendly takeover." They charged that the takeover was against the national interest of the United States, since the CDC was a foreign corporation owned by the Canadian government. It was also argued that members of the board of directors appointed by the CDC would face a conflict of interest when advising on Texasgulf's corporate policy.[81]

The CDC's purchase of a controlling interest in Texasgulf was at least as much a political act as an economic one, but it should not be interpreted solely as a federal government move toward the policy objective of increasing Canadian control of the mineral industry. Because the CDC is managed by a private board of directors and acts without cabinet or parliamentary approval, it cannot be seen as an arm of government for the direct implementation of federal policies. It would, however, have been surprising to find the CDC operating against government policy in the politically sensitive area of ownership of natural resources. Since its acquisition by the CDC, Texasgulf has also supported the policy objective of further processing through the commencement of construction of a large copper smelter and refinery in Ontario.

Foreign Investment Policy

Concern over extensive foreign ownership and control of the Canadian economy has increased steadily since the publication of the *Final Report of the Royal Commission on Canada's Economic Prospects* in 1957 and culminated in the creation of the Foreign Investment Review Agency (FIRA) in 1974.

Canadian government policy toward private foreign direct investment reflects the same tensions and contradictions that have affected the formulation of mineral policy. Opposing views on the nature of the international economic system lead to differing policy recommendations. Those who are suspicious of the bilateral relationship and seek to erect barriers against

foreign — particularly U.S. — investment might agree with the contention
that, since 1940, "Canada has stood alone, its independence exposed to the
penetrative power of American economic and military imperialism."[82] Supporters of the free flow of capital internationally, in contrast, are likely to
subscribe to the view that measures to restrict foreign investment are
"another attempt to blackmail successful alien risk-takers into paying
tribute to unenterprising but powerful local capitalists."[83]

A recommended course of action has been that Canadians should have
majority ownership and control of companies operating in the resource industries. A clear expression of this objective was made by the House of
Commons Standing Committee on External Affairs and National Defence,
commissioned in 1970 to study the question of foreign ownership in
Canada. The recommendation of the committee was that "Canadians
should control Canadian companies by owning at least fifty-one percent of
their voting shares. . . . It is particularly vital that we control our resource
industries."[84] Prior to the federal election of 1974, Prime Minister Trudeau
told voters that the Liberal Party was of the view that "new, major projects
in the natural resource field should have at least 50, preferably 60, percent
Canadian equity ownership."[85] The recommendation of majority Canadian
ownership for resource ventures has not been followed; and even in areas
solely under federal control, the government has required only that a mining company list its shares on a Canadian stock exchange before leases are
awarded.[86]

The Canadian mining industry, in contrast to other extractive and
manufacturing sectors, includes a number of major Canadian-owned companies operating both in Canada and abroad. Table 7.3 shows that, of total
assets of nearly $14 billion in 1974, approximately one-half were accounted
for by Canadian-owned companies in the private sector. Canadian ownership is also strengthened by the assets of Canadian government enterprises.
Among foreign-owned firms, U.S. companies predominate, but enterprises
owned in other countries, principally in the United Kingdom, account for a
substantial portion of industry assets. Table 7.3 also reflects the size and the
economic strength of Canadian-owned private mining companies, which
account for 50 percent of total assets and sales but earn over 65 percent of
industry profits. This relationship between assets and profits contrasts with
that found in most other sectors of the Canadian economy.

Despite the fact that neither the critics nor the supporters of foreign investment in Canada have succeeded in building an irrefutable case for their
respective positions, there has been a steady movement at both the federal
and the provincial levels toward limiting foreign investment. At the federal
level, FIRA acts as a screening mechanism to assess whether or not a particular investment is of "significant benefit to Canada."[87] Since an impor-

TABLE 7.3

Ownership in the Canadian Mining Industry, 1974

	United States		Other Foreign		Canadian Private Sector		Canadian Government Business Enterprises		Unclassified		Total
	Amount ($)	Percentage of Total	Amount ($)	Percentage of Total	Amount ($)	Percentage of Total	Amount ($)	Percentage of Total	Amount ($)	Percentage of Total	($)
Assets	5,507	39.5	1,155	8.3	6,976	50.0	162	1.2	143	1.0	13,943
Equity	2,792	37.7	594	8.0	3,886	52.5	94	1.3	41	.5	7,407
Sales	2,793	40.0	531	7.6	3,520	50.4	48	.7	87	1.2	6,979
Profits	477	26.7	131	7.3	1,173	65.6	7	.4	-7	—	1,781

Source: Department of Industry, Trade and Commerce, *Annual Report of the Minister of Industry, Trade and Commerce under the Corporation and Labour Unions Returns Act,* 1975, Part I, *Corporations* (Ottawa: Statistics Canada, 1978), pp. 140-54. The table was derived by subtracting the figures for mineral fuels from those for total mining. The amounts in the table represent metal mines except coal mines; non-metal mines, quarries, and sand pits; and services incidental to mining.

tant criterion in the screening process is the investment's effect on resource processing, a foreign investor need not expect resistance from FIRA if the investment leads to resource upgrading prior to export.[88] As of 1977, FIRA had posed little problem to foreign investors; in 1974-77 it had refused only one minor investment of the twenty-three mineral-related applications submitted to it for approval. Nevertheless, it is highly likely that FIRA would block any acquisition that threatened the nationality of a major Canadian-owned mining company. Even before the introduction of FIRA, Prime Minister Trudeau had personally stopped the threatened U.S. takeover of two Canadian resource companies: Denison Mines Limited in 1970 and Home Oil Company Limited in 1971.

A foreign-owned company operating in Canada that decides to enter a "related business" other than by the acquisition route is not required to seek the approval of the agency, however.[89] Consequently, a narrow definition of related business would become a method for blocking diversification by existing foreign-owned firms, while adoption of a broad definition of the term would reduce the scope for FIRA to control the level of foreign investment. With respect to mining, the further processing of Canadian ores is defined as a related business and hence is outside the purview of FIRA, provided the company's existing production makes up at least one-half of the total input into a new smelting or refining operation.

Conclusions

Canada has not yet developed and implemented a federal mineral policy sufficiently specific and detailed to guide its strategic and tactical decision-making. Conflicting jurisdictional claims between the federal and provincial governments, overlapping responsibilities among federal government departments, a limited planning role for government, and economic and political constraints at the international level have hampered attempts by the federal Department of Energy, Mines and Resources to develop an explicit national mineral policy. Consequently, the peak effort to lay down a federal mineral policy, the joint federal-provincial mineral-policy statement of 1974, was, of necessity, made flexible to the point of losing any value that it might have had as a policy guideline.

Using a less stringent definition of what would constitute a national mineral policy—one that would include government attitudes and actions that have created the public-policy environment of the mineral industry—it can be concluded that federal government policies and mechanisms have had a major effect on the growth and development of the industry and that such actions have been directed toward three broad economic and international trade objectives: to increase the level of investment and output in the mineral industry; to diversify export markets and investment ties away from the United States; and, through further processing, to increase the economic returns to Canadians from mineral exports. Each of these objectives holds the potential for conflict between the United States and Canada.

The policy instruments that have been employed, sometimes in a contradictory manner, have included taxation policy, developmental expenditures, commercial policy, government ownership, and control over foreign investment. Taxation has been the most important policy instrument for achieving the objectives of increased investment and output in the industry. Proposed changes in Canadian tax laws were of direct concern to the industry; but, in fact, the Income Tax Act of 1972 did little to detract from the achievement of these objectives. The lengthy and vocal debate over resource taxation that began with the final report of the Carter Commission in 1967 and continued until a reduction in provincial taxes after 1975 did not evoke protests or commentary from U.S. authorities.

Direct government assistance to mining companies to promote developmental objectives has led to only minor conflict. The imposition by the United States of quotas and anti-dumping duties on Canadian mineral exports in most cases reflects protectionist sentiments in the United States. Future conflict is possible if countervailing duties are imposed by the United States, but to date this has not been a problem in the mineral sector.

The goal of diversifying Canadian exports and trade ties away from the United States has not yet become an irritant in U.S.-Canadian relations, mainly because so little diversification has occurred. The wording and the tone of the 1972 "Third Option" policy and the 1976 Framework Agreements with Europe and Japan may have led some Americans to reassess the stability of the relationship, but Canadian attempts at diversification have not yet embodied the necessary commercial-policy mechanisms to make them work. For the foreseeable future, the Framework Agreements must remain statements of intent, useful only in changing attitudes in Canada and abroad regarding the advantages of closer trade and investment ties with Canada.

Further processing, a primary objective of Canadian mineral policy both before and since World War II, holds the greatest potential for conflict in U.S.-Canadian relations. The interest in resource upgrading is deep-rooted in Canadian economic policy, and enabling legislation for export controls was passed in 1974 to support the upgrading of resources. Export controls on non-energy minerals have not been used against the United States for other than Canadian price control purposes and could not, even if it were thought desirable, be used effectively until economic and supply conditions changed to give Canadian suppliers greater leverage in the U.S. market.

Even if it is difficult to define precisely what is meant when speaking of a Canadian federal mineral policy, this policy is clearly undergoing change. How far this change will go can be determined only by the interaction of a variety of influences, including the evolution of federal-provincial arrangements and international mineral-market trends. In the past, Canadian emphasis on encouraging mineral sector development as an engine of growth was quite compatible with U.S. interests. But Canadian policies may not be as compatible in the future.

Canada will clearly remain a net resource exporter for many years, while the United States faces the prospect of becoming more and more dependent upon foreign supplies to meet its resource requirements. Therefore, certain conflicts of interest between the two countries are virtually inevitable in the mineral sector. As modern industrial nations, both countries will be interested in price stability in commodity markets. But as a net exporter, Canada will naturally seek stability at higher prices than will the United States, an importer of numerous minerals.

Moreover, Canada is likely to be able to press much harder than in the past to achieve diversified developmental objectives from its mineral sector. In pressing for these objectives, Canada will undoubtedly meet strong resistance from the United States, as it has, on occasion, in the past. For example, the United States will not easily sacrifice employment opportunities to Canada to suit that country's mineral-upgrading aspirations and will no doubt use whatever means at its disposal to frustrate impending job losses. But the United States will find it more difficult to threaten credibly the imposition of barriers to Canada's market access if alternative sources of supply for the United States are also available only on more demanding terms of sale.

In short, Canadian federal mineral policy may well remain an exercise in ad hocary, but this exercise is likely to take on more consistency and to find a more hospitable environment within which primary objectives can be pursued.

Notes

1. The term "mineral policy" was first introduced into the *Annual Report* of the Department of Energy, Mines and Resources in 1970/71. The Department felt that a number of "complex" and "critical" issues had to be faced in the areas of orderly development of the resource base, expansion of domestic and foreign markets, capital availability, foreign ownership and control, and taxation. A "coherent" and "effective" mineral policy was said to be needed, and in 1971 the Department was restructured to "sharpen and emphasize this new thrust."

The need for an explicitly stated mineral policy had been foreseen earlier by mineral analysts in the Department, and the existence of a *de facto* policy could be inferred from departmental publications in the 1960s (see, for example, W. Keith Buck, *Mineral Development Policy,* MR 64 [Ottawa: Mineral Resources Division, Department of Mines and Technical Surveys, 1963]; and R. B. Toombs, *Canadian Minerals in National and International Perspective,* MR 75 [Ottawa: Department of Mines and Technical Surveys, 1964]).

In 1970 a set of specific objectives was published, listing fifteen elements for possible inclusion in a national mineral policy (see W. Keith Buck and R. B. Elver, *An Approach to Mineral Policy Formulation,* MR 108 [Ottawa: Department of Energy, Mines and Resources, 1970]; and W. Keith Buck, *Factors Influencing the Mineral Economy of Canada: Past, Present and Future,* MR 106 [Ottawa: Department of Energy, Mines and Resources, 1970]).

2. Department of Energy, Mines and Resources, *Towards a Mineral Policy for Canada: Opportunities for Choice* (Ottawa, 1974), p. 17. See also Department of Energy, Mines and Resources, *Mineral Policy Objectives for Canada: A Statement by Federal and Provincial Ministers Responsible for Mineral Policy* (Ottawa, 1973).

3. Department of Energy, Mines and Resources, *Towards a Mineral Policy for Canada,* op. cit.

4. As quoted in O. W. Main, *The Canadian Nickel Industry* (Toronto: University of Toronto Press, 1955), p. 81.

5. House of Commons, *Debates,* 3rd Sess., 22nd Parl., July 9, 1956, p. 5780.

6. Ibid., p. 5779.

7. John Davis, *Mining and Mineral Processing in Canada,* study prepared for the Royal Commission on Canada's Economic Prospects (Hull, Quebec: Queen's Printer, 1957), p. 326.

8. Department of Industry, Trade and Commerce, "News Release 47/73," Ottawa, July 23, 1973, pp. 1 and 4. See also Alastair W. Gillespie, "Canada's Industrial Future," *The Conference Board Record,* July, 1974, pp. 35-38. In March, 1974, it was reported that the Minister wished to see approximately $5 billion in new capital invested to upgrade Canadian natural resources prior to export (*Financial Post* [Toronto], March 16, 1974).

9. Senate, *Proceedings of Standing Senate Committee on Foreign Affairs: Thirty-Sixth Proceedings Respecting Canadian Relations with the United States,* 1st Sess., 13th Parl., May 27, 1976, Appendix A, Table 6, p. 36:31.

In an earlier period the Leader of the Opposition had pointed out that Canada's export trade was increasingly made up of unprocessed raw materials, with a decline, over the years 1946-54, from 52 percent to 40 percent in the proportion of industrial exports in fully manufactured form (see House of Commons, *Debates,* 3rd Sess., 22nd Parl., July 9, 1956, p. 5799).

10. Energy, Mines and Resources Canada, *Mining to Manufacturing: Links in a Chain,* MR 175 (Ottawa, 1978), pp. 56 and 58.

11. J. de N. Kennedy, *History of the Department of Munitions and Supply* (Ottawa: King's Printer, 1950), Vol. II, p. 103.

12. House of Commons, *Debates,* March 2, 1943, as quoted in D. Y. Timbrell and H. Anson-Cartwright, *Taxation of the Mining Industry in Canada,* Royal Commis-

sion on Taxation Study No. 9 (Ottawa: Queen's Printer, 1964), p. 113.

13. Canadian Metal Mining Association, *Submission to Royal Commission on Canada's Economic Prospects* (Toronto, 1956), p. 10.

14. As cited in Timbrell and Anson-Cartwright, op. cit., p. 118.

15. W. Keith Buck, *Mineral Development Policy*, op. cit. pp. 5-6.

16. *Final Report of the Royal Commission on Canada's Economic Prospects* (Ottawa: Queen's Printer, 1957), p. 229.

17. D. J. Daly, "Economic Appraisal of the Proposals for Tax Reform," memorandum prepared at the request of the International Nickel Company of Canada, Limited, reproduced in House of Commons, *Proceedings of the Standing Committee on Finance, Trade and Economic Affairs*, No. 64, June 16, 1970, Appendix D, p. 64:131-137. See also R. W. Boadway and J. M. Treddenick, *The Impact of the Mining Industries on the Canadian Economy* (Kingston, Ontario: Centre for Resource Studies, Queen's University, 1977), Chap. 6.

18. E. J. Benson, *Proposals for Tax Reform*, White Paper (Ottawa: Queen's Printer, 1969), p. 64.

19. Ibid., p. 65.

20. House of Commons, Standing Committee on Finance, Trade, and Economic Affairs, *Respecting the White Paper Entitled Proposals for Tax Reform, Eighteenth Report*, 28th Parl., 2nd Sess., October, 1970, p. 74. The Senate Committee had substantial reservations about the proposed tax changes (see Senate Standing Committee on Banking, Trade and Commerce, "Report on the White Paper Proposals for Tax Reform," *Journals of the Senate of Canada*, Vol. 116, Part 1, September, 1970, Appendix, p. 14).

21. Alan H. Rugman, "Risk and Return in the Canadian Mining Industry," working paper, University of Winnipeg, n.d.

22. Coopers and Lybrand, *A Comparative Study of Tax Systems and Their Effects on Foreign Mining Investments* (American Mining Congress, 1975), p. 5.

23. The interest that policy-makers have in comparative tax legislation and the difficulties in drawing conclusions from such studies were illustrated in 1952 by the Paley Commission. A comparative study of U.S. and Canadian mineral taxation could conclude only that "the metal mining industries seem to receive more generous treatment under the Canadian law whenever the 3-year exemption of new mines is available [but] in other cases the results of the comparison are not clear" (*Resources for Freedom* [the Paley Report], a report to the President by the President's Materials Policy Commission [Washington, D.C.: U.S. Government Printing Office, 1952], Vol. V, p. 32).

24. Price Waterhouse and Co., *The Winds of Change: Tax Increases for Mining* (1974), Figure 11, p. 32.

25. John H. De Young, Jr., "The Impact of Recent Changes in Canadian Tax Laws on the Mineral Industries," in U.S. Geological Survey, Office of Resource Analysis, *Comparative Study: Canadian-United States Resource Programs*, study prepared at the request of Senator Ted Stevens (Washington, D.C.: U.S. Government Printing Office, 1975), Chap. C, pp. 30-33. See also John E. Tilton, *The Future of Nonfuel Minerals* (Washington, D.C.: The Brookings Institution, 1977), p. 49.

26. Between 1884 and 1912 the federal government paid bounties totaling $17 million to encourage the production of iron and steel in Canada. Similarly, Ontario

paid a bounty of $1.00 per ton to companies making pig iron from ore mined in Ontario. (See E. S. Moore, *American Influence in Canadian Mining* [Toronto: University of Toronto Press, 1941], pp. 121-22.)

Direct operating subsidies have also been used in the past to offset the high costs of mining coal fields in depressed regions of Canada and to compensate for the artificially low official price for gold.

In 1948 the Emergency Gold Mining Assistance Act provided what was to be a temporary subsidy to the gold-mining industry. The act was repeatedly renewed, so that, by 1957, $112 million had been paid out; by 1971 over $300 million had been granted to Canadian gold-mining companies. (See Department of Energy, Mines and Resources, *Annual Report* [Ottawa, various issues].)

27. Total expenditures by the Department of Energy, Mines and Resources increased from $20 million in 1950 to over $1.3 billion in 1975 (Department of Finance, *Public Accounts* [Ottawa, various issues]).

Under the Roads to Resources Programme, approximately 3,000 miles of road were constructed to open up areas potentially rich in natural resources. Each province was allocated $7.5 million, for a total expenditure by the federal government of $75 million. (Department of Energy, Mines and Resources, *Annual Report,* 1967/68 and 1968/69 [Ottawa, 1968 and 1969].)

28. "RFC to Help Develop Ontario Ore Deposits," *New York Times,* January 13, 1943; and House of Commons, *Debates,* March 25, 1943, pp. 1575-78, and June 17, 1943, pp. 3761-63.

29. House of Commons, *Debates,* June 17, 1943, Vol. IV, p. 3761.

30. Ibid., p. 3762.

31. The mine was exceptionally profitable, and the company recovered all its investments within three years of starting production in 1965 (see Robert B. Gibson, *The Strathcona Sound Mining Project: A Case Study in Decision Making,* Background Study No. 42 [Ottawa: Science Council of Canada, 1978], pp. 20-24).

32. Ibid., pp. 25-26.

33. Department of Regional Economic Expansion, *Annual Report,* 1976/77 (Ottawa, 1977), Appendix B. As DREE has spent over $3 billion since its inception in 1969, it can be seen that, compared to other industrial sectors, the mineral industry has not received a disproportionate amount of financial assistance.

34. The relevant U.S. legislation calls for the imposition of countervailing duties whenever an imported product has been produced with any form of foreign government assistance judged to be a "bounty or grant."

35. A typical expression of support for the Imperial Preference System came from the Hon. J. A. MacKinnon, Minister of Trade and Commerce, before leaving to represent Canada at the 1947 trade talks in Geneva. The Minister reassured the House of Commons that imperial preferences would not be bargained away in exchange for tariff concessions from other countries, particularly the United States: "There is no intention to abolish imperial preferences, or to agree to large reductions in imperial preferences in exchange for meagre or nominal reductions in the tariff of the U.S. or other countries. . . . [It is] not simply a matter of trade but [is] an issue which may affect the large question of our relations with the British family of nations." (House of Commons, *Debates,* 3rd Sess., 20th Parl., Vol. II, March 26, 1947, p. 1759.)

36. House of Commons, *Debates,* 1st Sess., 21st Parl., March 28, 1950, p. 1219.

37. House of Commons, *Debates,* 1st Sess., 21st Parl., December 1, 1949, p. 2552. Similarly, the Hon. Douglas Abbott, Minister of Finance, told the House that, at Torquay in September, 1950, Canadian negotiators would seek a "better balance in our trade with the U.S., the sterling area, and Western Europe" (House of Commons, *Debates,* March 28, 1950, p. 1218).

38. Specific U.S. tariff reductions included the following: aluminum and alloys, from 2 cents to 1-1/2 cents per pound; lead, from 2-1/8 cents to 1-1/16 cents per pound; zinc ores, from 3/4 cents to 3/5 cents per pound; and zinc blocks and pigs, from 7/8 cents to 7/10 cents per pound (see House of Commons, *Debates,* 4th Sess., 21st Parl., Vol. III, May 8, 1951, p. 2827).

39. House of Commons, *Debates,* 3rd Sess., 22nd Parl., Vol. V, June 7, 1956, p. 4792. For a listing of U.S. tariff concessions on Canadian exports of metals and metal manufactures, see House of Commons, *Debates,* June 7, 1956, Appendix, p. 4835.

40. House of Commons, *Debates,* 3rd Sess., 22nd Parl., July 9, 1956, p. 5792.

41. House of Commons, *Debates,* 3rd Sess., 22nd Parl., June 7, 1956, Appendix, p. 4835.

42. House of Commons, *Proceedings of the Standing Committee on Finance, Trade and Economic Affairs Regarding the Kennedy Round Tariff Resolution,* No. 25, 2nd Sess., 27th Parl., February 13, 1968, p. 25-5.

43. See "The Kennedy Round: A Detailed Report," *Foreign Trade* 128, No. 1 (July, 1967): 6-12 and 19-23.

44. See Caroline Pestieau, *The Sector Approach to Trade Negotiations: Canadian and U.S. Interests* (Montreal: C. D. Howe Research Institute, 1976).

45. See "Stockpile Objectives for Selected Minerals over the Entire Life of the National and Supplemental Strategic Stockpiles," supplement to a statement by Simon D. Strauss on behalf of the American Mining Congress regarding stockpile goals announced by the Administration on October 1, 1976, before the Joint Committee on Defense Production, Washington, D.C., November 24, 1976.

46. Ibid., pp. 3 and 8.

47. For a discussion of the lead and zinc quotas, see Orris C. Herfindahl, *Three Studies in Mineral Economics* (Washington, D.C.: Resources for the Future, 1961), Chap. 3, pp. 37-63.

48. As cited in Canadian Metal Mining Association, *Submission to the United States Tariff Commission Presented on Behalf of the Lead- and Zinc-Producing Industry of Canada* (Toronto, 1960), p. 7.

49. Ibid.

50. See, for example, "U.S. Sulfur Producers Are Injured by Imports from Canada, Unit Rules," *Wall Street Journal* (New York), October 22, 1973; "Aluminum Producers Face Investigation by U.S. for Possible Anti-Trust Violations," *Wall Street Journal* (New York), November 4, 1975; and "Prices of Zinc Are under Study in Anti-Trust Case," *Wall Street Journal* (New York), May 18, 1976.

51. *An Act Respecting the Export and Import of Strategic and Other Goods,* 2-3 Elizabeth II, Chapter 27 (assented to March 31, 1954, as amended 1974), sec. 3 (a.1) and (a.2).

52. See Canadian Prices and Incomes Commission (John H. Young, Chairman), "Copper Price and Supply in Canada," Ottawa, November 10, 1970, pp. 19-22.

An early example of export duties on ores and metals is provided in *An Act Respecting Export Duties,* June 29, 1897, which allowed the Canadian government to impose duties—up to a specific limit—on nickel, copper, lead, and silver. (Provisions were also made for export duties on logs and pulpwood.) (See *Statutes of Canada, 1896-1897,* Chapter 17.)

53. Senate, *Debates,* May 6, 1974, p. 388.

54. Department of Energy, Mines and Resources, *Potash,* MR 156 (Ottawa, 1976), Figure 1, p. 3. Price is quoted in dollars per ton of K_2O equivalent.

55. Saskatchewan Queen's Bench, "Central Canada Potash Co. Ltd. and Attorney General of Canada v. Attorney General for Saskatchewan, Minister of Mineral Resources for Saskatchewan and Government of Saskatchewan," *Western Weekly Reports* 5 (1975): 193-328.

56. *Western Weekly Reports* 1 (1977): 487-525.

57. Embassy of the United States of America, "Aide-Mémoire," Ottawa, December 9, 1975.

58. Department of External Affairs, "Potash," text of a note from the Government of Canada to the Embassy of the United States of America, Ottawa, March 23, 1976.

59. In hearings before a Senate Committee the Director General of the Office of Special Import Policy admitted that he could not think of one non-agricultural product other than potash that might qualify for export controls under amendment a.2: "I think the answer is to be found in the potash situation that arose a few years ago. . . . [The] government felt that it was ineffectual, in as much as the Saskatchewan government took over the job of setting up [an] export control mechanism" (see Standing Senate Committee on Banking, Trade and Commerce, *Evidence on Bill C-4 to Amend the Export and Import Permits Act,* May 7, 1974, pp. 5:7 and 5:11).

60. *Framework Agreement for Commercial and Economic Co-operation Between Canada and the European Communities,* Ottawa, July 6, 1976, Art. II, sec. 1(b).

61. See Charles Pentland, "Linkage Politics: Canada's Contract and the Development of the European Communities' External Relations," *International Journal* 32, No. 2 (Spring, 1977): 207-31.

62. "Framework for Economic Co-operation," an agreement signed by the Prime Minister of Canada and the Prime Minister of Japan, Tokyo, October 21, 1976.

63. Ibid. See the section entitled, "Development of Trade," No. 3(c), p. 2.

64. Ibid. See the section entitled "Development of Economic Cooperation," No. 2(b), p. 2.

65. Notes for a speech delivered by the Hon. Don Jamieson, Secretary of State for External Affairs, at a luncheon given in honor of the foreign minister of Japan, His Excellency Iichiro Hatoyama, Vancouver, June 13, 1977, pp. 8 and 9.

66. Secretary of State for External Affairs, "Statement by Mitchell Sharp at the Sixth Session of the United Nations General Assembly," New York City, April 11, 1974, p. 3.

67. United Nations Conference on Trade and Development, "Resolution Adopted by the Conference," 93(IV): Integrated Programme for Commodities TD/RES/93(IV), June 10, 1976.

68. United Nations Conference on Trade and Development, Trade and Development Board, Integrated Programme for Commodities, Intergovernmental Group of Experts on Copper, 2nd Sess., Geneva, February 7, 1977; Study No. 17, submitted by Canada, "Consultative Producer-Consumer Body on Copper," TD/B/IPC/Copper/Ac L.19, March 23, 1977.

69. United Nations Conference on Trade and Development, United Nations Tin Conference, 1975, "Text of the Fifth International Tin Agreement As Established by the Conference at Its Final Plenary Meeting on June 21, 1975," TED/TIN.5/10, June 24, 1975.

70. Aspects of the uranium cartel have been described in a variety of newspaper and magazine articles. See, for example, S. Probyn and M. Anthony, "The Cartel That Ottawa Built," *Canadian Business* 50, No. 11 (November, 1977): 36; "Uranium Probe Papers Imply Ottawa Participant," *Globe and Mail* (Toronto), June 17, 1977; "Taking the Fifth," *The Economist*, June 18, 1977, p. 98.

71. The Canadian uranium industry is no stranger to governmental control. During World War II a joint Canadian-U.K. project was organized to investigate the possibility of creating an atomic war weapon. With the Americans studying the same concept, the future supply of uranium became an urgent problem. Consequently, the Canadian government, through the offices of the Minister of Munitions and Supply, C. D. Howe, secretly entered the stock market and quietly bought control of Eldorado Mining, one of the few uranium-producing companies in the world at that time. Today, Eldorado Nuclear Limited is a major entry on the list of twelve crown corporations owned by the federal government and engaged in mineral fuel development.

72. House of Commons, *Debates*, October 25, 1977, p. 218.

73. House of Commons, *Debates*, November 24, 1977, p. 1228.

74. House of Commons, *Debates*, June 17, 1977, p. 6785.

75. During World War II the federal government participated directly in the mining industry through Wartime Metals Corporation, a crown corporation organized in March, 1942, to explore for mineral deposits in Canada. Wartime Metals also became the instrument for very close U.S.-Canadian cooperation involving an imaginative arrangement whereby the U.S. government financed the capital investment and operating expenses of selected Canadian mines to meet U.S. mineral needs; Wartime Metals, on behalf of the Canadian Department of Munitions and Supply, supervised the development and operation of these mines. By the end of its three-and-one-half-year existence, Wartime Metals had brought fourteen mineral projects to fruition, eight of these as an agent of the U.S. government. (See Kennedy, *History of the Department of Munitions and Supply*, Vol. 1, pp. 506-18.)

76. In this agreement the company undertook to bring into production a mine capable of producing 525,000 tons of ore per annum and a concentrator capable of processing the ore prior to shipment. The mine was to operate for twelve to thirteen years and was to employ Inuit workers to the extent possible. The lead and zinc

concentrate was to be exported for smelting in Europe and the United States. (See *Agreement Between Her Majesty the Queen, in Right of Canada and Mineral Resources International Limited,* June 13, 1974.)

77. The other shareholders are Mineral Resources International Limited of Toronto, with 59.9 percent, and two European companies, Metal Gesellschaft AG. and Billiton, N.V., each with 11.25 percent.

78. Department of Indian Affairs and Northern Development, *Canada's North 1970-1980* (Ottawa, 1972), p. 29.

79. At the official opening of the Nanisivik mine, the Minister of Indian and Northern Affairs, Jean Chrétien, said: "This is a pilot Arctic mining venture involving many new concepts. . . . It is my hope that it will be a model for future mineral developments in the Arctic" (Department of Indian and Northern Affairs, "Communiqué: Speech Notes for the Hon. Jean Chrétien, Minister of Indian and Northern Affairs, at the Signing of the Nanisivik Mines Ltd. Agreement," Frobisher Bay, Northwest Territories, June 19, 1974).

In a 1977 speech to representatives of the Canadian mining industry, the parliamentary secretary to the Minister of Indian Affairs and Northern Development said that "the days of open-handed government assistance to the private sector of the northern economy are over. . . . Government will determine its participation in individual mining projects based on an evaluation of each proposal. It could conceivably become a majority partner in some mines." (*Globe and Mail* [Toronto], December 3, 1977.)

80. Canada Development Corporation, "Corporate Policy," in *Annual Report,* 1974 (Vancouver, 1975), p. 4.

81. Burgain G. Hayes, Jr., "Texasgulf, Inc., vs. Canada Development Corporation, 366 F. Supp. 367 (S.D. Tex. 1973)," *Texas International Law Journal* 9 (1974): 255.

82. Donald Creighton, *Canada's First Century: 1867-1967* (Toronto: MacMillan, 1970), p. 353.

83. Harry G. Johnson, *The Canadian Quandary* (Toronto: McGraw-Hill, 1963), p. 9. The debate over foreign ownership and control in Canada has generated a vast literature. The references to professors Johnson and Creighton have been selected to represent two of the main points of view concerning the pros and cons of foreign—largely U.S.—investment in Canada.

84. House of Commons, Standing Committee on External Affairs and National Defence, *Proceedings Respecting Policy Defence and External Affairs, Canada-U.S. Relations,* No. 33, July 13-27, 1970, p. 98.

85. As reported in *Canadian News Facts,* June 16-30, 1974, p. 1222.

86. Canadian Mining Regulations, S.O.R./61-86, as amended by ss. 45(5), (6), made pursuant to the Territorial Lands Act, R.S.C. 1970, c.T.-6 and the Public Lands Act, R.S.C. 1970, c.T.-29. Similarly, financial assistance for exploratory work in northern Canada is available only to companies meeting this requirement (see Northern Mineral Exploration Assistance Regulations, S.O.R./66-404, as amended by S.O.R./67-584 and S.O.R./69-346 enacted under The Appropriation Act, No. 9, 1966).

87. *Foreign Investment Review Act,* 21-22 Elizabeth II, Chap. 46, December 12, 1973.

88. "Factors to be taken into account include, *inter alia,* the effect of the acquisition or establishment on the level and nature of economic activity in Canada, including . . . the effect on employment, on resource processing, on the utilization of parts, components and services produced in Canada, and on exports from Canada" (*Foreign Investment Review Act,* sec. 2, subsec. 2(a)).

See also "Principles of International Business Conduct," devised in 1975 by the minister responsible for the administration of the act. Foreign-owned firms in Canada are advised to, *inter alia,* "extend the processing in Canada of natural resource products to the maximum extent feasible on an economic basis" (*Foreign Investment Review* 1, No. 1 [August, 1977]: 18).

89. Foreign Investment Review Agency, "Guidelines Concerning Related Business," consolidation of extracts from *Canada Gazette,* Part I, August 2, 1974, and March 19, 1977, Guideline 2, pp. 8-9.

8

Forces Underlying the Evolution of Natural Resource Policies in Quebec

GÉRARD GAUDET

Introduction

The purpose of this chapter is to describe the main factors affecting the evolution of policies toward the development of natural resources in Quebec. It is not our purpose to analyze in detail, and to pass judgment on, the validity of any specific policy or government action or of the whole set of such policies or actions. Our main objective is to assemble the factors that should be helpful in explaining the "why" of such policies or actions and their probable orientation in the medium term.

Lessons from the history of natural resource development in Quebec have had a considerable impact on the evolution of attitudes toward policy-making with regard to natural resources over the past fifteen or twenty years. It is appropriate, therefore, to review briefly the major historical forces that have shaped the development of natural resources in Quebec. The major part of the paper, however, is devoted to a description of the main economic-policy preoccupations that began taking form in the early 1960s and have now become part of the mainstream of thought in Quebec and to an attempt to relate the policy orientations in the field of natural resources to them.

Three dominant themes emerge from a survey of studies of Quebec's economy and from other analytical literature: the difficulty in reconciling the continued need for foreign capital with the desire to promote a greater integration of new capital investments into the Quebec economy; concern over the weakness of the interindustrial trade structure of the economy;[1] and concern with the participation of local entrepreneurship in the economic-development process. These concerns now seem inscribed in the political economy of Quebec as elements of continuity; although they do not allow us to predict the exact means of intervention by the government, they certainly allow us to understand better the motivation and the general orientation of future policy, particularly that in the field of natural resources, the backbone of the Quebec economy.

Historical Patterns

Forest and mineral resources, hydro-electric power, and labor have
provided the basis of Quebec's economic growth. Comparative advantages
in these areas have been exploited against a background of general
openness of the Quebec economy to the import of the complementary
factors of production—capital, technology, and entrepreneurship. These
factors were provided in a very large measure by U.S. firms, especially in
the period after World War I, when U.S. capital began to assume a
preponderant role following the decline of British investment in Canada.
The U.S. presence, however, was already being felt in Quebec at the turn
of the century.[2]

The growth process led to the development of three predominant types of
industries in Quebec.[3] The first is tied to the development of natural
resources and is very highly export-oriented, with principal markets outside
Canada, primarily in the United States. Included in this category are forest
and mineral products and other products highly dependent on the
availability of hydro-electric power. Table 8.1 illustrates the importance of
these industries in Quebec's exports to the United States. Seven of the
export categories reflect natural resources indigenous to Quebec.
Aluminum exports reflect the advantage to production in Quebec arising
from abundant and relatively low-cost hydro-electric power. Automobiles
and aircraft components are exported to the United States under special
trade arrangements.

The second type of industries, characterized by a relatively high labor
intensity, also contributes to exports, but in this case exports almost
exclusively to the rest of Canada, principally Ontario.[4] For example, the
textile, clothing, and furniture industries are now only marginally able to
withstand foreign competition, even with tariff protection, and constitute a
weak link in the Quebec economy.

A third group of industries includes those in which Quebec has no
particular international comparative advantage; however, for various
reasons, domestic markets consume a high percentage, if not all, of the final
product. Included here are the service industries and food and beverage
products.

U.S. capital and initiatives have played a major role, although not to the
same extent for all the products involved, in the development of the first
two groups of industries. However, the forces that have shaped their
development have to be viewed separately. Whereas in the second, labor-
intensive, type of industries, political forces and decisions—if only in the

TABLE 8.1

Major Quebec Exports to the United States, 1977[a]

Item	Quebec Exports	Total Canadian Exports	Quebec's Share of Total (percentages)
	(thousand Canadian dollars)		
Newsprint paper	860,594	1,869,417	46.0
Iron ores and concentrates	653,330	756,310	86.4
Passenger automobiles and chassis	398,651	3,948,142	10.1
Aluminum, including alloys	396,292	536,275	73.9
Aircraft engines and parts	151,712	168,711	89.9
Copper and alloys	147,913	196,751	75.2
Precious metals, including alloys	133,955	388,715	34.5
Woodpulp and similar pulp	126,522	1,218,688	10.4
Lumber, softwood	119,269	1,869,774	6.4
Asbestos, unmanufactured	105,961	138,168	76.7

[a]Exports as classified by province of lading.

Source: Statistics Canada, *Exports by Countries,* 1977 (Ottawa, 1978).

form of tariff protection—were clearly significant, market forces have been overriding in the resource-based industries. A historical perspective shows that very rarely have political decisions by the Quebec or the Canadian government tended to impede these market forces.[5] In the natural resource industries an attitude of *laissez-faire* clearly dominated, at least until the early 1960s.

With respect to the development of natural resources, it is a good working hypothesis to consider the Quebec economy as an integrated part of the North American economy. The development of natural resources in Quebec was marked mainly by economic, technological, and geographic factors, and the original impulse most often came from the United States.[6] Almost all the location decisions in the natural resource sector can be explained by the complementarity of the relationship noted earlier. U.S. firms brought the capital, the technology, and the management know-how. They found a good labor force and raw materials that could be extracted for use by U.S. industry or, if processed in Quebec, to satisfy U.S. markets. Political barriers, although sometimes a hindrance, were only a secondary consideration in this spatial development.[7] Given the relative size of the markets, the technology, and the amount of capital necessary, it was

perhaps inevitable that the development of natural resources in
Quebec—and in Canada generally, for that matter—historically had to
develop in the context of the overall North American economy.

Pulp and paper, hydro-electricity, aluminum, the base metals, and
asbestos are all cases in point.[8] The original development impulse always
came from an increasing U.S. demand. Given the heavy capital
expenditures required, U.S. demand was followed by a flow of U.S.
capital, accompanied by U.S. entrepreneurs and firms. Where Anglo-
Canadian firms became involved, it was seldom without the help of U.S.
capital and financiers.[9] Very rarely did the development initiative come
from indigenous entrepreneurs. Whatever the historical, cultural, or economic explanations,[10] this must be accepted as an important characteristic
of the history of Quebec's economic development. It is important because it
is a characteristic that has influenced economic policy-making since 1960
and is liable to continue to do so.

There is a widespread perception that French Canadian society has
historically hesitated to accept, and perhaps been totally opposed to, industrialization. There is validity in the notion that the influence of the clergy
and of conservative nationalist elements, who favored an agricultural and
rural orientation for the Quebec economy and society, had an important
bearing on the province's early development. This notion, however, provides an incomplete picture of the historical perception of economic
development in Quebec. Ever since the turn of the century, successive
governments, largely supported by liberal writers and by the liberal press,
have been favorable to the industrialization of Quebec,[11] an industrialization that was to rest on the economy's endowment of natural resources. The
following quotation from a speech by Premier Taschereau in 1927 provides
an eloquent summary of these attitudes toward, and strategies for, economic development, not only of that particular government, but of successive governments until at least 1960:

> We want to bring in industries, and we are ready to do all possible in that di-
> rection. We are not afraid of foreign capital. We invite foreign capital to join
> with us in developing our natural resources, and creating industries here. Let
> the capital of England and of the United States come here as much as it
> wishes and multiply our industries, so that our people will have work. Such
> capital is welcome. I am not afraid, and I will never be afraid that our French-
> Canadians will become Americanized because of an inflow of American capital.
> They have resisted other dangers and other trials, and as I have said many times,
> I prefer to import American dollars to exporting Canadian workmen.[12]

The economic-development model implicit in such a statement is quite
clear. The development of natural resources was seen as a primary force in

ensuring industrialization and a balanced economy for Quebec. Reliance was to be placed on the development of natural resources to stimulate industries and to create jobs, the principal goal of the government. However, the means of implementing this economic-development model seemed limited, given the small size of the internal market and the lack of local financial institutions necessary to channel the large amounts of capital needed. The most obvious strategy appeared to be to rely on continental market forces for the necessary growth impulse. This was an especially attractive strategy in that the North American economy, whose demand for imported natural resources was growing, was also ready to provide the entrepreneurship, technology, and capital.

From the very beginning, as the Quebec economy began to feel the thrust of the rapid industrialization of the North American economy, the objective of the Quebec government for its natural resource sector was one of maximum development, which was counted upon to serve as the principal moving force in the development of the economy as a whole and in its integration with the industrialized world. This objective was promoted by a policy of *laissez-faire* combined with the active seeking and encouragement of foreign, and especially U.S., capital and entrepreneurship.

Foreign investors were quick to respond and were largely responsible for the "take-off" of Quebec's economy. The growth of the natural resource sector was assured, as was a reasonable rate of growth of the economy as a whole. However, this initial reliance on foreign investors, who brought with them technology and entrepreneurship, quickly turned into a dependency relationship. Foreign investment, which in most industrialized countries constitutes a means of transmission of know-how and of modern technology, had very few of these secondary effects on Quebec and very little impact on the technical and managerial training of the local labor force. While this limited impact may be partly explained by socio-cultural factors, it is not unrelated to the policies of successive governments that have promoted continued dependence on foreign investment for maximum development of natural resources.

It is against this background that we must consider the policy orientations that appeared in the 1960s and that are likely to continue. Inasmuch as we can distinguish between growth and development, we might say that Quebec's economy had many of the characteristics of an underdeveloped economy. It had known growth, but not, to the same extent, development. Although the standard of living of the average Quebecker had grown at a rate comparable to that of most industrialized nations, the province lacked the coherent and well-integrated interindustry trade structure vital to any well-developed economy.

As the world economy entered a period in which international competition for existing markets was becoming more and more acute, access to large markets was becoming an important factor in location decisions, and new and competitive sources of natural resources were being put into production, it was bound to become apparent that the mere presence of natural resources and manpower would not be sufficient to assure the development of Quebec's economy. It was bound to become apparent also that the type of economic development that results from an almost complete reliance on foreign investment, besides creating a dependency that can diminish internal dynamism of the local economy, does not necessarily bring about the type of industrial structure that one would like to be able to count on in order to face a world economy characterized by rapidly changing conditions. That it would appears to have been an implicit assumption in the development strategy of Quebec governments during the first six decades of this century.

The "Quiet Revolution"

A period of important social changes in Quebec, the "quiet revolution," began with the change of government in 1960. Along with these social changes appeared a new awareness on the economic front. The change in attitude can perhaps best be grasped by comparing the following excerpt from a speech by Premier Lesage in 1963 with that of Premier Taschereau in 1927, cited earlier.

Economic progress . . . has occurred without us, Quebeckers. We have profited passively from it; we have collected marginal benefits from it, almost by accident. We have, somewhat despite ourselves, profited from the fact that the North American economic context was such that there was a need — in the United States, for example — for the natural resources that could be found on our territory. . . .

The result of this situation is that the movement of industrial activity in our economy depends in large measure not on what we decide to do or not to do, but rather on what groups foreign to our collective aspirations choose to do or not do. I obviously hold no grudge against Canadian, American, or European firms that have invested capital here during the past few years; they act quite logically in looking after their own interests first. As Quebeckers, we would act in the same way if we had large amounts of capital invested abroad. We have no intention, either, of refusing them access to our natural resources; on the contrary, we need them now and for a long time to come.

But the presence and the activity of foreign capital in Quebec have created among many people an ill-fated attitude which, if it were to be shared by every one of us, would aggravate our present dependence in Quebec. Indeed, many have come to think that the only way to promote economic progress in

Quebec is by a still greater inflow of foreign capital. They forget that this is only one possible source of progress, and that there exists in reality at least one other: our own participation in the economic life of the province.[13]

This statement, which would still receive wide support today as a broad diagnosis of the economic situation, is interesting because it provides, in a sense, a framework for an analysis of the new attitude to economic policy-making that was taking form in the early 1960s and still prevails.

Three themes are apparent in this passage. First, Quebec nationalism was compatible with a continued high degree of openness to foreign investment. Second, there was a major preoccupation with a perceived weakness in Quebec's industrial structure. Third, there was a concern that Quebeckers should participate more actively in the development of their economy. These themes are examined individually below.

Approach to Foreign Investment

Quebec's new attitudes toward economic policy-making reflect a refusal to close the door to foreign investment or to attribute all the ills of the economy to foreign investors. What is stressed is that economic development cannot continue to be based primarily on the capacity to attract foreign investment.

It is interesting to draw a parallel here between Canadian economic nationalism, which came into prominence during the late 1950s with the Gordon Report (1958), followed by the Watkins Report (1968) and the Gray Report (1972), and economic nationalism in Quebec, particularly vis-à-vis the United States. Although many aspects of Canadian foreign-investment policy at the federal level are still being debated across Canada, this series of reports culminated in the 1973 Foreign Investment Review Act, the first piece of Canadian legislation to propose some degree of overall regulation of foreign investment.

The official reaction from the Quebec government at the time is significant.[14] It reflected the fact that Quebeckers have not generally perceived the problems raised by foreign investment in quite the same way as have other Canadians — although Quebeckers are preoccupied by the dependence of their economy upon foreign initiatives, their reaction to the act was based more on the necessity of their getting involved in their own economy than on the enactment of legislation related to the nature and importance of foreign penetration.[15] The Quebec government criticized the lack of concern for regional economies inside Canada implicit in the provisions of the act. It feared that such legislation could be detrimental to Quebec's efforts to transform its own industrial structure. It felt that, in the present state of development of Quebec's economy, the participation of foreign investment should not be ruled out, especially investment that might bring about fruitful technological transfers, but that in any case it was up to Quebec to decide on its own needs and priorities. It feared that the criteria proposed, being Canadian in scope, could tend to reinforce the existing Canadian industrial structure to the detriment of Quebec's efforts to transform its own industrial structure and to stimulate the participation of local entrepreneurs in this transformation.

This reaction reflected more than a political strategy. Canada's and Quebec's brands of economic nationalism are fundamentally different. Quebec nationalism is "pro-québécois," since it can identify itself with a unique culture, reaffirmed by differences in values and traditions, and particularly in language, which is distinct from that of the rest of the North American continent. Canadian nationalism, on the other hand, tends to be more anti-American, since it seeks to preserve or promote cultural differences with the United States without the natural safeguard provided by a difference in language.[16]

Economic nationalism, especially vis-à-vis the United States, is therefore much less apparent in Quebec than in the rest of Canada, and this can be partly explained by cultural differences. But economic reasons are also important as an explanation of these differences in attitudes toward foreign investment. It is quite clear that, at the present stage of development of its economy, Quebec cannot afford to take as restrictive a position toward foreign investment as can Ontario, for instance—a point that is also true for the Maritime provinces. It has even been argued that the increase in U.S. investment in Canada has contributed to the reinforcement of the two nationalisms. On the one hand, English Canadian nationalism seeks a united front to restrict U.S. investment in Canada. On the other hand, Quebec feels that it needs U.S. investment (and other foreign investment) to maintain the rate of growth of its economy and to increase its independence vis-à-vis English Canada. Such investment would, it is argued, tend to reinforce the anti-American sentiment embodied in English Canadian nationalism.[17] The present constitutional crisis seems, however, to have revived another dimension of English Canadian nationalism, which Abraham Rotstein calls "mappism" and which is centered on themes of territorial integrity and territorial sovereignty of the central government.[18] This dimension is apt to overshadow that of foreign investment, at least for some time.

Quebec's Industrial Structure

A major preoccupation that surfaced during the 1960s and that remains at the forefront of current economic-policy discussions in Quebec is the weakness of Quebec's industrial structure. It has already been noted that the province's economic growth has not been accompanied by the development of a strong interindustrial trade structure. The predominance of foreign investors and foreign firms, particularly in the natural resource sector, has resulted in a situation where the economy has not benefited fully from the spread effect that this investment might have had.[19] There is little natural incentive for foreign firms to integrate into the local economy. Although, theoretically, the presence of foreign firms might have encouraged local suppliers to develop and to become competitive with foreign suppliers of these firms, this has not been the case. The spread effects have thus quite naturally tended to be oriented toward the home economies of the foreign firms. This process has left the local economy in a state of disequilibrium that could be described as a form of underdevelopment,[20] with a truncated industrial structure unable to adapt promptly to changes in external and internal demand.[21]

The primary sector, which in large measure still represents the basis of comparative advantage in the Quebec economy, accounted for 4.7 percent of gross domestic product (GDP) in 1974. The importance of this figure in any economy can be evaluated properly only by considering the backward and forward linkage effects on the rest of the economy. The primary sector itself is not, by definition, a sector with very high backward linkage effects, but it is usually expected to have a high forward linkage effect.[22] It is at the intermediate stage that both the backward and the forward linkage effects become important.[23] The local economy will benefit from these backward and forward linkage effects to the extent that the primary sector is well integrated into the interindustrial structure of the economy. In Quebec's case this degree of integration is not very high. Only about 30 percent of minerals extracted, for example, are directed toward the local secondary sector, the rest being exported before reaching the secondary stage.[24] Not more than one-third of the value added in the secondary sector can be attributed to the transformation of natural resources exploited in Quebec (this includes fisheries and agriculture, which account for a relatively important share).[25] The secondary sector itself accounted for only 31.8 percent of Quebec's GDP in 1974, a large part of which was attributable to the weak traditional industries (clothing, textiles, furniture, and so forth), which survive only with the help of tariff protection. It follows that a substantial part of the linkage effects that one would theoretically expect from the exploitation of natural resources is in fact exported.

The weakness of the industrial structure will certainly remain a major policy preoccupation for governments for years to come, especially since there are signs that the interindustrial structure could continue to weaken gradually.[26] There is certainly reason for concern in the fact that both the primary and secondary sectors have been losing ground simultaneously.

They represented, respectively, 8.5 and 40.4 percent of GDP in 1956, 6.4 and 36.1 percent in 1966, but only 4.7 and 31.8 percent in 1974.[27] It has been estimated that, if the present trend were to continue, these shares would fall to 3.2 and 25.8 percent by 1985, leaving 71 percent of GDP accounted for by the tertiary sector.[28] The development of the service sector is not in itself a reason for concern, since a well-developed service sector obviously constitutes an important element in the structure of any economy. What can be aimed for, however, is a situation in which the service sector is backed by a secondary sector that, while not necessarily large, constitutes a stable and dynamic element of the economy and is well-integrated with the natural resource sector.

Local Participation

A third major theme manifested in the 1963 speech quoted earlier is the need for Quebeckers to participate more actively in the development of their economy. Much has been written and said on this subject, which remains an important current policy issue. It is becoming widely accepted that lack of participation cannot be explained solely by cultural reasons. This interpretation would appear to be well-founded if one considers that the service sector offers a quite different picture than do the secondary and primary sectors. The service sector provides numerous examples of successful local entrepreneurs, which suggests that the explanation might be socio-economic as well as cultural. In other words, the lack of active participation of local entrepreneurs in the development process is due not to an inherent lack of entrepreneurship but to a lack of access to the necessary capital, technology, know-how, and information. This situation may have been further aggravated by a sense of dependence on foreign entrepreneurship that has developed from the continued presence of foreign firms.

The rejection of a primarily cultural explanation in favor of a socio-economic explanation opens the door to the possibility that the existing situation might be remedied by appropriate government action.[29] This possibility becomes all the more likely if one believes, as many do, that the passiveness of Quebeckers has not been unrelated to the lack of dynamism in the secondary sector.

Quebec's Policies Regarding Natural Resources

There still does not exist a specific set of policies that might be identified as Quebec's "natural resource policy." Moreover, it is not really clear that it would be useful to conceive a set of policies specific to this sector except as an integral part of a more general economic-development strategy. Two key elements of such a general strategy arise from the major preoccupations that have evolved in Quebec over the past fifteen or twenty years. The first is that a development model that presupposes that the maximum exploitation of natural resources inevitably generates growth and development is being viewed with increasing skepticism, if it has not already been rejected. This skepticism is being reinforced by the sudden awareness over the past four or five years — an awareness that seems to have been unleashed by the Club of Rome studies and the oil crisis and is in no way specific to Quebec — that maximum exploitation is not necessarily synonymous with optimal exploitation when dealing with non-renewable resources. Pressures have grown on governments to assume the role of managers of natural resources in such a way as to attempt to maximize the net social (as opposed to private) benefits to be recovered from the exploitation of natural resources.[30] These pressures have already been reflected in attempts by governments to capture through taxation a greater share of the economic rent associated with the exploitation of non-renewable resources.

The second clearly indentifiable element of a general development strategy is an active role for the state, a role that had long been avoided with a general policy of *laissez-faire*. The institutional infrastructure necessary has been in place in Quebec since the 1960s, a period that saw the creation of a number of public enterprises in various sectors of the economy, and particularly in natural resources. These are the Société québécoise d'exploration minière (SOQUEM), the Société québécoise d'initiative pétrolière (SOQUIP), the Société de récupération et d'exploitation forestière (REX-FOR), the Sidérurgie du Québec (SIDBEC), and, more recently, the Société de développement de la Baie James (SDBJ). These state enterprises will undoubtedly continue to be privileged tools of government intervention in the development process.

State Enterprises

The *raison d'être* of these state enterprises can be directly related to the major preoccupations already mentioned. They were conceived, at least in part, as a means of reducing the obstacle that large capital requirements seemed to create to the entry of Quebec enterprises into their own natural resource industries and as a means of promoting the development of local expertise in the field, which might in the long run have a beneficial impact on bringing about a better integration of the natural resource sector into the local economy. They were created not to replace private enterprises in their traditional role of resource allocation, but to supplement this role with objectives that private enterprises might not naturally pursue.

The best example is probably SOQUEM. As with any other exploration company, its stated goals are to "carry out mining exploration by all methods; participate in the development of discoveries, including those made by others, with power to purchase and to sell properties at various stages of development and to associate itself with others for such purposes; participate in the bringing into production of mineral deposits, either by selling them outright or transferring them in return for a participation."[31] It has no special privileges and has to conduct its business according to the rules of the marketplace. However, the objective of a greater participation by Quebeckers in the bringing into production of Quebec's mineral resources lies at the origin of SOQUEM.

SOQUEM now has a capital stock of $45 million. It has, since its creation ten years ago, embarked on 225 exploration projects, many of them joint ventures with private enterprises, which have resulted in five discoveries, three of which are already producing mines. It has also extended its activities to that of a holding company, with managing interests in two producing companies.[32] There is thus no doubt that SOQUEM has made its presence felt in mining exploration in Quebec, and it would not be surprising to see the company become more extensively involved in production in an attempt to further the goal of the participation of Quebeckers in all stages of the mining industry.

Pursuit of Further Processing

In terms of more specific issues that are likely to retain attention in the natural resource sector in the coming years, further processing is one of the most important. The further-processing issue is, of course, directly related to the concern for a greater integration of the sector into the interindustrial structure of the economy. There are signs that efforts are being made to apply the means of intervention in this direction on a case-by-case basis rather than to adopt a single approach to all situations. There is thus an explicit recognition that each case can differ enormously in terms of industrial organization, and especially in terms of markets. In iron and steel it seems that efforts will be concentrated on completing the vertical integration of SIDBEC. In pulp and paper the problem, already under scrutiny, is one of maintaining the competitiveness of existing processing activities. Although no definite decisions have been announced, indications are that the most likely intervention, if any, will take the form of incentives for plant renovation and modernization, probably through the use of subsidies. In the case of nonferrous metals, the present market situation precludes much hope of progress in terms of further processing in the short run. The most likely course of action in the long run is a pragmatic one whereby the government would seek arrangements with the private sector, especially in the case of major new developments. This would, within the limits of profitability, assure the maximum degree of processing in Quebec. However, copper in particular and zinc to a lesser extent are now relatively well-integrated, at least to the semi-finished stage, and the problem is one of the exhaustion of known reserves, which would entail serious economic difficulty for certain regions. For this reason efforts will be concentrated in the coming years on the promotion of exploration.

Asbestos: A Unique Case

The case of asbestos is unique in many respects.[33] It is unique in that Quebec is the world's largest producer, with over 40 percent of total world production, and close to 60 percent if the USSR is excluded. The total annual value of production has, over the years, paralleled that of copper for Quebec.[34] Asbestos is also unique in that over 95 percent of its production is exported as raw material, a proportion largely exceeding that for most other minerals, and therefore creates very few jobs. It is also of extreme importance to the economy of a particular region of Quebec (the southeastern region), although this feature is shared by the mining industry in general. Finally, it is unique because it has attracted specific political attention for many years. The pressures to "do something" about asbestos are almost as old as the mines themselves,[35] the first one of which began operations in 1877. What is, in fact, most surprising is not the recent decision to create the Société nationale de l'amiante, which will take over Asbestos Corporation,[36] but the fact that successive governments were able to avoid a political decision concerning asbestos for so long.

The situation most closely resembling in certain respects the present situation in asbestos is that of forest products at the turn of the century. In the face of both a growing demand for, and a shortage of, wood in the United States at that time, Quebec was already exporting 200,000 cords of pulpwood a year to the United States, and this volume was increasing at an annual rate of 25 percent.[37] In an attempt to force greater local processing, in 1910 the Quebec government, following the action of Ontario, put an embargo on the export of wood cut on crown land. The U.S. government immediately reduced—in 1911—the tariff on newsprint and then abolished it completely in 1913, with the result that U.S. firms established pulp and paper plants in Quebec.[38] It is interesting to speculate on whether such an approach might have been attempted for asbestos, had it been possible. It was not, however, for the simple reason that asbestos deposits have, historically, been the property of the mining companies themselves,[39] and it is hard to predict what the impact of such a course of action would have been. It is likely that its impact on local processing would not have been felt as much as in the case of pulp and paper because of quite different demand situations in the two industries. Because of the multitude of products in which asbestos can be an input, often in very small proportions, the demand structure is much more complex than that in pulp and paper and probably offers a much less favorable context for attaining a high degree of local processing.[40]

The possibility of creating a marketing board for asbestos has been raised from time to time, but rejected — partly, it seems, because of the problem of the ownership of the deposits and partly because it would have hampered an already well-functioning and complex international market while providing only a slight chance of any success in achieving the goal of greater local processing.

Any initiative for an export tax on raw asbestos would have had to come from the federal government, which has exclusive jurisdiction over international trade. And in the unlikely event such a tax had been imposed, it would probably have been regarded as an intrusion by the federal government into provincial jurisdiction over natural resources.[41]

Therefore, once the political decision to intervene in asbestos was taken — a decision in line with the increasing preoccupation with the long-term-development process of the Quebec economy — the means of action were more or less dictated by the situation. Also weighing heavily in the balance was the fact that creating a state-owned company involved in asbestos from extraction to eventual transformation responds to Quebeckers' preoccupation with becoming involved in a natural resource sector in which they have been almost totally absent.

The overall chances of success of the Société nationale de l'amiante in greatly increasing the proportion of the raw material transformed locally must be judged as modest. However, the particular solution adopted guarantees that, as long as the Société nationale de l'amiante is required to abide by the rules of the game in a competitive international market, whatever local processing it manages to create probably has a greater chance of being economically viable in the long run than had it been the result of government-imposed artificial market barriers. It remains to be seen whether this solution will be adhered to, but it generally has been to date with respect to SOQUEM.

Other Issues

Among other specific issues that will continue to attract attention in the natural resource sector are health and safety, working conditions in general, the environment, and taxation. These issues are, of course, in no way peculiar to Quebec; in fact, the Quebec government has tended to follow the lead of other governments, both provincial and federal, in dealing with them. This is true, in particular, of taxation, where Quebec presents a relatively stable picture. Mining duties remained unchanged, and relatively low, from 1935 to 1965. The 1965 revision brought about changes in the structure of the tax and an overall increase in rates, partially offset by deductions designed to encourage exploration and processing. Mining taxation was thus brought in line with that in other provinces. In 1965-66, for the first time, mining revenues exceeded the expenses of the Department of

Natural Resources, a department traditionally geared mainly toward providing services to the industry.

The 1975 revision of the Mining Duties Act followed revisions in Ontario, Manitoba, and British Columbia. The rate structure was again modified, and higher rates and greater progressivity in the top brackets and a higher basic exemption were introduced. The act included a new provision allowing for an income-averaging and -loss offset. New investment allowances were introduced to encourage exploration, development, and transformation activity, and the existing processing allowance was modified to encourage a greater degree of processing.[42]

Between 1972 and 1975 there were also important changes in the Quebec corporate income tax, and these had a significant effect on the mining industry. They more or less reflected the changes in the federal corporate income tax that followed the Carter Commission Report. These included the disappearance of the three-year tax exemption for new mines, the replacement of the automatic 33.3 percent depletion allowance by an earned-depletion system, the disappearance of the deductibility of the mining tax for income tax purposes, and changes in the depreciation rates of certain assets. The tax rate itself remained unchanged.

Although no major overhaul of taxation is in sight, it is to be expected that future revisions will reflect attempts to reconcile the objective of capturing an appropriate share of the economic rent inherent in the exploitation of non-renewable natural resources with that of stimulating further processing and economic activity in general. The present economic climate is likely to give more weight to the growing pressures from the industry, which feels it has been unfavorably affected by the recent tax changes.

Prospects

There is little doubt that private enterprise and private capital will continue to play the dominant role in the development of natural resources in Quebec.[43] It is already a fact, however, that this role will be partly shared with state-owned enterprises, which will act both as observers and as direct participants in the development process. These enterprises are at the core of the development strategy taking shape in Quebec. This means of state intervention was, of course, not invented in Quebec. It is becoming an increasingly popular means of intervention in many other traditional capitalist economies where it is felt that the lack of adequate internal markets, and of a sufficiently dynamic internal economy, tends to render inefficient the more conventional forms of intervention — taxation, protection, and controls, for example — on which large and highly integrated economies may rely.

The state-owned firm as a particular form of intervention is often seen as the best means of reducing barriers to the integration of local entrepreneurship into the economic-development process. What the impact of this means of intervention will be in the long run is hard to predict. The long-term viability of these firms, however, is likely to depend very much on their capability to adapt, like other firms, to the highly competitive rules of the marketplace. Inasmuch as success is measured in relation to initial objectives, it is important for the Quebec economy that a goal of long-term economic viability and self-sustained dynamism, rather than mere size, be retained in relation to the efforts to improve the industrial structure and to further the integration of the natural resource sector with the secondary sector of the economy.

Notes

1. A description of an economy's interindustry trade structure is provided by input-output tables, which show the linkages among different sectors (see *Le système de comptabilité du Québec: analyses intersectorielles de l'économie du Québec* [Quebec: Quebec Bureau of Statistics and Laboratoire d'économétrie de l'Université Laval, 1974]). The relative strength of a structure can be measured by the nature of existing linkages compared with the potential that could be attained in a more highly integrated economy. The presence of "holes" in this structure can reflect a lack of diversification in economic activity and the existence of important leakages in favor of other economies.

2. See Albert Faucher, "Le caractère continental de l'industrialisation au Québec," *Recherches sociographiques* 6, No. 3 (September-December, 1965).

3. For an attempt to classify a number of industries along similar lines, see André Raynauld, *Croissance et structure économiques de la province de Québec* (Quebec: Quebec Ministry of Industry and Commerce, 1961), Chap. 7.

4. Although data on exports to other regions of Canada are incomplete, recent estimates for 1973 show that, of known Quebec exports, 35 percent went to Ontario, 13 percent to the western provinces, and 6.8 percent to the Atlantic provinces. This compares with 27.6 percent to the United States, 8.6 percent to EEC countries, and 8.4 percent to other countries. (See Carmine Nappi, "La souveraineté, la structure d'exportation et le choix d'une politique commerciale pour le Québec," in Association des économistes québécois, *Économie et indépendance* [Montreal: Édition Quinze, 1977], pp. 151-75.)

5. The most notable exception is probably the decision of the Quebec government in 1910 to impose an embargo on the export of pulpwood from crown land. This case is discussed briefly later in this chapter.

6. For an interpretation of the early history of industrialization in Quebec, see Albert Faucher and Maurice Lamontagne, "Histoire de l'industrialisation," in René Durocher and Paul-André Linteau, eds., *Le retard du Québec et l'infériorité économique des Canadiens français* (Quebec: Les éditions du Boréal Express, 1971).

7. Faucher, op. cit.

8. For a description and analysis of the birth of some of these industries in Quebec and of the role played by U.S. capital and enterprise, see Faucher, op. cit.

9. Faucher (op. cit.) provides a number of examples.

10. Some of the major theses are developed in Durocher and Linteau, op. cit. See also Norman W. Taylor, "French Canadians As Industrial Entrepreneurs," *Journal of Political Economy* 68, No. 1 (February, 1960).

11. This is well documented for 1918-29, a period marked by rapid progress in industrialization and urbanization, in Yves Roby, *Les Québécois et les investissements américains, 1918-1929* (Quebec: Les Presses de L'Université Laval, 1976).

12. Ibid., p. 169 (original in English).

13. Excerpt from a speech by Premier Lesage in the National Assembly on April 3, 1963; see the preface to *La Politique minière du Québec: ses objectifs, son cadre, ses instruments* (Quebec: Planification Branch, Quebec Ministry of Natural Resources, 1966) (author's translation).

14. See Government of Quebec, Executive Council, *Le cadre et les moyens d'une politique québécoise concernant les investissements étrangers,* Rapport du Comité interministériel sur les investissements étrangers (Quebec: Quebec Official Publisher, 1973), pp. 195-203.

15. Judging from the official program of the Parti Québécois, the present government will also take a pragmatic approach in dealing with the problem of foreign investment. It explicitly recognizes the need for foreign capital and the importance of taking into account the characteristics of each sector in dealing with the problem.

16. See Jacques Henry, "La dépendance structurelle du Québec dans un Canada dominé par les États-Unis," in Albert Legault and Alfred O. Hero, eds., *Le nationalisme québécois à la croisée des chemins,* Collection Choix (Quebec: Centre québécois de relations internationales, Laval University, 1975). Cultural implications of foreign investment from a Canadian point of view are discussed in the Gray Report (see *Le rapport Gray sur la maîtrise économique du milieu national: ce que nous coûtent les investissements étrangers* [Ottawa: Leméac/Le Devoir, 1971], pp. 99-104).

17. Robert Gilpin, "Les investissements directs américains et la présence de deux nationalismes au Canada," *Études internationales* 2, No. 1 (March, 1971).

18. See Abraham Rotstein's Walter Gordon Lecture delivered at Laval University on January 26, 1978, and published in *Le Devoir* (February 2, 1978) under the title "De quoi le nationalisme canadien-anglais est-il fait?"

19. *Le cadre et les moyens,* op. cit., Chap. 2, *passim.*

20. Ibid., p. 36.

21. For a discussion of the implications for the Quebec economy, see Quebec Ministry of Industry and Commerce, *Une politique économique québécoise* (Quebec, 1974), pp. 27-34.

22. Albert O. Hirschman, *The Strategy of Economic Development* (New Haven: Yale University Press, 1958), Chap. 6.

23. Ibid.

24. See Direction des études industrielles, *Evolution et développement de l'industrie minière et de son intégration à l'économie du Québec* (Quebec: Quebec Ministry of Industry and Commerce, 1977).

25. This also includes the aluminum industry, which imports raw materials but utilizes considerable amounts of hydro-electricity.

26. Quebec Planning Development Bureau, *Analyse structurelle à moyen terme de l'économie du Québec,* Collection études et recherches (Quebec: Quebec Official Publisher, 1977).

27. See P. Fréchette, R. Jouandet-Bernadat, and J.-P. Vézina, *L'Économie du Québec* (Montreal: Les éditions HRW, 1975), Chap. 15.

28. Quebec Planning Development Bureau, op. cit., p. xiv.

29. Recent language legislation, if considered from a strictly economic standpoint, has had as objectives the further integration of foreign firms into the local economy and the reduction of obstacles to greater integration of local expertise into the economic-development process.

30. See, for example, *Mineral Policy Objectives for Canada: A Statement by Federal and Provincial Ministers Responsible for Mineral Policy,* 1973.

31. Quoted in Côme Carbonneau, "From Dream to Discovery or from Resources to Reserves," speech delivered at the annual meeting of the Canadian Institute of Mining and Metallurgy, Ottawa, April, 1977.

32. For a more complete evaluation of SOQUEM's first ten years by its president during those years, see Côme Carbonneau, op. cit. A brief account of SOQUEM operations is also provided in Rex Bosson and Bension Varon, *The Mining Industry and the Developing Countries* (New York: Oxford University Press, 1977), pp. 256-60. These authors refer to SOQUEM as "one of the more successful [government] exploration promotion efforts" (p. 144).

33. The asbestos industry in Quebec is examined in detail in Volume II of this project.

34. Quebec Ministry of Natural Resources, *L'Industrie minière du Québec* (Quebec, annual).

35. See Roby, op. cit.

36. The Société nationale de l'amiante is to have an initial capital of $250 million, part of which will go toward the acquisition of Asbestos Corporation, part toward research on new uses for asbestos, and part toward the opening of transformation plants with other, private companies. Asbestos Corporation at present is the second-largest of five producers in Quebec, with approximately 18 percent of production.

37. Faucher, op. cit., p. 230.

38. Ibid., pp. 230-31.

39. The rather complex historical issue of the property rights for these asbestos deposits is dealt with extensively in a Ph.D. dissertation under preparation at the Department of Economics, Laval University, by Robert Armstrong. The dissertation deals with the asbestos industry in Quebec between 1878 and 1929.

40. A recent study prepared for the Quebec Asbestos Mining Association has attempted to identify a number of asbestos products that could be manufactured in Quebec and to evaluate the extent to which this might be done (see Sorès Inc., *Étude des possibilités de fabrication de produits d'amiante au Québec* [Montreal, 1978]).

41. Such a possibility was raised at the turn of the century in the case of pulp and paper and was rejected for the same reason (see Faucher, op. cit., p. 230).

42. See Richard Carter, "Changements récents dans la taxation des ressources

minières au Québec," mimeographed (Quebec: Groupe de recherche en économique de l'énergie, Department of Economics, Laval Univeristy, 1977).

43. For the position of the present Minister of Natural Resources on this point, see his speech at the 34th Annual Conference of Provincial Ministers of Mines, held in Quebec, September 12-13, 1977, and reproduced in *Québec-Canada* 5, No. 6 (September, 1977).

9

Natural Resources, Economic Development, and U.S.-Canadian Relations: A Western Canadian Perspective

KENNETH H. NORRIE

Introduction

The dislocation experienced in raw materials markets in the early 1970s has revived old concerns about the finiteness of natural resource supplies being the ultimate constraint to long-term economic growth. This development has, in turn, produced a renewed interest in policies designed to minimize the disruptive economic impact of any future resource shortages. While there are nearly as many opinions as there are commentators on this topic, most discussions in Canada have revolved around such questions as the optimal rate of depletion — and hence export — of non-renewable resources; public versus private or domestic versus private foreign ownership; the division of economic rents among consumers, the private sector, and the various levels of government; and the place of raw materials and their further processing within the country's elusive "new industrial structure."

Canadian attempts to develop a new natural resource policy, however, cannot proceed independently of developments in the United States. This constraint arises primarily because of the large volume of trade in natural resource products between the two countries. The large U.S. corporate presence in Canadian natural resource industries — and the much smaller presence of Canadian firms in U.S. resource industries — adds to this interdependence. Thus any proposals by either country for policies that would

This paper was completed while on leave at Ekonomiska Historiska Institutionen at Uppsala University, Sweden. I would like to thank, without implicating in any way, Mike Percy, John Gray, Terry Levesque, and especially Yolanda Van Wachem for help in suggesting and securing background material and Carl E. Beigie and Alfred O. Hero, Jr., for comments on earlier drafts.

267

deviate significantly from current ones will be of keen interest to the other — which is, of course, the main theme of this series of studies.

Regional viewpoints are of particular interest in this context, since provincial governments can affect U.S.-Canadian relations regarding natural resources in two separate ways. First, overlapping constitutional responsibilities for resources, coupled with a federal government increasingly more willing (or compelled) to consult with provincial governments, have meant that resource-policy formulation in Canada has become a continuous round of trying to balance the conflicting viewpoints of the producing provinces with those of the consuming ones and with some vague concept of the national welfare. Thus even for those aspects of U.S.-Canadian relations, such as trade, where the Canadian position will ultimately be formulated in Ottawa, there is a need to judge what the various regions will lobby for and how vigorously and with what degree of success they will pursue their respective cases. Second, the fact that the provinces themselves — and especially, but not exclusively, the producing provinces — have considerable scope for action within their own areas of jurisdiction means their decisions have potentially significant national and international implications.

The western Canadian position has been given more prominence recently, largely because the commodity price boom of the early 1970s granted the region, at least temporarily, economic and political clout to an extent unmatched since the 1920s. The rapid increases in the prices of oil and natural gas, agricultural products, timber, and minerals in the early 1970s led to buoyant economic conditions for the four western provinces. While the course of events in these sectors since then has been somewhat uneven, the region is still in a relatively stronger position economically than in 1970. Increased power has stemmed largely from the monopoly on conventional oil and gas and on future energy sources such as oil sands, heavy oil, and coal at a time of high prices and uncertainty over future supplies. An enhanced political and economic status, coupled with a demonstrated willingness and ability to exploit it, means that western viewpoints and probable future policy directions on natural resource issues in the western provinces need to be taken explicitly into account.

The purpose of this chapter is to examine how the western provinces could affect future U.S.-Canadian relations with regard to natural resources, either directly through actions of their own or indirectly by influencing federal policies affecting the United States. The chapter provides a systematic analysis of western attitudes to resources and to economic development generally. It proceeds from this base to a discussion of specific areas where western aspirations will mean political demands or economic policies that would have a significant impact on U.S.-Canadian relations. For this purpose the western provinces' goals can be juxtaposed with those of other interest groups and with political power realities to consider how resource relations between the two countries might evolve. The advantage of this approach is that the basic western goals can be extrapolated to any of several different scenarios of economic circumstances and power relations.

We start by linking present western attitudes toward economic growth, resource development, and federal-provincial relations to the economic history of the region, with particular emphasis on the past ten years. Then recent policy measures of the individual governments to collect economic rents and to use them to try to diversify their economies are outlined, both to demonstrate current western goals and strategies and to help gauge future attitudes and policies regarding resource development and trade specifically. A final section attempts to draw implications of the western position for future U.S.-Canadian relations in the field of natural resources.

An Overview of the Western Provinces' Economic Development

The economies of the western provinces have always been intricately linked with the production and export of raw materials products to more industrialized areas. From the fur trade era through early timber and mineral production in British Columbia and grain exports from the Prairies to the current reliance on agricultural products, timber, oil and gas, and metallic and non-metallic minerals, the four western Canadian provinces have consistently been classical staple economies. The initial stimulus to capital and labor inflows was the emergence of conditions making the export of a raw or partly processed natural product feasible. The extent and the nature of the resultant economic growth then depended on the rate of expansion in the export sector and on the degree of development of ancillary or linked industries — industries engaged in further processing of the staple and in the provision of inputs to its production. An additional source of growth came from industries needed for providing consumer goods and services for the population drawn to the area. Subsequent economic experience depended on shifts over time in the demand and supply conditions for the staple, technological change within the sector, and dynamic changes in forces affecting location decisions for ancillary industries.

Alberta

Alberta's economic base rests heavily on two staples: agricultural products and oil and gas. Erik Hanson[1] has estimated that in 1964, 47 percent of personal income in Alberta was accounted for directly or indirectly by oil and gas, while another 35 percent was derived from agriculture. Shaffer[2]

270   KENNETH H. NORRIE

provides independent corroboration for this conclusion with his finding that nearly half of all jobs created between 1961 and 1971 were the direct or indirect result of the petroleum sector.

Food and beverage industries dominate the industrial structure of the province, but metal fabricating is also important because of the availability of natural gas as a fuel (see Table 9.1). There is some transportation equipment production, but this is largely an input to the petroleum industry. The well-developed construction and service sectors rely largely on oil and gas as well, both through employment automatically created in ancillary industries and through the spending of provincial royalties on public goods and services.

The other primary sectors are of significantly lesser importance. Forestry has been developing recently in connection with pulp and paper projects and an expansion of the wood-products industry, but the sector is, and will likely remain, important in local areas rather than on a province-wide basis. Alberta has no significant production of any metalic mineral at present, as can be seen from Table 9.2, although there is some interest in eventual exploitation of known iron ore reserves. Its large share of Canadian sulphur output, shown in the non-metals category of Table 9.2, is the by-product of stripping sour natural gas prior to distribution. Coal resembles forestry currently in its importance to certain areas within the province rather than to the economy overall; but unlike forestry, it promises to expand significantly over the next decade.

Saskatchewan

Saskatchewan provides an extreme example of a staple economy, with nearly total dependence on agricultural exports for its well-being. While there are no detailed studies of agriculture's contribution to income or job creation in this province as far as could be determined, one need only look at the economy in the late 1960s through 1971, when grain prices and sales were so depressed, and compare the situation to the years 1972-76 to see the decisive role the sector plays. Again the linkages from agriculture are clear in the predominance of food and beverage and machinery industries in the manufacturing sector, as shown in Table 9.1. But in contrast to oil and gas, agriculture does not require as much local-service-industry support, leaving Saskatchewan with the least well-developed tertiary sector of the four provinces.

Crude oil ranks second to agriculture in importance as a staple, and Saskatchewan had roughly 10 percent of Canadian production in 1975 (Table 9.2). The oil industry is largely operated as an offshoot of Alberta's, however, so the linkage development has mainly accrued to the latter province. Saskatchewan produces all Canada's potash, but this industry has not

TABLE 9.1

*Percentage of Total Manufacturing Employment Accounted for
by Main Manufacturing Industries, Western Provinces, 1975*

Province and Industry	Percentage of Total Manufacturing Employment
Alberta:	
Food and beverage	23.7
Metal fabricating	9.8
Wood	8.7
Transportation equipment	6.9
Printing and publishing	6.9
Saskatchewan:	
Food and beverage	30.3
Machinery	10.3
Printing and publishing	8.7
Wood	8.3
Metal fabricating	7.9
Manitoba:	
Food and beverage	20.3
Clothing	11.9
Transportation equipment	9.9
Metal fabricating	9.1
Machinery	8.9
British Columbia:	
Wood	28.2
Paper and products	14.7
Food and beverage	13.3
Metal fabricating	6.6
Primary metal	6.1

Source: Calculated from Statistics Canada, *Manufacturing Industries of Canada: National and Provincial Areas,* 1975 (Ottawa, 1977).

TABLE 9.2

Western Provinces' Shares of Canadian Output of Selected Minerals, 1975
(percentages)

Mineral Category	Manitoba	Saskatchewan	Alberta	British Columbia	Total, Western Canada	Total Canadian Production As Share of Respective Mineral Category's Total Output[b]
Metals: (35.9)[a]						
Nickel	26.3	—	—	—	26.3	23.0
Copper	8.8	1.1	—	35.3	45.2	21.5
Iron Ore	—	—	—	1.7	1.7	19.2
Zinc	6.1	0.4	—	9.4	15.9	18.2
Gold	2.9	0.9	—	9.5	13.3	5.6
Silver	2.5	0.2	—	15.9	18.6	3.7
Lead	—	—	—	20.2	20.2	3.3
Molybdenum	—	—	—	100.0	100.0	1.5
Non-metals: (7.0)[a]						
Potash	—	100.0	—	—	100.0	38.2
Asbestos	—	—	—	14.2	14.2	28.5
Elemental sulphur	—	0.2	98.8	0.9	99.9	9.8

Salt	0.3	8.9	—	21.8	6.4
Peat moss	11.2	4.9	16.0	33.5	2.4
Sodium sulphate	87.0	13.0	—	100.0	2.3
Gypsum	1.4	—	8.6	10.0	2.2
Quartz	14.2	6.4	2.0	23.9	1.4
Fuels: (49.9)[a]					
Crude oil and condensates	0.8	85.6	2.5	99.7	56.6
Natural gas	—	92.4	5.1	98.2	22.9
Natural gas by-products	—	97.2	2.0	100.0	11.8
Coal	—	31.2	58.3	91.1	8.8
Structural materials: (7.2)[a]					
Cement	5.1	9.8	10.5	28.4	34.6
Sand and gravel	7.5	11.1	13.7	35.8	31.8
Stone	1.1	0.6	5.4	7.1	21.1
Clay	1.8	11.1	7.4	24.4	8.2
Lime	5.3	8.1	4.2	17.6	4.3

[a] Category's share of total Canadian mineral production.

[b] For example, Canadian copper output, of which 8.8 percent was produced in Manitoba, 1.1 percent in Saskatchewan, and 35.3 percent in British Columbia, accounted for 21.5 percent of total Canadian metals output, which in turn accounted for 35.9 percent of total Canadian mineral output.

Source: Statistics Canada, *General Review of the Mineral Industries: Mines, Quarries and Oil Wells, 1975* (Ottawa, 1978).

had the kind of economic impact that was hoped for in the early 1960s. Other than potash, Saskatchewan's mineral production is limited to small quantities of lignite coal, uranium, and sodium sulphate and a little copper, zinc, gold, and silver from small northern mines. The forestry sector has made some advances in connection with the Prince Albert pulp mill and some sawmilling operations, but remains a small and localized factor.

Manitoba

Manitoba is also primarily an agricultural province, although it shows somewhat greater diversity than Saskatchewan. The manufacturing sector is proportionately larger than that of the other two Prairie provinces, largely because of Manitoba's historic role as a gateway to the West. Thus while it has a predominance of food and beverage industries, there is also an important clothing-production industry, one usually found in more populated industrial areas. Manitoba's service sector is also more developed than that of Saskatchewan and rivals that of Alberta, again a reflection of its unique service function to the grain economy. This entrepôt role, which gave the Manitoba economy considerable initial vitality, has slowly been eroding, along with agriculture's relative importance.

Forestry plays the same kind of marginal, localized role as in the rest of the Prairies, serving two pulp mills and some small sawmill operations. Manitoba is the most interesting of the three Prairie provinces in terms of mineral production. Its small slice of the Canadian Shield has yielded commercial deposits of nickel, copper, zinc, cobalt, gold, and silver, among others, with the first three — and especially the first — being of major importance. On the other hand, the province is totally deficient in energy sources other than hydro power.

British Columbia

British Columbia differs from the Prairies mainly in the greater diversity of its staple base and in its more highly developed service sector. The manufacturing sector is still underdeveloped relative to Canada as a whole and is dominated by the further processing of local raw materials. The forest-products industry is the key to the British Columbia economy. Logging is an important activity in and of itself, and the wood, paper, and paper products industries together accounted for over 40 percent of all manufacturing jobs in 1975. Agriculture and fishing are supplementary activities, and much less important than forest products. The well-developed service sector is the result partly of spin-off activities from staple and other industries, partly of British Columbia's relatively high per capita incomes, and partly of the continuing development of Vancouver as a port.

British Columbia is the most interesting of the four provinces in terms of mineral production, since the mining and processing of minerals represents the most important activity in the province next to forestry. Copper is the main metal, and British Columbia accounts for roughly 35 percent of total Canadian production. Coal ranks second and produces nearly 60 percent of Canada's total output. British Columbia has a comparatively small output of crude oil and natural gas, but the current high prices for these products make the value of output quite high. As Table 9.2 shows, British Columbia produces some quantities, sometimes quite significant ones, of nearly all the other main metallic and non-metallic minerals.

Trade Patterns, Instabilities, and Structural Adjustments

A long history of reliance on a staple export base has resulted in several dominant patterns in the economic growth of the western provinces. First, this region has always been oriented at least as much toward the international economy as to the rest of Canada, both as a market for staples and as a source of capital, technology, and entrepreneurship for resource development and infrastructure needs. Britain was the most important early link when the principal export products were fur and wheat, and Europe is still a main market for Prairie grains. But as the new industrial staples emerged after 1900, the market shifted primarily to the United States, and the incidence of U.S. direct investment increased proportionately. Today the United States is an important market for lumber and pulp and paper for all four provinces and especially for British Columbia. More than one-third of Alberta's natural gas production is currently piped south. At the beginning of the 1970s about one-half of western crude-oil output was exported to the United States, but this percentage has been reduced steadily since 1974 in accordance with federal energy policy and the extension of the Interprovincial Pipe Line to Montreal. In the absence of any major changes in policy or supply, these exports are to end completely in the early 1980s. The United States is also the main single market for Saskatchewan potash and for the metallic and non-metallic minerals of Saskatchewan and Manitoba.

The most recent development affecting exports from the western provinces has been the opening of new markets in the USSR and China for grain and in Japan for a wide variety of raw and semi-processed materials. Japan purchases nearly all the coal shipped from British Columbia and Alberta and has taken nearly all British Columbia's copper output until quite recently. It is also a market of lesser importance for fish, lumber, pulp, and some agricultural products. Furthermore, Japan has become an important source of foreign direct investment, especially in British Columbia and, to a lesser extent, in Alberta.

The western provinces have counted relatively less on central Canadian than on international markets. British Columbia plywood does find its main market within Canada, and about 20 to 30 percent of other lumber products are regularly sold internally as well. Natural gas has long found a market in Canada, and crude oil does so increasingly, for reasons mentioned above. Feed grains are sent east with the help of freight-rate subsidies,[3] and there are sales of lesser importance of some minerals such as copper and coal and of some semi-processed or processed agricultural products. Overall, however, the region maintains a rather large "trade deficit" with the rest of Canada because of the large volume of "imports" of manufactured products from central Canada.[4] In terms of aggregate economic growth, the welfare of the region has usually been (at least apparently) positively correlated with the degree of access of its raw materials exports to larger industrial countries and with the ease with which foreign capital and expertise could be acquired.

A second implication of the western provinces' economic base has been that the region and the provinces individually have experienced a very unstable economic existence. The demand for the region's staples tends to be highly volatile on international markets, being subject to tariffs, quotas, and especially to construction cycles and general fluctuations in industrial production. The cyclical, boom-bust pattern that results from this vulnerability imposes great costs of adjustment on residents — ranging from the psychological and economic costs of dealing with an uncertain income stream to migration costs in extreme downturns — which have been firmly etched into the minds of residents and, especially, of regional political leaders and spokesmen.

Aside from these short-term cyclical features, two of the provinces have experienced longer-run structural adjustments, and the same prospect has always been imminent for the other two. A low income elasticity of demand for staple products, together with relatively rapid rates of technical change within the industries, has led to absolutely falling levels of employment, most notably in agriculture. In the absence of other expanding sectors, displaced labor has emigrated. Thus Saskatchewan has had a net outmigration almost without exception since 1940, with Manitoba's experience being only somewhat less dramatic. Alberta was in the same position in the 1940s, when the Leduc and subsequent discoveries of oil and gas turned the province again into a net recipient of labor. British Columbia has experienced a net inflow of migration throughout the postwar period, in large measure from Saskatchewan and Manitoba, although the level has fluctuated considerably in response to changing economic conditions and has apparently declined in recent years.[5]

This displacement of employment from staple sectors has meant a concomitant winding down of ancillary sectors as well — the disappearance of the small Prairie town being the most visible example. The resulting out-migration has been remarkably rapid, with the result that the per capita incomes of Saskatchewan and Manitoba have remained quite close to the national average. From the viewpoint of national economic efficiency, this adjustment must be viewed favorably. But for those affected, for those remaining in areas undergoing the necessary adjustments, and for those in other western provinces still in the expansion phase of staple production but with a similar ultimate prospect, it is regarded differently. There are significant economic and psychological costs to migration; and provincial political leaders, civil servants, and businessmen are firmly enough mercantilist in attitude to regard an out-migration of population, however efficient in an overall economic sense, as a disaster. It would be a unique politician or bureaucrat indeed who saw his task as merely ensuring an orderly retreat in the face of a structurally declining economic base.

Recent Experience
Within a Staple-Based Economy

The economic fluctuations faced by the western provinces over the past ten years seemed to confirm the worst fears about both the short-term stability and the long-run viability of a staple-based economy. At the same time, however, the commodity price boom of the early 1970s, affecting as it did nearly all western Canadian export products, seemed to provide an opportunity to change this staple orientation. The complex of problems faced and negotiations undertaken during this period have forced at least some of the provincial governments into a political and economic sophistication heretofore lacking.

For Saskatchewan especially, but even for Manitoba, the years from 1967 to 1971 were some of the most trying since the end of the Great Depression. The International Wheat Agreement had collapsed and with it the export price of wheat. Traditional markets had been closed off, and unsold grain was piling up in record quantities. In addition, the potash construction boom was over, and the effects of overexpansion were being felt in excess capacity and falling prices. The South Saskatchewan River Dam project was completed as well, releasing yet more construction workers. With no strength in sectors such as mining or timber, the only recourse was emigration — nearly 28,000 from Saskatchewan alone in 1970, for example. Manitoba's more diversified agriculture and broader economic base generally somewhat cushioned the loss of wheat markets. But for both provinces the cyclical sensitivity and structural adjustment patterns inherent in staple production were experienced in the extreme in these years.

Events after 1971 produced a complete reversal in this situation. Crop failures around the world and poor anchovy catches off the coast of Peru drove the prices of wheat and feed grains to record high levels. As a result, net farm incomes in Saskatchewan increased nearly sevenfold in the space of a few years. Rising grain prices also created a demand for fertilizers, which reversed the depressed conditions in the potash industry. The oil price increases and the crisis atmosphere regarding energy increased the value of Saskatchewan's oil production significantly, and the unexpectedly strong world industrial expansion after 1971 came at a time of low inventories of industrial raw materials, producing rapid increases in the prices of minerals and forest products and leading to renewed activity in the mines and forests of northern Manitoba and Saskatchewan. The magnitude of these changes, coupled with the spread of their effects into all other sectors of the economy, was strong enough to reverse the long-prevalent pattern of net out-migration in both provinces.

The expansion was merely another in a long series of staple booms, however, differing from the past in magnitude but not in character, and as such was inevitably reversed. The forest- and mineral-products sectors were the first to suffer from the onset of world recession in 1974. Expanded harvests abroad brought grain prices down significantly; and this factor, combined with poor harvests at home, reduced farm incomes well below their recent record levels. Potash prices and sales declined along with grain prices, leaving only oil at its earlier higher value. Thus after a brief but spectacular respite for a few years, Saskatchewan and Manitoba apparently resumed their long-run relative economic declines.

In Alberta the situation has been somewhat more complex. The agricultural sector experienced much the same problems prior to 1971 as in Saskatchewan and Manitoba, although the diversified nature of Alberta's economy tempered the situation somewhat. The oil and gas sector remained strong throughout, meaning that Alberta did not experience any relative decline in population or income. But by the end of the 1960s there was a growing recognition — not least, significantly, by the new opposition leader, Peter Lougheed — that, in the absence of offsetting changes, Alberta was in for some major adjustments in the oil and gas sector and thus more generally. The last major discovery of oil had been the Rainbow field in 1965, and the geological prospects for any further major discoveries were very slim. As a result, the major oil companies were moving their exploration activities out of the province to the (then) more promising Arctic and east coast fields. Alberta's petroleum industry was clearly moving from the expansive phase to the mature-producer phase.[6]

This was an ominous development because the main employment impact of the industry stems from exploration and development rather than from production. The latter is a highly capital-intensive process requiring relatively little labor directly. With exploration and development winding down, the rate of job creation would be severely curtailed.[7] Some major changes were clearly necessary if the province were to avoid the long-run adjustments in employment, and thus in population, implied by this final phase of the industry. Since most of the industries providing services to the sector are owned locally, there was an unusually strong perception of the need for some kind of political solution.[8] Thus in Alberta as well as in the other two Prairie provinces, there was a heightened awareness of the implications of excessive reliance on staple exports, and a renewed determination to avoid them, just as the disruptions in commodity markets began to appear.

Alberta was the province most favorably suited to benefit from events after 1971..The increases in agricultural-product prices affected Alberta as they did Saskatchewan and Manitoba, but the major changes were in the prices and sales of crude oil and natural gas. With Alberta's near monopoly on these resources within Canada, provincial income would have increased substantially even without any taxation changes. The crisis atmosphere in energy and sharply rising prices led to increased exploration activities for new oil and gas supplies and created a renewed interest in the province's extensive steam and metallurgical coal deposits as well as in the nonconventional oil sands and heavy-oil deposits. High timber and pulp prices before 1974 also stimulated activity in the northern forestry regions. For a time, in fact, the major economic problem in Alberta was conceived to be just how to manage the pace of development so as not to place an undue strain on the province's labor market and infrastructure.

Continued high energy prices have sustained economic expansion in Alberta. The decline in agricultural incomes imparted a little slack to the economy, but the renewed search for conventional oil and natural gas reserves, secondary recovery activities in some existing wells, continued development of the oil sands and coal deposits, experimentation with heavy-oil deposits and with *in situ* techniques for oil sands, and petrochemical projects have combined to give the province a continued impressive rate of growth. An additional major stimulus has come from increased public spending from swollen royalty revenues. As one indication of this relative prosperity, immigration in the past few years has increased several-fold over levels typical of earlier booms.

British Columbia has also experienced a highly unstable economy because of its important forestry sector's dependence on the cyclically prone construction sector and because of the volatile pattern in markets for mineral products. The province generally fared well throughout the 1960s, even as the Prairies were suffering from collapsed grain markets, and certainly benefited from the commodity price boom of the early 1970s. The onset of the world recession in 1974, however, affected British Columbia more than the other western provinces because the demand for wood and mineral products slackened considerably while grain markets were strong for another two years. On top of this there was considerable uncertainty resulting from alterations in the province's resource-taxation legislation. The result of all this was what the Ministry of Economic Development called "a dramatic cyclical pause in [the province's] economic growth."[9] The unemployment rate, always relatively high because of immigration from other provinces, increased considerably, and the usually large net migration fell off substantially.

British Columbia had still not recovered from the recession in 1977, although the official review quoted earlier noted some improvement and was quite optimistic about the future. But the basic forestry and mineral industries are still in a relatively weak position and require a major expansion of the U.S., Japanese, and Canadian economies to improve their prospects. A hoped-for development of coal reserves in the northeast section of the province has apparently been postponed indefinitely, and there are no other major resource developments predicted for the near future. British Columbia officials are quite candid in their evaluation of the recent recession. There has been, to again quote the official review, "a reappraisal of the prospects for longer term growth in western industrial nations. As a result of this reappraisal there is a widening consensus that the high rates of growth experienced in the past may not be replicated in the future."[10]

Policy Motivations and Options

These characteristics of the nature and pattern of western economic development have had a profound impact on basic western attitudes to economic growth, resources, and trade. In turn, these attitudes have been translated into a consistent pattern of political demands for corrective economic policies throughout the postwar period, and especially in the past decade. Since these basic perceptions have so clearly affected the nature of the particular positions adopted and policies chosen, and will continue to do so in the foreseeable future, it is worth spending some time on them here.

The first point to note is that the region displays, through its spokesmen, what might perhaps best be described as a neo-mercantilist attitude toward economic growth. There is an almost unquestioned belief in the benefits of economic diversification, and especially of industrialization. This attitude clearly stems from the economic history of the region as discussed above. Industrialization is sought to provide jobs for those continually being released, or ultimately so threatened, from the staple and related sectors. Industrial pursuits, unlike staple production, are seen (correctly or not) to be labor-intensive and less susceptible to the vagaries of the business cycle. Industrialization, it is felt, would reverse actual or imminent population outflows and provide a measure of economic stability heretofore lacking. To the regional businessmen whose sales depend on the size of the local market or to the politicians and bureaucrats whose constituency size is a measure of their political power, these features are highly valued.

Since the region is economically unsuited for most kinds of market-oriented manufacturing industry, and is recognized as such locally — however reluctantly at times — the first priority for an industrialization policy is seen to be to try to increase the degree of further processing of staples prior to their export. Thus there have been numerous studies of, and support for, rapeseed-crushing plants, petrochemical plants, pulp and paper projects, saw mills, pet-food-processing ventures, and so on. Another obvious policy option is to try to increase the degree of local provision of inputs into the staple sector. Regional policies regarding iron and steel mills, agricultural implements, and oil field supplies are examples of such an approach. With respect to these two general approaches, the object has been to discover whether some form of government action could overcome an initial cost disadvantage relative to other more industrialized areas and permit the beginnings of what it is hoped would become a self-sustaining industrial expansion. Thus a preoccupation with the provision of jobs — especially in manufacturing, and necessarily mainly in industries closely linked to the main staple sectors — is the first major characteristic of contemporary economic-policy goals in the western provinces.

The other important legacy from past experience is the West's concept of its political status within the larger confederation. There is a tendency to view the relationship with the federal government and the "East" generally as one of continuous strife and adversity. Confederation is seen by many as a kind of "zero-sum game" where the distribution of a fixed stock of wealth is a function of regional political power, with the federal government's being at best indifferent to the West and at worst actively working against it. Again the roots of this sentiment go far back into western Canadian history. There was more or less continual resentment during the settlement of the Prairies over tariff, freight-rate, and land-disposition policies. Since World War II the list of irritants has included — in addition to renewed concern over freight rates and tariffs — taxation arrangements, government purchasing policies, the operations of the banking system, monetary policy, and even foreign-ownership and environmental policies. The basic antipathy has been exacerbated in the 1970s by the dispute over the pricing, taxation, production, and disposition of natural resources. Predictably, the result of these conflicts has been the emergence of strong and vocal provincial governments, notably in Alberta, the most affected province.[11]

This attitude toward the federal government is manifest in both resource developments *per se* and in the further processing of resources. With regard to the resource sectors themselves, the provinces have adopted a very rigid interpretation of the relevant sections of the British North America Act. Resource management is viewed as being primarily in provincial hands, to be carried out in accordance with the long-run aspirations of the province concerned. Federal interventions in the form of output, price, and tax policies are seen as inevitable but are greeted as unwarranted and illegal intrusions into provincial jurisdiction and to be tolerated only in exchange for concessions in other areas.

In terms of further industrialization based on resources, the situation is even more complex. There is a frequently expressed belief that federal policies on tariffs, railway freight rates, and government purchasing policies, for example, are discouraging the further industrialization of the West. Thus the obstacles to the desired broader industrial base are seen to include not only the acknowledged natural economic disadvantages but also additional artificial ones stemming from federal policies. Meatpacking, petrochemicals, rapeseed-crushing plants, perhaps iron and steel, and so on, are seen as examples of industries in which the West would have a comparative advantage in a more neutral policy environment. Some accounts go even further to suggest that the concentration of industry in central Canada is deliberate and systematic, being the original and consistent aim of national economic policies since Confederation.[12]

Collecting Resource Rents

One can discern two important types of economic policies pursued with renewed vigor since 1971 by the western provinces: moves to capture economic rents from the production of resources and the use of this revenue, as well as of regulatory powers over the industries, to attempt to shape the industrial structure of the region. We shall look at these policies in this section and the next, discussing briefly the chronology of events leading up to them and assessing their results. In each case the object is to demonstrate that economic and political goals have not changed, but that the sense of urgency behind them and the resources devoted to attaining them have. These developments are directly relevant to the main issue of U.S.-Canadian relations, since it is through taxation and regulatory powers over supply that the governments of the western provinces have their major impact on North American resource developments. They are too small, individually or even as a group, to have much of an effect on the demand side. Immediate past policies in these areas are a good indication of probable future trends, since they reflect the fundamental western goals and attitudes discussed earlier.

The main emphasis in what follows is given to pertinent developments in, and reactions of, the province of Alberta, although there are a considerable number of cross-references to Saskatchewan and a comparatively summary treatment of Manitoba and British Columbia. Alberta is the most interesting of the four provinces to study because of its dominant position in the supply of oil and natural gas, which has afforded substantial windfall economic revenues and economic bargaining power. In addition, the turbulent events of the early 1970s coincided with the election in Alberta of a young and technically and politically sophisticated government with a reasonably clear economic stratgy. Alberta's economic strategy is also of more general interest, however, since the province's actions reflect in most respects the aspirations of all the western provinces.

An objection might be raised that the western provinces are so dissimilar economically, geographically, and perhaps especially politically, that any aggregation is meaningless. There is no recourse, then, but to concentrate on each province individually.[13] However, it is important to remember that the reference here is to the broad goals of capturing resource rents and using them, together with regulatory powers over the industries, to try to induce a greater degree of staple-linked manufacturing activity. As discussed earlier, each province has had a similar enough kind of experience with a staple-based economy to concur in these general goals, if not always in the specific policies employed. Political differences among the four western provinces are easily exaggerated, at least when it comes to policies for economic growth and diversification. The government of any small and geographically peripheral resource-based economy has so little room to maneuver that policies adopted by any of the political parties tend to become indistinguishable.[14] It would be too extreme to suggest that political ideologies make no difference at all. But the harsh economic facts of life facing any western premier soon remove much of the freedom of action assumed to exist in party platforms and campaign speeches.

When it comes to discussing specific issues, as opposed to general aspirations, however, it is necessary to take into account the realities of power politics. The western provinces' desire for industrial diversification is expressed in their attempts to convince the federal government to alter its economic policies, including those dealing with natural resources. Under a charitable view of federal-provincial relations, this should not require resort to power politics. But the seriousness with which independent provincial initiatives need to be taken by those concerned with North American resource development depends primarily on the degree of economic power held by the provinces in any specific sector. That is, Alberta may be a model for western aspirations, but it is not necessarily one for success in realizing them. Here one is necessarily back to a case-by-case study, a point that will be examined in the final section of this chapter.

Energy Resources

The dramatic federal-provincial confrontations over the economic rents generated in the oil and gas sector are well known. One of the first moves of the new Lougheed government after its election in August, 1971, was to impose a tax on reserves of crude oil that had the effect of increasing the existing royalty rate from an average of 16.66 percent to about 22 percent. After the rapid and unexpected increases in the price of oil beginning in late 1973, the federal government introduced an export tax on oil shipments. This tax was set at 25 cents per barrel in September, 1973, and was adjusted in a series of steps to a high of $6.40 in 1974; since then, it has fluctuated considerably. The export tax had the effect of siphoning off all the additional economic rent and distributing it about equally to federal government coffers and to Canadian consumers in the form of a price lower than the world price.

The reactions in Alberta and Saskatchewan to this federal action were immediate. They scrapped the existing royalty agreements and replaced them with ones based on much higher sliding scales. The Alberta regulations that became effective on April 1, 1974, maintained the existing rate on the so-called "select" price of a barrel of oil — that is, a price calculated to cover costs plus a "fair" return to the industry. The base figure could be, and has been, adjusted upward to reflect rising costs. The difference between the actual or par price and this select price, theoretically equal to pure economic rent, was taxed at a much higher rate by applying a predetermined royalty factor. This latter figure was significantly higher for old than for new oil to allow for the fact that any new discoveries were likely to be in high-cost areas. Saskatchewan's rates were set higher than those of Alberta in view of the fact that there was little new exploration and development activity.[15]

The federal government responded to these provincial moves by disallowing the deduction of royalty payments to provincial governments from corporate-income-tax calculations. After much acrimonious exchange between Ottawa and the provincial governments and threats by the oil companies that exploration would cease entirely, a compromise of sorts was reached. Ottawa allowed additional generous write-offs for exploration and development, and the provincial governments adjusted their effective royalty rates downward. In addition, it was agreed that the domestic oil price would rise in a series of steps to the world price.[16] The decades-old western demand for access to the Montreal market was granted with the decision to extend the Interprovincial Pipe Line from Sarnia. Since then the federal-provincial political climate has improved somewhat.

In natural gas the principal actor has again been Alberta, with its dominant share of total Canadian production. The policy strategy was one of trying to raise the price, in this case to its BTU equivalent with oil, and to increase the share of the rent going to the province. The depressed price was a result of the fact that there was almost no competition in the purchase of gas, with TransCanada Pipe Line virtually in a monopsonistic position. The National Energy Board, in its concern over the long-run availability of Canadian gas supplies, had begun refusing export permits to competing buyers. The Alberta government responded by threatening to use the jurisdictional powers of its Energy Resources Conservation Board (ERCB) to withhold permission for gas exports from the province unless the buyers agreed to renegotiate the purchase price and by sponsoring competing purchases of gas at significantly higher prices, principally through Pan Alberta Gas. These moves have largely been successful, with the result that natural gas prices in Canada have been moving up, along with the price of oil.

A revised royalty system for natural gas came into effect January 1, 1974, but was soon replaced by a less ambitious one made retroactive to the same date. The principle behind the gas royalty is identical to that for oil. The existing rates are maintained on a base price, with the difference between it and the selling price being taxed at a significantly higher figure. The marginal rate increases in a series of steps as gas prices increase, with the maximum rate currently applied to gas selling for more than 72 cents per mcf. An entirely separate calculation, identical in form but at lower rates, is made for new gas.

The western coal industry was quite significant in the days of steam locomotives and before natural gas furnaces, but declined dramatically in the 1950s and 1960s. The high prices of oil and gas and concern over long-run supply have occasioned a renewed interest in coal, however. New power plants on the Prairies are to burn coal rather than natural gas, and even Ontario has begun contracting for western steam coal for the first time. But even more important, the metallurgical coals of the mountain areas have suddenly become significant. Long-term contracts for both Alberta and British Columbia coal have been signed with Japanese buyers. In addition, U.S. coal prices have been rising, and the U.S. government has been talking about eventually limiting exports, so Ontario's steel companies are beginning to look at western metallurgical coals as a possible supplement or even as an eventual replacement.[17] Thus while coal still plays a relatively minor role in the economies of the provinces, it has taken on a significant new importance that will almost certainly increase in the future.[18]

Expanding markets and rising prices have naturally created a renewed

legislative interest in this mineral. Alberta's response has been to implement a new and much more comprehensive set of regulations for coal activity.[19] A major feature of the legislation, which became effective July,
1976, is that it outlines clearly the areas where coal exploration and
development will be allowed. To this end the province has been divided into four zones, ranging from total exclusion of exploration and development
to active encouragement. But of more interest for present purposes is the
revised royalty schedule. The old flat rate of 10 cents per ton has been
replaced by a complicated sliding-scale formula that takes prices, capital,
and operating costs into account. There is a minimum royalty, but after that
taxation increases according to the economic rent generated. The effect will
be to increase significantly the provincial return from this revitalized sector. There are also measures to guarantee the employment of local labor
and materials as far as possible, to give Alberta's residents the opportunity
to invest in development of the resource, and to ensure that any further
upgrading takes place within the province.

Other Resources

Moves to capture additional economic rents in the other resource areas[20]
were generally more of a provincial government/industry confrontation,
although the federal government was inevitably involved also. The potash
case in Saskatchewan is perhaps the most illustrative here. A technological
solution to the flooding problems of the mines ushered in a rapid expansion
of the industry after 1962. By 1970 the construction phase was over, and
ten mines were in operation. It was immediately obvious that considerable
overexpansion had occurred. World prices dropped drastically, and the
mines operated at considerably less than full capacity. Finally an agreement
was reached between the companies and the Saskatchewan government to
implement a prorationing scheme for "conservation" reasons.[21] Total output was to be restricted to keep the price up, and each producing mine was
allotted a share of the total product. The scheme went into effect at the end
of 1969 and did apparently succeed in stabilizing the industry and raising
the price somewhat. But there was no new investment and thus little further
impact on Saskatchewan's economy, since the production of potash, as
compared to the construction of facilities, is very capital-intensive.

Under the depressed conditions there was little room for altering the
existing royalty structure. But with the rise of grain prices after 1971, the
demand for fertilizer — and thus for potash — increased dramatically. Prices
rose from $20 per ton to nearly $80 between 1969 and 1975. Production increased, and for the first time mines were approaching capacity production.
It was thus understandable that the new NDP government would attempt
to increase its share of the sudden windfall gains in this sector. It im-

plemented a tax on potash reserves designed explicitly to leave the producers only a normal rate of return on capital invested and to direct the economic rent to the province. The imposition of this reserve tax on top of the existing royalty and prorationing fees greatly increased the province's share of revenue from the sale of the mineral. At this time the companies, encouraged by the recent success of Central Canada Potash in challenging the prorationing scheme through the courts, filed suit, claiming the tax was unconstitutional, and shelved all expansion plans pending the outcome. It was then that, faced with the very real prospect of losing the suit and thus the considerable revenue it was collecting, the government decided to take over a portion of the industry.[22]

The federal government opposed the provincial government in two ways. It objected to the prorationing agreement on grounds that it interfered with clear federal responsibility for interprovincial and international trade. In this case Ottawa was actually a co-sponsor of the court challenge to the scheme. The other area of conflict was the nondeductability of royalty payments for corporate tax calculations, discussed above. This put an additional squeeze on the companies, adding to the mood of pessimism and confrontation already present in the province.

As for other minerals, prior to 1974 most provincial governments levied a special tax, over and above the provincial income tax on the profits of mining companies, to compensate them as owners of depleting assets. But the subsequent price increases in minerals and the suddenly large profits of the companies quite naturally led the provinces to attempt to capture a share of what were considered pure economic rents. The ensuing period was a confusing sequence of legislative proposals, revisions, implementations, amendments, and often subsequent abrogations. Alberta has no significant production of minerals beyond coal, so it was not involved in this process. Saskatchewan made no major changes in the taxation of either metallic minerals or coal, although it did increase the degree of public participation in the sector via a special crown corporation. In 1976 it introduced a two-tiered system for taxing uranium, composed of a basic royalty of 3 percent of gross sales and an additional graduated taxation of operating profit relative to capital invested at rates of up to 50 percent.

Manitoba's efforts have received the most publicity, largely because of the national prominence given to the Kierans report.[23] On April 1, 1974, the Manitoba government gave notice to the industry of impending changes in mineral taxation and temporarily raised the mining-profits tax from 15 percent to 23 percent. One month later an ambitious new royalty scheme was announced, and just as quickly denounced as excessive by the industry. After much lobbying,[24] the entire system was scrapped and replaced in January, 1975, by one based on company earnings. Profits up to a normal rate of return, currently considered to be 18 percent on invested capital, are taxed at 15 percent. Profit rates above 18 percent are subject to a 35 percent rate. The new act also has provisions for averaging profits over three years to take account of the highly cyclical nature of the industry's earnings. Thus Manitoba backed off significantly from its earlier position regarding the taxation of economic rents, but has still moved beyond the pre-1974 practices.

British Columbia's mineral taxation moves were undoubtedly the most dramatic. In 1974 the NDP government announced that on top of existing taxes there would be a basic royalty of 5 percent of the gross value of production plus a "super royalty" on minerals exhibiting large price increases. In the latter case, if the price in any period exceeded a basic value, set by the cabinet, by a factor of 1.2, 50 percent of the excess was payable to the Crown. The industry claimed that the effect of this scheme on top of the mining tax and the federal and provincial corporate profits taxes was to move the marginal tax rate beyond 100 percent. As a result there was a general suppression of investment in the industry, contributing to the serious British Columbia recession discussed earlier. Following a change of government the super royalty was abolished on April 1, 1976; and on January 1, 1977, there was a return to a mining-tax system based on company profits. The official taxation rate is set at 17.5 percent, but the effective rate is somewhat lower because of processing allowances. As in the case of Manitoba, then, the British Columbia government has backed down from its early position, but has still managed to increase the province's share of income from the production of depleting assets.

Summary

The western provinces have been reasonably successful in their attempts to increase provincial income from the production of natural resources. The degree of success, however, varies from resource to resource and from province to province. The most spectacular increases have been registered in oil and gas revenues in Alberta, which increased fivefold between 1972 and 1975 and are still rising. Saskatchewan's additional petroleum revenue is much less, but still represents a marked break with levels typical before 1973. For the other resource products, and thus for the other two provinces, the overall increases are much less dramatic, since the price increases — and thus the economic rent generated — were far less significant and much more transitory in nature. But generally speaking, the sudden appearance of these economic rents after 1971 and the apparent ability of the provincial governments to capture an increasing share of them have resulted in significant gains to provincial treasuries.

Putting Resource Rents to Use

The provincial governments are using their increased royalty revenues and their regulatory powers to try to restructure their respective economies. These efforts illustrate both the increasing tendency of the western provinces to view resource developments as part of a larger industrial strategy and the use of new institutional arrangements as a means of achieving their goals. Again, the specific actions of Alberta will be highlighted for reasons similar to those explained in the previous section.

A fundamental feature of Alberta's industrial strategy is the belief that considerable state intervention is necessary if significant changes are to be made to its industrial structure. As discussed earlier, this belief reflects in part the inherent economic disadvantages of a small, geographically peripheral economy in an industrialized North America. It also reflects the view (correct or incorrect) that federal government economic policies have contributed negatively to the level of industrial development in the province. Thus provincial government support is regarded as necessary, partly to meet the classical divergence of public and private benefits and partly to try to overcome artificial developmental barriers.[25]

Alberta has been employing two different kinds of tactics. One is the use of regulatory powers over the production and sale of natural resources, specifically oil and gas, to attempt to affect location decisions regarding industries engaged in resource processing. In the important case of oil and gas, the ERCB has been given jurisdiction over proposals for using Alberta's reserves, with a clear understanding that the province's fuel and industrial feedstock needs are to be met first. In effect, this has meant a clear signal to processing firms that an Alberta location would assure them secure access to petrochemical feedstocks while another Canadian location might not. This attempt to forestall competing, out-of-province ventures has even been extended to include the threat of prohibiting any shipment of oil and gas out of the province, although it is not clear whether such an action would be constitutional.

Alberta's Heritage Fund

The second tactic has involved the use of public funds to subsidize, or even to purchase outright, industrial ventures in an attempt to promote their establishment or local expansion. The major instrument for that purpose is the Alberta Heritage Savings Trust Fund, a multi-billion-dollar offspring of the taxation moves discussed above. Initially, $1.5 billion from general revenues were placed into the fund in 1976, with the declared intention of adding 30 percent of annual revenues derived from the sale of non-renewable resources plus accumulated interest on investments. Expenditures are to be of three types. First, 20 percent is to go to so-called capital projects within Alberta, such as medical facilities and research, irrigation, reforestation, and grazing land development. No explicit return is expected on these funds. Second, 15 percent is to be lent to other provincial governments or to projects with crown guarantees, with the sole intention of earning as high as possible a rate of return. Third, the remaining 65 percent is to be invested within the province to affect future industrial development. Investments of this type are to "yield a reasonable return or profit to the Fund" and should "tend to strengthen and diversify the economy of Alberta."[26] One use of these funds was to purchase Pacific Western Airlines (PWA).

The form of the government's participation in investment for industrial development is interesting. A special company, the Alberta Energy Company (AEC), was legislated into existence in October, 1974. The creation of AEC, whose shares are owned by both the Alberta government and private investors, was deemed necessary because the role of multinational corporations in Alberta's resource development had effectively precluded residents from investing directly in that development. In this respect, AEC is to play much the same role as the Canada Development Corporation and is obviously modeled along similar lines in its make-up and operation.

The AEC is currently involved in a wide range of activities.[27] It has purchased the mineral rights in the Suffield Block near Medicine Hat and has been awarding contracts there for shallow and deep-well drilling for both natural gas and oil. It has also assumed control of Alberta's interests in the Syncrude project. It holds the option, retained in the Syncrude negotiations, of purchasing from 5 percent to 20 percent of the Syncrude equity after the plant is fully operational. It has a two-thirds interest in AEC Power, Limited, the company created to construct and operate the plant to provide electricity and steam to the mining operation. And it has set up a wholly owned subsidiary, Alberta Oil Sands Pipeline, to construct and operate the pipeline to carry synthetic crude from Fort McMurry to Edmonton. Also in the oil and gas area, the AEC has assumed a 49.2 percent share in Pan Alberta Gas, Limited, which has contracts to deliver gas outside Alberta.

The other activities of AEC reflect the government's goals of diversifying the economy and allowing local participation in the process. Thus it has a 50 percent interest in Steel Alberta, which has taken over the government's 20 percent ownership of Interprovincial Pipe and Steel Company (IPSCO) of Regina. (The Saskatchewan government owns a further 20 percent of these shares, with the remaining 60 percent held privately.) The AEC has also recently become involved in both forestry and coal developments through a 40 percent interest in a joint venture with the Simpson Lumber Company for the development of a timbering and forest-products complex in the Whitecourt area and a 25 percent interest in a venture with Luscar for development of the Coal Valley property. The coal venture is to deliver two million tons per year of thermal coal to Ontario Hydro in addition to expected offshore sales. The manufacturing side is represented by the Petrochemicals Alberta Project (PETALTA), a joint venture currently investigating the feasibility of building a 1.1-billion-pounds-per-year benzene plant in Alberta, which would use pentanes-plus, a natural gas condensate, as a feedstock. This project has been given clearance by the ERCB.

The Syncrude project is a good example of the Alberta government's resolve to broaden the base of the economy.[28] The development of the oil sands deposits is clearly a key element in Premier Lougheed's industrial strategy.[29] The reserves contained therein, if it is ever feasible to exploit them fully, are immense and would free the province from dependence on the diminishing reserves of conventional supplies as an economic base. Synthetic crude is in a partially refined state already and is ideal as an input to petrochemical industries, another key element in the strategy. The construction phase provides considerable employment and has linkages throughout the rest of the economy. Even the operation of a plant requires a fairly substantial labor input per unit of output. For all these reasons, then, it was clearly imperative for Premier Lougheed that Syncrude go ahead and that additional plants of both the extraction and the *in situ* type follow. The form of the ultimate Syncrude agreement, with its complex of loans to companies, joint ventures, and public participation via the AEC, illustrates well the perceived need in the West for new institutional arrangements for large-scale resource projects.[30]

Petrochemical Objectives

The heart of Alberta's industrial strategy is the development of a world-scale petrochemical complex. The energy crisis of the 1970s appeared to change location factors for this industry somewhat in Alberta's favor. Significantly cheaper sources of inputs can offset a transportation cost disadvantage on final products, but there has been no evidence, at least as yet, that the province is planning to provide natural gas as a feedstock to local plants at prices lower than their opportunity costs in sales outside the province. The question of security of supply, however, was another matter. The government made it clear that it would actively use its power to regulate gas exports out of the province to deny feedstock supplies to new petrochemical projects in the East. If these projects were to be located in Alberta, however, they would be guaranteed access to feedstock inputs for the lifetime of the venture. In the confusing days of 1973 and 1974, this guarantee seemed of sufficient importance to alter location decisions. There was a rash of proposals put before the ERCB for approval, including plans for methanol plants, numerous fertilizer plants, and, most significantly, two world-scale ethylene plants. Many of these proposals were (predictably) withdrawn later, including one of the ethylene plants. But the methanol and several fertilizer projects have materialized, and the Alberta Gas Ethylene Company plant at Red Deer is under construction. The latter, when approved by the ERCB, was linked to several proposals to further upgrade a substantial portion of the output locally, although one of these companies has since announced its intention of suspending development for the present. Nevertheless, the province has clearly come out of the confusing years of the oil and gas price disruptions with a clear stake in the petrochemical industry.

Other Industrial Projects

The other industrial developments are more minor in character but entirely consistent with the general strategy. A natural backward linkage from conventional oil and gas, oil sands, and petrochemicals is the production of iron and steel products. To this end the province acquired the 20 percent interest in IPSCO mentioned earlier, with the intention of adding to its Alberta facilities. The purchase of PWA and the movement of the headquarters to Calgary are intended to give the province a stake in the rapidly expanding air freight and passenger business. In addition, there are numerous small-scale projects, such as rapeseed-crushing plants and sawmills, that are consistent both with broader diversification goals for the economy generally and with a decentralization away from the two main cities of Calgary and Edmonton.

The policy moves of the other provincial governments have not been nearly as extensive, mainly because they have had only a small fraction of the income Alberta has enjoyed. Saskatchewan's Energy and Resource Development Fund, established in 1974, is similar in nature to the Alberta Heritage Fund. The accrued resource revenues have been used to date as a source of capital for the purchase and opening of potash mines, not for industrialization projects as in Alberta. Saskatchewan's industrial ventures have been restricted to attempts to stimulate small, resource-related projects, such as food-processing plants, sawmills, and the expansion of the IPSCO facilities. There has been, however, a good deal of speculation in the province concerning heavy-oil development in the Lloydminster region.

British Columbia has had even less additional revenue to use for industrial investment than has Saskatchewan. This fact, plus the generally depressed state of the British Columbia economy in the past few years and the recent change in government, limits prospects for identifying an active industrial strategy akin to Alberta's.

Manitoba deserves special mention. Unlike the other three western provinces, it possesses essentially no oil, gas, or coal, so on energy questions its interests have been much closer to those of Ontario, breaking the usual western consensus on economic matters. Manitoba's industrial strategy might best be described as a kind of continuous holding action in those industrial areas that became established there. Time and again the Manitoba government, through the Manitoba Development Fund, has been required to invest in aircraft or bus production, for example — not always with totally satisfactory results. Thus these activities have represented attempts more to defend an existing base than to expand it, in contrast to the situation in Alberta. In other areas Manitoba's actions have been focused on more traditional staple-related activities. The government takeover and operation of the Le Pas pulp and timber complex is an example. The hydroelectric development of the northern rivers gives the province an activity and a chance at diversification lacking in Saskatchewan and Alberta, but exploited in British Columbia. Finally, Manitoba has been able to maintain and develop some of the specialized service functions in finance, insurance, and wholesaling that have given the province an additional measure of diversity.

Implications for U.S.-Canadian
Natural Resource Trade

What does this analysis imply for the future of U.S.-Canadian relations with regard to natural resources? This question can be addressed in two parts. First, to what extent do western attitudes, as described above, differ from the so-called national perspective, and how might this difference affect the ultimate form of any new national policy? Second, do the western provinces' reactions to recent events in the resource sector provide any grounds for anticipating major new unilateral actions by the provincial governments that would have significant national and international consequences?

The answers to these questions follow directly from the preceding analysis. The western provinces are currently preoccupied with promoting aggregate economic growth and, specifically, industrialization and diversification. Thus policies are directed in the first instance at influencing the growth of gross provincial product, aggregate investment, or total employment rather than at per capita growth. Given that these policies have achieved very little to date in the way of lessening dependence on the staple industries, the same primary concerns are likely to continue to dominate economic-policy decisions for some time. This means a continued emphasis on rapid and extensive development of existing and new natural resources, coupled with attempts to induce local processing of these resources. In pursuit of these goals, provincial governments are exhibiting an increasing degree of economic and political sophistication; they perceive efforts to develop resource projects as part of a larger strategy of industrial development; and they are insisting on becoming more directly and actively involved in a regulatory, and even an ownership, role.

The federal government, on the other hand, has been under increasing pressure to shift its attention from growth to efficiency, equity, and the quality of life generally. In the area of natural resources this focus would mean increasing emphasis on conservation, to ensure future domestic supplies, and on environmental protection. More generally, it involves emphasis on a more effective redistribution of income to slow-growth areas, a broadly conceived industrial strategy designed to rationalize secondary manufacturing, and perhaps a lessening—or even a reversal—of dependence on foreign-capital inflows. The types of measures required to achieve these ends are not necessarily always compatible with extensive economic growth, but they can be; and to the extent that they are and that Ottawa moves to adopt them, conflicts with the western provinces can be expected. Some specific examples may clarify the nature of these potential conflicts.

Income Redistribution

Consider income redistribution first. Attempts by the federal government to tax the economic rent of the resource industries and to redistribute it through equalization payments, oil price subsidies, or any other means will continue to be an especially contentious issue in federal-provincial relations. The western provinces, especially Alberta, have received much unfavorable press in the past few years, being depicted as obsessed with accumulating vast sums of money for its own sake and at the expense of poorer regions of the country. This is an unfair charge, however. Their actions have to be judged in the context of their concern about the implications of continued dependence on a staple economy. Windfall revenues are generally judged not as income to support higher consumption but rather as a means—and a very temporary one, given remaining reserves of conventional oil and gas—of perhaps breaking out of the staple mold.[31] One cannot overemphasize this point. Ottawa's attempts to appropriate and redistribute part of the economic rent from resource production are inevitably viewed in the West as a deliberate attempt to forestall its future industrialization. And as such these moves will continue to be bitterly opposed.

This apparently internal Canadian dispute is not without its implications for U.S.-Canadian relations. At one point the uncoordinated taxation efforts of the two levels of government were allegedly reducing the rate of return to resource companies (disproportionately U.S.-owned, as noted earlier) below alternatives available elsewhere. The result was a threatened or actual cessation of exploration and development activity in Canada, and a shift to the United States. The movement of oil and gas drilling rigs south and renewed interest in potash deposits in New Mexico and Montana provide the best examples of the situation. Taxation policies were amended in the face of these developments, and conflict shifted to the division of the residual economic rent between the federal and provincial governments. Given the importance the western provinces attach to this revenue and the federal government's commitment to regional income redistribution, however, any significant new changes in raw materials prices could lead to a repeat of the same type of problem for the resource companies.

There is likely to be substantially more agreement over the pricing of energy products in the future than there has been in the past few years. The producing provinces have naturally wanted immediate access to world prices for their raw materials. Royalty revenues are directly related to the price level, and high prices tend to generate more exploration and development activity and thus more employment locally. There was no disagreement over charging the international price for that portion of Canadian oil production exported to the United States, nor is there likely to be any in the future. But initially the federal government was opposed to a similar price increase for domestic shipments, mainly because of the inflationary implications. Ottawa's concern has slowly shifted to increasing the efficiency of present resource usage and to securing new reserves. The contribution of the price system to achieving both aims seems to have been accepted. Thus there is basic accord between the producing provinces and the federal government on the energy-pricing issue.[32]

The issue of guaranteeing adequate reserves for anticipated future Canadian needs has obvious potential implications for U.S.-Canadian resource arrangements. The federal government has already moved to curtail exports of crude oil and natural gas to the United States. In the former case there is ostensibly no real disagreement with the producing provinces, since the oil is simply being diverted to other buyers in eastern Canada at a price approaching the world price. But a significant part of the oil is to be sent to Sarnia as a feedstock for the Canada Development Corporation's Petrosar petrochemical operations. Alberta's plans for a petrochemical industry are naturally affected by this competition, and Premier Lougheed has threatened to prevent deliveries to the plant. Whether this action would be a violation of the British North America Act is not clear. If Premier Lougheed takes this action, the federal government would clearly have to intervene on

Petrosar's behalf to protect its jurisdiction over interprovincial trade. An alternative would be to allow Petrosar to import offshore oil. But this goes directly against current federal efforts to reduce eastern Canada's dependence on imports. Either way, the Petrosar case is an obviously unstable element in Canada's current oil policy.

In the area of natural gas the problems are potentially more serious. As we have already seen, the denial of new export permits by the NEB reinforced TransCanada's monopsony position with regard to the purchase of gas and thus tended to depress prices producers received. This problem was finally overcome by a concomitant exercise of regulatory powers within Alberta and the federal government's compliance with the demand that natural gas prices be set at an appropriate competitive level relative to those for oil. More serious is the fact that the denial of export licenses runs directly counter to Alberta's initiative to develop the petrochemical industry. The Pacific Northwest area in the United States is a potential market for Alberta's petrochemicals. At the moment, U.S. tariffs represent an obstacle to this trade. But Premier Lougheed has expressed a willingness to permit additional exports of natural gas to this energy-starved region in exchange for U.S. concessions on tariffs. To this end he has journeyed to the area and enlisted the support of some local leaders, including Senator Jackson. The U.S. government is also interested in the prospect, judging from speeches made in 1977 by Ambassador Enders.[33] If some kind of tied agreement of this sort could be reached in principle, a federal refusal to allow these gas exports could lead to a major political dispute. Even more likely is a confrontation over the fact that the federal government appears unwilling even to try to negotiate such an agreement.

A final concern in this area is the likelihood that subsidiary corporations brought in to develop oil sands and heavy-oil deposits will want to commit at least part of their production to parent corporations in the United States. This would, of course, run counter to the federal government's concern that these resources be developed for future Canadian needs. Refusal to allow these exports, at least before some threshold level of proven reserves is reached, could thus slow down, or even preclude, the development of what to Alberta and Saskatchewan are crucial new resources.

The potential for federal-provincial conflict is decidedly less serious for non-energy resources. For one thing, the provinces have less of a relative stake in these other areas, as seen in Table 9.2. Manitoba is a significant producer of nickel, which is an important Canadian mineral product, and cobalt, which is much less so. Other than potash, Saskatchewan is a main producer only of the relatively unimportant resource sodium sulphate. Alberta has no significant production of any non-energy mineral. The situation is different in British Columbia, which accounts for a significant share of Canada's production of copper, silver, lead, and asbestos. None of these resources play the same key roles in the provincial economies as do energy and potash in Alberta and Saskatchewan, respectively.

There are no apparent current differences of opinion over conservation for future Canadian needs versus maximizing the rate of provincial economic growth in the case of non-energy resources. Very little potash is consumed in Canada; in any case, the reserves are immense. Any conflicts in this sector will continue to stem from disputes over taxation, regulation, and nationalization. The West has wanted Canadian markets for its coal since the turn of the century and can be expected to press even harder for policies such as transportation subsidies that would allow it to supply increased domestic demand. A federal government decision to halt the development and sale of nuclear-power technology would affect Saskatchewan's uranium industry adversely, but it is difficult to envision this course being followed. The supply situation for forest and agricultural products appears to be such that there is no reason to expect the federal government to want to limit the rate of development or to control the price of these products in the near future. Both levels of government would appear to have a stake in expanding their production and export. Nor has there been much talk about restricting the rate of development or export of metallic minerals, although this could become an issue in certain specific cases in the future.

Foreign Investment and Ownership

Moving to another policy area, the western provinces are naturally going to be less interested than the federal government in policies to limit the inflow of foreign capital. Resource-development and industrialization projects currently under way or planned will require substantial amounts of capital. Like any frontier area still trying to promote extensive growth, the West would feel that restrictions on the inflow of capital would only make the cost of credit higher and thus reduce the viability of projects. In another vein, the West simply does not consider the substitution of eastern-Canadian-based banks or corporations for U.S. or Japanese credit sources much of a gain. If anything, western economic "nationalism" views provincial rather than national control as the first priority, as the existence of the AEC in Alberta attests.

There has been, however, a definite change in the manner in which the western governments regard private investment in resources, whether multinational or domestic. The skill with which provincial interests are determined and defended has increased. Resource matters have been given a greater priority within the governments, and there has been a special effort to increase expertise in the civil service and in regulatory agencies.

There is also a greater tendency to view resource projects as part of a larger overall development strategy and to try to obtain concessions on the degree of local input, further processing, and local financial participation. The extent to which this attitude will have a bearing on Canada's resource policy depends on the economic power the province possesses over the resource in question. Alberta could more successfully negotiate concessions tied to gas exploration, for example, than could Saskatchewan or Manitoba with respect to northern metal mines.

With respect to ownership, there has been a clear movement away from the old belief that resource development is purely a private-sector responsibility. But there has been no corresponding shift to the other extreme of public ownership *per se*. Rather, there is a willingness to experiment with new ways to increase public control over development, ranging from beefed-up regulatory agencies with broader powers and more sweeping mandates to joint public and private operations. Nationalization is seen as a move to be reserved for extreme cases. This tendency seems to be general across the four provinces, largely irrespective of political ideology. It should be noted, however, that this change in attitude toward public-sector involvement is not unique to the West, nor is it something that private companies necessarily oppose. The large capital costs and higher risks of many new resource projects, especially in energy, have increased the gains to all parties from risk-sharing arrangements.

In the western provinces the increasing reliance on public participation in major resource-development and industrial projects could be a source of future conflict (within the Canadian context). Alberta's purchase of Pacific Western Airlines is a case in point, as it opens the door to political disputes. The Saskatchewan Potash Corporation poses problems of another sort. There is a tradition, if not a constitutional prohibition, against one level of government taxing another. Yet the federal government is also understandably unwilling to give up its share of potash revenue. Furthermore, for Ottawa to yield on this point would open up the possibility of the use of provincial purchasing agencies as a device for avoiding federal taxes on other natural resources.

Industrial-Strategy Objectives

The last general area of interest to be discussed here stems from the considerable discussion in the past decade about the need for a new industrial strategy for Canada. Any major changes in this area would have significant implications for the United States. The West is important in this respect, since it can be expected to press for the strategy most consistent with its own goals. The exact meaning of the term "industrial strategy" varies from proposal to proposal, but the focus is almost always on what one could call the traditional or non-resource-processing secondary industries. That Canada's performance in this regard is dismal is granted by all serious observers. The most common recommendation is a bilateral-free-trade arrangement with the United States covering manufactured products.[34] A less commonly discussed alternative envisions a comprehensive package of taxation, foreign-ownership, and other measures as a precursor to eventual reciprocal, or even unilateral, tariff reductions.[35] Resources enter the discussion quickly because of the assumption that Canada is too concentrated in the raw materials and primary processing sectors to the detriment of employment, domestic ownership, and technological sophistication. The ultimate goal of most industrial-strategy proposals is to develop a comparative advantage in the high-technology, more fully-processed industrial products that are an increasingly important part of international trade.

The West's reaction to these proposals will depend on their specifics. The bilateral-free-trade proposal would probably be greeted relatively favorably, given the region's interest in having the United States end its cascading tariff structure on further stages of processing of petrochemical, wood, and agricultural products and because of the positive effect it would have on real incomes generally in the region. There is, in fact, the interesting possibility that the only version of a free-trade arrangement the United States would ultimately accept is one that the West would favor but Ottawa would not. The United States would presumably bargain for greater access to Canadian resources, especially energy, in exchange for opening its market to manufactured products. But this goes against current federal efforts to divert these supplies to eastern Canadian markets. The West and the United States are more likely to see mutual benefits in partial or special sector trade arrangements than is a Canadian or Ontario government interested in gaining general access to the U.S. market for a wide variety of manufactured goods. The proposed "deal" involving exports of natural gas is a case in point.

The formation of a North American free-trade area would not be unambiguously beneficial for the West if it tended at the same time to discourage closer economic relations with the Pacific Rim countries. These countries, especially Japan, are an even cheaper potential source of some manufactured products. More important, it was shown above that Japan, China, and the USSR are significant growth markets for products from all four provinces, and Japan's role as a source of capital and technology was also noted. To date the western provinces have not had much luck in marketing processed resource products, a problem shared with the rest of the world, at least as far as exporting to Japan is concerned. But as the frequency of provincial trade missions and the unanimity of their terms of reference attest, such a development is a key goal for the region. The danger is that the negotiation of a comprehensive commercial policy with the United States might involve restrictions on further arrangements with third countries. At a minimum, it might dampen the federal government's enthusiasm for any further major trade-policy changes or so effectively tie up technical personnel that no additional moves could be undertaken. It is not at all clear which trade strategy would be in the region's best long-run interests.

There would be very little interest in a significant investment of capital and effort to attain a comparative advantage in high-technology products whose development would only reinforce the industrial supremacy of the East. This is especially true if such a strategy also implied leaving the resource-processing industries to fend for themselves. It is in the latter area, if anywhere, that the region has a chance to increase its level of industrial activity. Westerners are likely to feel that a proportional amount of attention should be given to promoting the international prospects of industries whose natural location within Canada would be in the West, even if they are capital-intensive and involve a high degree of foreign ownership. Thus an industrial strategy that tends to downplay the future role of resource-processing industries in favor of more sophisticated consumer and capital-goods industries will not generate much support in the West.

Notes

1. E. H. Hanson, "Regional Employment and Income Effects of the Petroleum Industry in Alberta," paper presented at the Council of Economics, American Institute of Mining, Metallurgical and Petroleum Engineers, New York, 1966.

2. E. H. Shaffer, "The Employment Impact of Oil and Natural Gas in Alberta, 1961-1971," mimeographed (Edmonton: University of Alberta, 1976).

3. To the detriment of the western meat-packing industry, it has been argued.

4. For a discussion of this point with respect to British Columbia, see J. E. Peters and R. A. Shearer, "The Structure of British Columbia's External Trade, 1939 and 1963," *BC Studies* 8 (1970-71): 34-46.

5. See Government of British Columbia, Ministry of Economic Development, *1976 Review and Outlook* (Vancouver, 1977), p. 25.

6. The price increases for oil created a renewed interest in exploration in Alberta and resulted in some new discoveries, most notably in West Pembina. But these were not significant enough to alter the main point made here.

7. There was a parallel here with the adjustments in the agricultural sector during and after World War II.

8. Larry Pratt ("The State and Province Building: Alberta's Development Strategy, 1971-1976," in Leo Panitch, ed., *The Canadian State: Political Economy and Political Power* [Toronto and Buffalo: University of Toronto Press, 1977]) uses the term "new industrial elite" in reference to this group of Alberta businessmen, politicians, and bureaucrats.

9. For an attempt to model the consistent large majorities in the Alberta legislature as a response to these federal-provincial encounters, see T. Levesque and K. Norrie, "Overwhelming Majorities in the Alberta Legislature," mimeographed (Edmonton: University of Alberta, 1977), and T. Levesque and K. Norrie, "A Spatial Model of Sustained Overwhelming Legislative Majorities," mimeographed (Edmonton: University of Alberta, 1977).

10. See, for example, Western Premiers, "Capital Financing and Regional Financial Institutions," joint submission to the Western Economic Opportunities Conference, Calgary, July 24-26, 1973, p. 3.

11. Government of British Columbia, op. cit., p. 6.

12. Ibid.

13. Once this objection is raised, however, it is not at all obvious why one should stop at the provincial level. There are important economic and social differences between the southern urban areas of each province and the northern or interior ones, for example.

14. The Conservative government of Alberta has adopted a very active planning, and even public ownership, role as part of its industrial strategy, to the chagrin of some of its more conservative supporters. NDP administrations, on the other hand, have never been reluctant to rely on large multinational corporations in the resource sector, even to the point of offering what some of their followers regard as "sweetheart" concessions to attract them. Government/industry relations are typically more uncertain under NDP governments, as the Barrett years in British Columbia or the Saskatchewan potash dispute well attest. But at one point in 1974, in the immediate aftermath of the royalty revisions, the Lougheed administration was not held in much higher esteem by the petroleum industry either.

15. The Oil and Gas Conservation Stabilization and Development Act (Bill 42) establishing these higher taxation rates was challenged on constitutional grounds by Canadian Industrial Oil and Gas Limited (CIGOL), supported by the federal government. The Supreme Court ruled in favor of CIGOL in November, 1977, with regard to the sections of the act imposing a mineral income tax and a royalty surcharge but found the remaining sections valid. The judgment applies only to payments made by CIGOL since 1974, but it opened the possibility of further challenges totaling nearly $600 million.

16. The federal government's acquiescence in this was helped, of course, by the fact that, with declining exports to the United States, the revenue from the export tax was falling further and further behind the subsidies paid on imported oil into Quebec and the Maritimes. Ottawa was having to make up this large and rapidly growing difference out of general revenues. As Canadian oil prices are brought up to world levels, this subsidy will gradually disappear.

17. For a view that such action by the United States is extremely unlikely, see R. L. Gordon, *Coal and Canada-U.S. Energy Relations* (Montreal and Washington, D.C.: Canadian-American Committee, 1976).

18. Manitoba has no commercially feasible deposits of coal. Saskatchewan's coal is exclusively of the soft lignite variety suitable only for steam generation and is of such little value relative to bulk that it is not economical to transport it any distance. Alberta has both steam and metallurgical coal, the former on the prairies and the

latter in the foothills and mountain regions. British Columbia has the richest deposits of the mineral.

19. See Government of Alberta, Department of Energy and Natural Resources, *A Coal Development Policy for Alberta* (Edmonton, 1976).

20. A detailed account of the evolution of provincial government policies toward mining operations is given in a forthcoming series by the Centre for Resource Studies at Queen's University. I am grateful to the Executive Director, C. G. Miller, for making the preliminary versions of some of these available.

21. This was obviously merely an attempt to avoid a federal challenge on constitutional grounds. Reserves of potash in Saskatchewan are estimated to be sufficient for a minimum of 1,600 years at current production rates. For a discussion of two different estimates of these reserves, see Richard Shaffner, *HRI Observations,* No. 12, *New Risks in Resource Development: The Potash Case* (Montreal: C. D. Howe Research Institute, 1976), pp. 10-11.

22. This is the interpretation given by J. Richards in "The Significance of Oil and Potash As Regional Staples in Saskatchewan," paper presented at the National Policy and Western Development Conference, University of Manitoba, February 24-25, 1977. (See also Shaffner, op. cit., pp. 18-21.)

23. Eric Kierans, *Report on Natural Resource Policy in Manitoba* (Winnipeg: Planning and Priorities Committee of Cabinet, Government of Manitoba, 1973).

24. Or "consultation," as it is usually termed.

25. The social benefits can be interpreted as the demand for industrial activities *per se,* as discussed in H. G. Johnson, "An Economic Theory of Protectionism, Tariff Bargaining and the Formation of Customs Unions," *Journal of Political Economy* 73 (1965): 256-83.

26. The Heritage Saving Trust Fund Act, Bill 74, Legislative Assembly of Alberta, 1975.

27. Details are from Alberta Energy Corporation, *1976 Annual Report* (Edmonton, 1977), and Alberta Energy Corporation, *Interim Report for the Six Months Ended June 30, 1977* (Edmonton, 1977).

28. For details see Larry Pratt, *The Tar Sands: Syncrude and the Politics of Oil* (Edmonton: Mel Hurtig, 1976), or Judith Maxwell, *HRI Observations,* No. 10, *Developing New Energy Sources: The Syncrude Case* (Montreal: C. D. Howe Research Institute, 1975).

29. One might add the heavy-oil deposits in Alberta (and Saskatchewan) here as well, although at the time of writing little was publicly available about their economic status.

30. There has been considerable criticism in Alberta of the concessions made to the oil companies (see Pratt, *The Tar Sands,* op. cit.). But more recent evidence indicates that Alberta came out of the negotiations in a relatively good position and that it is Canadian taxpayers as a whole who will foot any bill (see John Helliwell and Gerry May, "Taxes, Royalties and Equity Participation As Alternative Methods of Dividing Resource Revenues: The Syncrude Example," in *Natural Resource Revenues: A Test of Federalism,* British Columbia Institute for Economic Policy Analysis series, ed. Anthony Scott [Vancouver: University of British Columbia Press, 1976]).

31. One should not overlook the absence of a sales tax in Alberta, or the recent lowering of the provincial income tax, when assessing the province's claim that these funds are to be channeled to investment.

32. It will be interesting to see whether the federal government will go even further and agree to the floor price for oil that some of the companies currently negotiating the terms for proceeding with additional oil sands plants are alleged to be demanding.

33. Judith Maxwell, ed., *Policy Review and Outlook, 1978: A Time for Realism* (Montreal: C. D. Howe Research Institute, 1978), Chap. 7.

34. See, for example, Economic Council of Canada, *Looking Outward: A New Trade Strategy for Canada* (Ottawa, 1975).

35. For a summary exposition and critical evaluation of this view, see R. J. Wonnacott, "Industrial Strategy: A Canadian Substitute for Trade Liberalization?," *Canadian Journal of Economics* 8, No. 4 (1975): 536-47.

10

Lessons from Bilateral Trade in Energy Resources

PAUL DANIEL AND RICHARD SHAFFNER

Trade in energy resources has been one of the major links in the U.S.-Canadian relationship in the post–World War II period. Canada has been an important source of both oil and natural gas for the United States, and the United States has, in turn, supplied a large share of Canada's domestic coal requirements. Canadian exports of uranium to the United States were also very significant until the mid-1960s, when an import embargo was imposed by the United States. Finally, there has been a steady, though modest, trade in electricity between the two countries, with the United States being the net importer in most years.

The world energy picture of the 1970s has changed dramatically from what it was previously. There is now a far greater awareness of the global limits to oil and natural gas resources (in recent years oil and gas have been supplying over 65 percent of primary energy needs in the United States and Canada), of the risks to national security that these limits pose for the short to medium term, and of the need to respond to these risks by developing alternative energy sources for the long term. The Arab oil embargo of 1973 and the subsequent fourfold increase in petroleum prices by the Organization of Petroleum Exporting Countries (OPEC) made unmistakably clear the fact that a tenuous situation existed; but even prior to these actions, U.S. policy-makers were becoming uneasy about the growing dependence of the United States on imported oil.

Both the United States and Canada now realize that they are in a state of transition as far as energy resources are concerned. Whereas, in the early days following the 1973 embargo, there was optimism that, with appropriate incentives, oil and gas resources in the two countries could be developed to overcome the "crisis," it is now acknowledged that a much more basic challenge exists. Conventional deposits of oil and gas are limited; other sources, such as tar sands and oil shales, will be very expen-

305

sive to exploit on a scale sufficient to supply a significant proportion of demand while meeting environmental safeguards. What the two countries face is the need to effect a shift to other basic energy sources, so that dependence on oil and gas can be lessened. The options being investigated include greater use of coal (which is in abundant supply in the United States and, to a lesser extent, in Canada); the further development of nuclear power through the use of breeder reactors, recycled spent fuel, and, eventually, nuclear fusion; and the introduction of various renewable energy systems based on solar, wind, wave, biomass conversion, and tidal sources. On the demand side of the equation, there has been emphasis on energy conservation by such means as increasing automobile gasoline mileage and better insulation in houses.

In the current environment, energy policy has become a central concern of the governments of the United States and Canada. The level of government regulation of both production and consumption of energy has escalated, and there has been an increase in direct government involvement through public spending on research and public participation in development projects. The governments of both countries have been faced with difficult choices as to the pricing of oil and gas owing to the trade-off between the immediate inflationary effects for the overall economy of higher prices and the need to have prices at levels that will induce new investment in energy. With the increased uncertainty about long-term energy supplies, decisions about trade in energy resources have also become very much more complicated.

As a result of the importance of energy to overall economic activity and the rising sense of concern over the security of energy supplies, a great deal has been written recently on energy in the U.S.-Canadian context.[1] When this series on U.S.-Canadian resources was being planned, the decision was made to focus principally on non-fuel resources, on which comparatively little recent analysis is available. However, because significant similarities between energy and non-energy resources do exist and because the extensive analysis of energy in the bilateral context has yielded some results that may well be relevant to non-energy resources, this chapter explores the possible implications of recent experience with energy resources that it may be useful to bear in mind when examining the broader resource questions focused upon in this project. The analysis in this chapter is taken primarily from experience with oil and gas because these are the resources that supply the largest shares of energy requirements and that have been most significant in bilateral trade. So much has transpired in the energy area that, to keep this paper to a reasonable length, it has been necessary to limit its scope to a highlighting of the major developments and a summary of some generalizations about trends.

Developments in U.S.-Canadian
Trade in Energy Resources

The importance of mineral fuels in overall trade between the United States and Canada has grown considerably in the past twenty years or so. In 1956, exports of mineral fuels represented only 2.6 percent of total Canadian exports and only 4.3 percent of total Canadian exports to the United States.[2] By 1975 these figures had risen to 16.3 percent and 22.3 percent, respectively.[3] Imports from Canada in 1975 provided the United States with 18.2 percent of its total imported mineral fuel supply.[4] This rising trade in energy resources was a reflection both of the geographical proximity of the two countries, which has made possible the construction of efficient means of transporting mineral fuels, and of the close corporate connections that exist between them. The growth of Canadian oil and gas exports has depended on the construction of major oil and gas pipeline distribution systems in Canada that link with U.S. distribution systems. Without such links to permit exports it would have been much more difficult, if not impossible, for Canadian suppliers to finance domestic distribution systems privately and would have resulted in higher costs of transportation to Canadian consumers. With respect to corporate interconnections, U.S. companies have played a major role in the development of Canadian energy resources; a principal reason for their interest in Canada has been developing resources to supply the large U.S. market. Statistics Canada estimates that 22 percent of the businesses operating in the Canadian mineral fuel industry in 1975 were controlled by U.S. interests and that these companies represented 60 percent of the industry's assets and 81 percent of its sales.[5]

Trade in Oil

Oil is the energy resource that has figured most prominently in the U.S.-Canadian context. During the 1950s and 1960s the focus of oil policy in both the United States and Canada was on expanding domestic production. Following the discovery of commercial oil fields in Alberta in 1947, the Canadian government sought to foster development of a domestic petroleum industry to encourage economic growth in an area that had been relatively depressed. The major stimulus initially took the form of federal corporate-income-tax laws that provided the industry with substantial development incentives.[6] At the time, there was such an abundance of cheap Middle Eastern and Venezuelan oil available that western Canadian oil was competitive only in the small markets of western Canada and adjacent U.S. states. To provide an assured market for the struggling Canadian oil industry, in 1961 the Canadian government introduced a National Oil

Policy that split the country into two markets—the area east of the Ottawa Valley would be supplied by imported oil, while the market west of the Ottawa Valley would be left exclusively to domestic producers.[7]

U.S. oil policy, meanwhile, was concerned about expanding domestic oil production for national security reasons. A flourishing oil industry had existed in the United States since the 1860s, but in 1948 the country became a net importer of oil for the first time. Moreover, the large U.S. oil companies were increasingly favoring relatively unexploited foreign sources of supply over scarcer domestic ones. Following a period of voluntary controls on the importation of crude into the United States, a mandatory program of controls was enacted in 1959. Because Canadian imports were "overland" and therefore considered less of a threat to security than "waterborne" imports, however, they were given an advantage under this quota system, with the result that Canada's share of the total import quota expanded steadily. In 1967 the governments of the United States and Canada agreed to limits on Canadian oil shipments to the United States, but because of the absence of an enforcement mechanism, the agreement was relatively ineffective.

The combination of the assured Canadian market resulting from the creation of the Ottawa Valley line and of steadily growing access to the U.S. market resulted in impressive growth in Canadian oil production in the 1960s, as Figure 10.1 shows. Toward the end of the decade, moreover, with Canadian oil reserves thought to be very large and greater access to the U.S. market still a Canadian objective, there began to be talk of working out a continental energy arrangement. While there were never any formal initiatives for such a plan, it seems likely that it was discussed informally in meetings between leading government officials of the two countries at that time. The concept was envisaged to include such elements as unlimited access by the United States to Canadian oil, a common price for oil in the two countries, joint security programs against interruption of imports, and joint commitments of capital resources to develop U.S. and Canadian arctic reserves and such non-conventional deposits as the Athabasca tar sands.[8] In 1970, however, the U.S. government unilaterally imposed quotas on imports of Canadian oil.[9] Even though the quotas were short-lived, they signaled a decisive turning away from cooperation on energy matters between the two countries. At about the same time a much more nationalistic attitude was emerging in Canada, an attitude that made any kind of "continental harmonization" politically unacceptable.

The dramatic shift in the oil-supply picture around the world in the early 1970s also made an oil deal impractical. With the peaking of U.S. oil production in 1972, it became evident that imports would have to be increased, at least until Alaskan oil could be brought on the market. Meanwhile,

FIGURE 10.1
Disposition of Canadian Oil, 1960-77
(million barrels per day)

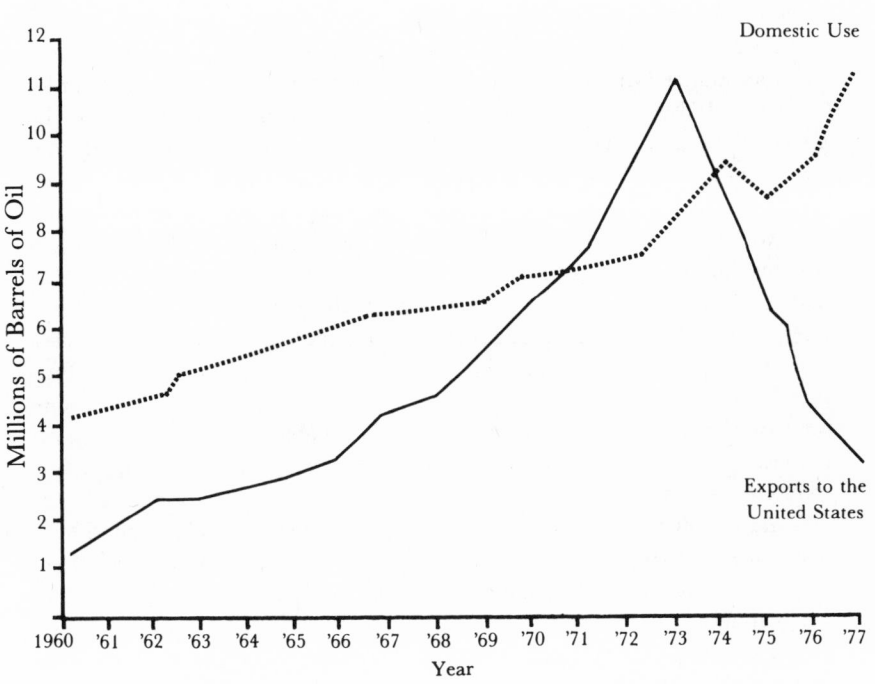

Source: Oilweek, October 15, 1973, and February 16, 1978.

demand was exceeding forecast growth because new environmental protection regulations were inducing a large conversion from coal to oil and gas for power and heat generation. Requests for Canadian oil by U.S. importers were so great that the U.S. government regularly allowed imports to exceed quotas. Finally, in early 1973, import limits were removed altogether.

Canada had been seeking unlimited access to the U.S. market for many years, but when that opportunity finally arose in 1973, it was unable to take advantage of it. Within a few weeks of the removal of U.S. import quotas, Canada had to impose export controls because of soaring U.S. demand. Not only was there concern about production capacity, but new assessments of Canadian reserves were revealing that previous estimates had been grossly optimistic.[10] In November, 1974, the Canadian government announced that exports to the United States would be phased out by the early 1980s, the level of exports during the phaseout period to be governed by a prescribed formula. Behind this decision was the projection by the National Energy Board (NEB)[11] that Canada would soon become a net importer of oil again (Canada had been a net exporter of oil for the first time in 1972 and 1973) and that in the 1980s Canadian production would become inadequate to supply the market west of the Ottawa Valley.[12] It had also been decided that — in order to reduce dependence on foreign supplies, which by this time had been quadrupled in price by OPEC — a pipeline with a capacity of 250,000 barrels per day would be built from Sarnia, Ontario, to Montreal. Thus western oil would supply part of the Canadian market east of the Ottawa Valley. To enable Canadian oil to meet domestic needs for as long as possible, some capacity was "shut in" by reducing exports.

Canada's phasing out of exports was a cause of considerable irritation to the United States, not only because it meant adjusting to new sources of supply, but also because Canada did not consult with the U.S. government when making its decision.[13] In providing the formula by which exports would be phased out, Canada was trying to let the United States know what to expect. Subsequently, Canada has endeavored to make its intentions even clearer by, for example, specifying the quantities of light and heavy oil that it will be able to make available.[14] The United States now appears to accept the fact that Canada's action was predicated on an oil-reserves situation not very different from its own and that Canada was essentially justified in taking the action it did.[15] There remain, however, the particular difficulties of the "northern tier" states, whose transportation facilities and refinery specifications have been geared to Canadian oil and who are threatened directly by the decrease of Canadian exports. Since 1976, Canada has cooperated in the operation of an oil-swap program by which western Canadian oil, in excess of the specified export allocation, is supplied to northern tier refineries in exchange for an equal amount of U.S. oil coming into eastern Canada. The amounts are small, but they have nevertheless given the northern tier states time to make the necessary adjustments in sources of supply and transportation systems.

Before leaving oil, it should be noted that another cause of irritation for the United States in the mid-1970s was Canada's levying an export tax on its oil exports to bring the price approximately in line with that charged by OPEC. Canada justified this action on the grounds that it had to import oil at world prices in its eastern market. What the Canadian government did, in fact, was use the revenue from the export tax to subsidize oil consumers east of the Ottawa Valley and to keep the domestic price of oil well below the world price. The United States objected to the export tax because technical factors that could not be accounted for in the tax made Canadian oil the most expensive foreign oil entering the United States and because it felt the subsidy would be used to provide Canadian industry with a trade advantage in the form of lower energy costs.[16] The implications of energy price adjustments are discussed in more detail later in this chapter.

Trade in Other Energy Resources

Natural Gas. Natural gas has historically ranked second in importance in U.S.-Canadian energy trade, but with the decrease in oil exports it moved ahead of oil in terms of the dollar value of trade in 1977. Canadian gas exports to the United States are granted on the basis of long-term contracts, whereas oil-export permits are only for thirty days. In 1970 the National Energy Board (NEB) authorized a contract for gas exports to the United States of 6.3 trillion cubic feet over twenty years, the largest contract ever granted by Canada. When it was subsequently discovered that the reserves figures on which the contract was based were seriously overestimated, there was a widespread public outcry in Canada over the sale. With the exception of a small amount to help the United States deal with a gas-supply emergency created by a period of extremely cold weather in the winter of 1976/77, the NEB has consistently refused to authorize new export sales since 1970.

Gas became a specific source of irritation in U.S.-Canadian relations when shortages developed in British Columbia's gas production in 1975 and, in order that domestic supplies would not be interrupted, the provincial government cut back gas exports to less than the contracted amount. At about this time the NEB indicated that a generalized reduction in gas exports under existing licenses might be necessary,[17] but the federal government also made it clear that Canadian gas consumers would share the burden of any gas shortages. The rate of growth of Canadian natural gas demand would be reduced so that U.S. obligations could be met as nearly as possible. As it has turned out, no further reductions in gas exports have been necessary. In fact, increases in gas prices have stimulated discovery of sufficient new gas reserves in Canada to make new export sales seem a distinct possibility.[18]

Coal. In contrast to the situation with oil and gas, the United States is a major exporter of coal, and Canada is one of its primary markets. Because Canada's only sizable coal deposits are located on the east coast and in the western provinces of Saskatchewan, Alberta, and British Columbia, U.S. Appalachian coal has long enjoyed a considerable cost advantage in Ontario, the major Canadian market. U.S. coal has consistently supplied over 50 percent of Canadian demand and has been split fairly evenly between thermal coal, mostly for Ontario Hydro, and metallurgical coal to meet the coking requirements of the country's steel industry. In 1950 Canada purchased over 80 percent of U.S. coal exports, but now ranks second to Japan as a destination for U.S. exports.[19] Overall, Canada is only a small net importer of coal, however, as it too has sizable exports, particularly to Japan. In 1977, for example, Canada imported 16.5 million tons from the United States while exporting 13.3 million tons, of which 11.4 million tons went to Japan.[20]

While Canadian demands on U.S. coal resources are quite small in contrast to relatively large U.S. demands on Canada's oil and gas output in the past and even though the United States has never placed, or threatened to place, embargoes on coal exports to Canada, moves to decrease Canada's dependence on U.S. coal are being taken. A new terminal at Thunder Bay to transfer coal from rail to ship will increase the capacity for transporting western Canadian coal to Ontario from 1.5 million tons a year to 6 million tons. In addition, Ontario steelmakers have been testing the metallurgical properties of western coal with an eye to increasing its use considerably by the 1980s. These actions seem more a reaction to the general perception of an energy-short world than to any specific threat by U.S. producers or by the U.S. government to restrict shipments. However, U.S. President Carter has made increased use of coal a main plank in his energy policy, and this could result in higher prices and a tight supply situation in the future.

Uranium. The United States and Canada are both major exporters of uranium.[21] Canada's uranium industry was developed primarily to supply the weapons programs of the U.S. Atomic Energy Commission (USAEC). In the mid-1960s the USAEC stopped buying foreign uranium, and the United States imposed a ban on the purchase of foreign uranium for its embryonic commercial nuclear-power market. The Canadian uranium industry, which had been supplying about a quarter of U.S. needs, was forced to close some mines and mills and probably would have shut down completely had it not been for a Canadian government stockpile program.[22] It has been only with the emergence of a worldwide commercial market for uranium in the mid-1970s that the Canadian industry has begun to recover. Because of concern about the ability of U.S. uranium reserves to meet long-term domestic requirements, the U.S. government initiated a program to relax import controls in 1977, with all restrictions to be removed by 1984.[23] This opens the door once again for Canadian exports to the United States. As in the case of oil and gas, however, exports will be conditional on domestic needs' being protected; Canada restricts its uranium exports to reserves in excess of thirty years' supply for all Canadian reactors in operation, under construction, or planned. Given present domestic requirements and existing commitments to other foreign purchasers, it appears that relatively little Canadian uranium will be available for export to the United States for a number of years.

Electric Power. Trade in electric power between the United States and Canada, which is made possible by the interconnection of the power-distribution systems in adjacent areas of the two countries, has existed since the early years of this century. Originally, firm contracts for uninterruptable power were common; however, in recent years sales have mostly been in the form of emergency backup power and seasonal exchanges. Canadian demand for electricity peaks in the winter, and U.S. demand in the summer. Although Canada and the United States export electricity to each other, in nearly every year since 1950 Canada has been the net exporter, and the United States the net importer. The actual volumes of exports, however, have been quite small—Canada has rarely exported over 5 percent of its production, and the United States rarely over 0.3 percent.[24] Net imports by the United States averaged only 0.5 percent of total U.S. production in the 1971-77 period.[25] The growing use of air conditioning in Canada, which is reducing the complementarity of the seasonal patterns of consumption in the two countries, suggests that, in the future, electricity exports will be directed more to easing temporary shortages than has been the case in the past. An expected slowdown in the growth in demand for electric power in Canada, moreover, has resulted in sufficient surplus generating capacity for the next few years to enable Canada to increase considerably its electric-power exports to the United States, should the demand arise.

The Energy Picture in Transition

The changes in U.S.-Canadian energy trade in the 1970s—notably the Canadian decisions not to allow new gas-export contracts and to phase out exports of oil and the U.S. decision to again allow imports of uranium — reflect the turmoil that has prevailed in the energy sector worldwide during this decade. In late 1973 the decision of some OPEC members to curtail production and to apply an embargo against several importing countries generated shock waves that are still reverberating throughout the world economy. In addition, within a period of a few months in 1973 and 1974, OPEC quadrupled the price of its oil exports. These actions showed the Western developed economies to be vulnerable on two counts: their physical dependence on imported oil and the potential economic dislocations, particularly in the form of balance of payments problems, created by the higher oil prices.

The initial reaction of the U.S. and Canadian governments to the threats posed by OPEC was to seek alternate sources of oil in order to reduce the potential impact of the producers' cartel. In 1974 the U.S. administration launched Project Independence, the goal of which was energy independence for the United States by 1980.[26] The emphasis of the program was on increasing domestic production of energy, particularly oil. The Canadian government, meanwhile, was reassessing its energy resources and, as noted above, found that oil reserves were far smaller than previously estimated. That the NEB did not at this time recommend an immediate stoppage of all exports, however, suggests that it felt that large new reserves would be found in Canada; the continued availability of export markets would help keep production levels at rates high enough to generate the cash flow required to find new, higher-cost reserves. "On balance," the 1974 NEB report stated, "it is the Board's opinion that the immediate cessation of all exports would not be in the best interests of Canada in terms of securing long-term energy supplies."[27]

It appears that the positions of both the U.S. and the Canadian governments in the period immediately following the 1973 embargo were the result of short-term, rather than of long-term, considerations. By 1976, though, there began to emerge a recognition that the energy problems could not be solved mainly by increasing domestic production of oil and gas. Instead, the emphasis in government policy began to shift to the need for comprehensive long-term energy planning. In early 1976 the Canadian government published a policy paper entitled *An Energy Strategy for Canada,* which established the objective of supplying Canada's energy requirements from domestic resources to the greatest extent practical.[28] While this report deals extensively with oil and gas in examining energy supply and demand prospects for the 1976-90 period, it also conveys the idea that there is a need to focus on "reducing the rate at which our energy requirements grow in the future" and on "substituting those energy forms which are in relatively abundant supply in Canada for those that are not."[29]

Advocacy of a coordinated approach was expressed even more clearly in the National Energy Plan introduced by the U.S. administration in April, 1977.[30] The plan identified the long-run task as the development of a new energy base "to have renewable and essentially inexhaustible sources of energy for sustained economic growth,"[31] and it placed the short-run questions in this larger perspective. In addition to devising pricing policies for oil and gas to stimulate domestic production, it put specific emphasis on conservation through the promotion of energy efficiency in industrial, transportation, and residential markets; on having certain industries and utilities convert from oil and gas to coal; and on promoting research in, and development of, such non-conventional renewable sources as solar energy. In general, the dimensions of the energy challenge and the programs that will be required to deal with it have been better articulated in the United States than in Canada. The National Energy Plan proposal, for example, sought systematically to incorporate relationships among such sectors as delivery systems, conservation, energy pricing, and interfuel substitution into the overall economic framework. On the other hand, the Canadian policy approach appears to have created an environment in which the transition could take place fairly quickly. This has undoubtedly been partly attributable to the fact that Canada is not as mature a producing region and has been able to place more emphasis on the prospects for its oil and gas resources, particularly in unconventional forms and frontier locations; but it is also attributable to pricing policies that created incentives to which the markets have quickly responded. In contrast, the U.S. pricing policy for natural gas was not settled until October, 1978, at which time the question of oil pricing was still subject to debate.

In short, the policy perspective of the U.S. and the Canadian governments on the energy problems they were confronting changed between 1974 and 1976 from a reaction to events to the need for a coordinated approach. This occurred because there was recognition of the fact that the two countries — and most of the countries in the world, for that matter — were faced with making a transition to a new energy base, that it would take ten years or more to achieve the transition, and that the transition could not be effected by relying mainly on conventional oil and gas supplies. Investment in new energy sources became recognized as the key to the transition. The higher price of oil on international markets provides an incentive for such investment, but the two governments have not been willing to leave the provision of future energy supplies entirely to the market.

Investment in Energy

Until 1973 the post-World War II period was one in which the world enjoyed abundant supplies of cheap energy, mainly owing to the availability of Middle Eastern oil. While estimates vary somewhat, it is now widely conceded that supplies of conventional oil will fall short of meeting demand sometime before the year 2000.[32] The energy resources that will have to be developed to replace conventional oil and, to a lesser extent, natural gas will be more expensive to produce than the resources currently being consumed. For this reason, a larger share of the world's total investment expenditures will be required to generate a given level of energy. The United States and Canada, furthermore, have indicated they want domestic energy sources to supply a higher proportion of total demand as protection against possible international supply disruptions. In many cases, the new energy alternatives will be of such technical characteristics that they can be far less easily transported than hydrocarbons. The combination of higher-cost energy sources and a goal of greater self-sufficiency suggests that investment in energy as a share of the two economies' GNP can be expected to grow.

A government study has estimated that, if Canada is to achieve its goal of energy self-reliance, annual capital investment in new energy sources will have to average between 4.9 percent and 5.2 percent of GNP between 1976 and 1990, compared to an average of 3.5 percent during the 1950-75 period.[33] In effect, during this fifteen-year period Canada's energy investment, as a share of national output, would be 40-50 percent greater than during the previous twenty-five-year period. Comparable estimates for the United States do not appear to be available as yet, but would probably show a somewhat similar pattern.[34]

The obvious risk a country takes by not increasing its investment in energy is that it will become increasingly dependent on imported supplies and that, in a time of global energy shortage, its economic performance will suffer. There are also dangers to increasing investment in energy, however. One is the possibility that real energy prices will one day fall and thereby make some newly developed energy resources uneconomic. OPEC's price for oil far exceeds production costs and could be lowered if OPEC countries decided they needed to do so to increase their sales. If a country's drive to increase domestic sources of supply is very successful in one area, moreover, it could push domestic energy prices lower and cause losses on other domestic energy investments.

A second danger in increasing energy investment as a share of GNP is the prospect that it will crowd out desirable investment of other types. This is not to suggest that the total amount of investment as a share of GNP is fixed—actually total investment can expand through either increased domestic saving (which can occur by a decrease in personal consumption expenditures and an increase in personal saving, by increased retained earnings by business, and by governments' increasing their revenues

relative to their expenditures) or increased use of foreign sources of investment funds. By definition, saving is always adequate to cover investment,
but if the demand for investment funds is too great, the cost of these funds
becomes so high that some projects cannot be undertaken. In the case of the
projected increase in energy investment needed in Canada between 1976
and 1990, the Canadian government study estimates that little in the way of
dislocations will result, for two reasons. First, some reallocation of investment patterns should be possible. Demographic factors will cause the share
of investment in residential construction, as well as the amount of government investment needed for educational and medical facilities, to fall. Second, domestic saving is expected to increase as a result of stronger
economic growth following the slow-growth performance of the mid-1970s.
As a result of these factors, the Canadian study concludes, Canada should
be able to meet its investment goals without increasing its reliance on
foreign funding.

It might also be noted that, if there is slack in the economy, the upsurge
in energy investment could produce a welcome stimulus to growth.

Another important consideration in evaluating the effect of increased investment in energy is whether the financing will be in the form of equity or
debt. Traditionally, petroleum companies have relied very heavily on internal financing because such a high proportion of their investment expenses
has been in high-risk exploration activity. Given the substantial cash flows
that the petroleum companies have been generating,[35] this pattern of financing is unlikely to change very much with respect to the production of conventional oil and gas. In financing specific large new development such as
oil sands plants and heavy-oil-upgrading plants, however, the petroleum
companies are likely to turn more to debt. The main obstacle in the initia-
tion of such ventures tends to be the large amounts of development capital
required; in the case of conventional supplies, in contrast, uncertainties
associated with exploration tend to be the limiting constraints. Debt financing will also be very important to the financing of the several major new
pipelines that may be built by 1990. The high initial capital costs of these
undertakings make them similar, from the point of view of financing them,
to electric utilities. A high proportion of energy investment has been for
electric utilities in the past, and this trend can be expected to continue.

While on the subject of sources of investment funds, mention should be
made of the possibility of direct participation by government in energy
development. The most prominent example of this approach was the
establishment of Petro-Canada in 1975 by the Canadian government.
Petro-Canada is a crown corporation set up to help Canada meet its
energy-supply goals by participating in the exploration for, and development of, new energy sources. The corporation is also expected to help the

government formulate public policies that better reflect the realities in the energy field and to provide a mechanism for increasing the extent of Canadian participation in the industry. Petro-Canada, by taking over the Canadian government's interests in several energy projects, has become involved in northern exploration for oil and gas, in oil sands development, and in the examination of possible northern gas transportation systems.[36]

Another case of government initiative was the establishment of the Alberta Energy Company Ltd. in 1974 by the Alberta government. The Alberta Energy Company is not a crown corporation — it is owned one-half by the provincial government and one-half by individual shareholders — and neither elected members of the government nor civil servants participate in its management. Its purpose is to give Canadians the opportunity to participate in the development of the resource and industrial bases of Canada and, in particular, of Alberta.

In the case of electric power, direct government participation is well established in Canada, where most of the major utilities are crown corporations. This is not true in the United States, where utilities are mostly privately owned. Regardless of the level of public ownership, however, government influence over energy investment can be great. A country's pricing policies are very significant in determining the overall level of investment in energy and the allocation of investment funds among energy sources. Pricing policies in the United States and Canada are discussed below. Tax policy, too, can be designed to influence investment. Under the U.S. National Energy Plan, for example, it was proposed to encourage investment in coal by levying a tax on those industrial and utility users of oil and natural gas that failed to convert to coal where the possibility of conversion existed. Canada's income tax system, meanwhile, is designed in such a way that oil companies can largely avoid paying federal income taxes on their share of the revenue for increased oil prices if they reinvest their earnings in exploration for new resources.

In summary, it is likely that investment in energy in the United States and Canada will grow as a share of GNP and that government will promote this growth. Government intervention in the economy may be justified when it is felt that market mechanisms are not producing results in the public interest. The actions of the governments of both countries indicate they feel that present uncertainties about energy prices, energy technology, and long-term supply security merit expanded government involvement in the energy field. What governments must be prepared to accept is responsibility for the costs of their particular energy goals, such as the possible negative effects on economic growth of being committed to using relatively high-cost energy resources and the possibility that certain investments in other areas will be crowded out. On the other hand, if the economy were to contain considerable slack in the years ahead, accelerated investment in energy would provide governments with a stimulus to growth.

Energy Pricing

Historically the transition from one energy resource to another has resulted from technological developments that have lowered the production costs, and subsequently the price to the consumer, of the new resource relative to the old. The present transition in energy is unusual in that the OPEC oil price—which, by virtue of the dominance of OPEC in world oil trade, determines the world price—is above the price that would prevail on a freely functioning market. For several years there has actually been a glut of oil on world markets—the high price having both stimulated increased production and induced demand-retarding conservation measures in many consumer countries. Thus the market is giving conflicting signals, and countries like the United States and Canada are put in the position of trying to prepare for the possibility of major oil shortages in the long term at a time when there are indications of a surplus in the short term.

To a large degree the United States and Canada have attempted to counteract the misleading signals of the market by adopting pricing policies that will provide incentives for the production of new domestic resources and the development of alternative sources. At the same time, the level of energy prices has been a major force behind the high rates of inflation the world has experienced in the 1970s. In establishing domestic energy-pricing policies, the two countries have consequently been forced into considering very carefully the trade-off between future energy supplies and current economic performance.

The initial reaction in the United States to the 1973-74 rise in oil prices was to adopt a system of partial price controls. To keep consumer prices reasonably low and to limit windfall gains on production from existing wells, the price of domestically produced "old oil"—the equivalent of the oil produced on any given lease in 1972—was controlled by setting a price ceiling. To provide an incentive for increased domestic production, meanwhile, the price of domestically produced "new oil"—oil produced on any given lease in excess of what was produced in 1972 and newly discovered oil—was allowed to vary to reflect production costs. A "composite" price of oil was calculated from the weighted average of the prices of imported oil and of "old" and "new" domestic oil. Because refiners had varying access to shares of high- and low-priced crude, an "entitlement" procedure was established so that all refiners would effectively pay the same composite price for crude. With the passage of the Energy Policy and Conservation Act in December, 1975, price controls were extended by the establishment of a price ceiling for new oil. Under the Energy Policy and Conservation

Act, controls were to last for forty months, during which time the President has the power to increase the composite price in line with the annual rate of inflation — plus, if he feels it justified, an additional 3 percent to create an incentive for developing higher-cost deposits or for encouraging enhanced recovery. The total annual increase in the composite price is limited to 10 percent.[37]

Under this sytem of price controls, the composite price of crude (that is, the acquisition cost to the refiner, including transportation costs from the wellhead) rose from $9.07 a barrel in 1974 to $11.96 a barrel in 1977.[38] While the United States has managed to keep the price of domestic crude, including that of new oil, well below the world price of oil to limit the inflationary effects of higher oil prices, the system of controls and entitlements has failed to encourage much of a shift to new domestic sources of energy. In fact, it appears to have subsidized oil consumption in the United States — because U.S. domestic crude production has been near capacity, the price consumers pay under the controls system is below the price the United States must pay for additional supplies. Increased demand for oil in the United States has thus been translated directly into increased demand for imported oil,[39] and oil imports have been the main ingredient of a large U.S. balance of trade deficit having worldwide economic implications.

There were three main elements in the oil-pricing strategy Canada adopted following the 1973-74 world price increase. First, it was decided to adopt a single price for oil throughout the country and thus to abandon the Ottawa Valley line, which had resulted in different prices in the domestically supplied western market and the import-supplied eastern market. Second, it was decided that, in order to minimize the potential inflationary effects of higher oil prices, the price in Canada should move gradually up to world levels over a period of several years. Third, a tax was added to the price of oil for export to bring its cost to the importer to about the same level as that of OPEC oil, and the revenue from the tax was used to subsidize the purchase of foreign oil by Canadians.[40] Oil prices in Canada have been raised in a number of discrete steps, usually of about $1.00 a barrel at a time, at intervals of from six to fifteen months. Throughout this process, Canada has kept its oil price below the composite price in the United States. The decisions on the increases have been mostly on the basis of a consensus between the federal and the provincial governments, with the provinces' positions being sharply divided between the oil-producing provinces — which would like to see the Canadian price rise quickly to the world price — and the non-producing provinces — which would like oil prices to remain as low as possible. On one occasion, when an agreement could not be reached, the federal government made the pricing decision unilaterally.

An important aspect of pricing policies for oil in Canada was the com-

petition between the federal government and the governments of the producing provinces for the revenues that the higher prices generated. Under
the Canadian Constitution the provinces own the resources located within
their boundaries. In late 1973 and 1974 the producing provinces increased
their royalties, so that they were collecting the bulk of the price increases in
oil and natural gas. They argued that, as owners of these depletable
resources, they were entitled to most of the higher returns being generated.
Their actions eroded the federal tax base in the petroleum industry to such
an extent that in May, 1974, the federal government announced that provincial royalties would no longer be deductible in the calculation of income
tax. This would have resulted in serious double taxation of the petroleum
industry, but shortly thereafter the two levels of government reached a
compromise that made a portion of the provincial royalties deductible for
income tax purposes.

While there has been nothing equivalent to the OPEC increase in oil
prices directly affecting the pricing of natural gas, there has been ample
reason for gas prices to reflect the general long-term precariousness of
energy supplies. Falling gas production has been at least as great a cause for
concern in the United States since 1973 as declining oil production, and
there was a period when the adequacy of reserves in Canada to meet contracts was very much in doubt. In addition, gas is a convenient substitute
for oil for many uses.

Natural gas sold to interstate pipelines in the United States has been
under federal price controls since 1954, while gas sold for consumption in
the state in which it is produced (that is, intrastate gas) has been
unregulated.[41] Not only have interstate prices not risen fast enough in the
1970s to stimulate much new gas production; they have also increased sufficiently less than intrastate prices that producers have been encouraged to
commit their gas to intrastate markets where possible, thus causing shortages in the interstate market. Moreover, because new, higher-cost gas is
"rolled in" with all previously discovered gas, so that even the price of intrastate gas does not really reflect the cost of new supplies, consumption at
prices below incremental costs has been encouraged. Thus U.S. gas-pricing
policy appears to have been relatively ineffective in either changing consumption patterns or encouraging new production. In Canada, meanwhile,
the federal government made elimination of the long-standing under-
pricing of natural gas relative to oil one of its main energy goals. In an
agreement reached in late 1975 with Alberta, the principal gas-producing
province, the price of gas for domestic use was moved to about 85 percent
of the commodity-equivalent value of crude oil. In addition, the federal
government indicated it would move domestic prices for gas toward 100
percent equivalency with oil while maintaining an appropriate competitive

relationship with oil. The increase in gas prices in Canada has been an incentive for the development of new gas reserves. The increase in gas supplies has spurred consideration of possible new exports to the United States and of an extension of the Canadian natural-gas-pipeline system to markets east of its present terminus in Montreal.

Because there was a close correlation between growth in energy consumption and growth in real GNP in the United States and Canada over much of the post–World War II period, a presumption built up that the two were rigidly dependent on one another.[42] It is very possible that this symmetry existed because the price of energy did not increase as rapidly as the price of most other items, thus making increased energy intensity the result of rational economic choices. In Canada's manufacturing sector, for example, the price index of fuels and electricity fell 30 percent relative to average wage rates over the period 1961-71.[43] The increase in energy prices since 1973 has been relatively greater than the increase in the prices of other inputs, with the result that a reversal of the trend toward great energy intensity can be expected. What is known about the price elasticity of demand for energy would seem to support this conclusion. The general results of a number of studies of the elasticity of demand for energy in Canada suggest that demand is responsive to changes in price at both the intermediate demand and the final demand levels, although the elasticity is greater for specific energy sources than for energy in total because of the possibility of interfuel substitution.[44]

Despite the fact that U.S. and Canadian pricing policies have been far from totally effective, there is no doubt that higher energy prices have caused energy consumption to fall relative to GNP growth since 1973.[45] Decreases in the rate of growth in energy consumption and the expectation that the elasticity of demand for energy will cause this trend to continue raise questions about the urgency for new investment in energy. Ironically, the ultimate impact of the pricing policies may be to reduce somewhat the need for the new investment in energy they were intended to stimulate. If this turns out to be the case, the energy transition the two countries are confronting may not be quite as difficult as it first appeared.

Bilateral Implications of the Transition

There have always been elements of both cooperation and noncooperation in the energy trade between the two countries with the balance constantly fluctuating. Cooperation has followed easily whenever parallel and reinforcing interests were perceived to exist. When important interests have clashed, however, discord has resulted.

Canada's decision in 1974 (mentioned above) to phase out oil exports to the United States is a prominent example of friction between the two countries over an energy issue. Subsequently, however, both countries have come to realize that they face a common transitional adjustment to new energy sources and quite similar energy situations. Americans now accept the fact that Canada does not have virtually limitless supplies of energy resources waiting to be developed, and Canadians realize they do not have quantities of energy sufficient to justify smugness in an energy-short world. The result has been the emergence of interest in a number of energy ventures based on U.S.-Canadian cooperation. While energy for long-term supply or for short-term-adjustment purposes has been central to this cooperation, other considerations have included the complementarity of transportation prerogatives in the two countries and interest in promoting efficient utilization of productive capacity.

Four main bilateral energy initiatives have occurred or come under consideration since awareness developed of the need for an energy transition:

1. In 1977 the governments of the United States and Canada signed an agreement to permit the construction of a natural gas pipeline to transport Alaskan gas across Canada to markets in the Lower 48 states. The plan also makes provision for Canadian gas from the Mackenzie Delta and the Beaufort Sea to be linked up for shipment to markets in southern Canada, should it be needed. At an estimated cost of $12 billion, the Alaska Highway natural-gas-pipeline project will be one of the largest either country has ever undertaken. The principal interests of the two countries in the project vary, however; the United States has been concerned mainly with the gas itself, while Canada has focused on the overall economic implications of constructing the pipeline. Consequently, during the negotiation of the agreement the United States was mainly interested in the effect that building the pipeline would have on the cost to the consumer of the delivered gas, while Canada's attention was on the benefits to the Canadian economy that would result from the contracts and employment generated during the construction phase.

2. With the increases in natural gas prices in Canada since 1973, there has been a large increase in gas exploration, resulting in the discovery of sizable new reserves, mainly in Alberta. It has been estimated that in 1977 and 1978 there were surpluses in productive capacity in Canada of 400 billion cubic feet (about 25 percent of actual production).[46] The gas surplus has sparked interest in new gas sales by Canada to regions in the United States where gas has been in short supply. Although the United States has contracts running into the 1990s to purchase Canadian gas, no contracts have been allowed by the Canadian government since 1970. Three possible gas export arrangements have been discussed: Canada could accelerate its sales to the United States under existing contracts to help ease supply problems in the United States until Alaskan gas becomes available; Canada

could export gas in excess of existing contracts on the condition that these supplies be made up when Alaskan gas starts flowing (this sort of arrangement is commonly referred to as a "time swap"); and contracts for entirely new exports could be drawn up if it were certain that Canadian demands could be more than adequately supplied by conventional and Mackenzie Delta–Beaufort Sea supplies. Any increase in exports, because it would tax the cross-border capacity of existing gas pipelines, would encourage the building of the southern portion of the Alaska Highway pipeline first (that is, the portion from Alberta to U.S. destinations). Moreover, each of the export schemes would improve Canadian gas producers' returns by permitting a higher level of capacity utilization and thus would be likely to encourage even more exploration in Canada.

3. The phasing out of Canada's oil exports to the United States caused serious supply problems for oil refiners located in the upper midwestern and northwestern (or northern tier) states. The long-range solution to the shortage is the construction of a pipeline that will enable Alaskan or off-shore oil to move into this area. Several specific projects involving Canada have been given consideration. One was for a pipeline to be built from a new tanker terminal at Kitimat, British Columbia, to Edmonton, Alberta, where it would link up with the existing oil delivery system from Canada to the United States. The probability that this project will not be needed to supply Canadian oil requirements and its unpopularity on environmental grounds have caused the Canadian government to effectively kill it.[47] A second project involved reversing the flow of the Trans-Mountain Pipeline to move oil from a tanker terminal at Cherry Point, Washington, to Edmonton—where, again, it would be linked to the existing pipeline network to the northern tier states. This proposal was eliminated with the passage in October, 1977, of an amendment to the U.S. Marine Mammal Protection Act that will prevent the necessary expansion of the Cherry Point terminal. A third possibility is building an oil pipeline along the route of the Alaska Highway natural gas pipeline, linking the Trans-Alaska Pipeline to the existing system at Edmonton. It is generally conceded that construction of such a pipeline would have to lag somewhat behind construction of the natural gas pipeline, which will not be completed until 1983 or later. It is possible that before then a pipeline will be launched along a route through the United States to supply the northern tier states.

4. As insurance against another oil embargo or production cutbacks by the major oil exporters, the United States is in the process of building up a stockpile of one billion barrels of oil. The cheapest way to store large volumes of oil is in natural underground caverns or in such man-made underground areas as worked-out mines. Because there are few suitable sites of this sort in the northeastern United States, the U.S. government has

expressed an interest in purchasing the use of possible storage sites in eastern Canada. Allowing the United States to store oil in Canada also would be likely to create the guarantee that Canada would require to enter into oil "time swap" arrangements with the United States. Such swaps would permit Canada to assist even more with the adjustment of the northern tier states to the phase-out of Canadian oil exports than is possible with the small "non-time" swaps that have been occurring since 1976.

Two main themes predominate in these initiatives for bilateral cooperation. One is the retention, to the extent that energy supplies make it possible, of the traditional pattern of energy flows (trade in coal is the exception) from Canada to the United States. The trade flows that have been considered include both those for long-term supply and those that will assist the United States to overcome short-term regional adjustment problems. The second concerns investment in Canada to service the U.S. energy-supply infrastructure in the form of transportation and storage facilities. An additional theme from which there could be much mutual advantage is technological cooperation and the coordination of research and development in the two countries. Canada has a lead in some areas, such as oil sands technology, while the United States leads in others, such as coal liquification.[48]

While these initiatives indicate a mutual concern for the problems that the energy transition creates, past experience indicates that several factors shaping the environment for bilateral cooperation must be taken into account. These include the following:

- Traditionally, the United States has paid for energy imports from Canada with exports to Canada of manufactured goods. Canada has increasingly resisted this trade pattern because it wishes to do further processing of many of its natural resource products. The government of Alberta, for example, has indicated it might make additional gas exports to the United States conditional upon increased U.S. imports of its petrochemical output and certain of its agricultural products.
- Canada's development of its energy resources has largely been financed by foreign capital and controlled by foreign companies, a situation that many Canadians resent. The Canadian government would regard with disapproval new activities in Canadian energy that enhanced this trend. On the other hand, it would undoubtedly be pleased if a trade surplus resulting from increased energy sales to the United States were to permit Canada to export capital so that it could repatriate some of the assets held by foreign interests.
- Both countries are likely to be wary of long-term contracts for

energy sales. British Columbia's abrogation of some long-term gas
contracts in 1975, for example, was a significant irritant in
U.S.-Canadian relations.

- In arranging bilateral deals, the negotiating process itself is fraught
with hazards, ranging from unilateral actions based on political ex-
pediency to incompatibilities with a country's international obligations. Reacting to Alberta's possible conditions for approving new
gas exports, for example, the United States has stated that the terms
of any agreement will have to be negotiated at the international
level, with the federal government of Canada being the appropriate
representative at these negotiations.

The transition to a new resource base is the challenge that has dominated
energy policy-making since the mid-1970s and will continue to do so until
at least well into the 1980s. Policies adopted individually by the United
States and Canada have started to generate some positive results, and the
apparent return of close bilateral cooperation on energy matters is an encouraging sign. Much remains to be done, however, and the task will be
made difficult by the shifting of priorities that inevitably accompanies a
country's changing economic fortunes.

The Principal Features of Energy Resources

As a result of the attention that energy prices and future energy sources
have generated in recent years, a disproportionately large segment of the
analysis of natural resources has been focused on energy. The project of
which this volume forms a part, on the other hand, concentrates on non-
energy resources. The main exception is this chapter, the purpose of which
is to indicate what has emerged from recent energy experience that may be
relevant to the analysis of non-energy resources. The remainder of this
chapter summarizes the main characteristics of energy resources as revealed earlier in the chapter and indicates the extent to which they are
either unique to energy resources or generally applicable to all types of
resources. The dominant features of energy resources are the role of energy
as a major force in the economy, the great strategic importance of energy,
the possibility of energy-resource depletion, the recent increase in government intervention in energy markets, and the pressures among different
levels of government within the same country that have been created by recent developments in energy.

The Economic Significance of Energy

The importance of energy resources to the economies of the United
States and Canada is well documented in Chapter 2 of this volume. In 1975

the value of mineral fuel (oil, natural gas, and coal) production in the United States was 76 percent of total mineral production and 29 percent of the total output of raw materials (minerals, forest products, and agricultural products). For Canada, these figures were 54 percent and 28 percent, respectively.[49] The extent of energy-resource use is also prominently reflected in the trade data of the two countries. In 1975 the United States imported $22 billion of mineral fuels more than it exported. By 1977 this energy-trade deficit had risen to $40 billion—principally as a result of $44 billion spent on oil imports—and was the major cause of an overall U.S. balance of trade deficit of $31 billion.[50] Mineral fuels comprised 16 percent of all Canadian exports in 1975, and 12 percent of total imports.[51] The impact that investment in energy resources can have on the economy—and, in particular, the effects of a possible 40-50 percent increase in Canada over the next few years—has already been shown to be very significant.

In terms of their role in the economy, individual non-fuel resources are not nearly as significant as energy resources. In 1975, production of copper and iron ore, the leading non-fuel minerals in the United States, represented only 2.9 percent and 2.6 percent, respectively, of total mineral production, and only 1.1 percent and 1.0 percent, respectively, of total raw materials production.[52] The value of the leading agricultural commodity, cattle and calves, was 10.6 percent of total raw materials production. A similar picture exists in Canada, where the most important non-fuel mineral products, nickel and copper, represented 8.7 and 8.3 percent, respectively, of total mineral production in 1975, and 4.6 and 4.3 percent of total raw materials production. Wheat, the leading agricultural commodity, accounted for 10.8 percent of total raw materials production.

Some non-energy resources, because they are produced largely for export, are relatively more significant than energy resources in terms of their impact on international trade balances than in terms of production. This applies to wheat and to a variety of metals and non-metallic minerals in Canada. It applies to a much lesser extent in the United States and is limited primarily to molybdenum, uranium, phosphate rock, and certain agricultural products.

With respect to the specific economic impact on the development of certain regions of a country, there would seem to be fairly close similarity between energy and non-energy resources. In Canada, in fact, the emergence of resource industries has been crucial to the development of particular areas of the country. The main difference between the energy and non-energy resource industries in regional development is mostly one of scale: a new metal mine may turn around the economy of a local area, but the discovery of oil or gas can greatly influence the economy of a whole province, as it has in the case of Alberta since 1947. In Canada, development of export markets for resources, whether energy or non-energy, has often been essential in attaining the economies of scale in production needed to permit the realization of regional growth opportunities.

Strategic Considerations

Energy is of great strategic importance because abundant supplies are essential to the operation of a modern industrial economy and to meet basic human needs. Shortfalls in energy would precipitate serious disruptions in economic activity by causing cutbacks in the operations of production and transportation systems. They could also lead very quickly to social crisis. The scale on which energy resources are consumed and the degree of specialization involved in their use mean that substitution among energy sources is not readily feasible in the short run. The volume of energy consumption also makes stockpiling on a scale large enough to prevent supply interruptions very expensive. Even the stockpile of one billion barrels of oil that the United States is in the process of creating represents less than half of that country's yearly imports. The low short-term feasibility of substitution and the high cost of stockpiling mean that countries that rely on external sources of supply are highly susceptible to supply disruptions; for them, security-of-supply considerations are crucial. It has been U.S. concern about the security of supply of its oil imports that has resulted in preferential policies favoring Canadian oil.

Some non-energy resources are at least as susceptible as energy resources to interruption by foreign suppliers. In general, however, the impact of such interruptions is not as serious. The possibility of supplies' being limited by cartels and embargoes exists for all types of resources, but in the case of non-energy resources, substitutes usually can be found. In addition, because the volume of material used is likely to be much smaller than in the case of energy resources, stockpiling of non-energy-resource materials is often more feasible. A stockpile not only protects a country against short-term interruptions of supply but also gives it some flexibility in adjusting to substitutes if the supply interruption is expected to be lengthy.

Concerns about Exhaustion of Resources

One of the central concerns behind the transition in energy on which this chapter has focused is the fear that world oil and natural gas resources are running out. While forecasts of when conventional oil and gas supplies at current, or close to current, prices will actually become inadequate to supply world requirements vary, depletion of these resources is clearly considered by most experts to be approaching.[53] When concern about the depletion of a non-renewable resource has emerged in the past, the price of that resource has risen to stimulate discovery of deposits, to make economic the use of previously unprofitable deposits, and to encourage substitution, thus defusing any perceived crisis. Increased oil and gas prices since 1973 have led to many new discoveries, including large reserves in Mexico and China, but the fear of depletion remains. As existing producing areas have become fully developed, exploration has had to shift to areas that are physically much more difficult to explore, such as in the Arctic and off-shore, and to areas that have a limited geological potential for oil and gas. The discoveries that have been made in these areas, moreover, tend to be small in relation to total world demand.[54]

The one energy source for which depletion is not considered to be a problem for many years is coal. The United States is particularly well-endowed with coal, which is estimated to constitute 90 percent of its conventional energy reserves.[55] Among the other energy sources, hydro power is non-depletable, but there remain in North America few sites suitable for development. The amount of energy derivable from uranium, meanwhile, is quite uncertain, not only because there may still be large sources of supply that have not been discovered, but also because the extent of recycling, which would greatly increase the energy from a given amount of fuel, is yet to be determined.

Depletion of non-energy resources does not seem to be a cause for concern in the foreseeable future. There appears to be ample land to produce the agricultural and forest products required, and it is generally accepted that the higher prices, which induce new discoveries and encourage re-cycling, will keep the world supplied with mineral products for generations to come. The one major exception to this optimistic view is evidence that the world may be reaching a limit in production from its fisheries as a result of having treated them for so long as a common-property, renewable resource.

Government Intervention

The strategic importance of energy and the attendant concern about depletion of oil and gas reserves have resulted in extensive government intervention in energy markets. Prices have been set at levels to give producers some incentive for new investment, while consumers, especially certain groups, have been protected from the immediate impact of higher world prices. Policies have been pursued to assure the greatest possible degree of security against interruption to supplies from foreign sources. In addition, Canada has established limits on sales of its oil and gas resources. Canada's hesitancy in approving new gas sales to the United States when it had excess productive capacity in 1977 and 1978 illustrates the control governments have been willing to exert over market forces.

One explanation for the widespread government involvement in energy is the high political profile of energy, especially since 1973. Although governments have also intervened in non-energy resource markets, they have generally done so to a lesser degree and at a more measured pace. The relative absence of supply problems in the markets for non-energy resources has meant that governments have been under far less pressure to act on behalf of domestic producers and consumers. Much more typical of government involvement has been the establishment in Canada of agricultural marketing boards as a response to what was perceived to be a long-standing problem of income instability for producers. In the non-fuel mining industry, intervention has tended to be oriented toward modifying the economic impact of a single dominant industry in a region—for example, the employment effects on a community when a resource business shuts down.

The involvement of different levels of government in energy-resource markets has resulted in conflicts among them. This has been particularly true in Canada, where, since 1973, problems have included decisions on the pricing of oil and gas and on the allocation of the economic rents from the sale of resources among the federal and provincial governments and producers. With respect to pricing, producing and consuming provinces have frequently been pitted against one another, with the federal government acting somewhat in the role of mediator—its position being determined by its perception of the best interests of the country. With respect to the distribution of rents, a major confrontation between the producing provinces and the federal government arose in 1973-74, when the provincial governments raised their royalties so that they might derive extra benefits from higher oil prices and the federal government retaliated against this attack on its tax base by declaring royalties to be non-deductible for income tax purposes. The same conflict applied to the taxing of some non-energy resources. This particular federal-provincial conflict has been resolved, but because some responsibility for resources rests with the provinces and some with the federal government, conflicts among levels of government seem bound to emerge periodically. The decision Canada faced in 1977 and 1978 regarding whether to allow new sales of natural gas to the United States is typical—the producing provinces wanted to sell the gas because it would be to their economic advantage as owners of the resources, but the federal government felt constrained to hold back sales until it could determine whether they would be in the long-term economic interest of all of Canada.

Lessons for the Bilateral Resource Relationship

This review of the main characteristics of energy resources suggests that the energy experience of the 1970s is of fairly limited relevance to non-energy resources. Energy-resource issues differ from most other resource issues in both degree and kind. Energy production is vastly more important as a form of economic activity than the production of individual non-energy-resource materials, and the volume of energy consumption is so great that trying to safeguard against supply interruptions by stockpiling is highly impractical. The need for the continuous availability of energy, essential to the operation of any modern industrial economy, makes energy unique among natural resources in terms of strategic importance. A shortage of any resource material will hurt some industries, but a shortage of energy will hurt all.

Despite these fundamental differences, there are two lessons of some significance for non-energy resources that can be derived from the recent energy experience. One is the obvious lesson that, when a resource material is in short supply on a global basis, the United States and Canada tend to concern themselves far more with their domestic needs than with the supply problems of each other. Cooperation is dependent on some evidence that both countries can benefit from working together, a situation that was gradually perceived to prevail with respect to the energy problems of the 1970s. The long-standing close bilateral relationship—a relationship that tends to be tighter when the two countries face a common threat[56]—may have encouraged the process of cooperation, but national interests were clearly dominant.

The second lesson is the likelihood of government's intervening in the market for a resource if the interests of the country are perceived to be at risk. The governments of the United States and Canada have become involved in the pricing of energy resources such as oil and natural gas in order to be able to balance the interests of producers and consumers whenever they perceive the markets incapable of doing so. Government involvement in non-energy-resource industries may tend to be less oriented toward the total market for a commodity; but in their concern to protect jobs in an industry, to collect the economic rent from a depletable resource, or to provide some sort of regional stimulus, governments can make their presence felt quite strongly.

Recent energy experience provides an encouraging example of U.S.-Canadian cooperation. The two countries appear to have overcome what in 1973 and 1974 appeared likely to become the source of a major rift in relations. Subsequently, they have shown their willingness to work together against some common energy-supply problems—for example, in adjusting to scarcer supplies of oil, Canada was willing to phase down its exports to the United States rather than cut them off—and to continue to export energy resources to the other where those exports do not jeopardize long-term domestic needs—for example, Canada is continuing to export natural gas to the United States, and coal continues to move in the opposite direction. To the extent that bilateral cooperation in energy continues to exist, the prospects for trade in non-energy resources will probably be enhanced.

Notes

1. For general reviews of U.S.-Canadian energy trade, with particular reference to oil and natural gas, see J. Alex Murray, ed., *North American Energy in Perspective,* Proceedings of the Canadian-American Seminar, University of Windsor, November 14-15, 1974 (Windsor, Ontario: University of Windsor, 1975); Ted Greenwood, "Canadian-American Trade in Energy Resources," in Annette Baker Fox, Alfred O. Hero, Jr., and Joseph S. Nye, Jr., eds., *Canada and the United States: Transnational and Transgovernmental Relations* (New York: Columbia University Press, 1976); James McKie, "United States and Canadian Energy Policy," in Campbell Watkins and Michael Walker, eds., *Oil in the Seventies: Essays on Energy Policy* (Vancouver: The Fraser Institute, 1977); and John E. Carroll and Marcia Valiente, "Energy and Canadian-American Relations," *Journal of Natural Resource Management and Interdisciplinary Studies,* March, 1978.

In addition, the Canadian-American Committee has recently sponsored studies dealing specifically with coal, uranium, and electricity in the bilateral context. They are: Richard L. Gordon, *Coal and Canada-U.S. Energy Relations* (Montreal and Washington, D.C.: Canadian-American Committee, 1976); Hugh C. McIntyre, *Uranium, Nuclear Power, and Canada-U.S. Energy Relations* (Montreal and Washington, D.C.: Canadian-American Committee, 1978); and Mark Perlgut, *Electricity Across the Border: The Canadian-American Experience* (Montreal and Washington, D.C.: Canadian-American Committee, 1979).

2. Dominion Bureau of Statistics, *Trade of Canada,* December, 1957 (Ottawa: Queen's Printer, 1958).

3. See Chapter 2, Table A.3.

4. Ibid.

5. Statistics Canada, *Corporations and Labour Unions Returns Act,* Report for 1975, Part I, *Corporations* (Ottawa, 1978), Table 3.

6. These tax provisions, which remained in effect until the tax reform of 1971, included automatic depletion allowances of one-third of taxable production income, deduction of lease and royalty payments to provincial governments, deduction of all exploration and development expenses, and a three-year tax exemption on the revenue from new wells.

7. The division of the country into two markets was recommended by a Royal Commission on Energy (see Royal Commission on Energy, "Second Report," mimeographed, July, 1959) chaired by Henry Borden.

8. McKie (op. cit., pp. 253-55) provides a description of the prospective energy arrangement.

9. In February, 1970, a U.S. Cabinet Task Force on Oil Import Control released a report entitled *The Oil Import Question: A Report on the Relationship of Oil Imports to the*

National Security (Washington, D.C.: U.S. Government Printing Office, 1970), in which it recommended that tariffs be placed on Canadian oil imports until July, 1972, when, if a pact relating to energy matters could be concluded, Canadian oil would be allowed to enter on an unrestricted basis. The U.S. administration did not follow the recommendation and instead imposed the import quotas.

10. The first government report indicating serious estimating errors was National Energy Board, "Potential Limitations of Canadian Petroleum Supplies," mimeographed, December, 1972.

11. The National Energy Board, which was established in 1959, is a federal government regulatory agency with broad responsibility over the hydrocarbon and electricity sectors. Its functions include preparing forecasts on production and reserves; control and licensing of exports and imports of natural gas, electricity, and — since 1973 — oil; and advising on the construction of pipelines. Until 1973, it oversaw the operation of the National Oil Policy.

12. The decision was based on the analysis contained in National Energy Board, *In the Matter of the Exploration of Oil* (Ottawa, 1974); further analysis was supplied in National Energy Board, *Canadian Oil: Supply and Requirements,* September, 1975.

13. This view is contained in Canadian-American Committee, *A Time of Difficult Transitions: Canada-U.S. Relations in 1976* (Montreal and Washington, D.C., 1976), pp. 46-47.

14. National Energy Board, *Canadian Oil: Supply and Requirements,* February, 1977.

15. Canadian-American Committee, *Bilateral Relations in an Uncertain World Context: Canada-U.S. Relations in 1978* (Montreal and Washington, D.C., 1978), p. 65.

16. See Canadian-American Committee, *Difficult Transitions,* op. cit., pp. 44-45.

17. National Energy Board, *Canadian Natural Gas: Supply and Requirements,* April, 1975.

18. The NEB launched a round of hearings in October, 1978, to assess the status of Canada's gas reserves, on the basis of which it will decide whether to recommend new gas exports.

19. Gordon, op. cit., p. 11.

20. Statistics Canada, *Exports by Commodities,* December, 1977 (Ottawa, 1978).

21. Uranium is the subject of a case study in Volume II of this project.

22. In addition, there is fairly certain evidence that between 1972 and 1975 Canadian uranium producers, at the specific request of the Canadian government, participated with producers from France, Australia, South Africa, and Britain in a uranium cartel that set minimum and maximum prices for uranium and decided on market shares. For a brief description of the cartel and the concerns that have been expressed about it in the United States, see Canadian-American Committee, *Bilateral Relations,* op. cit., pp. 86-89.

23. For a review of the U.S. supply-demand situation for uranium, see McIntyre, op. cit.

24. Perlgut, op. cit., Tables 1 and 2.

25. Ibid., Table 2.

26. There was, however, no single agreed interpretation of what independence meant in this context. "To some, energy independence is a situation in which the

United States received no energy imports i.e., it produces all of its energy domestically. To others, independence is a situation in which the United States does import to meet some of its energy requirements, but only up to a point of 'acceptable' political and economic vulnerability." (Federal Energy Administration, *Project Independence: A Summary* [Washington, D.C., 1974], pp. 18-19.)

27. National Energy Board, *In the Matter of the Exploration of Oil, op. cit.*, p. 4-4.

28. Energy, Mines and Resources Canada, *An Energy Strategy for Canada: Policies for Self-Reliance* (Ottawa, 1976).

29. Ibid., p. iii.

30. Executive Office of the President, *The National Energy Plan* (Washington, D.C.: U.S. Government Printing Office, 1977).

31. Ibid., p. ix.

32. For example, see Workshop on Alternative Energy Strategies, *Energy: Global Prospects 1985-2000,* Carroll L. Wilson, project director (New York: McGraw-Hill, 1977).

33. Energy, Mines and Resources Canada, *Financing Energy Self-Reliance* (Ottawa, 1977), p. iv.

34. The emphasis that has been given in Canada to the overall impact on investment of the changing energy base is perhaps a reflection of an underlying concern about whether it will stimulate new, large-scale foreign investment—a longstanding issue in Canada. Another study of future investment in energy is J. R. Downs, *The Availability of Capital to Fund the Development of Canadian Energy Supplies* (Calgary: Canadian Energy Research Institute, 1977).

35. See "The New Diversification Oil Game," *Business Week,* April 24, 1978, pp. 76-88.

36. Petro-Canada has acquired the Canadian government's equity in Panarctic Oils Ltd. (45 percent at December 31, 1976) and in Syncrude Canada Ltd. (15 percent) and has taken over its commitment to the Polar Gas project.

37. The President may, however, propose to Congress that the composite price rise by more than 10 percent if he feels that a higher price would lead to greater production.

38. U.S. Department of Energy, *Monthly Energy Review,* August, 1978 (Washington, D.C.: U.S. Government Printing Office, 1978), p. 58.

39. U.S. crude-oil imports increased at an average annual rate of 22.7 percent in the 1973-76 period, while oil imports in virtually all other major industrial countries were falling (see "Annual Report of the Council of Economic Advisors" in *Economic Report of the President,* January, 1978 [Washington, D.C.: U.S. Government Printing Office, 1978], p. 187).

40. As exports of oil to the United States began to be phased out, revenue from the export tax became insufficient to provide all the oil compensation payments called for. To help fund the deficit, in 1975 the federal government applied a special excise tax of 10 cents per gallon on sales of motor gasoline for non-commercial use. This tax was reduced to 7 cents per gallon in September, 1978, as an anti-inflation measure.

41. As a result of the energy bill passed by Congress in October, 1978, federal price controls will be extended to intrastate gas, but federal controls on the price of

all newly discovered gas, both intrastate and interstate, will be lifted in 1985.

42. Over the 1958-73 period, energy consumption in the United States grew at an annual rate of 4.0 percent, while real GNP grew at an averate annual rate of 4.1 percent ("Annual Report of the Council of Economic Advisors," op. cit., pp. 181 and 258). During the same period, aggregate Canadian demand for energy increased at an annual rate of 5.1 percent, while real GNP grew at an annual rate of 5.0 percent (Statistics Canada, *Detailed Energy Supply and Demand in Canada* [Ottawa, various issues], and Statistics Canada, *National Income and Expenditure Accounts* [Ottawa, various issues]).

43. Ernst R. Berndt, "Canadian Energy Demand and Economic Growth," in Watkins and Walker, op. cit., p. 58.

44. For a review of studies on the elasticity of demand for energy, see Berndt, op. cit., pp. 58-68.

45. Over the 1974-77 period, total energy consumption in the United States grew 1.4 percent, compared to a growth in real GNP of 8.3 percent. In Canada, total energy consumption grew 9.4 percent, while real GNP increased 12.8 percent.

46. National Energy Board, *Reasons for Decision: Northern Pipelines* (Ottawa, 1977), p. 1-81.

47. The National Energy Board estimates that domestic supplies of oil are such that Canada will not have to augment its existing oil-importing capacity until after 1995 (National Energy Board, *Canadian Oil: Supply and Requirements,* September, 1978 [Ottawa, 1978]).

48. One possibility for joint R&D in the energy area is the proposal for working together on nuclear fuel cycles that would serve as an alternative to the breeder reactor (Canadian-American Committee, *Safer Nuclear Power Initiatives: A Call for Canada-U.S. Action* [Montreal and Washington, D.C., 1978]).

49. Chapter 2, Table A.1.

50. U.S. Department of Commerce, *Survey of Current Business* (Washington, D.C.: U.S. Government Printing Office, various issues).

51. Chapter 2, Table 2.3.

52. Data in this paragraph are taken from Chapter 2, Table A.1.

53. For a review of world oil and gas reserves and resource potential compared to demand, see Workshop on Alternative Energy Strategies, op. cit., Chaps. 3 and 4.

54. For example, the Prudhoe Bay discovery in Alaska was estimated to contain 26 trillion cubic feet of saleable natural gas at the time the decision was taken to build a pipeline to bring the gas to the Lower 48 states (National Energy Board, *Reasons for Decision,* op. cit., p. 2-168). In recent years, consumption of natural gas in the United States has been about 20 trillion cubic feet per year; the Prudhoe Bay gas discovery therefore represents supplying the equivalent of less than 1-1/2 years of domestic demand.

55. Executive Office of the President, op. cit., p. 63.

56. The notion that relations between the United States and Canada reflect the extent of common external problems is presented in Canadian-American Committee, *Bilateral Relations,* op. cit., pp. 7-25.

11

What Are the Issues?

WILLIAM DIEBOLD, JR.

Of all things, an indiscreet tampering with the trade of provisions is the most dangerous, and it is always worst in the time when men are most disposed to it; that is, in the time of scarcity. Because there is nothing on which the passions of men are so violent and their judgement so weak, and on which there exists such a multitude of ill-founded, popular prejudices.

—Edmund Burke, "Thoughts and
Details on Scarcity" (1795)[1]

Perhaps, if this study had been undertaken a few years earlier, this caution of Burke's would have had to be underlined in every chapter. But by now the limits of the *Limits to Growth* are well known, OPEC is seen in a perspective that for the most part emphasizes the differences between oil and other natural resources rather than their similarities, and the prices of most minerals have once again demonstrated both the chronic problem of instability and the plausibility of the old saying that what goes up must come down. To be sure, it would be foolish to draw the conclusion that there can be no such thing as scarcity. In laying out these issues in Chapter 1, Carl Beigie shows why the very difficulty of making reliable long-term forecasts makes it prudent to assume that constraints on the supply of some materials and higher real costs of extraction will exist sometime in the future. Moreover, we can be sure that at least some people in the world will from time to time act as if there were significant shortages. In the process they can create a variety of difficulties for others and may bring on the problems they fear.

The shadows of recession created an opposite risk for the authors of this volume. The complacent consumer—whether an individual, a businessman, or a government—is an important character in the earlier chapters. He is as responsible as anyone for the fact that although, from time to time during the first three-quarters of this century, difficulties with raw materials supplies led many people to advocate strong and farsighted national raw materials policies, their advocacy dissipated once the flow of

337

materials resumed and came to be taken for granted again. Writing under limitations of space as well as time, our authors have had to find a perspective that takes account of good times and bad and of a large element of uncertainty. There is some comfort in Keynes's remark, "Economists must leave to Adam Smith alone the glory of the Quarto, must pluck the day, fling pamphlets into the wind, write always *sub specie temporis,* and achieve immortality by accident, if at all."[2] Immortality aside, our team has had to worry about weaving together work on interlocking and sometimes overlapping topics by people of diverse backgrounds. The process has contributed much to the shaping of this chapter, which, while not a summary of the earlier chapters, depends heavily on them.

Several chapters in this volume concentrate on the economic aspects of the raw materials industries, and others, on the processes by which governmental policies affecting the industry are shaped. Though only two deal explicitly with the history of U.S. and Canadian policy, all of them taken together can be said to tell us how we reached the present situation. The case studies of selected materials in Volume II (which were available in early draft when this chapter was written) carry the analysis down to specific situations. Drawing on all this material and occasionally going beyond it, this chapter is best seen as one author's interpretation of the nature of the problems raised by the place of raw materials in U.S.-Canadian relations. As part of the collective study, it also poses some of the policy problems that will be dealt with in Volume III.

The Basic Bilateral Resource Relationship and the Problems It Creates

Thumbnail Sketch of the Relationship

Trade and investment in raw materials make up a major part of the economic ties between the United States and Canada. That nexus constitutes the largest set of foreign economic relations for each country. Consequently, problems in raw materials relations will influence — for better or worse — general relations between the two countries, while at the same time many problems of raw materials relations will be specific manifestations of larger questions about the relationship between the two countries.

The raw materials tie is vital to both countries, but the flows are not balanced. The difference in size of the two economies makes that inevitable, but there is much more to the matter, as Richard Shaffner's figures in Chapter 2 make clear.[3] Raw materials production is far more important to the Canadian economy than to that of the United States. Canada is a net exporter, and the United States is a net importer. In many cases the

United States provides the largest market for Canadian exports — quite often over half. Even when the U.S. share is lower — as in the cases of nickel, zinc, copper, and asbestos — Canada provides a very large share of what the United States imports; Canada simply sells more of these resources to the rest of the world. Among the minerals studied by Shaffner, phosphates provide the only case for which Canada is reliant on imports from the United States.

Foreign-owned companies are important in the Canadian mineral industry, and among them U.S.-owned companies predominate. As Garth Stevenson points out in Chapter 6, however, foreign ownership is heavier in energy than in non-fuel minerals. Indeed, in the field of non-fuel minerals, firms that are largely Canadian-owned are among the world's largest — notably Alcan, Canadian Pacific Investments (Cominco), Inco, and Noranda. (However, the U.S. presence in Alcan and Inco, at least, is strong enough in management, finance, and minority stock ownership not to go unmarked in Canada.) While some of the U.S.-owned companies operating in Canada sell widely around the world, in most cases a high proportion of their production moves to the U.S. market, often as an essential ingredient of vertically integrated production and processing. Indeed, the evidence is quite clear that much U.S. capital moved into Canadian raw materials production to obtain supplies for the growing U.S. market (see Jacob Kaplan's figures in Chapter 4 relating to the postwar surge). Although there has been some limitation on investment by foreigners, a substantial part of the growth of Canadian mineral production since 1945 has been induced by U.S. demand, financed by U.S. funds, and carried out by U.S.-owned companies.

While this thumbnail sketch emphasizes the asymmetry of U.S.-Canadian raw materials production, it also shows that a simple comparison of numbers is misleading. Clearly, the moral of what has just been said is that Canada is of exceptional importance to the United States as a supplier of raw materials. Geography is a factor, as is the cost of transportation (not the same thing); so are favorable supply conditions and production costs — part of the complementarity that D. J. Daly emphasizes in Chapter 5. In a larger sense, U.S. companies have found it natural to go to Canada when they need more raw materials, and U.S. government policy has been based on the same kind of considerations. As Kaplan points out in Chapter 4, in formulating its stockpiling policy, the United States has clearly assumed that Canada is a secure source in much the same sense as is the United States itself. One need not spend time looking for documentary evidence of how widespread this view is and how it has affected U.S. thinking. There can be little doubt that a disturbance of the line of supply of many Canadian minerals to the United States would have a greater impact than would trouble with supplies from other countries.

Although the bilateral raw materials relationship is a central one for both countries, it is neither static nor isolated. Western Europe and Japan have increased their investment in raw materials production in Canada, and Canadian exports to these areas have increased faster than to the United States. At the same time, U.S. dependence on imports of raw materials is increasing — and not just in energy — so its imports from overseas have risen. Many of the same companies that produce raw materials in North America operate all over the world. On occasion this fact leads some Canadians to think that even Canadian-owned companies give preference to overseas production. But difficulties and disturbances in developing countries have given a boost to exploration in North America. If the world is entering a period when concern with raw materials supplies will increase, major producers like Canada are bound to have their importance in the world economy enhanced. They gain strength and are presented with new opportunities — and that is bound to influence the bilateral relationship.

Sources of Conflict

Such an intimate and asymmetrical relationship is bound to create many difficulties. On the Canadian side the large U.S. presence has helped stimulate economic nationalism, a loose term for a wide range of attitudes and policy prescriptions that command varying degrees of allegiance within Canada. On the basis of the evidence in this volume it would be difficult to argue that the production of raw materials has excited stronger emotions of nationalism than have other kinds of economic activity, though this has often seemed to be the case in other parts of the world. What cannot be doubted, however, is that the magnitude of raw materials production and its dispersal over so wide an area of Canada must contribute substantially to the worry that heavy dependence on U.S. investment and markets limits the ability of the Canadian government to manage its national economy — a task for which any democratic government must take responsibility, whether it pursues an "interventionist" or a "hands-off" attitude. Another, more explicit set of problems concerns the terms on which foreign firms are to operate and how the costs and gains of their activities are to be divided.

From the late 1960s to the late 1970s, Canadian governments took a variety of measures to cope with such problems. The worst fears of exploitation through foreign control should have been ended by the vivid demonstration in the mid-1970s that the disposition of Canadian oil was determined by the Canadian government and not by U.S.-owned oil companies. The terms on which foreigners can invest in Canada are set by the Foreign Investment Review Agency, which is specifically charged to ensure that the benefits for Canada from such investment are adequate. The

Canada Development Corporation exists to establish a Canadian interest where that seems desirable or to help Canadian companies deal with foreigners. Another public corporation, Petro-Canada, provides initiative, information, and a presence in the oil and gas industry. Some of the provinces have similar companies. Taxing power is used, at the federal and provincial levels, to ensure that an adequate share of the earnings of foreign-owned companies stays in Canada.

Naturally, Canadians are not unanimous about the effectiveness of these arrangements, the standards applied by FIRA, the level of taxation, and how large a public presence is desirable in the production of raw materials. It is beyond the scope of this chapter to enter into that discussion, although what Canadians do may cause reactions in the United States. As far as the two governments are concerned, relatively few troublesome issues have arisen from these matters, except during the early stages of the oil crisis. But there is no doubt that herein lies a range of questions that will be, inescapably, on the permanent agenda of U.S.-Canadian raw materials problems.

U.S. views of these matters are not altogether clear-cut. So much U.S. capital is invested in Canada that the treatment of U.S.-owned firms is bound to have an effect on the U.S. economy. What is not so clear, however, is where the line is to be drawn between those matters the U.S. government must treat as affecting the public interest and those in which essentially the private interests of U.S. businessmen are at stake. Traditional policies of protecting nationals abroad go only so far and are bound to fall short of encompassing the intricate economic relations of the two countries. There are questions, too, about how Washington should treat U.S. foreign investment in general and whether the same approach should apply to Canada as to other countries. Closely related to all this is a kind of underlying uncertainty in the United States about how to react to economic nationalism in Canada; this arises partly from U.S. unfamiliarity with Canadian nationalism but is wearing off.

A second set of inescapable problems concerns trade. In spite of the importance of the U.S. market to Canada and of Canadian supplies to the United States, both governments have at one time or another interrupted the flow of raw materials. The Canadian government limited the export of oil in the 1970s and, as Donald Patton points out in Chapter 7, equipped itself in 1974 with the power to prevent the export of raw materials if that became necessary to encourage processing in Canada. It has long been a sore point with Canadians that the U.S. tariff falls more heavily on finished products than on semi-manufactures and more heavily on semi-manufactures than on unprocessed raw materials, thus protecting processing in the United States and discouraging it in Canada. Gérard Gaudet points out in Chapter 8 that in 1910 Quebec banned the export of logs cut on crown land to encourage the establishment of domestic sawmills. Ontario had already done so. Then the U.S. changed the tariff. John Ashworth, in Chapter 3, Patton, and Kaplan have discussed a number of cases of U.S. action against imports: quotas on lead and zinc, antidumping and countervailing duties against potash and other products, and the closing of the uranium market. In earlier days the U.S. restriction on oil imports from Canada was a source of conflict. While the explanation of U.S. actions has usually been the pressure of domestic interests, the list of questions to be covered in any discussion between the two governments will continue to include such more consistent expressions of policy as the tariff structure, anti-dumping standards and procedures, and the definition of forms of government help that will escape countervailing duties or be interpreted as subsidies requiring their use.

Areas of Mutual Interest

It would be a mistake to limit the list of raw materials questions between the United States and Canada to those relating to conflicts of interest and policies. There clearly are major common interests and prospects of mutual gain to be considered. For example, what combination of measures will do most to attract capital, increase production, improve efficiency, and yield higher revenues in the production and use of raw materials? Should the governments try to assure reasonable stability of prices, markets, and levels of activity? How should the costs of developing transportation facilities and other infrastructure be shared? Security of supply to the user and security of market to the seller are complementary, not conflicting, interests — but are difficult to provide on a lasting basis. A simple step can start a dynamic progression. If the United States set up stockpiles of some materials for the purpose of stability and not just security (or for not altogether clearly stated purposes), Canada might think it would receive some costless benefits but would also be uneasy about how some future U.S. government might use its added market power to influence Canadian production or prices. In return for assurances, the United States might reasonably suggest that Canada share the cost of stockpiling, and the normal Canadian riposte would be to ask for a voice in policy and management.

Maximizing efficiency and sharing the gains equitably are not the only issues to be examined. There is the basic approach to raw materials — are they to be used at whatever going rate economic activity requires and sold at what the market will bear? Or is conservation — however defined — to set the maximum rate of exploitation? Is there some other way to protect the interests of future generations? How much weight is to be given to their interests, and at whose expense? Environmental standards, the restoration of mined-out areas, the many trade-offs between quality and quantity, and the difference between who pays and who benefits are all matters that have to be settled. Many of these matters could perhaps best be left entirely to the producing country — environment being the most likely candidate — but the effects of one government's actions on the other country cannot be ignored, and other matters plainly require something close to explicit agreement. Perhaps as much as anything, one might say that a question of equal importance to what is decided is who is to make which decisions.

It is probable that these common problems will be a more important part of the U.S-Canadian raw materials agenda in the future than in the past. This is not because Pollyanna is likely to take over the formulation of policy in Washington or Ottawa or because there is the prospect of a revival of contented continentalism. It is partly because actions once regarded as matters of individual behavior have come to require some degree of government sanction. Old relations have been challenged, and real or potential conflicts of interest underlined; common interests and opportunities for mutual gain therefore have to be made equally explicit if a balanced course is to be found.

It is perhaps foolhardy to speak of lessons from the energy experience before it is over, but in early 1979 it seems reasonable to draw a few conclusions from the story told by Paul Daniel and Richard Shaffner in Chapter 10. Americans have learned that Canada is not a limitless source on which they can draw at will, while Canadians have learned that foreign domination of their raw materials industries does not prevent them from exercising their sovereign powers over their resources. Both peoples have been reminded how heavily their bilateral relations can be shaped by what happens in the rest of the world. The initial disputes and difficulties that were inevitable when old relations were abruptly changed and sharp conflicts of interest were brought to the surface have been moderated by the passage of time and the fuller understanding by Americans of Canadian views and interests. On both sides of the border a similar set of issues has come to the fore as the two countries try to work out a sensible approach to their future energy needs. There will continue to be arguments about sources of supply, levels of production, transportation systems, the financing of investment, and prices, but they have much more to do with the working out of common interests than with exercising command and control in situations where one country can gain only at the expense of the other.

The sequence of events in energy is hardly likely to be repeated for other materials. Still, it suggests points that the authors of Volume III will wish to take into account as they try to work out policies that will satisfy the national interests of both the United States and Canada — an essential requirement of all lasting solutions. But when they come to define national interests, they will have to take two more circumstances into account. The first is the complexity of the process by which both the United States and Canada define their national policies and of the way in which less-than-national interests directly shape the activities of the raw materials industry. The second is that the United States and Canada cannot approach their common raw materials problems without paying close attention to the broader international setting.

Broad Perspectives

"Gold is where you find it" may have been a Klondike proverb,[4] but it is true of every mineral in every place and has a great deal to do with the problems of the raw materials industry. On the economic side the facts are familiar, from the risks of exploration to the tying up of talent, technology, and money for years before mines pay, and from the costs of transportation to questions about where ore should be smelted and metals refined and processed. But geography is also a matter of politics, and not simply in the sense that international relations are often involved. Perhaps no single point emerges more strikingly from the chapters in this volume, and in more different ways, than the diffusion of power and influence over the raw materials industry in the United States and Canada. The pluralism of both countries is a familiar fact, but in mineral matters it seems to take an especially marked form. It is not just a question of the mines being in one jurisdiction and the markets in others, with transport across still other areas. It involves federalism and regionalism; the place of origin of capital, labor, and management; the role of public or private power; and the division of power, influence, interest, and perspective within each of the two federal governments.

Jurisdictional Issues

In their chapters, Ashworth, Stevenson, Gaudet, and Norrie highlight certain jurisdictional factors in the context of the two countries' resources; in their historical pieces, Kaplan and Patton provide further details. The case studies in Volume II will throw some light on how business is affected by the division of authority through pyramided taxes, the application of different standards in different places, uncertainty as to what regulations will apply, and—sometimes—the opportunity to exploit differences among regulatory authorities. For the authors of Volume III there are difficult questions: Do effective raw materials policies require the United States and Canada to resolve conflicts over jurisdiction? What kinds of policies work best (or worst) when overlapping jurisdictions cannot be avoided? Is it possible to simplify policy-making and at the same time to give adequate weight to all the factors and interests that have to be taken into account?

The most important aspect of the jurisdictional problem is quite different in the two countries. In Canada the main issues center on the division of powers between the federal government and the provinces; in the United States the relevant division is between Congress and the executive branch. Thus jurisdictional difficulties are less important in the United States as long as there is no positive policy requiring legislation. The Canadian version of the jurisdictional problem, in contrast, is more pervasive; it affects taxes, operating conditions, and the general run of business and so makes a good deal of difference to the conditions in which the production of, and trade in, raw materials are regularly carried on.

The Policy-Making Structure

An element of the problem common to both countries — the fact that different ministries or departments are interested in different aspects of what the mining industry may do — must be taken as a normal condition, not likely to be changed. Societies have multiple ends, many of which conflict; representative governments have to reflect these differences in a variety of ways. The weakness lies not in these multiple ends but in the lack of means of arriving at timely conclusions (when conclusions are necessary) or — what may be more serious — in the discrepancy between the weight given to different agencies and the importance of the interests or points of view they represent. Here the argument that the Department of the Interior in the United States and the relevant departments in Ottawa and the provincial capitals tend to be close to industry and imbued with its views becomes a matter of importance. Not that they should be anti-business, or even stress the adversarial approach proper to an anti-trust division, for instance. What is needed is objectivity, technical expertise, and critical intelligence — a very difficult combination to obtain in the civil service when the rewards for two of the categories are a fair amount higher in private employment. Nor does it follow that the objectivity called for is always neutrality about the claims or requirements of an industry; if there is no one inside the bureaucracy capable of seeing an issue through the eyes of the industry, or able to support its contentions when they are correct, it is unlikely that public policy will be what it should be. Moreover, if — as many people believe — the stimulation of raw materials production, perhaps under adverse natural conditions and with rising costs, becomes important to the U.S. and Canadian economies, then the public interest may be served by ministries that are in some sense "pro-industry."

This type of issue may already be upon us. It is a common complaint in the mining and forest-product industries that new standards of environmental protection and the procedures for enforcing them have created burdens that have reduced not only profits but production and investment in future capacity. Even if one makes a generous allowance for special pleading, it would be surprising if there were not some substance to the complaints. There is almost bound to be delay as an increasing number of approvals are required, many of them concerned only with certain aspects of an activity, without an agreed system for dealing with basic trade-offs. Uncertainty is inherent in the right of a variety of interested parties to appeal, sue, and otherwise call into question decisions made at an earlier stage. It is natural in this process that the agencies concerned with particular issues—water, air, reforestation, and so forth—should deal only with their particular specialities, but the result is unsatisfactory. The basic problem for governmental policy is to strike the right balance by making relevant trade-offs within a set of sometimes conflicting desiderata that the body politic has decreed. It will be a major task for the designers of policy machinery in Volume III to suggest how these trade-offs can best be made with expedition and with some assurance that, once made, they will hold for a reasonable period of time.

Division of Powers

The diffusion of decision-making need not be all bad. There are good theoretical and practical arguments for putting difficult problems into the hands of those most affected by them. Who, after all, is better qualified to make decisions about the environment than those who live in it? But what they do affects the jobs and revenues of others, and there is the question of who pays the social costs of production. So the relevant area for decision-making grows larger. Other issues enter the decision-making process: the conservation of supplies and the interests of the next generation. We arrive quickly at some of the most fundamental political and constitutional issues—the competence question, or who decides what, and behind it the question of competence competence—who decides who is to decide? Although the usual answer is the nation-state, this is not always altogether accurate.

In Canada the challenge is explicit: the provinces have, or claim to have, powers over raw materials issues that in the United States would undoubtedly belong to the federal government. These powers concern not only the environment and taxation but investment and production. Moreover, a province's clearly established powers can be used to reach into gray areas or to increase its influence on what the federal government does in dealing with the rest of the world in trade or in political relations. Alberta, for example, has expressed a wish to link the sale of gas with reductions in the U.S. tariff on petrochemicals. A province's pressure to get more processing for itself can take this activity away from another province. While the problem of the division of powers is particularly acute in raw materials, it extends to a wide range of issues. The coming into office of the Parti Québécois in 1976 posed the question of sovereignty itself. While the actual separation of Quebec, or a parting to be followed by a re-association of some sort, may be unlikely, or at least remote, the possibilities of greater autonomy are not, and that may well mean an increase in the already considerable powers of provinces over raw materials across the country. Involved are not only the discrepancies and the uncertainty of multiple jurisdictions or the way business is treated, but the ability of the country to formulate and carry out international as well as domestic economic policies.

In the United States the situation is different. Even if the congressional challenge to the President's freedom to conduct foreign policy were to become less sharp than it has been in recent years, the President's ability to conduct economic policy without legislation or other congressional action would still be very limited. Local and regional interests can become quite powerful. The interrelation of domestic and foreign economic issues increases the range of issues that Congress can deal with and adds to the complexity of working out measures of bilateral cooperation. As the experience with energy has shown, the result may be a failure to act or a sharp limitation on what is possible. Another typical result is for Congress to require one action and refuse to permit another, with results that amount to a patchwork, at best, and a series of contradictions, at worst.

Multiple jurisdictions and the division of powers also affect the efforts each government makes to appropriate as large a share as it can of the benefits of raw materials production, processing, and trade. What is a "fair" distribution between states, provinces, the United States, and Canada? There are no absolute answers, and certainly none that apply across-the-board to all products or even to all instances of dealing with the same product. The answer can only be a negotiated one that takes into account not only shifts in bargaining power and the rise and fall of activity in the industry but also the different combinations of political and economic interests pursued by the various units. While taxes provide an obvious measure, governments also attach value to employment, expenditures by companies and employees that keep localities prosperous, exports from their territories, and the like.

One result of this competition among governments may be to put unintended burdens on industry through cumulative taxes and a variety of other requirements. But the process may work the other way. Congress may provide tax exemptions the executive might deny. In Canada, provinces interested in jobs and development have pressed FIRA to permit foreign investment that other Canadians might oppose on "nationalistic" grounds. While business may sometimes benefit, uncertainty about these matters — which is exacerbated by the number of governments involved — is not likely to be constructive as far as investment and other business behavior are concerned.

More is involved in these matters than the current division of gains between private and public interests or between one public authority and another. There can also be long-run consequences for the raw materials economy of North America. Unduly heavy taxation may reduce supply in the long run by discouraging investment. Too much government help may create a bad allocation of resources, throw a hidden burden on other tax-payers, and even lead to international trade disputes. A major dispute in Canada in recent years has been whether Canadian tax laws unduly favor mining over manufacturing, as Patton and Daly have pointed out. In the United States the depletion allowance, which reduces corporate income taxes, has long been a target of critics and a precious asset for oil companies and others in the extractive industries. To judge whether immediate issues will have these long-run consequences is very difficult for both government officials and objective observers. Except in the most blatant cases, the balance of return, risk, alternative uses of funds, need for the material, and so on, requires a complex business judgment; at the same time, the businessman is engaged in a bargaining process with the public authorities in which he alone has the power to bring about certain constructive results, but both parties, separately or together, can do a good deal of damage.

Private Interests

In Volume III a chapter on private business will make a vital contribution to this project's examination of how governmental policies are shaped. Much of the time the main decisions about the production, distribution, and use of raw materials in the United States and Canada are made by private companies in pursuit of their own interests in conditions shaped only partly by governments. The purpose of that chapter is not to obtain the "opinion" of business on matters of public policy or economics — that is easily enough done — but to understand how key business activities are conducted and which are the crucial decisions. The long-run commitment of funds, people, and organizational skill needed to produce and sell raw materials makes issues more complex than the simple calculation of spreads between known costs and prices or the division of earnings among profits, taxes, and interest. There is a need to balance long-run commitments with the ability to respond to changes in the markets. Nor is it only a matter of what the producing companies think; there are also users, bankers, and sometimes independent processors to be taken into account. To commercial risk has to be added the uncertainty about future policies of governments — usually several of them.

Business behavior depends in part on the structure of an industry. The production of raw materials frequently requires large firms and typically leads to oligopoly, and sometimes monopoly. The possibility of overseas competition—whether in third markets or through imports into North America—of new entrants, or of diversification among major companies (as energy producers go into metals, for example) has a major bearing on how firms are likely to react to measures by which governments try to shape national raw materials policies. So do government-business relations themselves—a matter of considerable complexity when two national governments are involved, to each of which many firms have to be responsive and whose priorities are not likely to be identical. Indeed, the shaping of national policies may itself lead to a divergence in views about the most desirable organization of industry. An American for whom the anti-trust tradition dominates is, for instance, a very different political animal from a Canadian concerned primarily with national companies and, if necessary, cooperation among smaller companies to build up national strength and efficiency. What is done on one side of the border affects the other side and may create conflicts within a firm. To think clearly about long-run policy, we also need to know when a U.S.-owned firm in Canada is treated as a Canadian firm and when it is not.

Volume III will also take up the matter of labor unions. Here, too, organization crosses the border, since a substantial number of the workers in Canadian raw materials production belong to unions affiliated with U.S. organizations, while others belong to independent Canadian unions. How much such affiliation, or the lack of it, affects labor attitudes toward raw materials issues is not at all clear except on a few points, but there is no doubt that the emphasis on job creation and security will be a mainspring of union activity in the two countries. It will both shape national policies and sometimes create conflicts, especially if it seems that the jobs being created in one country are being taken away from the other.

In Canada the established view that secondary industry creates more and better jobs than primary industry—which is challenged by Daly in Chapter 5—is a key factor in shaping raw materials policy but presents itself differently to members of a particular union accustomed to doing certain kinds of work than to a disembodied "work force" whose occupation is ultimately to be determined. The question of the labor force required for future raw materials production in Canada is also one that cannot be neglected. Daly shows its importance in high turnover and increasing labor costs, especially in remote regions. The chances are good that this problem will grow as more remote ore bodies have to be worked at higher costs. To the extent that underground mining is involved, one should reflect on the rather general tendency for workers in rich countries increasingly to avoid that kind of employment if they can. At some point, questions about the recruitment of a labor force may lead (as they have in the past) to questions about immigration.

This rough sketch of interest groups, overlapping jurisdictions, and the diffusion of power indicates some of the complications the authors of Volume III will face, not only in suggesting how the two countries should work out their raw materials policies but in describing their substance. There is a positive value in the diversity described here as a better means of discovering the real interests of Americans and Canadians than is possible when simpler concepts of "national interest" are applied, which conceal many real conflicts of interest among domestic groups and compromise the gains of some and the losses of others. For example, a closer look shows that, while buyers and sellers have some opposing interests (a higher or a lower price), they also have a strong common interest (no market, no supply). Investors and those they employ in a foreign country have a common interest that is in conflict with that of the "nationalist" of one country who says the foreigner should be kept out and that of the labor union of the other that says capital should be kept at home. Naturally, such cross-border affinities have some influence on the determination of "national interest" in each country, but might not common and conflicting interests that cut across the border have a greater influence on national behavior than they would in two more separate economies? It has been said that the fabric of U.S.-Canadian relations is so closely knit below the governmental level that the substance of the relations between the two countries is more likely to be found there than in the usual catalog of interstate relations.[5] This is largely true of raw materials relations. Whether that circumstance can be translated into the maximization of the total welfare of the people in both countries is not certain, but it is not impossible.

The International Setting

Just as the analyst of U.S.-Canadian raw materials relations must look below the surface of "national interest," he must also look beyond the bilateral framework with which he starts. Important as they are to one another, the United States and Canada both have major economic relations with the rest of the world that affect their bilateral raw materials ties. There is almost always a competing supplier and an alternative market. For Canada, diversification of foreign trade and investment has always seemed a constructive way to moderate its built-in dependence on the United States; the expansion of its raw materials exports to Japan and the European Community and investment in Canada by these countries have been a marked feature of the 1970s. There are aspects of the growth of

U.S.-Mexican relations in raw materials and energy that may touch on Canadian interests. For importing and exporting countries, contractual commitments between producers and buyers contribute to stability but narrow the fields in which government policy can directly shape trade. In times of shortage they can add to the problems of government trying to determine whether and how to allocate supplies. Another part of the story is Canada's raw materials investment in developing countries. But there is no need to expand on so obvious a set of relations, only a need not to forget them.

Negotiating Stances

A more complex matter is what will happen if either country or both countries take a strong and active position in international negotiations as a producer or a consumer of raw materials. There they might find themselves engaged in conflicts over some materials but on the same side with regard to others, such as bauxite, tin, rubber, and wheat. Thus far that kind of divergence has been largely avoided, in part at least because negotiation about commodity issues has been less tense than seemed likely only a few years ago and because the organization of producer groups has moved more slowly than some had predicted. But it is also partly the result of fairly circumspect policies on the part of both governments, especially Canada.

There was probably never a serious possibility that Canada would "join OPEC." (Would it have been welcome?) But to Americans, Canada appeared to get something of a free ride from OPEC's success in increasing the oil price—a view that lost some of its plausibility when it was realized that Canada probably could not be a net exporter of oil for long. In a world expecting other raw materials shortages, however, the question had to be asked whether Canada might use its strong export position to join, or even lead, associations of producers of other minerals. As Patton shows, the Canadian government has decided not to join such movements in iron ore and copper, preferring such arrangements as the tin agreement, in which both producers and consumers would belong.[6] Since the United States also took the view that each product should be looked at separately and favored consumer-producer agreements (if any), the differences between the two countries have been secondary. Uranium—the subject of a case study in Volume II—is the exception and is correctly seen as a special case, but what that means for the future is not clear.

In a democratic country it is never wise to assume that current policies are immutable. It seems likely that some Canadians will urge a future government (or even a rather autonomous province?) to join forces with other producers of a given raw material. How that would affect U.S.-Canadian relations is impossible to say without hypothesizing a whole series of circumstances about the material in question plus quite a few other

things. Presumably, an estimate of the U.S. reaction would enter into the
Canadian decision. The case for believing that the current policy may
prove durable is that it offers a good deal of flexibility and takes account of
realistic considerations — such as that there are few cases where producers
alone are likely to be able to create another OPEC; that consumer-producer
arrangements have more promise of stability; and that different commodities require different kinds of treatment. The current stance also helps
overcome the somewhat misleading treatment of raw materials issues as
being primarily issues between rich and poor countries — which, as Patton
points out in Chapter 7, puts Canada in an ambiguous position.

The Multilateral Framework

Another international dimension that has to be kept in mind concerns the
extent to which some bilateral raw materials issues are being dealt with by
the United States and Canada on a multilateral basis. The OECD code
concerning the behavior of multinational enterprises can be seen as having
some bearing on investment relations and on the U.S. corporate presence
in Canada.[7] But national and provincial legislation, plus specific arrangements between Canadian authorities and U.S. companies — and
perhaps a few understandings between the two governments — seem a good
deal more concrete and go further than the code.

The situation is different with regard to trade. Since 1946, GATT has
provided the principal negotiating framework and the multilateral rules that
largely shape the trading relations of the two countries. In the Tokyo
Round (which was still under way as this was written), raw materials
tariffs, non-tariff barriers, rules about anti-dumping and subsidies,
and — possibly — principles concerning access to supplies are being actively
negotiated. Within the multilateral negotiations there is room for a certain
amount of bilateral bargaining, and it has been reported that the United
States offered an arrangement that would remove many of the duties that
Canadians see as most damaging to their wish to process more raw
materials at home.[8] If the formula under which that reduction would be
made proved unacceptable to Japan and the European Community,
however, the two North American partners might find that, in the end,
they had made less progress on this bilateral issue than they were prepared
for (since, under the rules of GATT, they cannot discriminate against other
members). Canada advanced a concept of negotiation by sector especially
adapted to dealing with individual raw materials, but the idea does not
seem to have gained much support from other nations.[9] At this point, it is
impossible to judge to what extent the outcome of the Tokyo Round's efforts to deal with non-tariff barriers will help to overcome the kinds of problems the two countries may face in their raw materials trade. One must

wonder, for example, how far a subsidy code would go in reducing the risk of a quarrel over the use of U.S. countervailing duties against the types of aid Ottawa or a province might provide to stimulate mining or processing.

Should the Tokyo Round fail, or simply fall far short of dealing with the main problems arising in raw materials trade between the United States and Canada, the two countries would face the question of whether to try to work out bilateral arrangements compatible with GATT — and possibly even the question of whether to continue with the basic multilateral formulas that have guided their trade policies during the postwar period. To speculate on such possibilities is impractical here. It should not be overlooked, however, that mixed in with the question of what is to be done multilaterally or bilaterally are perennial issues about the "special" relationship between the United States and Canada: Canadian objections to the "continentalism" ascribed to U.S. policies and thinking; the matching preference for multilateral agencies; the U.S. dilemma of holding to global principles that are hard to apply, on the one hand, or of arguing that Canada is an exception, on the other; and the internal Canadian dispute between those who see the quest for special treatment as accentuating dependency and those who regard it as not demeaning but inevitable. GATT eases such problems, but it is not so clear that they can be avoided if the United States and Canada set about formulating broad national raw materials policies.

Comprehensive National Policies?

Running through the chapters in this volume are references to the lack of a general U.S. or Canadian policy on raw materials, except for brief periods or in connection with one or another set of circumstances. The implication is quite strong — and in a few cases spelled out — that the lack of a broad strategy is "a bad thing" — that, if there had been such policies, there would have been less trouble. The tacit assumption is that they would have been the right policies, aimed at the right objectives, and that they would have worked. This is a fairly large assumption, but it is certainly true that, if people had been a little more thoughtful, if they had looked ahead a little more carefully and steadily, they could have avoided some difficulties that were encountered later. Nor is this entirely a matter of hindsight. Quite often the broad picture was well understood at the time; several starts were made, but then the effort petered out. It is also clear that limited policies served only partial purposes, were somewhat contradictory, and lacked long-term aims. The assumption is that a broader policy would have been more consistent.

It is natural — probably inevitable — to feel and think in these terms, especially for analysts whose concern is with public policy. And there can certainly be no gainsaying the hope of shaping such a policy—provided, that is, the term "policy" is broadly conceived as being concerned with results, so that there is no implication that the government must itself undertake to do everything or have a hand in everything instead of sometimes leaving well enough alone. It is necessary, too, to bear in mind that policies have costs as well as benefits—they involve choices that mean foregoing certain things and making trade-offs that will not universally commend themselves. To arrive at national policies, democracies have to go through a political process that balances interests and compromises points of view. The results may be substantially different from what the advocates of a comprehensive policy had in mind at the outset.

Still, to ignore a problem because one might arrive at the wrong solution is neither intellectually tenable nor socially responsible. It is a task of Volume III to try to suggest sound policies for dealing with raw materials—policies that can include deliberate decisions to do nothing about some issues. The final task of this chapter is to suggest to the authors of that volume some approaches for their consideration. First, however, a word has to be said about what the interrelation of the two putative national policies—U.S. and Canadian—might be.

North American Interrelationships

The basic dilemma is obvious enough. The interconnections of the U.S. and Canadian raw materials economies are so great and so important to each country that neither can sensibly form national policies without taking substantial account of the interests, wishes, and power of the other. At the same time, intricate national processes make that difficult and will, as a rule, give less weight to the interests of the other country than would be desirable. Almost any major policy steps taken by either country will have an impact on the other and may stimulate a reaction. While it is conceivable that a process of blow and counterblow will produce an agreed, constructive result, the greater risks of damage are obvious. A key question, therefore, for the authors of Volume III is how, if at all, some coordination of aims and means can be attempted. Perhaps, as was suggested earlier, the diffusion of divergent interests throughout the two economies, with the resulting connections across borders, will yield better results than would come from the formulation of a comprehensive policy on a purely national basis. But these interests will not make the process any easier.

It is not enough to talk generally of "cooperation." To Americans, that term would probably suggest secure supplies; expansion of production to meet consumption; the freedom of U.S. firms to explore, mine, and ship from north of the border; tax rates that encourage this activity; and so on.

In the perspective of many Canadians, their country had little choice but to "cooperate" that way in the past, but times have changed. They see little virtue in a "continentalism" based on grossly discrepant supply and demand. Similarly, a "partnership" between two countries so different in size will be less than tempting for the smaller unless it is quite sure that it has the means to insist on a balance of advantage in those things most important to it. Efforts to achieve this assurance are almost bound to emphasize the retention of ultimate national control over the use of domestic supplies and the right to independent judgment about particular actions taken by the United States or, at any rate, by U.S. companies. But these measures, along with those intended to maximize Canada's share of the return from raw materials activities, have to take into account U.S. interests and reactions: taxation and the regulation of business affect investment and the financing of development, limits on production and exports are related to the assurance of markets, and so on. Prescriptions for cooperation have to take account of substance as well as process.

The Scope of National Approaches

The question of balancing advantages leads inevitably to the question of what materials are to be the objects of the national policies so often recommended. Is it a matter of all raw materials, of minerals, or of certain minerals? As each country gropes for a national energy policy, it can be assumed that questions pertaining to oil, gas, coal, and — perhaps — uranium and tar sands will be looked at differently from those pertaining to lead, zinc, copper, iron ore, and aluminum and that these metals will be seen differently from other products. Uranium cannot be looked at without regard to nuclear security; and in a reasonable world, fertilizers would be thought of in relation to world food policies. Whatever the specific considerations, there are inescapable questions about the bargaining positions of the two governments with regard to each product and to the consequences of treating them separately or together in one combination or another. Bargaining apart, the mention of these differences — one could add others in forest products — is a reminder that the very concept of a "raw materials policy" will require some scrutiny, whether the emphasis is on national or on international measures.

Once that point has been clarified — or perhaps before — another and more fundamental question will arise: How does a raw materials policy relate to the rest of national economic policy? In Canada, at least — and perhaps someday in the United States — that question can be answered only in terms of an industrial policy or an industrial strategy. Is the traditional emphasis to be retained on the need for more secondary industries, using high technology and providing jobs? Or will Daly's argument about

Canada's comparative advantage in the production of raw materials lead to
the conclusion that the country will be better off moving in that direction?
Will the governments of Canada—for the provinces will certainly have a
hand—look for interventionist measures to move toward what they want,
or will they let market forces settle the matter? And how will agriculture be
treated? The same questions will surely confront Americans, although they
may not recognize them in the same terms. Both countries will also face two
of the basic problems posed by pluralistic democracies—to attain consistency and to make trade-offs that satisfy the largest public good.

Alternative Prospects

The Go-Slow Approach

There is little support in the chapters in this volume for the belief that
fundamental difficulties in the U.S.-Canadian raw materials relationship
are imminent. Instead, there has been—between the inception of this project and the conclusion of this chapter in early 1979—a kind of diffused
easing of the atmosphere as far as bilateral relations are concerned. There
are, of course, a number of concrete issues between the two governments—there almost always are—and one could list a series of specific
issues that may not be far below the surface. All this is normal in the relations of two closely linked economies and needs to be mentioned here only
because it raises the question of whether the situation calls for major new efforts and innovations in policy or approach in either country or in both
working together. That something of the sort is needed in energy is already
accepted, but none of the other fears of the early 1970s about major shortages, struggles for resources, and so on, have lasted. There is concern
about whether prices are too high or too low and whether there will be adequate investment to bring forth future supplies. But these are not major
worries affecting U.S.-Canadian relations.

Given the numerous difficulties already touched on concerning the formulation of satisfactory national policies, and even more of achieving effective international cooperation in shaping them, it would not be
unreasonable to conclude that it is really unnecessary—and probably unwise—for either the United States or Canada to undertake now any major
new comprehensive efforts to deal with raw materials problems at home or
abroad. This is not to say such problems will not exist in the future. The
suggestion is only that no clear and present need for action has been
demonstrated, whereas the ability of the two countries to cope with most
problems when they arise is a fact of life. The conclusion is not an argument for complacency but for the kind of pragmatism that comports fairly

well with the economic and political practices of the two countries.

Anticipating New Conflicts

In the eyes of many people such a conclusion would be far too short-sighted. While the alarms of the early 1970s might have been exaggerated, they would argue, there are real problems that will manifest themselves again as time passes — and, particularly, as the world economy comes out of its protracted slump. Difficulties are likely to be more frequent and more troublesome in the future than in the past. Not all raw materials issues have a great effect on U.S.-Canadian relations, but some do; and in any case the two countries may be able to cope better with some issues if they anticipate them. The responsible course, in this view, would be to prepare to meet these contingencies. Without gambling on predictions of just what will happen when, one could improve the capacity to deal with problems as they arise. One way would be to improve the warning system. Improved information and analysis of trends, more government-business consultation, and a sharing of assessments between the governments would be sought. The "warning" might also focus on proposed government or business measures in one country that might have an effect on the other, or on the building up of concern among particular interests about practices being engaged in by the other party. Trade problems, in particular, can sometimes be made more manageable if identified long enough in advance. In trade — or, indeed, in a whole range of governmental measures affecting business — a commitment to consult with the other government would have much to recommend it (if this is not already undertaken on a multilateral basis in GATT or the OECD, as might come to pass). And even without a commitment, a practice of advance consultation might be developed.

Expanding Supply Potentials

With or without this kind of contingency planning, a third, more positive approach might recommend itself. To reduce the risk of future shortages and the attendant difficulties, one ought to consider what can be done to ensure the production of adequate supplies of raw materials in the long run. At first sight this might seem to be one of those matters in which, as Burke put it in the passage cited earlier, "it is in the power of government to prevent much evil; it can do very little positive good." But this may be wrong. Probably not many Americans or Canadians would think in terms of their governments' becoming major producers of raw materials (although there is an interesting question about the use of government-owned enterprises to stimulate activity that private firms may, for one reason or another, hold back from or to assume local participation of the sort Gaudet ascribes to SOQUEM and other Quebec corporations). But as Beigie argues in

Chapter 1 of this volume, in recent years the planning environment has become increasingly unstable from the point of view of the producer, and that is something that governments *can* influence. The very large sums involved, the long time between initial investment and substantial output, and the further delay in securing adequate returns on the original capital make the production of raw materials different from other kinds of economic activity. Exploration and prospecting add to the lead time and to the uncertainty.

All this means that entrepreneurs must have some sense of confidence about the future rules of the game and about world demand. No government can guarantee conditions. As suggested earlier, North America may be a preferred area for investment because it is inherently more stable and less risky than many other places where raw materials are to be found. Still, it does not follow that the governments of the area, including provincial and state governments, can do whatever they like without causing a reduction in the rate and amount of investment. There is not much to be learned by simply asking businessmen what their requirements are by way of security and return; somehow the interplay of private calculation and public policy has to be taken into account. It involves not only political stability and some continuity in policy but also the basics concerning the sharing of rents and thus the whole balance of taxes and regulation. If the hypothesis of increasing real costs for much raw materials production holds, there may well develop a case for a higher degree of government activity in such matters as the financing of infrastructure (especially transportation) and regional development and — perhaps — insurance, equity participation, or other forms of support for private financing.

Measures to ensure adequate production blend with limits on production for conservation purposes; with measures for supply renewal, such as organized cutting and reforestation; and with the establishment of conditions of production by setting environmental standards. The opening of unexploited territories to prospecting or mining (a U.S. as well as a Canadian issue) also falls into this category. How far the concerns of the two countries — or of the producing and consuming areas in either — can be blended, and by what means, become matters of considerable difficulty that advocates of this course of action will have to consider.

They will need to look also at the regulation and encouragement of investment by national, provincial, and — perhaps — state governments. This activity is not likely to be abandoned, but the way it is exercised can make a great difference to almost all the other issues affecting raw materials in the long run. Even when the main concern is revenue, it can be troublesome to determine when the matter can be safely left to bargaining between the relevant governments and the private producer and when the public interest of other areas (not just another country but other regions of the same country not sharing in the take) is sufficiently affected to warrant bringing them into the discussion. The country from which the investment comes may also attempt to regulate the activity.

Whereas in the past the United States has not had well-defined major policies in this field, the situation may be changing. Interest in raw materials supplies would seem to warrant promoting investment by insurance, guarantees, credit, and so forth, as long as one felt the resulting supplies would be available even in times of shortage. Resistance to foreign nationalization might be stronger than in the past. Raw-materials-producing companies might find ways of reducing their vulnerability abroad. One school of thought in the United States holds that, because equity investments are inherently vulnerable, the government should refuse to insure them and should instead direct all its support to arrangements in which U.S. firms simply provide management and technical services as a contractor. There has been much interest in the part the World Bank and other international financial institutions could play in improving confidence.

A contrary approach to foreign investment is to discourage it because it results in the "export of jobs." In the United States that argument has focused mainly on manufacturing, but the same reasoning applies to raw materials when foreign production would compete with U.S output, especially in a declining sector. It would certainly come up if U.S. companies were pressed to process minerals abroad and had to close down domestic facilities to do so. In other circumstances, however, it could be argued that investment in raw materials abroad helps maintain the level of jobs in the United States by providing essential imports for industry. Changes in U.S. taxation of foreign investment are obviously relevant, along with any general tendency to increase government observation of the movement of capital, technology, or management abroad, which could have a number of causes, including an energy program of a certain sort.

Many of these matters may also be dealt with by general international agreements. But even if nothing of this sort takes place, the way these matters are handled by the United States and Canada will affect North America's supply of raw materials.

Dealing with Barriers to Trade

A related question on the supply side—especially for the United States, but also for Canada for some products—concerns the use of export controls by the other country. In the absence of official controls, private companies may become allocators of supplies, and in that case their freedom of action to do as they please and the criteria according to which they operate may become matters of public concern. To what extent these questions have to be left to each government to deal with when the occasion arises and to what extent there can be prior arrangements, at least about the criteria to be employed, are fundamental policy questions. A possibility not to be excluded is that questions of access or sharing might be agreed on when major investments were made, whether the principal interest was that of the capital supplier or his government. A further question is how the commitments of either the United States or Canada to third countries (or to investors from third countries) would affect the other's access to supply.

The natural counterpart of access to supply is access to markets, something that must also be discussed as part of U.S.-Canadian raw materials relations. The question of reconciling both countries' commitments to equal trade treatment, with exceptional measures to deal with the exceptional relations between the United States and Canada, may look somewhat different if the trade measures are part of a novel and sustained effort to put the raw materials economy of North America on an improved basis. This may also be true of financing mineral development by advance commitments to buy the output for a period of years, of the use of buffer stocks and stockpiles, and of other arrangements aimed at creating stability.

There may also be a need to distinguish between long-run stabilization arrangements and the more drastic measures taken in periods of recession: for example, some European governments have helped maintain employment by subsidizing production of some products for stockpiling. It will, in general, be necessary in the policy studies of Volume III to consider what should be said and done about cyclical questions and how far it is reasonable to abstract from them in shaping long-run policies.

Further Processing

The processing issue will require special attention. It affects trade, investment, security of supply, the division of benefits, local interests, the environment, and most other issues, including the general industrial strategy of both countries. It poses the question of whether to approach such issues by general rules or on a case-by-case basis, since the cases differ so greatly (as the studies in Volume II will surely show). If tariffs and other trade barriers were removed (including export controls), could matters be left to negotiations between companies and the governments of the producing areas, or is there an additional public interest that should be asserted? Tax concessions or subsidies intended to stimulate processing in Canada might well seem like unfair competition to U.S competitors and might lead to countervailing measures. Is it conceivable that governments and industry would be able to agree on some pattern or principles?

Concluding Observations

Not every issue has to be settled between the two governments. But most will at least have to be examined. For some issues the possibilities of broader international action, going beyond what the two governments can do, are much greater than for others. The handling of less-than-national interests raises difficult questions about the organization of the two governments; relations between government and business; and, indeed, how each democracy conducts itself. This recapitulation makes it sound as if the tasks of the authors of Volume III will be impossible to perform. That may be so. But there is also a way of reducing the task, one in which the studies of Volume II will help. This section has been written more in terms of a systematic than of a historical analysis, with the emphasis on the ways in which one might approach some difficult problems. But perhaps not all these problems need be approached. Not all are equally urgent; the suggestion that some may be dealt with by waiting to see if they arise implies that some may not have to be dealt with at all — at least by public policy. It is quite possible that the effective handling of a few key issues may reduce the others to a secondary or manageable status. A quite different possibility is that U.S.-Canadian relations will become so strained as to make it all but unthinkable that the two governments can cooperate. Even then, however, what one did would affect the other, and it is hard to see how either could shape a national raw materials policy in isolation.

Notes

1. Edmund Burke, *The Works of the Right Honourable Edmund Burke,* ed. Humphrey Milford, *The World's Classics* (Oxford: Oxford University Press, n.d.), Vol. VI, p. 2.

2. J. M. Keynes, *Essays in Biography* (London: Macmillan, 1933), p. 212.

3. We concentrate here on non-fuel minerals. The much-studied energy relation will be drawn on at various points. The complex situation with regard to forest products requires the detail of a case study, found in Volume II. Agriculture, in which the United States is the more important producer and exporter, is subject in both countries to a whole array of policies that cannot be taken up in this chapter.

4. So called by Merrill Denison, "Klondike Mike: An Alaskan Odyssey," in S. R. Colombo, ed., *Colombo's Canadian Quotations* (Edmonton: Hurtig, 1974), p. 14.

5. A discussion of the continuing interplay of factors within "this transcending, transnational, public-private mix" runs throughout John Sloan Dickey's *Canada and the American Presence: The United States Interest in an Independent Canada* (New York: New York University Press for the Council on Foreign Relations, 1975).

6. Canada has joined a consumer-only association — the International Energy Agency — but its current and future energy import needs, plus the Agency's emphasis on mutual assistance and on avoiding a confrontation with the producers, may have

helped overcome doubts as to just where Canada belongs.

7. See "Guidelines for Multinational Enterprises" and related declarations and decisions in Organisation for Economic Co-operation and Development, *International Investment and Multinational Enterprises* (Paris, 1976).

8. For example, Hyman Solomon, "U.S. Offers a Tariff Deal," *The Financial Post* (Toronto), January 28, 1978.

9. Caroline Pestieau, *The Sector Approach to Trade Negotiations: Canadian and U.S. Interests* (Montreal: Canadian Economic Policy Committee, 1976).

Index

DATE DUE

	MP 728